THE GAMBLING MANIA ON AND OFF THE STAGE IN

PRE-REVOLUTIONARY FRANCE

COMPILED, ANNOTATED AND EDITED

BY

Tamara Alvarez-Detrell, Ph.D.
Associate Professor, Foreign Languages
University of Central Arkansas

and

Michael G. Paulson, Ph.D.
Visiting Lecturer, Foreign Languages
University of Arkansas at Little Rock

UNIVERSITY
PRESS OF
AMERICA

Library of Congress Cataloging in Publication Data

Alvarez-Detrell, Tamara.
    The gambling mania on and off the stage in pre-revolutionary France.

    Bibliography: p.
    1. French drama--17th century--History and criticism.
2. Frendh drama--18th century--History and criticism.
3. Gambling in literature. I. Paulson, Michael G.
II. Title.
PQ528.A4 1982   842'.4'09   81-43819
ISBN 0-8191-2586-5
ISBN 0-8191-2587-3 (pbk.)

We dedicate this book to our special friends

Dr. Azzurra B. Givens

and

Dr. Dorothy L. Hoffman

with love and appreciation

ACKNOWLEDGEMENTS

The authors wish to acknowledge the following individuals whose help was indispensable for the preparation of the present study: Drs. Azzurra B. Givens, Dorothy L. Hoffman, Joseph L. Allaire and Joseph Plescia of The Florida State University, whose suggestions, comments and criticisms have been invaluable; Raymond A. McAuley of San Diego, California, whose first-hand acquaintance with the games of chance provided insight into the topic; the librarians and staff at the various universities visited in the preparation of this book, especially those at the Bibliothèque Nationale (Paris), The Florida State University, the University of Miami, Florida International University, the University of South Florida, the University of Central Arkansas and the University of Minnesota. Finally, we wish to thank the Research Committee of the University of Central Arkansas for a mini-grant to help defray some of the costs of research at the Bibliothèque Nationale.

NOVEMBER 25, 1982   TAMARA ALVAREZ-DETRELL
                           MICHAEL G. PAULSON

TABLE OF CONTENTS

PREFACE

Gambling has been defined in multiple ways, from various points of view, to include sociological, psychological, and pathological. This study will be based on these as well as other viewpoints in the attempt to reach a definition encompassing the many facets of gambling and the people who engage in it. We will present a spectrum of _joueurs_ and _joueuses_ as found in the literature of seventeenth and eighteenth-century France. The examination will ascertain the socio-psycho-literary impact of the gambler type. We intend to go beyond the common definition of the gambler as a person who engages in games of chance, in order to determine instead what characteristics constitute the individual who becomes a gambler. It is not our intention to isolate the gamblers within their individual frame of life, but rather to analyze them in the perspective of their times and their situations. These situations created by gamblers, which in turn may produce gamblers, will be related to the historical framework in order to establish a rapport with contemporary life. The historical background necessary to realize this comparison of literature and society is presented as introductory material.

One major work which relates drama and finances is Forkey's <u>Role of Money in French Comedy</u>.[1] Gambling, however, is only a chapter in this critical volume, since the author's aim is to present a variety of roles played by money in French theatre. He gives a brief but interesting picture of the male and female gamblers as literary figures during the reign of Louis XIV, but his approach is sociological and he makes no attempt to relate the gaming to the literature.

According to our investigations, it appears that the present study will be the first socio-psycho-literary presentation of the gambler during the reigns of Louis XIV and Louis XV viewed in direct relation to the social changes and reforms of pre-revolutionary French society. Literary critics such as Lancaster and Adam have analyzed plays which deal with gambling and gamblers, but exclusively as works of literature. No attempt has been made to present the gambler either as a factor or as a result of his own society. We will produce psychological, social and literary evidence to indicate the complexity of the gambling neurosis.

The saying that a picture is worth a thousand words has its practical application to literature in general and to our topic in specific. To demonstrate this "gambling mania," it is indeed necessary to see it first hand; with this concept in mind, we have included in our text a seventeenth-century play, Raymond Poisson's <u>Les Femmes coquettes</u>, which shows many of the tendencies and characteristics described elsewhere in our book. Here, as elsewhere, we observe the original orthography of the period and hope that the reader will enjoy both the theory behind gambling as well as one of its principal manifestations.

[1]Leo Forkey, <u>The Role of Money in French Comedy During the Reign of Louis XIV</u> (Baltimore: The Johns Hopkins Press, 1947).

[2]Henry Carrington Lancaster, <u>French Tragedy in the Time of Louis XV and Voltaire</u>, 2 vols. (Baltimore: The Johns Hopkins Press, 1950) and also his <u>A History of French Dramatic Literature in the Seventeenth Century</u>, 9 vols. (Baltimore: The Johns Hopkins Press, 1936-1940); Antoine Adam, <u>Histoire de la littérature française au XVIIe siècle</u>, 5 vols. (Paris: Del Duca, 1949-1956).

INTRODUCTION

1.   Origins of Gambling.

Gambling seems to have existed among all races. Evidence of it has been found in Egyptian paintings and in the tombs of the Egyptian people. Sometimes the practice was even attributed to the gods. It was popular among the ancient Chinese, became a madness among the Hindus,[1] and provided a common diversion among the ancient Persians; it was said that even the Huns were ready to gamble at all times.[2]

The astragalus was the ancestor of the die; this "knuckle bone" or "huckle bone" is defined as "a bone in the hind leg of cloven-footed animals which articulates with the tibia and helps to form the ankle joint."[3] The bones of sheep were generally used, but those of the antelope were especially prized for their superior elegance. Archaeologists have determined that these bones were used for gambling purposes as far back as the sixteenth century B.C.[4]

The Hebrews gambled only by drawing or casting lots; there is no indication of the way the lots were drawn, but we may assume the use of dice in the cast.[5] This type of gambling must have met with religious dictates, since we find no word against it in the Bible. The custom dated from very early times in the Hebraic tradition, for in Leviticus 16:8 Aaron cast lots on goats, in Numbers 26:52, 55, 56 the division of the Promised Land was expressly and divinely ordained by an appeal to chance, and in Acts 1:26, Matthias, one of the Apostles, was chosen by lots. There are many more references to the use of "the lot" throughout the Bible.

Gambling prevailed in civilized Greece;[6] Aristotle, in his <u>Nichomachean Ethics</u> (Book IV) ranked gamblers with thieves. Philip of Macedonia favored the gambling vice, although he recognized its corruptive nature. Homer included gambling in both the <u>Iliad</u> and the <u>Odyssey</u>, as did Aristophanes in some of his comedies.

The first gambling instrument among the Greeks was the astragalus; later Palamedes invented dice and taught the game to his fellow countrymen during the siege of Troy.[7] In the course of time, the sides of the astragalus were numbered and made of onyx or ivory.

1

Subsequently the Tessera, or cubical die, similar to the one now used, came into vogue; it was made of ivory, bone, porcelain or stone.[8]

Gambling was closely associated with the mores of the Roman Empire and its emperors; Augustus, Nero, Claudius and Caligula were passionately addicted to gambling.[9] Eventually, of course, the addiction reached the populace, becoming common among the soldiers. The city of Pompeii reveals a vivid picture of gambling as it was two thousand years ago; dice made of ivory, porcelain, stone, even loaded dice, have been found among the ruins. In one of the taverns, a series of wall paintings shows two players seated on opposite sides of the gambling table with a dice box; they then quarrel over the cast of the dice and are finally thrown out of the establishment by the tavern-keeper.[10]

Other excavations in Roman soil offer silent proof of the intense love of the people for games of chance. Pavements of porticos, baths, basilicas reveal gambling tables engraved or scratched on the stone or marble slabs, or on any flat surface accessible to the public. Evidence is found in the Forum, in the corridors of the Coliseum, on the steps of the temple of Venus and even in the House of the Vestals.[11]

The development of gambling in the Roman Empire is definitely associated with its decline, since in spite of the severe laws against it, there was hardly a more common pastime. Cicero placed the gambler on the same level with the adulterer, but indulged in gambling in his later years. Augustus and Nero played for very high stakes, while Caligula confiscated innocent people's property to support his vice. Claudius had his carriages modified for the convenience of his game of dice and even wrote a book on the subject.[12]

Tacitus, in de Moribus Germ, tells us that the ancient Germans would not only hazard all their wealth, but even stake their personal freedom upon the throw of the dice:

> And he who loses submits to servitude, though younger and stronger than his antagonist, and patiently permits himself to be bound, and sold in the market, and this madness they dignify by the name of honour.[13]

The English have been known for their propensity for gambling, just like the Russians, Italians,

Spaniards and Germans; the use of dice in England dates from the advent of the Saxons and the Danes. In early English times there was gambling with dice among the lower classes as well as among the nobles and clergymen, although edicts were promulgated attempting to control the vice. The Letter Books of the Corporation of London during the thirteenth and fourteenth centuries give us several examples of the wide-spread appeal of gambling and the various legal attempts at controlling it.[14] Its popularity, however, lingered on until Elizabeth I's time and even later; during the reigns of Charles II, James II, William III and Queen Anne, there were many notorious gamblers.

2. Gambling and Religion.

The relationship which exists between gambling and religions is very close indeed. Gambling emerged out of religion; its roots are in religion.[15] Pagan priests were among the first to use dice when they wished to consult the gods. According to Greek mythology, the gods themselves used the astragalus to determine who should rule the different regions.[16] The use of gambling to explain the unknown is at the core of mythology and of many religions.

How did gambling become secularized? Greek legends explain that on one occasion, Tyche, the goddess of Fortune, was raped by Zeus; a girl was born as a result. This child delighted in inventing gambling games and in watching the chaos and quarrels which they incited among men. Tyche provided the infant with houses lit with ever-burning lamps. The brightness of the lights could be seen through the windows and constantly attracted passers-by to enter and gamble with the goddess of chance. Egyptian legends also mention the secular and religious aspects; for instance, it is said that a gamble between the Moon and Thoth, the god of Night, resulted in the fact that the calendar year has 365 days and not 360.[17]

We have already seen how, in the Judeo-Christian tradition, gambling was a common system for determining the will of Jehovah. All civilizations have similar myths and practices related to gambling. The will of the gods is explained by chance; dice and lots settle doubts about destiny and risks. According to Huizinga, religion, judicial systems and games all have common origins.[18] It is interesting to note that gambling-like activities are common and strong elements in private judicial procedures and religious practices,

3

but that as soon as gambling becomes secularized and is no longer associated with religion, it is condemned. Religion may fear gambling when it cannot assimilate it into itself only because gambling provides another way of explaining the unexplainable, but the two practices parallel each other in very striking ways. We will briefly examine some of these aspects now and refer to them in the analysis of individual gamblers when we examine the plays dealing with gambling.

Since gambling emerged from religious divination, it also borrowed some of the paraphernalia; the ceremonies surrounding the use of the "equipment" are therefore interrelated. A casino closely resembles a church in its remoteness from common everyday life; opulence reigns everywhere. The style of speech differs from social language, while people follow unusual patterns of behavior. During the complex rituals, the followers submit willingly to a superior being, be it Tyche or God.

There are other outward signs obvious even to the casual observer. The gambler who wears a good-luck charm and a church-goer who wears a crucifix are both seeking some special favor from the superior being. The invocations of gamblers can even be compared to church prayers. Gamblers often claim the existence of a system to succeed, and they search for this "system" which, if interpreted correctly, serves as a guide much in the same way as the Bible or Prayer Book guides the life of the believers.

Religion in general and Christianity in particular have strong ties with gambling. The gambler and the Christian act in a similar manner; both attempt to impose and exert external and internal control over events, usually unsuccessfully. The religious person has a set of rigid beliefs; the gambler has an inexhaustible credulity. Both share a belief in an external being, much more powerful than themselves, whose favors they seek. They believe that this being can be influenced by physical and psychological activities here on earth (i.e., by amulets and prayers). In gambling and in Christianity, one clearly sees the presence of the father surrogate: fate or God, and of the mother surrogate: luck or the Madonna.[19] The attitude of the believer toward the surrogate and the way in which he tries to influence it, constitute interesting and important elements of his behavior.

Conviction plays a determining role in both

4

the religious man and the gambler. The latter is an inveterate optimist who believes that he will win, even though his experience and logic tell him otherwise. The former relies on "faith," an unexplainable, irrational confidence, unshaken by all arguments. It is the winning itself that counts, for every victory represents "the triumph of good over bad."[20]

The religious person and the gambler engage in activities dominated by fantasies and dreams. The former seeks eternal life in paradise; the latter seeks eternal wealth in the form of a "big win." Both are willing to endure suffering in order to attain these elusive goals. Thus, magic and mystery remain at the core of gambling and religion, as Huizinga points out:

> Luck may have a sacred significance; the fall of the dice may signify and determine the divine workings; by it we may move the gods as efficiently as by any form of contest. Indeed ... for the human mind the ideas of happiness, luck and fate seem to lie very close to the realm of the sacred.[21]

Finally, we must note the social aspect of such behavior, for the activities must be conducted with other people. The ceremonials or rituals involved are not created by the individual; the rules of the game, like the conventions of worship are already set and the players or worshippers stick to pre-established form or forms. Gambling, like religion, has the marks of a universal neurosis.[22]

3. Gambling in France.

Early French annals indicate that the idle lords of feudal times dedicated themselves almost exclusively to gambling in defiance of laws enacted against the vice; members of royal families played dice, while other noblemen often gambled away their property. Charles VI was a particularly heavy gambler; during his reign the Hôtel de Nesle, open only to the nobility, became famous for its gambling catastrophes.[23] The price paid for the privilege of gambling there was often one's honor or one's life.

The military camps were not immune, since gambling went on even when the enemy was near. Lost fortunes often placed the country's safety in compromising situations, and sometimes the commanders gambled away

5

the money which was to be the soldier's pay. In spite of its dissemination, however, gambling was not yet the source of social upheaval it would become in later times. The majority of the people were still more likely to go hunting or get involved in jousts and tournaments than in games of chance.

With the invention of cards a change in the kind of amusement was brought about.[24] At first, more time was lost than money, but they attracted the attention of clergymen and magistrates who were concerned with the gambling in the royal palaces and noble mansions. Their concern seemed justified for the games preceded the moral decline of the nobility as cheating became a common practice. The games were not yet detected among the middle or lower classes.

The situation was worsened by the fact that several French monarchs enjoyed the presence of cheats at the gaming table. Louis XI, for instance, was impressed by cleverness and sharp wit and did not object to thieves or cheaters, provided they showed originality in their actions. Henry III was not interested in games of chance, but established dice-rooms and card-rooms in the Louvre just the same. High stakes soon became the vogue as French and foreign gamesters gained admission into the Royal palace without any difficulty, while thousands of francs changed hands thanks to the King's generosity.[25]

Manifested at an early age, Henry IV's passion for gambling set a most pernicious example for his subjects to follow, since what he lacked in cunning and skill he made up for in greed. Gambling reached epidemic proportions and resulted in the ruin of multiple well-to-do families. To his court belongs the dubious honor of having simplified the exchange of gambling funds by using written vouchers for loss and gain, a sure way to speedy ruin. Although strict laws against gambling existed, special permissions could be secured from the courts for the right price. It was also during the reign of this popular monarch that the frenzy of gambling seemed to catch the people at large; members of all trades and professions, from the highest to the lowest succumbed to the temptation.

Henry IV's only object in gambling was to win. In contrast with his royal greatness in other matters, he could not tolerate losing at the gambling table, so that those playing against him had to either lose their money or incur the royal displeasure. In such occur-

rences, the King would insist on a _revanche_ until he
finally was the winner:

> After winning considerably from the King, on
> one occasion, Bassompierre, under the pretext
> of his official engagements, furtively de-
> camped: the King immediately sent after him;
> he was stopped, brought back, and allowed to
> depart only after giving the _revanche_ to His
> Majesty.[26]

Needless to say, gamblers were in high favor
during the reign of Henry IV. One, for instance, received an honor never bestowed upon dukes or princes;
he was allowed to enter the court yard of the royal
mansions in his carriage in order to gamble with the
Queen.[27]

In order to take care of gamblers from all social classes, the _Académies de Jeu_ were established.
From the nobleman down to the lowest peasant, people
rushed incessantly to these gambling houses where nearly every day someone was financially ruined. Great social affliction ensued, compounded by the law-suits
and the usury practices which accompanied the vice.
Dufresny's comment on the choice of the word _Académie_
for this kind of establishment is worth noting:

> Je ne sais pas pourquoi les lieux publics où
> l'on joue ont usurpé le beau nom d'académie,
> si ce n'est qu'on y apprend quelquefois, aux
> dépens de tout son bien, à gagner subtilement
> celui des autres.[28]

In the long run, this widespread gaming benefited only
the owners and keepers of the gambling establishments,
for the gamesters willingly paid high rents for the
use of small rooms, even closets, where they could indulge in their passion. In spite of the strictest
laws, the vice flourished thanks to magistrates who accepted bribes and looked the other way.[29]

Louis XIII was not a gambler and was against
all games of chance; during his reign, therefore, the
court did not openly set a bad example. Indeed, laws
against gambling were revived, penalties were enforced,
and gambling houses in Paris were shut. Unfortunately,
while these measures checked the practices of the people, the nobility went on gambling as before, albeit
in secret.

Louis XIV's long reign was a period of great accomplishments in many respects, yet it was also at that time that the gambling mania swept through the country. As we shall see, it was particularly marked during the late seventeenth and early eighteenth centuries.

Games of chance developed in France in the Middle Ages because they constituted a distraction from the boredom of a sedentary life in the castles in time of peace. The practice was not opposed by the Church then, since on many occasions the profits went for the upkeep or the building of monasteries and cathedrals. Leo Forkey remarks that in the seventeenth century,

> gambling first became widespread in the army camps where the soldiers, like the nobility of the Middle Ages, used games of chance to relieve a humdrum existence. The passion for gambling spread from the army camps to the French populace in general. It grew by leaps and bounds in the course of the century and was influenced by the vast amount of money in circulation. Under Louis XIV gambling had a prominent place at Court; from there it spread throughout the city of Paris, and later to the French provinces.[30]

The attitude of the Church in the seventeenth century paralleled that of the Middle Ages. While Cardinal Richelieu had vigorously opposed the vice, his successor, Mazarin, helped make gambling popular. He knew just how to combine gambling with his political designs, so that during his Régence, he used games of chance to ruin his enemies financially.[31] According to Steinmetz, Mazarin

> introduced gaming at the court of Louis XIV in the year 1648. He induced the king and the queen regent to play, and preference was given to games of chance. ... Cardinal Mazarin played with finesse and easily drew in the king and queen to countenance this new entertainment, so that everyone who had any expectation at court learned to play at cards.[32]

With the increasing popularity of games of chance, the number of families who fell into ruin and disgrace multiplied rapidly. The damaging effects of gambling, however, went beyond the mere financial repercussions, as tempers became excited and whole nights were spent at this diversion, resulting in great harm to health. Games of physical skill, such as tennis, were rejected in favor of the more glamorous, though less healthy, games of chance. As a result, weakness and sickness replaced good health among the gamblers.[33]

Intellect and wit also suffered because of this form of amusement. Prior to the popularity of gambling, the nobility was intent on improving the art of conversation. In order to accomplish this goal, ancient and modern books were widely read and discussed, memory and reflection were much more exercised. With the advent of the gambling vice, the nobles abandoned all intellectual activities, became more ignorant, and their conversations grew duller. Furthermore, respect went out with wit, as men and women spent whole nights together engrossed with their games of chance. Dufresny gives us an idea of what the gambling scenario was like in that age:

> On bannit de ces lieux privilégiés, non seulement la subordination et le respect, mais encore toutes sortes d'égards, de compassion et d'humanité; les coeurs y sont tellement durs et impitoyables, que ce qui fait le douleur de l'un y fait la joie de l'autre.[34]

More laws were enacted against the vice, and the Parlement de Paris repeatedly promulgated edicts to stop gambling (6 July 1661; 16 September 1663; 29 March 1664, 23 November 1680; 15 January 1691; 8 February 1705).[35] The government also imposed a fine of three thousand francs, of which a third went to the poor, a third to the king, and a third to the informer who denounced the offender. Nevertheless, it was very difficult to enforce these laws because the passion for gambling possessed all. The aristocrat, the bourgeois, the peasant and even the magistrates, all gathered around the gambling table.

It was during the reign of Louis XIV that gambling played its most important role in the history of France. Life was then centered around the Court at Versailles, where gambling was one of the main activities. Social convention imposed games of chance upon the noblemen and the continuous playing for high stakes drained their purses. Crippled by gambling debts, the nobles would then spend all their time at court, waiting for the opportunity to obtain a favor from the

King. This was just another way in which the absolute monarch controlled the nobility.

> Le Roi sait très bien ce qu'il fait; en dépit des interdictions officielles, il laisse faire et même encourage visiblement ce jeu effréné de Versailles. C'est un moyen très simple pour lui de domestiquer sa noblesse; le courtisan défait sollicite une gratification, une pension; on la lui accorde sous quelque prétexte, et le voilà enchaîné pour le reste de ses jours.36

An essential part of the routine of Court life, as planned by the King, was the Grand Appartement. Everyone would gather there three times a week for an evening of entertainment and games called, appropriately enough, Appartement. Versailles itself resembled a casino at times and was referred to as ce tripot.37

Dangeau, a well-known gambler at the court of the Sun King, wrote the following description on January 5, 1690:

> Le soir, à huit heures, on entra dans le grand appartement; on y joua jusqu'au souper, et on rejoua encore après souper jusqu'à deux heures; il y avoit cinq tables pour les dames, et une pour les seigneurs. Les tables étoient tenues par le Roi, par Monseigneur, par Monsieur, par Madame et par Mademoiselle; M. de Chartres étoit à la table de Monseigneur; le Roi, Monseigneur et Monsieur furent rois chacun à leur table.38

Dangeau's journal is saturated with gambling anecdotes from the court of Louis XIV. Most members of the royal family, as well as the courtiers, were active participants, as we can see from the entry for November 18, 1690: "Après son dîner, le Roi mena les dames dans son cabinet, où il leur donna des bijoux à jouer au tourniquet, pendant que Monseigneur et Monsieur jouoient au lansquenet."39

From the same entry we obtain names such as Madame la Princesse de Conti, Madame de Maintenon, la Princesse d'Harcourt, Madame de Dangeau and Madame de Beauvilliers. The list is endless, and each of these ladies received jewelry from the King to account for her winnings. On January 6, 1691, Dangeau wrote:

> La Reine d'Angleterre joua au portique et puis
> au lansquenet ... et puis le Roi rentra aux
> appartements, vit jouer Monseigneur au lans-
> quenet, et se retira à minuit. Monseigneur
> demeura encore longtemps à jouer.[40]

On April 20, 1700, he adds that the King, "sortant du
conseil, vint faire un tour à la loterie de Madame la
Duchesse de Bourgogne."[41] It is evident that she
found loteries to be a most enjoyable pastime, judging
by the numerous allusions to her weakness encountered
in the course of our research. It must be noted that
Lady Luck did not always favor the Duchesse the way
the King did:

> Madame la Duchesse de Bourgogne devoit dix ou
> douze mille pistoles de jeu, qu'elle se trou-
> voit hors d'état de pouvoir payer présentement
> ... et Sa Majesté prit en même temps le parti
> de faire payer toutes les dettes du jeu de
> Madame la Duchesse.[42]

Most of the nobles played for high stakes and
when they lost, they fell into despair, cried and
cursed unless the King were present, in which case
they would more or less control themselves. Cheating
was a common practice and incurred no shame. In addition, the majority of the games required but little
skill, so that most anyone could play.

On July 29, 1676, Madame de Sévigné spent a
day at Versailles and was so impressed by the glamor
and glitter of the court gambling that she wrote the
following account to her daughter:

> A trois heures ... ce qui s'appelle la cour de
> France, se trouve dans ce bel appartement du
> Roi. Tout est meublé divinement, tout est
> magnifique.... Un jeu de reversi donne la
> forme et fixe tout... Mille louis sont ré-
> pandus sur le tapis, il n'y a point d'autres
> jetons. Je voyais jouer Dangeau; et j'admirois
> combien nous sommes sots auprès de lui. Il ne
> songe qu'à son affaire, et gagne où les autres
> perdent; il ne néglige rien, il profite de
> tout, il n'est point distrait; en un mot, sa
> bonne conduite défie la fortune... Enfin on
> quitte le jeu; on n'a du tout point de peine
> à faire les comptes.[43]

There was an Italian game called <u>hoca</u> or <u>hocca</u>, a sort of roulette at which people lost such enormous sums, and which was generally so crooked, that in the seventeenth century, it was finally forbidden in the Papal States.[44] When this game eventually made its way from Italy into France, La Reynie, chief of police in Paris, unsuccessfully prohibited the game. Unlawful to the point of being under penalty, it was defiantly played at court: "Le hoca est défendu, sous peine de la vie, et on le joue chez le Roi! Cinq mille pistoles avant le dîner, ce n'est rien."[45]

The penalties for gambling were indeed so severe that as a rule they were not enforced, and therefore failed to repress the very crime against which they were directed. When Louis XIV died, almost three-fourths of the nation thought of nothing but gambling. The excitement of playing had turned into a madness which caused thousands of <u>pistoles</u> to be lost in the course of a single evening. During the reign of Louis XV, an ordinance went into effect in an attempt to stop the craze; it was enacted on December 28, 1719, and it prohibited the games of dice and cards under penalty of a three thousand <u>livres</u> fine. Unfortunately, the ordinance was never enforced and on April 16, 1722, the government authorized eight new gambling academies in Paris.

During the minority of Louis XV, a Scotsman, John Law, became Comptroller-General of France. Known as Jean Lass to the French, he undertook to restore the finances of the nation by introducing the gamble of the stock exchange. Although M. Lass was a gambler, the system itself was not gambling in the proper sense of the word, but under its guise fortunes were made and lost in a few hours. The nation eagerly poured its finances into this "game" and by extension grew more interested in the games of chance. More gambling houses were opened than ever before, only this time they were given a more suitable name in France: <u>Enfers</u> (Hells in England). Most of them were located in Paris, but some appeared in the <u>faubourgs</u>. Improper behavior was excused by the excitement that reigned everywhere. Gambling was set up in the mansions of foreign ambassadors, as well as in hotels. Suicides abounded, bankruptcy prevailed, and duels were fought on account of gambling debts.

In 1775, the lieutenant of police in Paris licensed gambling houses, decreeing for the first time that all profit would be directed to the contruction of hospitals.[46] This measure, however, in no way affected the operation of the illegal _enfers_. In 1778, gambling was again prohibited in an attempt to control the increasing number of crimes, but it was still popular at court and in the residences of the ambassadors.

Gambling kept pace with the general moral corruption which rose to its peak during the reign of Louis XVI. During the Revolution, gambling houses were frequently prosecuted, but in general the rigorous laws and vigilant revolutionary police were no more successful than their aristocratic predecessors. Indeed, the troubles of the Revolution and of the Empire helped increase the desire of the French to gamble. Fouché, minister of police, employed spies at the gambling houses and received hundreds of thousands of francs for licensing these establishments.[47] Not only did he draw a healthy revenue from a vice, but also used it for his own political aims and goals. It can therefore be stated that gambling went on during and after the Revolution much the same as it had in pre-revolutionary times.

In the course of our work, gambling as we have seen it in French society will be related to the literary characters who indulge in the vice. In so doing, we will analyze the reasons at the basis of their behavior, as well as examine the results of their actions on themselves and on the other characters of the plays. We are aware of the fact that our outline of gambling from the onset of recorded history to revolutionary France is somewhat sketchy. However, we must admit that, as Alfred Marquiset states: "On a toujours joué, on jouera toujours. Il faudrait maints in-octavo pour raconter l'histoire du jeu à travers les siècles."[48] Since our interest lies mainly in the France of Louis XIV and Louis XV, it is there that we intend to concentrate the development of our chosen topic.

NOTES TO THE INTRODUCTION

[1]Ernest B. Perkins, Gambling in English Life (London: The Epworth Press, 1950), p. 7. Perkins mentions that in ancient Hinduism, the Rig-veda was a poem which dealt with the tragedy of the gambler.

[2]Clemens France, "The Gambling Impulse," The Psychology of Gambling (New York: Harper and Row, 1974), pp. 116-118.

[3]John Ashton, History of Gambling in England (New York: Burt Franklin, 1968), p. 3.

[4]Perkins, p. 7.   [5]Ashton, p. 4.

[6]Andrew Steinmetz, The Gaming Table. Its Votaries and Victims (New Jersey: Patterson Smith, 1969), I, 59-61.

[7]Ed Reid, The Green Felt Jungle (New York: Trident Press, 1963), p. 58.

[8]Steinmetz, I, 62.   [9]Ashton, ch. 4.

[10]Perkins, p. 8.   [11]Ashton, p. 8.

[12]Steinmetz, I, 67.   [13]Ashton, p. 12.

[14]Ibid., p. 13.

[15]John Halliday, The Psychology of Gambling (New York: Harper and Row, 1974), p. 47.

[16]Ibid., p. 48.   [17]Ibid., p. 49.

[18]Johan Huizinga, Homo Ludens. A Study of the Play-Element in Culture (New York: Roy Publishers, 1950), pp. 46, 57, 76.

[19]Halliday, p. 55.   [20]Huizinga, p. 56.

[21]Ibid.   [22]Halliday, p. 54.

14

[23]Steinmetz, I, 67. [24]Ibid., p. 72.

[25]Ibid., pp. 74-76. [26]Ibid., p. 81.

[27]Ibid., p. 83.

[28]Charles Dufresny, Amusements sérieux et comiques (Paris: Editions Bossard, 1921), p. 128.

[29]Steinmetz, I, 85. [30]Forkey, pp. 34-35.

[31]Ibid., p. 11. [32]Steinmetz, I, 87.

[33]Ibid., p. 88. [34]Dufresny, p. 124.

[35]Forkey, p. 35.

[36]Georges Mongrédien, La Vie de société aux 17e et 18e siècles (Paris: Hachette, 1950), pp. 103-104.

[37]Nancy Mitford, The Sun King: Louis XIV at Versailles (New York: Harper and Row, 1966), p. 64.

[38]Philippe de Courcillon, Marquis de Dangeau, Abrégé des mémoires (Paris: Treuttel et Wurtz, 1817), I, 301.

[39]Ibid., p. 353. [40]Ibid., p. 359.

[41]Ibid., II, 196. [42]Ibid., p. 198.

[43]Madame de Sévigné, Lettres (Paris: Bibliothèque de la Pléiade, 1960), II, 153-155.

[44]Mitford, p. 65. [45]Sévigné, I, 876.

[46]Steinmetz, I, 102-105. [47]Ibid., pp. 106-107.

[48]Alfred Marquiset, Jeux et joueurs d'autrefois (Paris: Editions Emile-Paul Freres, 1929), p. 7.

...the front part of the
...and the hard palate are the organs
...
...the back of the tongue
...also its classification in this case
...the organs of articulation [g], [ɣ], [k]
...
...important to remember that the place of artic...
...ation is given according to the passive or...
...the place or manner in which... that often the
...itself to the active organ... is a label...
...between two organs...
...a relative compared activ...
...

...

...consonants are...
...

...

...

...

...

3. ...fricatives... inject what... these sounds are a... closure which is... that... through a passage... yielding sounds... ...[f], [v]
...[θ]...le
fric...with... in the passage by
air through the mouth are known
...which are
...ss/zzzz sounds

16

CHAPTER I

THE JOUEUSES

The universal appeal of gambling is well reflected in comedy. Gambling as an occupation or an
amusement forms the central or predominant theme in
several plays of manners and it occupies a secondary
place in scores of others. Furthermore, gambling constitutes a very important element in the literary transition from the comedy of character to the comédie de
moeurs.

In the latter part of the seventeenth century,
the French money play contributes an important element
to the evolution of French theatre. The late 1600's
show a renewed interest in the comedy of manners and
the comedy of character. The role of society becomes
more relevant as the playwrights seek their inspiration in the complex economic and social conditions of
the period. Since the stage situations reflect contemporary events, the characters find their prototypes
in real-life models.

During the years, the importance of money becomes obvious as the people who possess it are all
powerful; thus, it is only natural for wealth to play
such a dominant role in the contemporary comedies. The
roles in these works were those of thieves, rogues and
gamblers; we are primarily concerned with the latter
category.

The games of chance and their effects on society are presented by the playwrights throughout the
entire reign of Louis XIV, though there is marked increase in the decade 1690-1700. In general, the authors use gambling to introduce interest in their
works and to give a feeling of contemporary reality,as
many of its aspects are portrayed on the stage with
vivid realism. The authors present the mores of the
time; thus preaching and moralizing are, as a rule, of
secondary importance and on occasion, merely coinci-
dental. In this chapter we shall present a picture of
the joueuse, or female gambler. It is our purpose to
relate the social and literary aspects of these gamblers, as well as analyze their individual character.
The plays, which cover the period from 1664 to 1692,
will be discussed in chronological order in an attempt
to follow the evolution of social reaction to the practice of gambling.

The basis for these comedies can be found in the society of the times. At the beginning of the seventeenth century, during the reign of Henry IV, the literary salons were much in vogue as places where budding poets, dramatists, and épistoliers could present their work to an interested audience for objective criticism and evaluation. Active discussion, wit, and polished conversation were praised and encouraged.With Louis XIV, some of this changed; his interest in the arts paired with his generosity, made him an avid patron and financial sponsor for many artists, thus decreasing the need for private patronage and private intellectual gatherings. The people who had frequented the salons found themselves without a pretext for meeting. Eventually, however, the reunions were resumed for a different purpose, as non-intellectual pursuits and pleasures replaced literary activities. Gambling was one of the newly founded pastimes which fascinated the people at these social rendez-vous.

The literary salons of le Grand Siècle had been founded and directed by women who could then freely enjoy the company and friendship of men without incurring social censure. Likewise, their replacements, the institutions known as Académies de jeu were, for the most part, hosted by women.1 The female gambler, therefore, was a logical development of social change. The joueuse found herself as actively involved in gambling as her predecessor had been in literature. Her activities, however, were frowned upon by many of the contemporary critics. Charles Dufresny was shocked at their behavior:

> Jamais l'amour n'a causé tant de désordre parmi les femmes que la fureur du jeu. Comment peuvent-elles s'abandonner à une passion, qui altère leur esprit, leur santé, leur beauté, qui altère ... que sais-je, moi?2

Nicolas Boileau, who has something to say about everything, does not let the joueuses get by without criticism. He devotes part of his tenth Satire to the female gambler and her nefarious habit:

Chez elle, en ces emplois, l'aube du lendemain
Souvent la trouve encor les cartes à la main.
Alors, pour se coucher les quittant non sans peine,
Elle plaint le malheur de la nature humaine
Qui veut qu'en un sommeil, où tout s'ensevelit,
Tant d'heures sans jouer se consument au lit.3

18

Not all comments were this adverse as can be seen in the following except from the <u>Mercure galant</u> of August 1695, which recommends: "Vous avez raison, Mesdemoiselles, de vouloir apprendre le trictrac.C'est un fort beau jeu et qui est plus à la mode que jamais. On le joue beaucoup à la cour et à Paris."[4] Charles Kunstler, a modern historian, thinks that "les femmes de ce pays sont extrêmement joueuses" and further remarks that "on joue partout à Paris. Les femmes, surtout, sont comme fascinées par le jeu."[5] Keeping these mixed feelings on gambling in mind, we shall now examine three seventeenth-century comedies which deal mainly with this vice as seen in women.

1. La Forge's <u>La Joueuse dupée</u> (1664).

Chronologically, <u>La Joueuse dupée ou l'Intrigue des Académies</u> is the first play to be based entirely on the gambling mania. This one-act work, in verse, is more of a simple, direct dialogue than a comedy proper. The very uncomplicated plot is as follows: Clidamant is in love with Cléonice, daughter of Valère and Uranie, the <u>joueuse</u>. Knowing that the latter is too involved in her games to bless their union, Clidamant tricks her into gambling with a friend of his. While the game is in progress, the couple elopes, only to run into the girl's father. They are brought back in the house where Valère consents to their marriage.

The literary style of <u>La Joueuse dupée</u> is careless at times and the versification often faulty and clumsy. Its value, therefore, lies mainly in the information it provides on gambling, and in the vivid picture it paints of its development. The play is an excellent portrayal of contemporary society reflected in literature; it presents the <u>joueuses</u>, the frenzy for dice and cards, a game in progress, and the cynical acceptance of cheating.

The foundations of this comedy are social. It is based on the practice of holding open gambling <u>Académies</u> in certain private residences. As we have seen before, this custom was widespread due to the passion that existed for gambling during the latter part of the seventeenth century. The public <u>brelans</u> were not enough and they were more likely to be subject to the anti-gambling laws which were enacted from time to time.[6] These regulations could not be enforced so well in the private mansions where much of this activity could then go on undisturbed.

Many of the writers of the time were openly a-
gainst the vice and the proliferation of these establishments. La Bruyère expressed his concern for pos-
terity's reaction to the Parisian craze by making this
parallel with Rome: "L'on entendra parler d'une capi-
tale d'un grand royaume où il n'y avait ni places pu-
bliques, ni bains, ni fontaines, ni amphithéâtres, ni
galeries, ni portiques, ni promenoirs, qui était pourtant une ville merveilleuse."7 He continues his detailed condemnation of the popular pastime by attack-
ing the various services available in the Académies,
for the right price:

> L'on dira que tout le cours de la vie s'y pas-
> sait preque à sortir de sa maison pour aller
> se renfermer dans celle d'un autre; que d'hon-
> nêtes femmes, qui n'étaient ni marchandes ni
> hôtelières avaient leurs maisons ouvertes à
> ceux qui payaient pour y entrer; que l'on a-
> vait à choisir des dés, des cartes et de tous
> les jeux; que l'on mangeait dans ces maisons,
> et qu'elles étaient commodes à tout commerce.8

It was indeed the custom to leave money on the gaming
table to take care of the expense of the cards, dice,
etc. This was an accepted practice in all gambling
houses, public and private. It is interesting to note,
however, that the private Académies were notorious for
charging exhorbitant prices, much more so than the public brelans. In La Joueuse dupée, Uranie is a consum-
mate gambler who lives exclusively for her vice. Even
though she does not appear on stage until the fourth
scene, her passion is the topic of discussion throughout. Time not spent on gambling is time wasted; it is
her sole activity, her only pastime. Let us examine
the effects of her obsession on those around her.

Her husband, Valère, is infuriated by the fact
that she neglects him for her game:

> Que d'un pauvre mary l'avanture est cruelle,
> Quand il est embasté d'une telle femelle.
> Et que je suis niais de souffrir, par amour,
> Qu'une femme s'occupe à jouer tout le jour!9

His plight goes beyond economic reasons as he questions
his wife's marital fidelity:

> Au lieu de vous tenir à vos propres affaires,
> Vous y passés les jours avec les nuit entières,
> Et Dieu sçait à quel jeu vous joues le plus fort,

Quand vous avés appris que le bonhomme dort.
(sc. 7)

In real life, as well as in drama, gambling many times serves to camouflage questionable behavior. In the case of Uranie, her obsession is legitimate since nothing more appeals to her outside her vice. The gambler is not particularly interested in romance, as the two passions just do not seem to go well together. This aspect of the vice, true for both male and female gamblers, shall be analyzed in other plays as well. Some psychologists venture that "gambling may be, among other things, a sublimation of sex, or at least a psychological substitute."10

Three centuries prior to modern psychology, however, La Bruyère had made a similar statement in regard to the joueuse:

> Il est étonnant de voir dans le coeur de certaines femmes quelque chose de plus vif et de plus fort que l'amour pour les hommes, je veux dire l'ambition et le jeu: de telles femmes rendent les hommes chastes; elles n'ont de leur sexe que les habits.11

Lisette, the suivante, feels the effect of her mistress' actions. Since she is expected to follow Uranie everywhere and obey her wishes, her schedule becomes erratic. She elaborates on the harm done to her health by the odd hours she is forced to keep, and complains of lack of sleep, food and all comfort:

> C'est trop endurer, ma constance est à bout:
> N'avoir point de repos, ne dormir point du tout,
> Sans oser dire un mot, souffrir un froid extrême,
> En dépit de ses dents jeusner plus d'un caresme.
> (sc. 1)

In the simple, practical mind of the servant, non-routine behavior is unexplainable: "faire du jour la nuit, et de la nuit le jour" (sc. 1) is something Lisette cannot understand. Her role, however, goes beyond pointing out the evils of the vice, for she gives us a glimpse of society. Usurers are her target and our attention is briefly pointed at these individuals who make a living from the weaknesses of others.

Love is a very minor underlying theme in the play. As a matter of fact, love is presented as the alternate behavior for gambling, though sometimes dependent on it; while Uranie gambles, Cléonice loves. This is emphasized by Valère when he comments: "l'une perd tout mon bien, et l'autre est amoureuse;/Cléonice est coquette, et sa mère est joueuse." (sc. 7)

Lisette is instrumental in getting the two lovers together, yet love still depends on gambling. Clidamant uses gambling as a stepping stone in obtaining Cléonice's love. He admits the foolishness of his behavior, but understands the importance of keeping the gambling mother on his side, or at least indifferent to her daughter's desires: "Uranie est joueuse; il faut, par son malheur,/ Ou ne point voir sa fille, ou flatter son humeur." (sc. 2) Though not a gambler at heart, Clidamant gambles as a means to gain Cléonice's love; furthermore, he gambles on the outcome of his ruse.

Clidamant's valet, Turlupin, is in love with Lisette, in a parallel situation with his master's. In scene 2 he provides some comic relief reminiscent of the Spanish _gracioso_, by reciting some well-known proverbs in reverse, and thus giving origin to the term _turlupinade_. In addition, he portrays the society of the times by illustrating several methods of cheating to which his master has fallen victim: use of mirrors, marked cards, distractions, etc.

The character of the Marquis should be included in this discussion of cheating, since he is brought into the game precisely because of his ability at less-than-honest gambling. Very likely, he is a _faux marquis_, a usurper of a noble title, who has adopted it as a consequence of the court life under Louis XIV. Of all titles falsified in this way, that of marquis seems to have been the favorite and is therefore the target of ridicule by writers of comedy. Our marquis is a good _railleur_ and an expert liar. Clidamant summarizes his qualifications: "Sçavoir entretenir et Bacchus et l'Amour,/ Hanter l'Académie, et paroistre à la cour." (sc. 2) In our play, the Marquis and gambling go hand in hand. In scene 3, he elaborates on the subject of cheating, mentions several incidents and brags about his accomplishments in great detail. In the same scene he describes the game of _trictrac_, quite fashionable among the nobility. He resorts to his prodigious memory to enumerate the various popular games of the time and lists thirty-five of them in scene 5. He then proceeds to give a brief history of the _jeux_. Finally, in his portrayal of his society, he comments on the female gambler:

Ne nous accusés point: dans le siècle où nous
                                   sommes,
Les femmes sont au jeu plus fortes que les hommes;
En France, en Angleterre, en Espagne, et partout,
On les y voit tousjours tenir le meilleur bout.
                              (sc. 4)

The joueuse is not always above cheating and,
according to our marquis, is more adept at it than the
joueur. Women, he says, abuse the respect due them to
cheat shamelessly and they do not hesitate to use
their charms to their advantage. (sc. 4) Furthermore,
they lure men into gambling with them by emphasizing
their losses and hiding their winnings under their
skirts. A trace of préciosité is provided by Polixène,
who in a world of prosaic gamblers, prefers the poetic
ideal of the theatre. Her brief appearance toward the
end of the play is a reflection of real life. Gambling rivals drama, as the court's preference slowly
shifts toward the game and away from the play. Through
the eyes of Polixène we witness an attempt to prove
the superiority of the theatre, a sensible, entertaining pastime, over all others.

Polixène makes a casual entrance in scene 5,
and we are told that "ces yeux sont charmans! ce sont
de vrais soleils," and that "sa grace est divine." But
shortly afterwards she takes her stand and declares
that gambling is confining and that life is, indeed,
at the theatre:

C'est à la comédie où l'on voit le beau monde,
Attiré par les vers d'une Muse féconde:
Les sçavans de leur art y rencontrent les loix,
Et les Princes enfin y vont ouyr les Roys.
                              (sc. 5)

Unfortunately, the vice wins and Polixène, like the
others, gives in to Uranie's wishes to gamble. In contrast to the précieuse's wit and ability with words,
the joueuse shows lack of polish, and even admits her
ignorance: "De l'esprit j'en ay peu;/ Mais je me pique au moins de jouer un beau jeu." (sc. 6)

In spite of the defense of the theatre and the
underlying love theme, it must be concluded that gambling is the very heart of the play. Through its presentation of different gamblers, of cheating and of an
actual game in progress, La Forge offers us a tableau
where we can see the role that vice played in his soci-

ety. In this first attempt at dramatizing the practice, there is no moralizing and no character portrayal; gambling itself constitutes the means and the end.
Although the effects of the vice on the characters are
clearly depicted, we are not told what is right or
wrong, moral or immoral in their actions. The reader
must draw his own conclusions, for the author offers
none.

2. Dancourt's La Désolation des joueuses (1687).

This one-act play in prose owes its existence
to a government decree prohibiting the game of lansquenet. Dancourt turns to the contemporary scene for
inspiration and material, building his work around the
effect that this law has on his characters. This comedy differs from La Joueuse dupée in that it does not
present any scenes of gambling in progress, since it
had been outlawed. But the addiction to the vice is
emphasized even more and the reader is faced with a
Parisian society weakened by its passion for games of
chance.

The intrigue, again quite simple, develops
mostly in the first three and the last tow scenes. The
remaining nine scenes present in great detail the con-
sternation caused by the prohibition of the game. According to the play, the law affects only lansquenet,
but the other games just cannot console the gamblers.

The uncomplicated plot is as follows: Dorimène, the joueuse, is addicted to gambling and wants to
marry her daughter, Angélique, to a gambler. The latter turns out to be an impostor and the daughter is
finally allowed to marry the man she loves--provided he
learns to gamble. By minimizing the plot, Dancourt can
develop the subject more than his predecessor. In a
few scenes the author gives us a large picture of gambling and a variety of gamblers. The unity of the play
lies, not in the intrigue, but in the study of the
vice.

The evils of lansquenet are illustrated by the
disorder brought into a respectable household. The
game affects all, and Lisette, the servant, cannot help
but express joy at the law forbidding the game:

> Je sais bien pour moi, que si j'avais gouverné
> la police ... on ne parlerait plus de ces mau-
> dits jeux, qui causent tant de désordre, et qui

m'ont fait passer tant de nuits sans me cou-
cher.12

Angélique's comment is even more relevant, as it provides us with a contemporary reaction to the custom of
holding gambling Académies in private homes. She expresses her concern over the people who constitute the
habitués:

> Le jeu même ne me déplairait peut-être point si
> fort, si l'on jouait ailleurs que chez sa mère:
> mais, que cette maison soit une Académie ou-
> verte à toutes sortes de gens; que tout ce
> qu'il y a de fainéants, de ridicules et d'ex-
> travagants, pour ne rien dire de plus fâcheux,
> soient les bienvenus dans ce logis. (sc. 1)

Her exasperation is easily understood, since
the constant comings and goings of these unwelcomed
guests do not allow her a single moment of privacy.
Furthermore, she is prevented from expressing her own
feelings of disapproval to these individuals by the
very fact that so many of them lose, and therefore,
owe her money. Angélique would gladly sacrifice the
income from gambling in exchange for some peace and
quiet. It must again be noted that in addition to the
money which the hostess "earned" in the games, there
was the fee charged for the use of her house, dice,
cards, etc., all of which constituted a considerable
amount.

Dorimène neglects her daughter and therefore
remains unaware of the latter's amorous preferences.
Gambling and love are on opposite sides in this play,
for the man Angélique loves does not care to gamble,
while the one her mother has chosen for her is an inveterate gambler. Dorante, her lover, describes the
gambler as follows: "Le chevalier est un aventurier
tombé des nues, qu'on ne connaît que par le jeu, et qui
ne subsistait que par là, comme mille autres de son
caractère." (sc. 2) Dorante is determined to show
that, although he pretends to be a chevalier, his rival
is nothing more than an impostor.

The chevalier de Bellemonte constitutes a good
example of the chevalier d'industrie, an individual in
real life who serves as the author's target in a multi-
tude of plays. He is an adventurer who assumes a title
(usually that of chevalier) and is introduced into high
society through his association with women. In this

25

play Dancourt gives us little more than a rough sketch of his type; yet, although his character is not well developed, he does represent a social aspect of the times when money plays so important a role that it tempts men to assume false identities. Many times their disguises are not discovered; in this play, however, he had to be unmasked to save Angélique from ruining her life. His falseness contrasts with Dorante's honesty.

The concept of cheating at gambling parallels the idea of using disguises to conceal one's true identity. There are two cheats and masters of disguise in this play: one is the <u>chevalier d'industrie</u>; the other is Merlin, Dorante's so-called valet. The unity of the situation is clearly emphasized by the fact that Dorante can see through both masquerades; furthermore, he takes advantage of them by playing Merlin against Bellemonte, since one <u>fripon</u> can easily recognize another. Even Merlin evaluates the illusion of their identities: "on change de personnages dans le monde. Tantôt on est marquis, tantôt chevalier, puis marchand, quelquefois abbé, financier souvent. Que sais-je moi?" (sc. 3)

Dorimène's character shows more complexity than our previous <u>joueuse</u>. She is warped by her love of the game, but she exercises some prudence by not risking the thousand <u>écus</u> fine for breaking the law. Her indifference to Angélique and her squandering of the family fortune on her games, however, more than upset this proof of sound judgment. Her main role is as hostess of an <u>Académie</u> where the <u>habitués</u> constitute an assorted representation of social behavior. It must be noted that, not being a comedy of character, the <u>personnages</u> are typed, and our main concern remains with the study of manners, in this case gambling.

The fact that gambling was not limited to France and the French, even under Louis XIV, is a topic of discussion in the play. With the prohibition of <u>lansquenet</u>, Paris suffers the loss of a very important segment of its population: the gamblers. The universality of the vice saves them, however, for England is then paradise for an adept gambler, and afterwards "quand nous aurons épuisé l'Angleterre, nous passerons en Hollande. Il y a de bonnes bourses en ce pays-là." (sc. 5)

It is difficult to establish whether these peo-

ple gamble because of a need for money or because of
an addiction to the vice. Nevertheless, we shall now
examine some of the possible reasons for their behavior. It provides an excuse to be sociable; the guests
expect to see their friends at the gatherings and express disappointment when the routine is altered. The
comtesse is upset when she arrives at the usual time
and finds no one there: "Où est tout notre monde aujourd'hui?" she asks in scene 6. The meaning of the
possessive adjective is all too obvious: the world of
the gambling house is their only world, unreal but
safe and sure.

The countess first calls attention to the
snobism present in their society by expressing her
feelings on the bourgeois, whose manners are different
and, of course, inferior, from those of the gens de
qualité. In her opinion, the former's gambling debts
do not carry as much prestige as the latter's. When
she is informed of the regulatory measure against her
favorite game, lansquenet, she reacts in a dramatic
way: "c'est comme si l'on défendait de dormir." (sc.
7) She finally accedes to the reality of the situation, but in her own terms: "Ces publications sont
pour le peuple, pour les laquais, pour la canaille, à
qui l'on fait bien de défendre certains jeux qui ne
sont fait que pour les gens de qualité." (sc. 7)

Apparently, preference passes from one game to
another among the upper class; lansquenet is the fashionable pastime and therefore too good for the common
people. The countess' evaluation of the law is proved
wrong by the arrival of the intendante, who assures
all those present that the law concerns everyone;
there are no special privileges for anyone. The intendante, who is also a snob, is given to fainting
spells and is desperate to gamble so she can recoup
her losses before her husband finds out. The fainting seems to parody the frequent évanouissements of
the heroine of novel and tragedy. Lisette revives her
by waiving a pack of cards in front of her; this action
shows the author's cleverness and provides a moment of
good comedy in the midst of all the ridiculous happen-
ings. Where medicine fails, the remedy is "un jeu de
lansquenet, et il n'y a point de joueuse que cela ne
ressuscite en moins de rien." (sc. 8)

Most of the habitués show disrespect for the
law and insist on going ahead with the game as planned.
Dorimène opposes the suggestion since she alone, as the

hostess, would be the one facing the fine. The reason for their insistence is clearly stated; they all want to win back their money. The logical fact that they cannot all be winners is not even considered. On the contrary, each player is convinced that this is the one opportunity needed to break even and that afterwards there will be no more gambling ever. The following excerpt is a good example of the gamblers' attitude:

> ---Après cela, je vous promets de renoncer au jeu pour toute ma vie.
> ---Mais, Madame, si vous continuez à perdre?
> ---Mais, Madame, je gagnerai indubitablement.
> (sc. 8)

Even though the play is meant for entertainment and no moral judgment is expressly stated, it is difficult to overlook the implications of the protagonists' actions and their words. Most gamblers are optimists by definition, playing cheerfully again and again, although even in a fair game the odds are against them. This very optimism often brings about their ruin.

The fact that the gamblers are convinced of their immediate change of fortune is explained by John Cohen as the "gambler's fallacy." He summarizes this attitude as follows:

> The longer the run of failures, the more convinced he is that the next outcome will be successful. But after a run of successes he does not necessarily expect a reversal to failure. The gambler's relation to success is quite different from his relation to failure.[13]

The promises made by the _habitués_ of Dorimène's gambling _Académie_ seem to follow this pattern. They vow to quit gambling for stakes, as soon as they recover their losses.

An element of dishonesty and violence is introduced by the character of the crude _caissier_. He has a more valid reason for being upset at the prohibition of _lansquenet_, since he has helped himself to 25,000 francs from his bank to help finance the gambling of others; now that this activity has been suspended, he has no way of recovering the money. He is the only one among the guests who threatens the others and himself with violence; he will commit suicide as he cannot face the punishment for his actions. His bad manners and his use of words add color to the scene:

> Je suis ruiné si l'on ne joue; mais, ventre-
> bleu! vous jouerez les uns et les autres jus-
> qu'à ce que je sois payé de ce qui m'est dû.
> Je suis au desespoir, voyez-vous, et j'ai déjà
> voulu me pendre trois fois depuis ce matin.
> (sc. 9)

Eraste is brought on stage to explain the value of lansquenet. It seems that gambling in general
and lansquenet in particular played a very important
role in seventeenth-century France; scene 10 serves as
the literary mirror for this social behavior. The
young man points out the various inconveniences that
will result, since the game often is a disguise to de-
tract attention from other activities; for instance,
young men would borrow money at usurious rates of interest in order to live in luxury, yet would be able
to explain their way of life in terms of good luck at
the games: "le père ... admirait le bonheur de son
fils et l'utilité du lansquenet." (sc. 10) In addition, women who received expensive gifts from their
lovers could explain to their husbands that they had
won them at lansquenet; furthermore, the reputation of
many women could be protected for a long time by pretending they were out gambling: "et le lansquenet me
servait à ménager la réputation de vingt femmes que je
considère." (sc. 10) The prohibition of the game affected not only the real gambler, but also those who
pretended to be gamblers.

It cannot be denied that gambling had become a
habit to those people; in real life, gambling constituted a very important part of the daily routine of
the nobility, as pointed out by La Bruyère as he condemned the lack of imagination of the joueuses:

> Elles comptaient autrefois une semaine par les
> jours de jeu, de spectacle ... elles allaient
> le lundi perdre leur argent chez Ismène, le
> mardi leur temps chez Climène, le mercredi
> leur réputation chez Célimène.[14]

The final development of the play is the discussion of ways in which the law could be evaded; gamble they must, even though they fear the possible penalty. They consider playing on the roof, or in a cel-
lar where they would be out of sight; gambling on a
boat floating down the Seine River is a more original
suggestion, but not as desperate as leaving for Eng-

land, where gambling is still allowed: "On prend un
bateau au Pont-Rouge, et l'on va, jouant, jusqu'à
Saint-Cloud." (sc. 12) The most logical solution has
its drawbacks; they could meet at some old abandoned
house in the faubourgs, but in order to avoid suspicion, "l'assemblée ne se tiendra pas toujours au même
endroit, et l'on se promènera de faubourg en faubourg." (sc. 12). In spite of family responsibilities,
regardless of social class, against public regulations, they must gamble. The one factor common to all
of them is the game, so the physical location of the
activity is not as revealing as their attitude. The
comtesse best summarizes the general feeling in scene
12: "si je joue tant qu'il me plaira, je jouerai le
jour et la nuit assurément."

3. Dancourt's Les Bourgeoises à la mode (1692).

        Les Bourgeoises à la mode, a five-act comédie
de moeurs, is considered one of Dancourt's best plays.
Its dialogue is more natural and more dramatic than
that of his earlier works, and in spite of some loose
threads which remain unexplained at the end, it is
well structured. The complexity of its plot results
from the central motivating force, i.e., ambition
manifested in the passion for gambling. Two bourgeoises, Angélique and Araminte, need money in order
to become femmes de qualité. Since their husbands
will not willingly facilitate the necessary funds, the
women resort to deceit in order to extort money from
them; each of the husbands is blinded by his love for
the other's wife. The intrigue is complicated by the
selfish servants, Lisette and Frontin, and by Angélique's naive stepdaughter, Marianne, and her lover,
the chevalier. Madame Amelin, the pawnbroker, saves
everything and everyone at the end of the play.

        Knowing that gambling is the best means to
climb the social ladder in seventeenth-century Versailles, the two bourgeoises want to host an Académie
which would attract the right people and be fort à la
mode. Angélique's husband, M. Simon, is only a notaire; Araminte's husband, M. Griffard, a simple com-
missaire. In order to ascend in society they must not
associate with other femmes de robe, but seek the company of femmes d'épée: "Je ne veux voir que des
femmes de qualité ... des femmes d'épée. C'est mon
faible que les femmes d'épée."[15] As part of the image
they have to create and maintain, they must ride in
handsome coaches and hold parties at their homes; all

these activities cost money, of course:

> Je vais dépenser de l'argent puisque j'en ai.
> J'ai besoin de mille choses, des tables, des
> cornets, des dés et des cartes. Il faut de
> tout cela dans une maison où l'on veut re-
> cevoir compagnie. (act 2, sc. 4)

But the expenses constitute an investment which brings
fame and the right kind of visitors; a woman who
lavishes money and entertains her gambling guests is
very much in demand: "C'est une femme de fort bon
sens, qui aime les plaisirs, le jeu, la compagnie; et,
depuis deux jours, je me suis avisé de lui persuader
de donner à jouer chez elle." (act 1, sc. 1)

Among the various kinds of people anxious to
attend Angélique's Académie we find "deux Marquises,
une Comtesse, un Partisan, trois Abbés, autant de fai-
néants, ce Commis de la Douane et ce petit Epicier."
(act 2, sc. 2) Although we never witness an actual
game in progress, the gambling spirit is alive and
present throughout the comedy.

We shall compare some of the remarks made by
the characters in this comedy with opinions expressed
by present-day psychologists on the subject of gambling. For example, Clyde Davis explains that "the
winnings should be squandered on non-essentials which
you ordinarily cannot afford as there is no fun in
buying necessities."[16] This parallels very closely
Lisette's comment on her mistress' gambling habits:
"c'est une chose sacrée que l'argent du jeu; diantre,
ce sont des fonds pour le plaisir, où l'on ne touche
point pour le nécessaire!" (act 1, sc. 12) This attitude abounds among gamblers, so it is not unusual
that both the servant (the playwright's spokesman) and
the psychologist observe it. Bossuet has noticed it,
too, and deplores the practice as irresponsible: "Les
dettes de jeu étaient 'privilégiées.' Et comme si les
lois du jeu étaient les plus saintes et les plus in-
violables de toutes, on se pique d'honneur d'y être
fidèle."[17]

As the title indicates, the play claims to represent la vie quotidienne in middle-class circles, a
life characterized by intrigue, gambling and deceit.
Les Bourgeoises à la mode is primarily a comedy of manners and therefore, even though the characters are
firmly outlined in Act I, they become types and not

individuals. Dancourt pictures society as sordid; his impression remains subjective, of course. The dramatist describes the world that he knows, tinted by his own prejudices and attitudes; the actuality of his play results from his concern with topics of contemporary interest. A writer of comedy finds it easier to portray vice than virtue in order to provoke laughter, and irresistible to engage in a little exaggeration. The interest of the play stems from the variety of social types presented, but a large part of its merit lies in the spontaneous dialogue.

Most of Dancourt's observations are accurate as the characters find their sources in real life in the aspirations of the Parisian bourgeoisie. The bourgeoises aspire to be femmes de qualité; the chevaliers d'industrie will do anything for the right price; the dishonest usurers benefit from all the corruption; gambling is the favorite pastime. We may accept cautiously the naive daughter just out of the convent, and the cunning soubrettes and valets.

The ambition of the wives contrasts with their husbands' contentment in their mediocre professional class. Male ambition appears only in the unpleasant chevalier d'industrie who pretends to love women as long as they help him stay among the nobility. Frontin's definition accurately reflects this fact:

> L'heureuse chose que d'être né avec de l'esprit! Oh! pour cela, Monsieur le chevalier est un des premiers hommes qu'il y ait au monde. Le jeu, les femmes, tout ce qui sert à ruiner les autres, est ce qui lui fait faire figure; et tout son revenu n'est qu'en fonds d'esprit. (act 1, sc. 2)

The chevalier detects women with money, declares his love, and sometimes even marries them. Who marries these rogues? young ingénues, just out of the convent, whose naiveté about life conceals a precocious, unsatisfied curiosity. These girls have evolved since Molière's time; they now appear independent of parental control, willingly discuss married life more openly, and often take the initiative in the love affair. The influence of the suivante on the personal life of the young woman has replaced parental influence. Lisette herself explains how the new system works:

> Aujourd'hui les manières sont bien différentes: on prend seulement l'aveu de la petite fille;

on tâche d'avoir l'agrément de la fille de
chambre, et quand on ne peut plus cacher la
chose, on en informe la famille. (act 1,sc. 3)

Regardless of who holds the greatest influence on the
girl, it seems that the <u>chevalier</u> is rewarded, not punished, for his deceitful ways.

The cynicism of the author is best reflected
in the servants, the only ones who really triumph in
the end. Although they generally conform to Molière's
type, they have evolved toward selfishness. Frontin
for example looks at life cynically, closely watching
his own interests. "Je suis le garçon de France le
plus employé. Valet de chambre de l'un, laquais de
l'autre, grison de celle-ci, espion de celle-là ...
je suis presque toujours pour et contre." (act 1,sc.3)
Lisette is intelligent and quickly stacks the odds on
her side. She usually gives good advice to her mistress and often helps her in her love affairs. There
is no sentimental attachment, no feeling of loyalty,
no sharing between them, however, because greed and
money have come between them.

In this world of dishonest and selfish people,
kindness is provided only by an intelligent and compassionate businesswoman, Mme Amelin the pawnbroker.
Although not an <u>entremetteuse</u> by trade, she otherwise
belongs to the same group of interesting characters as
Frosine of Molière's <u>L'Avare</u>. Her love for the Chevalier, her son, shows a maternal instinct rare in
seventeenth-century French comedy; this affection
raises her from the type to the individual.[18] She disapproves of her son's dishonesty, but, proud of his
achievements, she willingly forgives him and secures
his future. In this pretentious world of the comedy,
she is ironically the only one who has any money. Her
fortune comes from the needs and ambitions of the people who gamble, but she alone is the real winner.

Gambling, a manifestation of the corruption of
society, once again serves as an excuse for other actions. It attracts the <u>gens de qualité</u> to Angélique's
household, for "tout Paris viendra chez vous sitôt
qu'on saura qu'on y joue" (act 4, sc. 3); it also attracts money. Lisette is able to obtain much needed
cash for her mistress from Araminte's husband by telling him that the money will only be accepted as gambling "conscience money." This constituted a common
practice among gamblers who cheated and were later
bothered by a guilty conscience; they would simply

send an anonymous letter with the amount which had been acquired dishonestly.

> Les joueurs sont un peu sujets à caution. Et Madame n'a pas joué toujours avec les plus honnêtes personnes du monde ... Envoyez-lui de l'argent qu'elle puisse recevoir comme d'un remords de conscience de quelque fripon converti. (act 3, sc. 9)

Angélique likes to have gambling parties because of the social prestige; her husband wants her to hold this social activity in order to keep her at home more often. Her illusions reach ridiculous proportions, as she dreams of "similar" events held at Louis XIV's Versailles:

> Il me faut de la musique trois jours de la semaine seulement; trois autres après-dînées, on jouera quelque reprise d'hombre et de lansquenet, qui seront suivies d'un grand souper, de manière que nous n'aurons qu'un jour de reste, qui sera le jour de conversation. (act 4,sc.6)

Her kind of grand scale entertainment cannot be afforded on her husband's income. But she reminds him that one of the benefits of hosting gambling parties is that they become financially self-supporting. Indeed, we have already seen that a _joueuse_ is assured an income.

As the interest in materialism increases, we witness a deterioration in the family structure. No trust exists between husband and wife, no love for the children, no respect for the parents. The decay of the high classes and the family forecasts the triumph of the lower classes and the servants. Vice conquers virtue, and although gambling is one aspect of this play, it symbolizes the general attitudes and mores of the characters. It holds their actions up for the reader's judgment with moralizing, but the disastrous effects of greed and ambition are all too obvious.

In this chapter we have seen three late seventeenth-century comedies, all little known, but which portray the effects of gambling on society, as reflected in literature. When possible, the social and the literary have been paralleled, compared or contrasted. Psychology has been brought into the examination only twice, but as we continue the socio-literary analysis in Chapters II and III, psychology will play a greater role. In our attempt to explain the reasons behind the behavior of the _joueurs_, we shall see social and family pressures mirror national pressures, and create a character whose neurosis is manifested in his gambling.

NOTES TO CHAPTER I

[1] Edmond Beaurepaire, "Les Maisons de jeux au Grand Siècle," *Mercure de France*, 83 (1910), 442.

[2] Dufresny, p. 127.

[3] Nicolas Boileau, *Oeuvres poétiques* (Paris: Flammarion, 1703), p. 80.

[4] Georges Mongrédien, *La Vie quotidienne sous Louis XIV* (Paris: Librairie Hachette, 1948), p. 102.

[5] Charles Kunstler, *La Vie quotidienne sous la Régence* (Paris: Librairie Hachette, 1960), p. 197.

[6] Beaurepaire, p. 442.

[7] Jean de La Bruyère, *Les Caractères* (Paris: Garnier, n.d.), p. 11.

[8] Ibid., p. 11.

[9] François V. Fournel, *Les Contemporains de Molière* (Paris: Firmin-Didot et Cie., 1876), p. 310. Henceforth, all quotations from *La Joueuse dupée* will be taken from this edition and will be indicated by the scene number.

[10] Clyde Davis, *Something for Nothing* (Philadelphia: J.B. Lippincott Company, 1956), p. 24.

[11] La Bruyère, p. 127.

[12] Dancourt, *Théâtre choisi* (Paris: Librairie Garnier Frères, n.d.), p. 44. Henceforth, all quotations from *La Désolation des joueuses* will be taken from this edition and will be indicated by the scene number.

[13] John Cohen, *Behaviour in Uncertainty and Its Social Implications* (New York: Basic Books, Inc., 1964), p. 60.

[14]La Bruyère, p. 123.

[15]Dancourt, _Théâtre choisi_, p. 318. Henceforth, all quotations from _Les Bourgeoises à la mode_ will be taken from this edition and will be indicated by the act and scene number.

[16]Davis, p. 26   ·   [17]Kunstler, p. 197.

[18]Arthur Tilley, _The Decline of the Age of Louis XIV_ (New York: Barnes and Noble, Inc., 1968), p. 96.

CHAPTER II

LE JOUEUR

Gambling in French comedy under Louis XIV and Louis XV provided an element of realism. In order to achieve this aim, the authors added the _femmes d'intrigue_, counterfeiters, usurers and cheats to the gallery of gamblers; their practices depicted on stage mirrored their models, so active during the reigns of both monarchs. We have previously noted that on occasion entire plays were built around this particular aspect of society. In Chapter I the _joueuses_ were seen in both French comedy and society; Chapter II will present, in Regnard's _Le Joueur_ (1696), a portrait of the male gambler as a young, relatively harmless amateur.

As we examine the play we shall notice a definite change from the works studied in the previous chapter, due to a more conscious attempt on the part of Regnard and other playwrights to analyze character as well as manners. Though society remains very much alive, instances of self-analysis increase and character portrayal becomes more descriptive. The interest in manners toward the end of the seventeenth century, however, prevailed over the interest in character. As the dramatists turned to the contemporary scene for inspiration, they felt obligated to include the manifestations of gambling which played such an important role in the national life of France; but while Bossuet and Bourdaloue preached and La Bruyère satirized, the playwrights did not concern themselves with moralizing at all. There is no judgment, only faithful portraits of the situations. The interpretation of the events presented in the play is left up to the reader or audience.

Interest in gambling is one of the most fundamental traits of human nature. The urge to risk a little in the hope of gaining much, the desire to get something for nothing is universal.[1] In all civilizations known to us the popularity of gambling has appeared evident; Davis explains what makes it so attractive:

> In a gambling transaction nothing of value is produced or transported or jobbed or wholesaled or distributed, that on a basis of sheer

chance one individual seeking to gain something
for nothing ventures some legal tender and loses while another individual also seeking something for nothing wins.[2]

Traditionally, studies on gambling have been concerned
with whether it is good or evil, moral or immoral,
right or wrong. In our study gambling is concerned
instead in terms of its role and function in society
and its effects on the individual. As we look more
closely at the joueurs, we will once again attempt to
relate them to other aspects of their particular situation in relation to themselves, their family, and
their society.

The majority of the psychological works related to gambling have been devoted to the abnormal or
addicted. Curiously enough, the male gambler seems to
be more affected by this malady than his female counterpart; literature of the period under study corroborates this opinion. In general, the joueurs are
given more complex characters than the joueuses and
their emotional instability has more serious consequences. Gambling, however, does not always accompany
an abnormal personality, since normal people also gamble. Neither are all the gamblers studied neurotic,
sick or emotionally unstable.[3] As a matter of fact,
our analysis in Chapters II and III will clearly show
a progression, as we follow the development of a "gambler" from youth to maturity, from carefree comedy to
fatal tragedy. We shall relate them to their respective milieu, and explain why each situation differs
logically from the other.

Psychological studies on the subject have established two kinds of gamblers; one type is emotionally stable, the other unstable. On the basis of this
evidence, it can be inferred that there exists a cor-
relation between gambling and normal behavior, as well
as gambling and abnormal behavior. The difference between the two types lies in the fact that the abnormal
kind participates in gambling to the exclusion of all
other activities.[4] It has not been established beyond a doubt, however, that gambling is "instinctual"
or "natural"; it has been shown in the Introduction
that whenever people have been organized in groups or
units, whatever the civilization, ancient or modern,
gambling also has existed. We have searched for possible explanations for this phenomenon, and all we can
conclude at this point is that gambling is a basic

human activity.

The fact that Jean-François Regnard was born into a rich family and inherited a considerable fortune at an early age is reflected in his five-act comedy, Le Joueur. His carefree ways and happy lack of obligation are mirrored in the "things-will-take-care-of-themselves" attitude of Valère. Of all the authors presented in our study, Regnard is the one whose life most closely influenced his work. Like his hero, he received a good education and enjoyed lavish entertainment. Both Regnard and Valère took things in stride and never allowed the situation to have the best of them. They enjoyed the pleasures of life and saw no reason to deprive themselves; both of them were also gamblers.

Regnard's relatively short life was one of indulgence, gambling, adventure and romance. He could always see the bright side and was never burdened by responsibility. His philosophy of life, reminiscent of Rabelais, is relevant because he practiced what he preached in his own life and in his works.

Les dames, le jeu, ny le vin,
Ne m'arrachent point à moy-même;
Et cependant je bois, je joue et j'aime.
Faire tout ce qu'on veut, vivre exempt de chagrin,
Ne se rien refuser, voilà tout mon système;
Et de mes jours ainsi j'attraperai la fin.[5]

Le Joueur is a high comedy in the tradition of Molière. Although there is no deep psychological character analysis, it can be classified as a comedy of character as well as a comedy of manners. In spite of the tragic view of the gambler, its tone rings gay because the initial stages of the vice do not necessarily result in serious consequences. Regnard's style is vivacious, graceful and picturesque; the play is well balanced and constructed. The influence of society seems obvious in the theme and the situations. The influence of Descartes, Molière and Racine will be studied later.

When Regnard, encouraged by the success of his shorter plays, decided to write a high comedy in verse, he chose to study a fashionable vice, the passion for gambling. Being a casual gambler, he understood the important role of gaming in French society of the late seventeenth century. It was a madness for which everything was staked: jewels, mansions, money and honor; it flourished in the _salons_ as well as at Court, but suffered serious competition from the public _brelans_ which had emerged everywhere in Paris. Regnard himself is known to have frequented the _brelan_ of the Loyson sisters. _Le Joueur_, instantly accepted by the public, caused brief animosity in 1697; the theme, after all, was the very vice which the royal police had repeatedly tried to curb. _Trictrac_, the favorite game in the comedy, had been declared unlawful several times after 1639, but the King and his Court were the prime offenders.[6]

Although we do not witness an actual game in progress, Regnard's play explains several facets of the art and uses some of its terms in the speech of the characters. The comedy emphasizes the fact that all social classes meet about the green felt table. This merely parallels the dubious speculations in the Paris of the times where many people were ruined daily at the card table, and where the aristocracy often found itself in the company of unscrupulous adventurers and seekers of fortune. In _Le Joueur_, the game of _trictrac_ gathers bourgeois and marquis alike, the high and the low, obliterating caste.

We can briefly summarize the play as follows: Valère, the inveterate gambler, is engaged to Angélique. His love, however, constantly fluctuates as his devotion to his fiancée alternates with his devotion to cards. He promises to stop gambling and he breaks his promise every time; Angélique, wearied of his incorrigible ways, decides to marry Dorante instead. The simple plot is well organized and reaches a logical conclusion, enriched by a variety of situations and characters which make it a comedy worthy of its name.

The son of a rich man, Valère depends on his father for financial assistance. Even though it sometimes becomes difficult for the young man to raise the necessary money to pay his gambling debts, he never regards his losses as serious. He has no obligations, no family responsibilities: "Comme Regnard lui-même, Valère n'est qu'un amateur, un enfant gâté qui tâte du jeu comme des autres plaisirs de la vie."[7] There is no deep psychological analysis of the gambler-type, for there is no depth in the character itself. Like Regnard, Valère is an amateur, a novice at the green table who falls prey to the cheating of crooked gam-

blers. We never see him gamble on stage; he does not
even seem to know how to play, "Parbleu, je te saurai,/
Maudit jeu de trictrac." (act 1, sc. 5)[8] Nevertheless
his excitement blinds his reason and he continues his
wagering convinced that the next attempt will be successful. The carefree youth of Regnard's gambler excuses his actions: "Le héros de sa pièce n'est qu'un
jeune homme, sans responsabilité familiale, soumis à
l'autorité d'un père qui l'empêche de disposer de sa
fortune; son vice ne peut donc avoir de graves consé-
quences."[9] These factors turn this play into a comedy
rather than a tragedy; we see in Le Joueur the lighter
aspects of the gambling mania. After all, a passing
fancy made Valère rename his valet Hector, after the
Jack of diamonds (act 3, sc. 4). In Chapter III of
this study, Béverlei will present the more tragic consequences of the gambling addiction.

In order to add the necessary dramatic elements
Regnard shows betting in conflict with love; young,
handsome and brave, Valère looks a worthy lover. But
because of his gambling habits he has been evicted
from the paternal house, and is constantly pursued by
numerous creditors. Since he cannot pay, he must borrow funds from usurers and is eventually ruined. His
emotions fluctuate, so that when he has no money he
loves Angélique, but when he is winning he loves only
the games.

---Son feu pour Angélique est un flux et reflux.
---Elle est après le jeu, ce qu'il aime le plus.
---Oui c'est la passion qui seule le dévore;
Dès qu'il a de l'argent son amour s'évapore.
(act 1, sc. 2)
This inconsistency is one of the best-known traits of
his character and the cause of his ruin, as his ser-
vant remarks,

Quand l'argent renaît, votre tendresse expire.
Votre bourse est, monsieur, puisqu'il faut vous le
Un thermomètre sûr, tantôt bas, tantôt haut, dire.
Marquant de votre coeur ou le froid ou le chaud.
(act 1, sc. 6)

Valère's speech toward the end of the play resembles
that of an ardent lover thinking only of his beloved,
but we should keep in mind that he has no money left:

Ah! Charmante Angélique, en l'ardeur qui m'embrasse,
A vos seules bontés, je veux avoir recours!

Je n'aimerais que vous;m'aimeriez-vous toujours?
Mon coeur,dans les transports de sa fureur extrême,
N'est point si malheureux,puisqu'enfin il vous aime.
(act 4, sc. 8)

The preceding lines contrast sharply with his philosophy just after winning at the gambling table, when he
values his bachelor's "freedom" and shuns all responsibility:

Je ne suis point du tout né pour le mariage:
Des parents, des enfants, une femme, un ménage,
Tout cela me fait peur; j'aime la liberté.
(act 3, sc. 6)

It is not so much that he is against marriage, but
that he is attracted to the glamor of gambling:

Il n'est point dans le monde un état plus aimable
Que celui d'un joueur: sa vie est agréable;
Ses jours sont enchaînés par des plaisirs nouveaux;
Comédie, opéra, bonne chère, cadeaux.
(act 3, sc. 6)

Valère does not overlook the easy companionship of the
ladies as one of the attractive aspects of the game:
"Chaque jour mille belles lui font la cour par lettres, et l'invitent chez elles." (act 1, sc. 2) The
fact that the <u>brelans</u> were often places "où de jeu et
d'amour on tient boutique ouverte," (act 1, sc. 2) is
affirmed by Beaurepaire in his study on gambling
houses.[10] Finally, gambling brings together all
classes in disregard of social condition, thus aveng-
ing injustices of birth. Like many other forms of
socially disapproved pleasures, it tends to override
class differences.

Le jeu rassemble tout: il unit à la fois
Le turbulent marquis, le paisible bourgeois.
La femme d'un banquier, dorée et triomphante,
Coupe orgueilleusement la duchesse indigente.
Là, sans distinction, on voit aller de pair
Le laquais d'un commis avec un duc et pair.
(act 3, sc. 6)

Valère's addiction to the games is accurately and con-
cisely described by Nérine: "il a joué, il joue et il
jouera toujours" (act 1, sc. 2) becomes obvious
throughout the play and is later reinforced by "Quiconque aime, aimera; et quiconque a joué, toujours

joue, et jouera." (act 4, sc. 1) Both emotions are addictive (act 5, sc. 1); unfortunately, Valère's addiction to gambling is stronger than his addiction to love.

The apparent conflict between love and gambling lacks gravity; our hero is neither a real lover nor a real gambler, "Il est bien plus un fils de famille, un jeune homme à la mode, qu'un joueur. Ce qu'il aime dans le jeu ce n'est pas l'émotion qu'il donne, c'est la richesse qu'il procure."[11] Valère acts immaturely and irresponsibly without true character. His personal conflict lies between his weakness for the "rich" life of the bettor and his desire to establish a comfortable marital relationship. Even his father comments on his lack of romantic ardor: "Vraiment, pour un amant,/ Vous faites voir, mon fils, bien peu d'empressement." (act 4, sc. 14) When he finally loses Angélique at the end of the play, he shows no emotion and philosophically admits that "le jeu m'acquittera des pertes de l'amour." (act 5, sc. 12) Cailhava believes that the social situation of Valère detracts from the value of the comedy and diminishes the impact of the study of a gambler: "Le Joueur de Regnard, qui n'est pas maître du bien de son père ... qui n'a pas de fortune par lui-même ... qui n'est qu'un petit brelandier, peut alarmer seulement les écoliers."[12]

Amateur though he may be, Valère is familiar with the gambler's code of ethics and knows that his gambling debts must be paid and given priority over other forms of obligations. From the sociological point of view this practice has another significance; the certainty that the loser will pay his debts, for to win without cashing in one's winnings makes no sense.[13] Gambling can only be profitable and worth its while with the continued assurance of getting paid, and Valère knows it: "Damon m'en doit encor deux cents (louis) sur sa parole" (act 3, sc. 6); he counts on this money as a sure thing. He shares another characteristic of gamblers, the most sacred use of gambling money; his winnings to not pay bills, debts, creditors, wages or even redeem pawned goods: "Rien ne porte malheur comme payer ses dettes." (act 3, sc. 8) Indeed when his servant reminds him that they have enough money to recover Angélique's portrait, the gambler replies: "Nous verrons ... je dois jouer tantôt." (act 3, sc. 6)

Uncertainties and superstitions control a gambler's life. Irrational optimism abounds, "La Fortune est pour moi dans ce jour" (act 2, sc. 14), accompanied by a belief in Luck: "J'ai dans le coeur ... un bon pressentiment;/ Et je dois aujourd'hui gagner, assurément." (act 3, sc. 13) Finally, with the grim reality of defeat all too obvious, a mysterious Fate or Destiny (not the gambler's actions) carries the blame:

Je te loue, ô destin, de tes coups redoublés!
Je n'ai rien à perdre, et tes voeux sont comblés
. . . .
As-tu jamais vu le sort et son caprice
Accabler un mortel avec plus d'injustice?
(act 4, sc. 13)

He has gambled and lost, proof that Lady Luck does not favor him any more. As Cohen explains, "gambling is essentially a provocation of Fate, a contest with Destiny, which is forced to decide for or against the player."14

The character of Dorante, too good to be true, remains a galant type and never develops into a real individual. Like the <u>héros de roman</u>, he always shows polite respect for the opposite sex (act 4, sc. 8). His generosity is bestowed on anyone deserving it, servants included (act 3, sc. 1) and his understanding knows no bounds, even when his love for Angélique is rejected (act 3, sc. 1). He is not the jealous type (act 5, sc. 1) and definitely not the <u>amant ridicule</u> so often portrayed in Molière's comedies. He provides the comedy with a character contrasting with Valère. Throughout the play Dorante is very much in control of his feelings and the situation, whereas Valère falls apart in desperation. The former is older and wiser ("Lui, c'est un homme d'ordre" (act 1, sc. 2)), while the latter is younger and foolish. However, youth and disorder do offer temptation: "L'Amour se plaît un peu dans le dérèglement." (act 1, sc. 2) The influence of Descartes on the comedy is apparent in the conflict of reason (Dorante) versus passion (Valère):

---Que Dorante a pour lui Nérine et la raison.
---Et nous avons l'amour. Tu sais que d'ordinaire,
Quand l'amour veut parler, la raison doit se taire.
(act 1, sc. 2)

Dorante understands his position well and

knows that youth attracts youth: "La jeunesse toujours
eut des droits sur des belles;/ L'Amour est un enfant
qui badine avec elles." (act 3, sc. 2) He does not
even pass judgment on Valère's gambling. His age is a
liability which he accepts; should he obtain Angélique
he would have nothing to brag about: "Et lorsque de
ses feux je sens quelque retour/ Je dois tout au dépit
et rien à son amour." (act 3, sc. 1)

Géronte typifies the bon père who disapproves
of his son's behavior, but who nevertheless loves him
tenderly. Even though he shows anger on occasion, he
gives the impression that his threats will not be carried out. He is a likable, colorful character who
adds a sense of humanity to the comedy; he is a good
man, not without some faults. Valère's gambling ir-
ritates him:

Pour la dernière fois,mon fils,je viens vous dire
Que votre train de vie est si fort scandaleux,
Que vous m'obligerez à quelque éclat fâcheux.
                                    (act 1, sc. 7)

The father offers insight into the role of gambling in
late seventeenth-century French society: "à présent
le jeu n'est que fureur:/ On joue argent, bijoux, maisons, contrats, honneur." (act 1, sc. 7) Aware of the
realities of a gambler's life, he points out to his
son that in gambling, "Il faut opter des deux: être
dupe ou fripon." (act 1, sc. 7) Ready to forgive the
young joueur, he would like to see him marry well, for
"Angélique est fort riche, et point du tout coquette."
(act 1, sc. 7)

The one flaw in Géronte's character causes him
to derive pleasure from his brother's misfortune. His
harshness toward Dorante, his brother, parallels his
kindness to Valère. The following statement of Géronte is cruel and unnecessary: "Et j'aurai deux
plaisirs à la fois, si je puis,/ De chagriner mon
frère et marier mon fils." (act 1, sc. 9) Perhaps Géronte realizes the moral superiority over his son and
therefore favors the latter.[15] He appears understanding and compassionate to his brother only when Dorante is depressed (act 3, sc. 3).

The father agrees to pay Valère's debts as
soon as the gambling stops, for he fears a gambler's
fate. "S'il est quelque joueur qui vive de son gain,/
On en voit tous les jours mille mourir de faim." (act
1, sc. 10)

An element of farcical comedy is introduced in act 3, scene 4; when Géronte listens to the reading of the list of the créanciers whom he has offered to pay, he becomes impatient and repeatedly hits the servant, causing papers to fly all over the stage. His actions are reminiscent of scenes between Cléante and La Flèche in Molière's L'Avare. Above all else, Géronte is an affectionate father, whose happiness knows no bounds when he believes that his son has changed his ways: "Ah! qu'un père est heureux, qui voit en un moment/ Un cher fils revenir de son égarement!" (act 4, sc. 16) This comment provides an instance of dramatic irony, for the audience knows that Valère still gambles. When brought back to reality, Géronte's affections turn to anger. His feelings are hurt by his son's actions, but it still seems unlikely that his threat will be carried out:

> J'ai peine à retenir le courroux qui m'agite.
> Fils indigne de moi, va, je te déshérite;
> Je ne veux plus te voir, après cette action,
> Et te donne cent fois ma malédiction!
>   (act 5, sc. 6)

Angélique appears to be genuinely in love with Valère, but in reality her love looks like a whim. The realization that gambling means more to him than she does hurts her pride, but their separation seems to cause her very little emotion. Her feelings for Valère are capricious rather than passionate, cool rather than furious. At first, she decides to break up with Valère and tries to convince her suivante that her decision is final: "Nérine, c'en est fait, pour jamais je l'oublie;/ Je ne veux ni l'aimer, ni le voir de ma vie." (act 2, sc. 1) Maybe she is too convincing to be sincere: "Ne viens point désormais, pour calmer mon dépit,/ Rappeler à mes sens son air et son esprit." (act 2, sc. 1) Obviously she still feels a very strong attraction for the young man, so that when he arrives, her determination weakens and her tone becomes tender. She wants a promise of reform, which Valère gives readily, but as she hands him a small portrait of herself framed in diamonds, she warns him: "Ne me trompez donc plus, Valère; et que mon coeur/ Ne se repente point de sa facile ardeur." (act 2, sc. 11) For a time at least, she believes that his weakness for gambling will be cured: "Le temps le guérira de cet aveuglement." (act 4, sc. 1) She finally realizes that her fiancé is a gambler above all else and will not keep his word to her: "Quoi, ton maître jouerait, au mépris d'un serment?" (act 4, sc. 2) she asks the valet. Furthermore, Valère does not value her love, only gambling; when he pawns her portrait, she learns a lesson. Her <u>suivante</u> warns:

> S'il met votre portrait ainsi chez l'usurier,
> Etant encor amant, il vous vendra, madame,
> A beaux deniers comptants,quand vous serez sa femme.
> (act 5, sc. 6)

Angélique plans to seek revenge, for unlike her literary predecessors, this young woman is not naive. She ingeniously tricks the <u>joueur</u> into admitting his actions and unsuspectingly renouncing his intentions to marry her, while at the same time she promises her hand to Dorante. She declares that whoever possesses her portrait will possess her: "Quiconque a mon portrait, sans crainte de rival,/ Doit avec la copie avoir l'original." (act 5, sc. 7) The dramatic irony of the situation must not be overlooked, for everyone with the exception of Valère, understands the full meaning of Angélique's words.

Although young and somewhat inexperienced, Angélique is not <u>une ingénue candide</u>. She has no angelic traits despite her name as she repeatedly shows her sister, <u>la comtesse</u>, no mercy. Her hostility toward the countess is barely justified by the latter's eagerness to take her lovers away from her. She sarcastically reminds her sister of her age: "Après un si long temps de pleine jouissance,/ Vos attraits sont à vous sans contestation." (act 2, sc. 2) Angélique shows even more cruelty to her sister upon the revelation of the marquis' true identity. Mordant sarcasm and lack of compassion prevail in her comment: "Vous aviez là, ma soeur, un fort illustre amant."(act 5, sc. 4)

Descartes' influence on the comedy becomes obvious as Angélique's passion occasionally triumphs over her reason; she recognizes that her feelings for the <u>joueur</u>, though not real love, are nevertheless strong. Her reasoning ability is powerless when faced with her emotions: "La raison, les conseils ne peuvent m'en distraire:/ Je vois le bon parti, mais je prends le contraire." (act 4, sc. 1) Her ardor will be cooled considerably when she learns that her precious portrait has been <u>prêté sur des gages</u>. With hurt pride, she turns down Valère and offers her hand to Dorante, out of spite--not for love; as she walks away

from the rejected young man, her last words betray her
bitterness:

> A jamais je vous laisse.
> Si vous êtes heureux au jeu comme en maîtresse,
> Et si vous conservez aussi mal ses présents,
> Vous ne ferez, je crois,fortune de longtemps.
> (act 5, sc. 9)

If Valère and Angélique are not very lively
characters, their servants are instead dynamic and
full of life. Regnard shows their relative importance
by the number of scenes in which they appear: Hector
appears in nine more scenes than Valère; Nérine out-
numbers Angélique by seven scenes.[16] The valet and
the suivante are vivacious, witty and loyal to the
joueur and his fiancé, respectively. Unlike the servants studied in Chapter I, they identify with their
masters. Their emotional attachment resembles that of
the valets and suivantes of Molière's comedies. The
few basic differences between them help add variety
and color to the comedy and create funny situations.

Hector's role owes its importance to his re-
partee rather than to his actions; he is indeed rather
inactive, as will be seen when compared to Nérine. His
speech is usually amusing, sometimes clever, but he
does not do anything that will either favor or hinder
his master's love affair. He opens the comedy in
grand fashion with the well-known monologue where he
dreams of the fortune which could be his if only his
master were not a gambler:

> Il est, parbleu, grand jour. Déjà, de leur ramage
> Les coqs ont éveillé tout notre voisinage.
> Que servir un joueur est un maudit métier!
> Ne serai-je jamais laquais d'un sous-fermier?
> (act 1, sc. 1)

Once again, the author uses the servant to illustrate
the inconveniences associated with a gambler's life:
lack of sleep, lack of comfort, lack of money.

Nérine, on the other hand, greatly assists her
mistress and her actions contribute movement to the
plot; her principal role is to express opposition to
Angélique's marriage with Valère and preference for
her union with Dorante.[17] Nérine is an intrigante,
Hector a confidant. When they appear together at the
beginning of the play, they give the reader a chance

to study their differences and similarities. The suivante is ready to act, the valet to speak cleverly; she demands to see Valère and Hector replies: "Va, mon maître ne voit personne quand il dort." (act 1, sc. 2) This play on words is an absurdly true statement for neither his master nor, for that matter, anyone else, can see anyone when sleeping. He merely tries to gain time by fibbing, to cover the fact that his master has not yet returned. To Nérine's persistence, he must finally indirectly confess the truth: "avant qu'il se lève,/ Il faudra qu'il se couche." (act 1, sc. 2). She accurately describes the situation: "Autour d'un tapis vert,/ Dans un maudit brelan, ton maître joue et perd," (act 1, sc. 2) and furthermore explains the reason for her visit: "Par ordre très exprès d'Angélique, aujourd'hui/ Je viens pour rompre ici tout commerce avec lui." (act 1, sc. 2)

They both claim to have control over the young woman's feelings for different reasons; Nérine sides with Dorante, "un amant fait et mûr" (act 1, sc. 2) and Hector, of course, with Valère: "Les filles, d'ordinaire,/ Aiment mieux le fruit vert." (act 1, sc. 2) The soubrette adds that Dorante has the qualities "d'un fort bon caractère,/ Qui ne sut de ses jours ce que c'est que le jeu" (act 1, sc. 2), but Hector is quick to point out, "Mais mon maître est aimé." (act 1, sc. 2)

Regnard repeatedly uses Hector in order to present elements of contemporary society which allow the reader a glimpse of the late seventeenth-century life in France. When the valet refers to Mme La Ressource as "le plus juif qui soit dans tout Paris" (act 2, sc. 14), his grammatical mistake is sociologically accurate: there were then many Jews in Paris who came from Algeria or the Orient and who practiced usury as a means of earning a living.[18] Later on in the comedy when Hector reads a ledger of expenses incurred by his master in order to keep his high standard of living, he makes it clear that although apparently superfluous, these costs are necessary and expected of a young man like Valère (act 3, sc. 4). Finally, it is the laquais who brings up the existence of a number of teachers (trictrac, music, singing) who constitute an active part of a young man's education (act 1, sc. 6).

From the beginning of the comedy, it becomes apparent that Nérine is a faithful servant and that she wants her mistress' bien-être above all else:

"Je ne souffrirai pas qu'on trompe ma maîtresse." (act
1, sc. 2) She is une personne d'action and will take
the necessary steps to insure a better life for Angélique away from gambling. She declares that

> Je fais la guerre ouverte; et je vais, de ce pas,
> Dire ce que je vois, avertir ma maîtresse
> Que Valère toujours est faux dans sa promesse.
> (act 1, sc. 2)

A more serious character than Hector, burdened with
the responsibilities of reveal the evils of gambling,
Nérine's appearances usually lack humor. She does
create lighter moments when she farcically pretends
to be Valère'trying to regain Angélique's love (act 2,
sc. 1), but she is at her best when using irony on
those she despises (Valère, the Marquis, the Comtesse).
Her main role, however, remains to criticize the gambling vice in a fashion that will not offend the reader; she does not moralize, she merely points out facts.
Regnard uses this character's potential very well, as
when Nérine angrily tells her mistress:

> Eh bien! madame, soit; contentez votre ardeur.
> J'y consens. Acceptez pour époux un joueur,
> Qui, pour porter au jeu son tribut volontaire,
> Vous laissera manquer même du nécessaire.
> (act 4, sc. 1)

She then proceeds to describe the gambler's tempera-
ment: "toujours triste ou fougueux, pestant contre le
jeu,/ Ou d'avoir perdu trop, ou bien gagné trop peu."
(act 4, sc. 1) Furthermore, the material and financial insecurity brought about by gambling causes endless marital arguments:

> Qu'on voit à chaque instant prêt à faire querelle
> Aux bijoux de sa femme, ou bien à sa vaisselle,
> Qui va, revient, retourne, et s'use à voyager
> Chez l'usurier, bien plus qu'à donner à manger.
> (act 4, sc. 1)

Nérine makes one last effort in order to save Angélique from a miserable existence with Valère:

> S'il met votre portrait ainsi chez l'usurier,
> Etant encore amant, il vous vendra, madame,
> A beaux denier comptants,quand vous serez sa femme.
> (act 5, sc. 6)

These strong words of advice are finally heeded.

It must be added that occasionally the suivante acts with insolence toward those whom she dis-
likes; e.g., the countess and the marquis. She often
interferes in matters which do not concern her, usually in asides (act 2, scs. 2, 4, 9, 11, 19) directed
to the audience, possibly the parterre. Nérine's role
is thus sometimes analogous to that of the chorus in
the plays of antiquity.[19]

If Regnard's plan for Hector was simply to
create an amusing character, he succeeded. The valet's
comical ability stands out in the reading of the list
of creditors to Géronte (act 3, sc. 4), and in his
mock-heroic account of Valère's encounter with gambling. Hector shows an alert mind when he recognizes
the marquis' speech as regional (act 4, sc. 12). He
also repeatedly acts as Valère's conscience, urging
him to act with more feeling (act 2, scs. 14, 15; act
3, scs. 6, 8). One of his final remarks, however
witty, destroys the theatrical illusion; when asked to
explain the confusion caused by the portrait, he responds: "par ma foi, je n'ose;/ Ce récit est trop
triste en vers qu'en prose." (act 5, sc. 8)

Although quite active throughout the comedy,
the Marquis and Angélique's older sister, the Countess,
have no effect upon the main plot. Their presence
does not help the reader gain a better understanding
of the joueur, nor of the perils of the gambling passion. Furthermore, their presence violates the unity
of action by unnecessarily complicating the situation.
They owe much to Molière; they are amusing and humor-
ous and have a certain individuality. They parallel
Valère and Angélique, but the contrast between the
relatively sincere love of the younger couple and the
almost grotesque relationship of the older one remains
sharp.

The Marquis is a chevalier d'industrie, a fake
as well as an impostor and adventurer. He assumes a
borrowed name and profits from the affection of a susceptible lady of means; ultimately he is betrayed by
someone acquainted with his past life. He speaks with
pride of his ancestry which he can trace to the déluge
(act 5, sc. 4), but speaks of the Court with contempt.
Lenient considers him "un mannequin plutôt qu'un caractère."[20] He has come to Paris to seek his fortunes
and has been rescued from prison by his cousin. He has
ascended in society thanks to his constant boasting
of a non-existent aristocratic ancestry and by taking
advantage of wealthy older women.

More of a caricature than a real person, the countess does not constitute a serious rival in Angélique's amorous relationships. She seems sincere when she advises her sister not to marry Valère because: "Rien n'est plus à craindre dans la vie,/ Qu'un époux qui du jeu ressent la tyrannie." (act 2, sc. 2). She also expresses her preference:

> J'aimerais mieux qu'il fût fueux, avaricieux,
> Coquet, fâcheux, mal fait, brutal, capricieux,
> Ivrogne, sans esprit, débauché, sot, colère,
> Que d'être un emporté joueur comme est Valère.
> (act 2, sc. 2)

Her mood changes rather quickly, however, when she realizes that Angélique has renounced Valère; she herself will marry him, then. She explains her reasons in a long tirade, remarkable for its realistic tone; a widow, she has kept and cherished a portrait of her late husband for years, but "qu'est-ce qu'un portrait, quand on aime bien fort?/ C'est un époux vivant qui console d'un mort." (act 2, sc. 2)

The countess' use of language touches on false modesty: "On sait sur les maris ce qu'on a d'empire" (act 2, sc. 2) and, "On a certains attraits, un certain enjoûment." (act 2, sc. 2) The affected use of on instead of je exudes prudishness. Like Corneille's heroines, she refers to the whole of her outstanding qualities as "mon mérite." (act 2, sc. 3) To the marquis' ridiculous statement that she and Angélique look like twins, she replies "Qu'il est sincère." (act 2, sc. 4) She becomes even more of a pitiful figure when, rejected by Valère, she throws herself at Dorante, who politely refuses her (act 4, sc. 7); in act 4, scene 9 she asks the marquis to marry her, only to find out soon afterwards that he is an impostor, unworthy of such an honor (act 5, sc. 4). Her indiscriminate attempts to find a man to marry render her grotesque.

The marquis, not as lifeless a character as the Comtesse, appears more likable and amusing. The son of a huissier, he pretends to be of noble ancestry; he is the type of the pseudo-noble so often portrayed in the comédies de moeurs of the times.

Claiming to be acquainted and bored with life at Court, the marquis gives a glimpse of what it entails: "Ma foi, la cour m'ennuie;/ L'esprit de ce pays n'est qu'en superficie." (act 2, sc. 4) He criticizes the protocol associated with the Roi Soleil and his entourage, while inflating his own ego:

> J'ai de l'esprit, du coeur, plus que les seigneurs
> de France:
> Je joue, et j'y ferais fort bonne contenance;
> Mais je n'y vais jamais que par nécessité,
> Et pour rendre au roi quelque civilité.
> (act 2, sc. 4)

In the same account he proceeds to explain that flattery rules at court and that hypocrisy reigns everywhere. He does not paint a very favorable picture, since he aims not at being objective, but at building himself up in the eyes of the countess.

True to the type of the <u>chevalier d'industrie</u>, he declares his love to lonely older women in order to maintain his high style of life.[21] He enjoys boasting about his romantic conquests: "la grosse comtesse" in act 2, scene 5; "cette jeune duchesse" in act 2, scene 6; and "cette femme de robe" in act 2, scene 7. He says, however, that they are only temptations (to which he willingly succombs) and that he loves only the Comtesse: "Et quand de mon amour je vous fais un aveu,/ Madame, il est trop vrai que je suis tout en feu." (act 2, sc. 4) His fire, of course, is kindled by his desire to belong to the very same nobility which he so ardently scorns.

A coward at heart, he puts on courageous airs as he challenges Valère to a duel, but when the fight becomes imminent, the Marquis tries to back out; he is a true <u>fanfaron</u>. Act 3, scene 9, is remarkable for the long self-praising tirade which Valère witnesses; his conceit shows in this line from that scene: "je suis parfait en tout." Since his vanity outgrows his valor, he attempts to talk himself into behaving in a brave and dignified manner: "Courage, allons, marquis, montre de la vigueur." (act 3, sc. 9) In his well-known monologue, he examines his good fortune and good qualities: "Quel bonheur est le tien! Le ciel à ta naissance/ Répandit sur tes jours sa plus douce influence." (act 4, sc. 10)

His aspirations to a life full of pleasures end abruptly when his real identity is revealed. This event follows the theatrical tradition of the <u>chevalier d'industrie</u>, as has already been presented in Chapter I of this study. The agent on this occasion is the Marquis' own cousin, a <u>revendeuse à la toilette</u>, appropriately called Mme La Ressource. A hard-hearted usurer, she lends her money only on <u>gages</u> of indisputable value, such as diamonds:

Je puis, maintenant, prêter en conscience;
Je vois des diamants qui répondent du prêt,
Et qui peuvent porter un modeste intérêt.
(act 2, sc.14)

Wanting to make a good impression from her "humble" state in society, she quickly points out that her black dress indicates her recent widowhood; she realizes that, otherwise, black can be worn exclusively by the nobility.

Mme La Ressource's presence is always justified. Her first appearance is important because then Valère pawns Angélique's diamond-studded portrait (act 2, sc. 14). Her last appearance is essential for it reveals Valère's indiscretion (act 5, sc. 6) and the ancestral origin of the pseudo-marquis (act 5, sc. 4): "Je l'ai démarquisé bien loin de son attente/ J'en voudrais faire autant à tous les faux marquis." She plays her role well and is true to life, a realistic borrowing from contemporary society. Usurers constituted an important part of French life of the time.[22] Their presence became even more essential as a result of financial debts incurred by losing gamblers.

Regnard gives an accurate description of the type, in society as well as in literature, of this descendant of La Celestina and of Molière's Frosine:

Habile en tous métiers, intrigante parfaite;
Qui prête, vend, revend, brocante, troque, achète,
Met à perfection un hymen ébauché,
Vend son argent bien cher, marie à bon marché.
(act 5, sc. 2)

The influence of Molière on Regnard appears more obvious in the scene of the creditors, M. Gallonier (<u>le tailleur</u>) and Mme Adam (<u>la sellière</u>). With tears in their eyes they have come to Valère's household to ask humbly for payment of the money due them (act 3, sc. 7); their behavior and the skill with which they are refused seem to be inspired from the scene of M. Dimanche in <u>Dom Juan</u>. Furthermore, the value of this scene rests on its social truth and its contemporaneity; gamblers incur debts in order to keep up appearances, yet they are unwilling to settle them.

A new character appears on stage: M. Toutabas, a professional gambler who teaches others how to cheat the odds, "docteur dans tous les jeux, et maître de trictrac." (act 1, sc. 10) Although his presence does nothing to advance the action, there is ample justification for his existence in that he provides a glimpse of contemporary reality. This _maître_ is more farcical than comical and highlights his entrance on stage by a misunderstanding: he assumes Géronte to be Valère. The social accuracy of the character is obvious in the following comment: "On trichait à la Cour, on trichait à la Ville, on trichait partout. Il y avait même des gens dont c'était le métier d'enseigner l'art de tricher."[23] Taught by some, learned by others and approved by all, cheating was called "prendre ses avantages."[24] It gained in popularity very rapidly as gambling became a national epidemic. The fact that cheating was widespread is also apparent in the art of the times, in George de la Tour's _Le Tricheur_, for instance.[25] This painting portrays two men and two women gambling around a table where cards and gold coins lie in a disorderly fashion; one of the men is hiding two cards in an obvious attempt to turn the odds in his favor.

Cheating took place in the public _brelans_, in the _Académies_ and in private gambling gatherings, but the example was set by the Court at Versailles; there the "peu de scrupules que beaucoup de gens du bel air apportaient au jeu"[26] was well known. According to Toutabas, cheating and gambling should therefore be an integral part of everyone's education: "Qu'un enfant de famille, et qu'on veut bien instruire,/ Devrait savoir jouer avant que savoir lire." (act 1, sc. 10) A young man, he says, has no need to know how to sing or dance; he should know how to become rich. He lists the virtues of gambling, its advantages for young men, for young women's reputations, for the _chevaliers d'industrie_ and, of course, for the usurers. Losing is impossible if his teachings are followed: "Je sais, quand il le faut, par un jeu d'artifice,/ D'un sort injurieux corriger la malice." (act 1, sc. 10) French society in the late seventeenth century accepted and condoned cheating on and off stage; cheating at cards is an art for Toutabas and he elaborates the technique in great detail (act 1, sc. 10).

It has been said that _Le Joueur_ is not too interesting because the gambler himself is not rich, because his losses do not have very tragic effects;[29]

perhaps there is even a lack of depth in the play. Nevertheless, Regnard "a bien saisi les traits essentiels d'un caractère de joueur, absorbé et incorrigible, marqué d'une sorte de fatalité."[28] In the tradition of Molière, he avoids a sentimental conversion by his gambler; he presents his material objectively. Valère does not repent; he is not punished. There are some minor inconveniences brought about by gambling, but there also are some pleasurable experiences. The absence of a moral and the author's aim to entertain make Le Joueur one of the best comedies of its time.

[1]Davis, p. 18.   [2]Ibid., p. 10.

[3]David Allen, The Nature of Gambling (New York: Coward-McCann, Inc., 1952), p. 31.

[4]Ibid., pp. 30-31.

[5]Jean-François Regnard, Le Mariage de la folie, in Oeuvres de Regnard(Paris: Pierre Didot et Firmin Didot, 1801), II, 242.

[6]Alexandre Calamé, Regnard: sa vie et son oeuvre (Paris: Presses Universitaires de France, 1960), pp. 281-282.

[7]Ibid., p. 285.

[8]Jean-François Regnard, Le Joueur, in Oeuvres de Regnard (Paris: Pierre Didot et Firmin Didot, 1801), I, 90. Henceforth, all quotations from Le Joueur will be taken from this edition and will be indicated by act and scene number.

[9]Calamé, p. 283.

[10]Beaurepaire, pp. 447-448.

[11]Calamé, p. 285.

[12]M. de Cailhava, De l'Art de la comédie (Paris: Didot, 1772), I, 46.

[13]Herbert A. Bloch, "The Sociology of Gambling," American Journal of Sociology, 57 (1952), 220.

[14]Cohen, p. 55.

[15]Lancaster, A History of French Dramatic Literature, IV, no. 2, 742.

[16]Hector appears in seven scenes in act 1, three in act 2, 12 in act 3, six in act 4 and six in act 5; Valère appears in four scenes in act 1, five in act 2, eight in act 3, two in act 4 and six in act 5. Nérine appears in one scene in act 1, 11 in act 2, three in act 3, five in act four and nine in act 5; Angélique appears in two scenes in act 2, four in act 4 and 11 in act 5.

[17]Lancaster, A History of French Dramatic Literature, IV, no. 2, 742.

[18]Mongrédien, p. 102.   [19]Calamé, p. 288.

[20]Charles F. Lenient, La Comédie en France au XVIIIe siècle (Paris: Hachette, 1888), p. 40.

[21]Lancaster, A History of French Dramatic Literature, IV, no. 2, 742.

[22]Mongrédien, p. 103.   [23]Beaurepaire, p. 445.

[24]Ibid.

[25]Le Tricheur by George de la Tour is found in the Louvre Museum, Peintres français du XVIIe siècle, RF 1972-8.

[26]Beaurepaire, p. 444.   [27]Cailhava, I, 46.

[28]Charles-M. des Granges, Le Théâtre au XVIIIe siècle (Paris: Hatier, 1962), p. 732.

CHAPTER III

BEVERLEI

It has been stated that Regnard's comedy Le Joueur would be a very philosophical play if the main character had a family, children and a job or a fortune to lose.[1] Under those circumstances, however, the pièce would become a tragedy. This indeed happens when Regnard's entertaining comédie goes to England: it becomes impregnated with sombre thoughts and tragic events in the form of Edward Moore's play The Gamester (1753).[2] A few years later, in 1786, the play returns to France as Béverlei, tragédie bourgeoise by Saurin; the laughter cannot disguise the bitterness, the melancholy and the anguish of this eighteenth-century joueur.

Moore's play is a moralistic middle-class tragedy with a touch of sentimentality; the growing French attraction for the new genre of drame bourgeois probably accounts for Saurin's interest in making this adaptation of the English tragedy.[3] Although the French playwright indicates his work as imitée de l'anglois, the two tragedies differ. For instance, in the French play, a new character appears, the child; in addition, the dramatic ambiance is intensified by the fact that Béverlei's arrest and suicide are acted out on stage. The use of these techniques magnifies the feeling of horror in Saurin's tragedy and constitutes some of its most spectacular elements.

Charles Cotton's definition of gambling and study of its effects, represents the best possible introduction to this chapter. The 1674 quotation, although lengthy, follows in its entirety because it will help place the reader in the proper frame of mind for a better understanding of Béverlei.

> Gaming is an enchanting witchery, gotten betwixt idleness and avarice: an itching disease, that makes some scratch the head, whilst others, as if they were bitten by a Tarantula, are laughing themselves to death: or lastly, it is a paralytical distemper, which seizing the arm the man cannot chuse but shake his elbow. It hath this ill property above all other vices, that it renders a man incapable

61

of prosecuting any serious action, and makes
him always unsatisfied with his own condition;
he is either lifted up to the top of mad joy
with success, or plung'd to the bottom of despair by misfortune, always in extreams, always
in a storm; this minute the gamester's counte-
nance is so serene and calm, that one would
think nothing could disturb it, and the next
minute so stormy and tempestuous that it
threatens destruction to itself and to others;
and as he is transported with joy when he
wins, so losing he is toast upon the billows
of a high swelling passion, till he hath lost
sight of both sense and reason.[4]

Although one sees no games in progress, the
gambling takes place in private residences and not in
the public <u>Académies</u>. The passion for gaming has
reached such high proportions that the public establishments do not suffice, so private homes must provide gathering places for those interested in risking
their money.[5] It is this kind of <u>brelan</u> that Béverlei
frequents and where he meets his ruin. Were the game
honest, the odds would still be against him; but the
widespread cheating predominant in these activities
make it impossible for him to win. We have already
established previously that cheating is accepted at
Court as well as in the aristocratic mansions; in this
tragedy, the <u>bourgeoisie</u> merely imitates the unscrupulous practices popularized by the nobility.

La Bruyère furnishes an accurate description
of these <u>brelans</u> and refers to them as "pièges tendus
à l'avarice des hommes, comme des gouffres où l'argent
des particuliers tombe et se précipite sans retour,
comme d'affreux écueils où les joueurs viennent se
briser et se perdre."[6] Well aware of the dishonesty
in these establishments, the seventeenth-century mor-
alist analyzes them philosophically:

> C'est un sale et indigne métier que de tromper,
> mais c'est un métier qui est ancien, connu,
> pratiqué de tout temps par des brelandiers.
> ... L'enseigne est à leur porte, on y lirait
> presque: Ici l'on trompe de bonne foi ... Qui
> ne sait pas qu'entrer et perdre dans ces mai-
> sons est une même chose?[7]

He cannot help but marvel at the steady number of
<u>dupes</u> who visit the brelans, none the wiser for their
experience.

In **the Satire contre les maris**, Regnard give a detailed picture of what one can find in a brelan:

Entrons dans ce brelan où s'arrête à la porte
Des laquais mal payés la maligne cohorte.
Vois les cornets en l'air jetés avec tansport,
Qu'on veut rendre garants des caprices du sort. [8]

He describes the typical joueurs in detail: "Vois ces pâles joueurs, qui, pleins d'extravagances/ D'un destin insolent affrontent l'inconstance." (La Satire, p. 159) It will be seen how closely Beverlei resembles this sketch of the gambler; similarly, Regnard prophetically warns the gambler's wife about the nefarious consequences of his behavior: "Infortuné joueur, il perdra tous tes biens,/ Qu'un contrat malheureux confond avec les siens." (La Satire, p. 158)

In the Introduction to this study, we have traced the roots of gambling to ancient history; we have likewise demonstrated that it can and does sometimes constitute an innocent pastime, a recreational activity devoid of evil. In Chapter Two, we showed that gambling is not necessarily a form of neurosis, since normal people have gambled since the beginning of time and still do today. In Chapter III, we shall examine that other kind of gambler: the pathological neurotic. From the sociological viewpoint, "gambling emerges as a form of social pathology only when there is widespread resentment against it because of the psychological or social problems which it creates." [9] It appears that it is not gambling per se, but gambling taken in a social context that is pernicious. When a person becomes an inveterate gambler, his actions have serious repercussions on those around him; this addict then neglects family, personal and social responsibilities. He no longer functions like a "normal" individual. He is generally condemned because of his "failure to perform the normal productive functions ordinarily expected of him," [10] rather than for his gambling. If his addiction had no consequences, it would not be deplored. Most western cultures approve of leisure activities, provided that they be second to productive ones, i.e., work. The so-called "responsible" endeavors carry more prestige than recreational ones; in addition, the non-productive undertaking must not be socially destructive. This philosophy predominates in an economically-oriented society.

In the eighteenth century, France was becoming just that kind of a nation: concerned with finances, more conscious of money needs and unnecessary waste. This viewpoint, of course, depended to a large degree upon the social class; among the wealthier upper classes gambling never carried a stigma. However, for the poor and for the struggling middle-class, this unproductive activity was strongly condemned. As we mentioned in the Introduction, John Law's efforts to restore stability to French finances during the minority of Louis XV resulted in an economic catastrophe for many. This disaster was followed by a breaking down of public morals and standards. Although illegal and condemned, gambling became commonplace as people tried to recover their lost fortunes; together with frantic gambling, cheating and usury flourished. The rich gambled for amusement, but the <u>bourgeoisie</u> needed to win.

This atmosphere of social distrust and baseness characterizes life in France in the second half of the eighteenth century, the time <u>Béverlei</u> appears. Steinmetz mentions in his work t h a t suicides and base deeds are commonplace. Social conditions force people to gamble gamblers in turn become unproductive members of that same society which then labels them as undesirable. Only in 1778, ten long years after these detrimental conditions are exposed in Saurin's play, is gambling strictly prohibited once more. In the meantime, the crimes and misfortunes, suicides and bankruptcies proliferate as a result of widespread corruption and misguided ambition.[11] Since gambling itself does not directly produce deteriorating effects upon man or society, its real danger lies in the fact that it interferes with "the normal assumption of responsibility which organized society compels."[12] In addition, this activity can create a major social problem because it eventually attracts lawless and unscrupulous elements, such as the character Stukéli in the play under study.

<u>Béverlei</u> is a tragedy in five acts, written in free verse. Stage directions throughout the drama emphasize the run-down condition of what was once an affluent household: "Le théâtre représente un salon mal meublé, et dont les murs sont presque nus, avec des restes de dorure."[13] Béverlei, the <u>joueur</u>, is married and has a son, Tomi. His unmarried sister, Henriette, lives in the same household, and is courted by Leuson. Stukéli, an unscrupulous rogue, pretends to be Béverlei's friend; Jarvis, the old servant, has recently been dismissed for lack of money.

We shall examine the play by acts, emphasizing the characters' contrasting attitudes and the interrelatedness of their actions. This approach will provide a clear understanding of the causes and consequences of gambling. It will also furnish a literary analysis of the work, together with close character study. We shall be able to determine whether the term "pathological gambler," defined earlier in this chapter, can be applied to Béverlei; we shall also look at the corruptive elements which abound in this literary work just as they did in the contemporary society.

In Act 1 all the characters are present except Béverlei; much is learned about him, however, because the others discuss him and his change in behavior. Saurin's gradual presentation of Béverlei intensifies the dramatic moment and provides an opportunity to gain insight into the gambler's personality as well as into the individual character of the others. The first four verses seem to parallel those of Le Joueur, but the mood is obviously different; a tone of sadness and despair rings in the language and attitude of the characters. The gambler has not yet come home: "il ne vient point!/ Quel tourment que l'inquiétude." (act 1, sc. 1)

Mme Béverlei and Henriette are well delineated early in the first scene, the former naively idealistic, the latter sharply realistic. Mme Béverlei's love for her husband blinds her to his faults; she truthfully admits that their financial difficulties stem from his gambling, but she forgives him. She readily accepts their sudden poverty: "Ses meubles, ses tableaux, ses glaces, sa dorure,/ ... Ce sont besoins du luxe, et non de la nature." (act 1, sc. 1) She pities her husband, but cannot hate him; after all, "Il n'a qu'un seul défaut" (act 1, sc. 1): gambling. When confronted with the fact that Béverlei's behavior sets a negative example for the child, she convincingly explains that Tomi will profit from the experience and will never give in to the same temptation. She occasionally shows signs of lucid intelligence and expresses her thoughts with a philosophical air: "Le bonheur, dont souvent l'on ne poursuit que l'ombre,/ C'est le contentement du coeur." (act 1, sc. 1) Being a very sensitive person, she truly understands her husband's precarious situation, maybe even too well: she can see Béverlei torn apart by remorse because he is making those whom he loves unhappy. She piously prays for a miracle: a reformed husband. She remains loyal to him, teaches their son not to pass judgment on his father, but to love him and accept him as he is. Her unselfish love makes her vulnerable to malice and her inner peace is shaken by rumors; although she refuses to openly admit it, she becomes suspicious and a bit jealous at her husband's all-night absence.

Henriette's character contrasts with that of Mme Béverlei; she loves her brother and sister-in-law and detests the condition to which they have been reduced. She feels that she could easily learn to hate the one who has caused them to "Tomber de l'opulence, au sein de la misère." (act 1, sc. 1) Her rôle provides a sensible and realistic viewpoint to counterbalance her sister-in-law's overconfidence; she becomes Saurin's <u>porte-parole</u> and presents his ideas on the evils of gambling and its effects on the family:

> Funeste amour du jeu!
> Combien de fois après l'aurore,
> Vous l'avez vu rentrer, maudissant dans vos bras
> Cette avare fureur qui l'agitoît encore?
> (act 1, sc. 1)

The fact that gamblers keep uncommon hours has been discussed in Chapters I and II; this behavior can be justified by lack of clocks or other means of telling time at most gambling establishments, so that gamblers very quickly get disoriented in that respect. Psychologists, however, explain this phenomenon in terms of an attempted return to infancy.[14] Most social human activities--eating, sleeping, working-- are more or less regulated in the adult world; gambling does not fall into this pattern. The gambler rejects the time-conscious adult world and returns, probably subconsciously, to the less-structured world of the child.

According to Henriette, it is not only the erratic schedule of the gambler's life that is harmful; even more significant is the worsening of her brother's general behavior since he developed the addiction to gaming. She provides some insight into Béverlei's pre-gambling life: "La passion qui le dévore/ Bannit toute vertu, tout sentiment du coeur" (act 1, sc. 1); previously, he loved his sister and adored his wife, but his feelings have changed. Henriette remembers Béverlei as a youthful and charming individual; she wonders what happened to "cette grâce, cette noblesse, et milles autres dons enchanteurs?/ Les veilles, les

chagrins ont flétri sa jeunesse." (act 1, sc. 2) His
gambling habits harm his mental and physical health.
Present-day sociologists agree in their evaluation of
a gambler's behavior: "It is not uncommon to find occasional evidences of neglect of diet and sleep ...
and of personal appearance."15

Henriette's perception of reality causes her
to suspect Stukéli, who by introducing Béverlei to
gambling, has brought nothing but misery to the family.
Béverlei's attachment to this man reminds us of M. Orgon's worship of the hypocritical Tartuffe in Molière's
play of the same name. The sister understands the
ways of gamblers, knows that reform is almost always
impossible, and realizes that any funds available will
feed his appetite for the games; she is not ashamed to
express fear that her own dowry might have already
been gambled away, since "un joueur n'a rien de sacré."
(act 1, sc. 1) Her unselfish concern becomes apparent
early in the play; she is worried not so much about
her own future as about her sister-in-law's well-being. She openly accuses Stukéli of falseness and
blames him for her brother's addiction:

Pouvez-vous vous dire son ami,
Quand son goût pour le jeu par vous est affermi,
Quand vous encouragez son vice?
(act 1, sc. 3)

She loves Leuson, but will not marry him until her
family situation improves; her sense of honesty and
responsibility demand that she share Mme Béverlei's
misfortunes: "de l'amour puis-je goûter les charmes?
... je vais essuyer ou partager ses larmes." (act 1,
sc. 9)

Jarvis, the faithful servant, remains loyal to
Béverlei even though the master fired him when he
could no longer pay for his services. Already an old
man, he has been with the family since his youth and
served the household under the gambler's father. Sentimental in his older years, he reminisces of better
times when laughter reigned everywhere; indirectly, he
provides a favorable portrait of Béverlei as a child.
Of all the characters, Jarvis expresses his feelings
the most; his master's fate moves him to tears. He
remembers him as a baby in his arms, the son of a
proud and honest man, and indicates his desire to spend
his old age serving Béverlei and his family. Like Mme
Béverlei, Jarvis wants to share the gambler's misfor-

tunes and help him conquer his weakness for games of chance; his loyalty is boundless.

The servant tells how Béverlei as a child was kind and generous to the poor; the boy could not comprehend why poverty existed. He had made a promise to Jarvis:

Je veux, si je suis jamais roi,
Qu'en mon royaume tout abonde:
Je rendrai riche tout le monde.
(act 1, sc. 2)

It is not unusual for a child to imagine himself a king, a person with power to do as he wishes; besides, his ambition seems to be caused by a generous desire to make everyone rich and therefore happy. Modern psychologists, however, offer a different explanation; they associate the child's desire to control the lives of many, were he king, with a feeling of omnipotence, manifested in adulthood by an addiction to gambling.[16] This harmless childhood wish for boundless power develops into a neurotic illusion of omnipoetence in adulthood. The gambler has a constant compulsion to test out Fate; consciously or unconsciously, he believes "in his right to ask Fate for special privileges, and he mistakes his strong yearnings for a lost omnipotence for the feeling that he is, in fact, omnipotent."[17]

The immediate cause of Béverlei's downfall is his so-called friend, Stukéli, who shows a hypocritical concern for the gambler; he repeatedly lures Béverlei to gamble and finally to stay out all night at a brelan. When pressured, the scoundrel admits having left our hero "chez Vilson, avec des gens qu'à connoître il n'est profit ni gloire,/ Il ne m'en a pas voulu croire." (act 1, sc. 3) He conveniently forgets to mention that it was he who took Béverlei there in the first place. A man of no scruples, he seeks to create a feeling of mistrust between Mme Béverlei and her husband by assuring her of Béverlei's faithfulness to her. She ought not to believe the rumors. The rumors are, of course, false, for Stukéli himself has just started them in order to worry the poor woman. Pretending to protect his friend's "secret," he says just enough to arouse her suspicions: "je vois,/ Que vous connaissez trop le monde/ Pour écouter les vains propos." (act 1, sc. 5) Finally he leaves the troubled wife with the thought that "indiscrètement je

vous ai fait connoître/ Ce que de vous apprendre il
n'étoit pas besoin." (act 1, sc. 5)

Stukéli's true motives become apparent in a
monologue in which he explains his plan to seek revenge against the family. He had been in love with
Mme Béverlei long before she became the gambler's wife;
although she has obviously forgotten the incident, he
cannot forget having been rejected. He believes that
if he can destroy the husband, he will then be able to
win the wife's affections:

Madame Béverlei, vous avez oublié
Qu'avant que par l'hymen votre sort fût lié,
Vous avez dédaigné ma flamme.
Sous le voile de l'amitié,
J'ai déjà ruiné le rival que j'abhorre
Dans le coeur de sa femme il faut le perdre encore
Le perdre ... la gagner ... c'est mon double
    projet.   (act 1, sc. 6)

Leuson, Henriette's suitor and an honest man,
intervenes in order to correct the situation. Interested in the welfare of his fiancée's family and ac-
customed to the realities of everyday life and its
struggles, he is well aware of the corruption which
exists everywhere in the country. He knows that op-
portunists always search for likely victims: anyone
with money and not much common sense. The dupe this
time is, of course, Béverlei. Leuson openly refers to
Stukéli as a hypocritical liar, interested only in
pursuing his own plan (of which Leuson is however unaware), and showing no concern for a man whom he says
is his friend. The good man blames the scoundrel, not
only for introducing Béverlei to gambling, but for
making him the victim of deceitful and dishonest practices:

On veut que chez Vilson,
Vous ayiez avec Machinson
Une secrète intelligence,
Vous vous enrichissez, dit-on,
Lorsque Béverlei se ruine.
                (act 1, sc. 7)

The cheating aspect of gambling constitutes a
very prominent element of the play, for it makes the
gambler an unsuspecting victim before he even places
his first bet. Of the works analyzed in this study,
Béverlei is the only one wherein gaming has degener-

ated to such baseness; unfortunately the situation on stage merely reflects the situation off-stage, the real world as shown in the preceding chapter. Corruption closely follows the need for money and for a way of "striking it rich" quickly, since the use of dishonest means might help a person get rich more quickly. Regardless of whether it represents a desire to control the odds or to show some power, the origins of cheating parallel those of gambling itself. Reid briefly remarks that in 1000 B.C. the pagan priests used dice to consult the gods, but "even then there were characters who tried to outwit divinity by loading the cubes."[18]

Leuson's nobility of character justifies his behavior toward Stukéli; if necessary, he will answer the latter's challenge to a duel in order to protect his friend's life and future. Henriette's suitor realizes the danger of the situation, since he is dealing with a man of little or no scruples, but his determination compels him to uncover the truth: "J'ai démasqué le traître. Il sait, le scélérat?/ Que Leuson le connoît, et dans le coeur il tremble." (act 1, sc. 9) He analyzes people well, recognizes Stukéli as a "lâche au coeur faux, à l'oeil timide et sombre" (act 1, sc. 9), and someone who "n'a jamais su porter tous ses coups que dans l'ombre,/ Je crois à sa valeur comme à sa probité." (act 1, sc. 9) Leuson hopes to have enough proof to send him to prison.

Act 2 brings all the characters on stage, although not at the same time; it presents an attempt on their part at self-analysis. In order to enhance the dramatic aspects of the situation, Béverlei appears alone at first, a disorderly sight to the audience. He examines his life as a gambler and compares it to the happiness of his pre-gambling days; although he praises common sense, he admittedly lacks it. The tone of the monologue remains sad and depressing; our hero is very low emotionally and unable to get out of his desperate situation.

Béverlei presents a pitiful figure as he approaches his own home, afraid to enter it; more than fear, however, guilt and remorse burden him:

Ciel, voici ma maison, et je crains d'y rentrer,
A ma femme, à ma soeur, je n'ose me montrer.
J'ai tout trahi, l'amour, l'amitié, la nature.
(act 2, sc. 1)

Basically a good man, he cannot justify his evil behavior; his irresponsible actions have brought grief
to those he loves dearly, yet he seems incapable of
controlling his vice. He surely despises what he has
done:

> A tout ce qui m'est cher, à moi-même odieux,
> Sans dessein, sans espoir, errant à l'aventure,
> La honte et le remords me suivent en tous lieux.
>   (act 2, sc. 1)

Although Béverlei cannot penetrate his innerself, he
does reveal several interesting factors worthy of more
detailed study:

> O du jeu passion fatale?
> Ou plutôt, vil amour de l'or!
> Eh! qu'avois-je besoin
> d'en amasser encore?
>   (act 2, sc. 1)

He is lucid enough to realize that his addiction might
reflect a need to become rich instead of to gamble per
se. Then another disturbing thought enters his mind:
he had wealth when he started gambling, he had no need
for more. Was it then ambition, weakness or something
else which started him on the road to vice?

In his writings, La Bruyère explains that although he knows about the type of gambler who cannot
control his vice, he has no pity for such a person:

> Mille gens se ruinent au jeu, et vous disent
> froidement qu'ils ne sauraient se passer de
> jouer: quelle excuse! ... Serait-on reçu
> a dire qu'on ne peut se passer de voler,
> d'assassiner?[19]

Considering games of chance as one of the lowest manifestations of human behavior, he sees no possible re-
demption for the gambler; after all, the money used
for gambling should instead go for feeding and clothing the unfortunate family: "poussé par le jeu ...
il faut même que l'on se passe d'habits et de nourri-
ture, et de les fournir à sa famille?"[20]

Marquiset provides a more objective analysis
in his study of the joueurs: "Ils jouent pour éprouver ces émotions ardentes qui les font passer en quelques instants de la joie au désespoir, ils jouent in-

souciants de la faim, du sommeil, de la vie, de la pensée."21 The scholar seems to share Béverlei's concern for the true reasons behind his vice; ambition is not always the motivating force: "On croit que le gain est le seul but ... erreur! Les joueurs jouent pour jouer."22

Saurin does not wish to portray a repulsive person; instead he wants to show the effects that the passion for gambling can have on a good, decent, kind fellow. For instance, the author uses Jarvis in order to accentuate the positive qualities of Béverlei; after all, such an excellent and loyal person could serve only the best of men. This joueur is a worthy man, or at least he was until he succumbed to his temptation; he experiences remorse and guilt, but cannot or will not change his behavior.

The meeting between Jarvis and Béverlei affords the latter the opportunity to describe the kind of atmosphere usually found at the private brelans, where corruption breeds freely:

> cette horrible maison,
> Ce gouffre où l'avarice égorge ses victimes,
> Où parmi l'intérêt, la bassesse et les crimes,
> Règne le désespoir, la malédiction.
> (act 2, sc. 2)

For all his criticism of the treatment received, the gambler keeps going back for more punishment. Fully aware of the damaging consequences that his actions have on his family, Béverlei remains incapable of correcting his behavior:

> J'ai passé cette nuit cruelle,
> Dans les convulsions d'un malheur obstiné
> A maudire cent fois le jour où je suis né.
> (act 2, sc. 2)

This mental impotence characterizes all gamblers. Bloch thinks that an interesting psychological feature of gambling is the enormous hold it exerts upon the individual's personality: "Once addicted, even though the gambler may recognize the harm his practice is causing his family, he will nevertheless continue to follow his bent."23

Béverlei has a very low opinion of himself after leaving his wife and child: "Que partout on me nomme époux ingrat, cruel,/ Frère sans amitié, père sans naturel." (act 2, sc. 2) Jarvis quickly assures him, however, that his fears are unfounded for his loved ones pity him but do not despise him:

> On vous regarde comme un homme
> Qui dans un précipice, en rêvant, s'est jeté:
> Le meilleur des humains (c'est ainsi qu'on vous
> Et partout plaint et regretté.   nomme)
>   (act 2, sc. 2)

Unable to cope with his shame or face his family, he unwisely decides to consult his "friend" for advice.

We realize the difficulty of trying to judge Béverlei. He seems insensitive toward his family and friends, since he makes them suffer so much, but perhaps he is only a dupe, willing to put his whole life in the hands of a virtual stranger. When Jarvis reminds him of Mme Béverlei's concern

> Elle a bien des chagrins, mon cher maître; et
> Je jurerois que votre absence   pourtant
> De tous ses maux est le plus grand.
>   (act 2, sc. 2)

he simply retorts: "A Stukéli je dois parler,/ Avant de me rendre auprès d'elle." (act 2, sc. 2) Some fools never learn.

Saurin's theatrical ability and deep psychological understanding of human nature become apparent in the characterization of the base scoundrel, Stukéli. A villain, he nevertheless arouses certain admiration; his actions are despicable but his cleverness in manipulating Béverlei provide some of the best lines of the drama. Our gambler's blind faith in him puts him completely at his mercy. Despite evidence to the contrary, Béverlei believes Stukéli to be incapable of evil.

Stukéli is the middle-class counterpart of the chevalier d'industrie already studied in Chapters I and II. The latter is a fake who moves among the aristocracy and gains prestige among men by using women; the former is a false friend who moves in bourgeois circles and exploits a man's weakness in order to obtain the woman he wants. Both the chevalier and Stukéli operate under false identities: nobility in the one case, friendship in the other; both use people and take advantage of moral weaknesses to attain their not-so-honorable goals. Their true intentions are eventually discovered by someone who genuinely cares for the victims.

Stukéli's cunning contrasts sharply with Béverlei's credulity; the villain increases the gambler's feelings of guilt by repeating that he has sacrificed his own wealth in order to support his friend's habit. He conveniently forgets to mention that he is responsible for Béverlei's addiction. In order to drain the dupe's finances, our rogue pressures him into risking not only his own money, but his sister's fortune and his wife's jewelry. Stukéli carries out his plan very cleverly:

> STUKELI
> On veut des sûretés. En avez-vous quelqu'une?
> Quant à moi, je n'ai rien qui puisse être engagé:
> Vous avez épuisé ce que j'eus de fortune.

> BEVERLEI
> Vous m'êtes venu tendre une main secourable,
> Et moi, doublement misérable,
> J'ai dans le même abîme entraîné mon ami.
> (act 2, sc. 3)

The gullible gambler does not realize that what he took was not a helping hand, but bait.

In his baseness, Stukéli suggests borrowing money from Jarvis or selling Mme Béverlei's jewelry which he describes as "ces bijoux, brillants et super-flus,/ Que notre vanité prend sur le nécessaire." (act 2, sc. 3) Shocked, Béverlei opposes both suggestions as improper of an "honnête homme." Obviously, however, the scélérat's perseverance and wit will win in the end. First he instills fear by mentioning the threat of creditors and imprisonment: "Que plus d'un créancier peut, d'un moment à l'autre,/ Faire d'une prison mon séjour et le vôtre" (act 2, sc. 3); then he creates feelings of guilt by accusing the gambler of ingratitude:

> Mets ce que j'ai fait en oubli;
> Laisse-moi dans le précipice.
> Je ne presse plus un ingrat.
> (act 2, sc. 3)

finally he lures the poor man back into the glamor of gambling:

Je suis sûr qu'aujourd'hui la fortune volage
Tourneroit de notre côté
J'ai des pressentiments dans l'âme,
Dont je garantirois l'infaillibilité.
                    (act 2, sc. 3)

Some characteristics of the pathological gambler stand out in the preceding quotation: sense of omnipotence, superstition and an irrational optimism. Dostoevski, in his short novel, The Gambler, queries: "Is it really impossible to approach the gambling table without becoming infected with superstition?"[24] Bergler, a present-day authority on gambling as a neurosis, explains that "there is a basic interconnection between superstition and the omnipotence wish."[25] He explains his theory as follows: "Dealing with the unpredictable, the gambler must be illogical and therefore, superstitious."[26] At the same time, however, on the unconscious level "we discover his fanatical belief in infantile megalomania (society and education have forced the gambler) to repress his conviction of his own omnipotence to some degree."[27] According to the psychologist, this is clearly demonstrated in the gambler's attitude when gambling: "he expects that he will win because he wants to win. When a gambler places his stake he is 'ordering' the next card to win for him, in the complete illusion that he is omnipotent."[28]

There are other parallels between the psychologist's theories and Saurin's main character. According to Bergler, the gambler is an inveterate optimist; i.e., "his belief in ultimate success cannot be shattered by financial loss, however great."[29] Béverlei does precisely that throughout the play and it brings about his downfall; he has lost everything but admits that "l'espoir m'enflamme." (act 2, sc. 3) Again, according to Bergler, another sign of neurotic gambling manifests itself in the exclusion of all other activities: "the pathological concentration overshadows everything else--vocation, love, hobbies."[30] Béverlei's behavior fits the pattern perfectly; he has neglected love, family and friends for the deceiving glitter of the games of chance.

Saurin repeatedly delays Béverlei's return home in order to build up the tension and the drama of the situation. First, he encounters Jarvis, then he meets with Stukéli; finally, as he approaches the door, his sister stops him just outside to discuss his behavior. She expresses her concern for her own wealth, entrusted to him long before he started to gamble; she would now like to have it returned: "mon dessein n'est plus qu'il reste sous la garde/ D'un homme qui si mal a conservé le sien." (act 2, sc. 5) She wants the truth, even if it is bad news, "Rendez-moi mes effets .../ Ou bien, s'ils sont perdus, daignez me l'annoncer." (act 2, sc. 5) She can accept her own ruin, but suffers because her sister-in-law and nephew have been left penniless. Henriette reproaches her brother and curses the passion which has brought misery to her loved ones; she resents the unfairness of the situation and feels that the gambler should be the only victim of his own addiction: "Si le mal sur vous tomboit, comme le blâme." (act 2, sc. 5) Curiously enough, although Béverlei harshly criticizes himself, he does not accept negative comments from others: "Vos reproches viennent trop tard;/ Sans pouvoir les guérir, vous ouvrez mes blessures." (act 2, sc. 5)

Bergler explains that self-criticism is only part of the neurotic behavior exhibited by the pathological gambler; the psychologist calls the pattern the "mechanism of orality," for he again attributes the behavior to a regression to an infantile feeling of omnipotence.[31] The gambler resents the lack of real omnipotence and his action then follows a pattern. First, "the psycho-masochist unconsciously provokes or misuses situations in which he is defeated, rejected, denied,"[32] as illustrated by Béverlei's continuous attempts at gambling in a corrupted brelan. Then, "unaware that he himself has been responsible for these defeats and rejections, the pathological gambler strikes out in righteous indignation, and apparently in self-defense, against the world's cruelty and injustice."[33] We have seen Béverlei become impatient and angry with those who really love him. "Then follows profound self-pity; Fate has handed him a raw deal."[34] In the play under study, the gambler goes through periods of deep depression, feeling sorry for himself and his misfortune.

Bergler emphasizes that only the aggression and the self-pity are conscious; the provocation of Fate remains at the unconscious level and the gambler does not realize that his action is deliberate. The psychologist further explains that gambling (at a level such as Béverlei's) can become a dangerous neurosis, since the "gambler does not gamble because he consciously decides to gamble; he is propelled by uncon-

scious forces over which he has no control. He is an
objectively sick person who is subjectively unaware
that he is sick."[35] This explains why Béverlei cannot
stop gambling no matter how badly he consciously
"wants" to quit.

When Béverlei finally sees his wife and child,
they do not reproach him; they show him only love and
understanding. Saurin adds the child Tomi in order to
bring out elements of sentimentality; the boy's candid
and honest expression of his feelings affords a re-
freshing sight contrasting with the corruption and
suffering which pervades the play. By necessity, however, his words are sad: "J'ai bien eu du chagrin!/
... C'est que maman tantôt elle pleuroit." (act 2,
sc. 6) Although touched by his family's attitude, our
gambler still remains unaware of who his true friends
are. He disregards everyone's praise of Leuson and
considers him disloyal, an idea implanted by Stukéli's
astuteness. Saurin presents Leuson favorably: "Voici
monsieur Leuson, dont le zèle et les soins/ Ne se
peuvent trop reconnoître" .(act 2, sc. 7); but when
Leuson criticizes Stukéli, Béverlei, in his usual
naive fashion, jumps to defend his "honor": "Un ami
qui périt pour venir à mon aide/ Oser l'appeler traître, et l'oser devant moi!" (act 2, sc. 8)

Béverlei's inability to distinguish the loyal
friend from the hypocritical villain and his refusal
to consider himself in error, constitute the tragic
flaw of the play; his own blindness brings about his
downfall. Unable to see Stukéli's true character behind the mask of friendship, Béverlei praises his
generosity and unselfishness; he even feels responsible for Stukéli's supposed "financial ruin" and thinks
he should make amends even though this "friend" blames
him for his alleged misfortunes:

> J'ai causé sa ruine.
> Tout le bien qu'avoit Stukéli
> Dans mon naufrage enseveli.
> Mon ami ne peut pas attendre.
> Dans l'amertume de son coeur,
> Il m'a reproché son malheur.
> (act 2, sc. 8)

A true friend, of course, would not have made such an
accusation.

Toward the end of act 2, the unscrupulous Stukéli strikes again, successfully; he arouses Béverlei's

feelings of guilt by sending a letter where he mentions his intentions to leave the country; he closes with the following words: "hâtez-vous de venir recevoir les adieux de votre ami ruiné." (act 2, sc. 10) The gambler foolishly reasons that the only honorable thing to do is to follow his friend into exile: "J'ai causé son malheur, je dois le partager." (act 2, sc. 10) Somehow, he does not feel the same responsibility toward his wife's malheur, which he has caused and which he definitely should share. Only after Mme Béverlei suggests pawning her diamonds to rescue Stukéli does he agree to stay; he quickly offers a solemn promise to stop gambling in exchange for her unselfish generosity: "Mais vous ne jouerez plus? Cela m'est bien promis?/ C'est à quoi mon époux expressément s'engage?" (act 2, sc. 10)

In act 3 optimism appears almost as strong as pessimism, and a ray of hope permeates the otherwise gloomy atmosphere; one contributing factor is the love affair between Leuson and Henriette. Intelligent and energetic, they love and respect each other and are concerned for each other's well-being:

En vous connoissant mieux, Leuson
Ce qui fut un penchant est devenu raison.
Avec vous je préférerois
La plus simple cabane au plus riche palais.
(act 3, sc. 5)

He wants reassurance that her feelings will not change with the years:

On connoît mal, d'abord, l'humeur, le caractère;
Ses défauts son cachés sous le désir de plaire.
Je crains que par le temps les miens produits au
(act 3, sc. 5)   jour.

Sure of her affection for him, Leuson tells her the truth about her fortune; her brother has gambled it away. In a very noble manner he has spared Henriette an embarrassing situation; had she known the truth beforehand, her pride would have kept her from marrying the man she loves. She recognizes this fact:

Vous avez surpris ma promesse.
De votre procédé j'admire la noblesse
Peut-être vous m'allez accuser d'être fière,
Mais je crains de vous trop devoir.
(act 3, sc. 5)

She wants to marry her social equal and believes that
Leuson should not be burdened with the debts of her
family. Once again his generous nature prevails:

> Quelle erreur! Eh quoi! belle Henriette,
> Entre deux coeurs qui ne font qu'un
> Peut-il subsister quelque dette?
> (act 3, sc. 5)

There is another high moment in the tragedy,
however brief, when Béverlei decides to stop gambling:
"j'abhorre le jeu;/ De le fuir à jamais devant vous je
fais voeu." (act 3, sc. 7) He announces more good
news; their much awaited funds from Spain have ar-
rived and the money can help pay their debts. Of
course, it can also create new ones. Mme Béverlei re-
joices in their change of fortune, while Béverlei promises to change his ways:

> J'abjure à vos pieds cette fureur honteuse
> Et je prends le ciel à témoin
> Que je ne veux avoir désormais d'autre soin
> Que d'élever mon fils et de vous rendre heureuse.
> (act 3, sc. 8)

Although he sincerely intends to reform, his characteristic lack of judgment will lead him back into
temptation. With this newly-acquired capital, he must
first settle his gambling debts: "D'une dette pressante il faut que je m'acquitte." (act 3, sc. 8)
Sociologists indicate that this behavior typifies gamblers:

> Primary is the "gentleman's code"--that gam-
> bling debts must be paid and given priority
> over other forms of obligation. ... This may
> be a survival of the aristocrat's code of
> the "debt of honor."[36]

We observe Stukéli in action as he works his plan to
perfection in act 3. At the beginning (sc. 2), he
makes Mme Béverlei suspicious of her husband, while
toward the end (sc. 9), he helps Béverlei walk into
his total ruin. He is conspicuously absent from the
remainder of the act. Aware of his power, he boasts:
"J'ai tout au mieux joué mon rôle!" (act 3, sc. 1) In
order to increase Mme Béverlei's troubles, he confes-
ses with an air of false innocence, that he has never
received the diamonds sent to him to pay off debts;
instead he seems reluctant to reveal that they might

79

have gone to "une indigne rivale." (act 3, sc. 2)
Although she will not admit it openly, the poor woman
burns with jealous fears, instilled by the scoundrel's
insinuations: "Je ne sais ... Il se répand des bruits
.../ Nous sommes dans un siècle ... on a vu des maris
..." (act 3, sc. 2)

Mme Béverlei's outrage at Stukéli's behavior
surprises him; a friend should not betray a trust. Because of her reaction, he briefly loses his composure
and almost the argument. When the hypocrite mentions
in triumph that

L'amitié m'imposait silence:
Il faut parler. Je sers la beauté, la vertu
....
De son secret, lui-même, il m'a fait confidence.
(act 3, sc. 3)

she replies without hesitation: "Ainsi de votre ami
trompant la confiance,/ Près de sa femme, ici, vous
venez l'accuser?" (act 3, sc. 2) His action affects
her deeply, causing her to lose all respect for him.
She finally sees him in the true light of a traitor, a
faux ami. To show her contempt she uses the tutoie-
ment:

Choisis d'être perfide ou calomniateur
....
Je te crois tous les deux
....
Va, de ta bouche impure
Ne viens plus en ces lieux distiller le poison.
(act 3, sc. 2)

Unfortunately, she will never communicate her discovery to her husband. Upset by the malicious gossip,
and excited by the arrival of the funds from Spain,
she forgets Stukéli's baseness. As act 3 approaches
the end, Béverlei again falls victim to the scoundrel
who, like a force of evil, seems to be everywhere. At
the precise moment when Béverlei leaves the house with
his newly-found fortune, he just happens to appear and
rekindles his passion for gambling.

The subtlety of Stukéli's technique merits a
detailed analysis; he has arranged for the creditors,
whom Béverlei intends to pay off, to be engaged in a
game "chez Vilson." The scélérat presents a very
tempting description of the place:

80

La partie est considérable;
Des flots d'or roulent sur la table;
Avec quelque bonheur on feroit un beau gain.
                    (act 3, sc. 9)

Since Béverlei resists the temptation, Stukéli must
then make his suggestions more attractive,

La fortune,il est vrai,n'est pas toujours cruelle.
Tu parois en grâce avec elle;
Avec discrétion on pourrait la tâter
....
Ce n'est point mon avis.
                    (act 3, sc. 9)

But this _is_ precisely his advice to Béverlei, hidden
under his hypocritical mask; the villain keeps up his
pretenses to the end and "insists" that they not go to
the _brelan_ in order to avoid the weakness that might
overcome the _joueur_. The latter's response, uttered in
the form of a question, seems to carry a premonition
in itself:

Me crois-tu donc si foible, et que sur un tapis
Un peu d'or me tourne la tête,
Que mes yeux en soient éblouis?
                    (act 3, sc. 9)

    The answer to that question becomes all too
obvious as act 4 opens into a dim and gloomy setting;
Béverlei, on the verge of madness, cannot sink any
lower. He has just lost everything:

J'ai tout perdu: rien ne me reste
Que d'affreux désespoir qui trouble ma raison;
Ma fureur va jusqu'au délire.
                    (act 4, sc. 1)

Cohen agrees that gamblers "become choleric and testy
if they lose and they break many times into violent
passions, and oaths, imprecations and unbeseeming
speeches, little different from mad men."[37] Misfortune ultimately forces Béverlei to see the situation
clearly and to curse his unworthy friend. He has lost
his self-esteem and cries, "Nuit, tu ne peux cacher un
coupable à lui-même/ O désespoir! ô honte extrême!
(act 4, sc. 2) Like most people addicted to gambling,
he has finally risked too much. Bergler's psychological interpretation of this behavior states that a
gambler will slowly increase his stake; sometimes the
money risked should go to feed his family but "sooner

or later every gambler loses his head, forgets his good intentions, and risks everything on one card--only to lose. Some inner compulsion drives the gambler to repeat these actions which cannot be logically explained."[38]

Saurin never actually shows the gambling house or a game in progress; he never describes the gloomy atmosphere of gambling. In the <u>Satire contre les maris</u>, however, Regnard paints an interesting picture which can apply to this drama:

> Vois cette table ronde,
> Autel que l'avarice éleva dans le monde,
> Où tous ces forcenés semblent avoir fait voeu
> De sacrifier au noir démon du jeu.[39]

To this kind of place our gambler keeps returning until he has nothing else left to lose.

As Béverlei's despair mounts, so does his anger at Stukéli: "j'ai vú l'artifice/ Et qu'en montrant le précipice,/ Tu savois inspirer la fureur d'y courir" (act 4, sc. 1); he knows that his "friend" wants to destroy him, but he does not know why. As his thinking clears, the gambler realizes that he has been cheated:

> J'ai ... un violent soupçon.
> De scélérats c'est une bande,
> Dont la caverne est chez Vilson.
> Ma perte n'est pas naturelle.
>   (act 4, sc. 1)

Davis corroborates the fact that a losing gambler becomes furious when he discovers that his losses are the result of dishonest practices: "The crooked operator of a gambling game is not only committing theft of the victim's money but may be stealing what amounts to the victim's state of grace."[40]

Béverlei must have unconsciously at least suspected cheating in the games, for he was never allowed to win. Although it seems unlikely that a person would choose to keep on losing, sociologists believe that the situation occurs often:

> Sometimes gamblers willingly go into a rigged
> game with the knowledge that the game is fixed
> and that they must lose. This voluntary sub-

mission to fate is easily transformed into the
wish that such humility should be rewarded.[41]

This theory does not seem too far-fetched, in view of
Béverlei's behavior. For the first time in the play,
this gambler finally begins to show real aggressive
behavior; previously, his personality pattern had remained passive. Since a radical change in attitude
would seem artificial, even though Béverlei does not
trust Stukéli any longer, he still does not like Leuson. Instead, his rudeness to the good man evolves
into violence; he accuses his real friend of hypocrisy
and of being after his sister for her fortune (which
no longer exists): "Moi présent, il proteste qu'il
m'aime,/ Et loin de moi sa bouche ose me diffamer."
(act 4, sc. 3) Leuson indignantly rejects the accusation: "Je ne dis jamais rien qu'en face/ Je ne sois
prêt à soutenir." (act 4, sc. 3) Béverlei remains
blind to the irony that his accusation of Leuson accurately describes Stukéli.

Angry about his losses, desperate about the
fate of his family, Béverlei draws his sword on Leuson
who cooly informs him of the true cause of his disgrace: "Ta folle confiance en un vil scélérat/ De
tout ce qui t'est cher a causé la ruine." (act 4, sc.
3) Overcome by despair, Béverlei asks to be killed
and thus end his misery. At this point Leuson leaves,
realizing that the duel is part of Stukéli's plan to
get rid of one of them or perhaps both. Saurin's
talent for the dramatic becomes increasingly obvious
as Béverlei stands alone on a dark street with a sword
in his hand, talking to himself and seriously considering suicide as the end to his unhappiness; the slow
approach of his loyal servant interrupts his fatalis-
tic thoughts. A brief return to religion accompanies
Béverlei's downfall; as he hands Jarvis the sword, he
thanks Heaven for having sent the old man to his rescue (act 4, sc. 5).

Unable to blame others for his misfortune, Béverlei curses Fate and thinks that an "infection" of
Bad Luck plagues him: "La ruine, l'horreur, la malé-
diction,/ De tout ce qui m'approche est le cruel par-
tage." (act 4, sc. 5) In reality, it is not his
"destiny," but his poor judgment, of course, which has
led him to his present state. Jarvis' presence
strikes a note of sentimentality which will reach its
high point with the arrival of the gambler's wife; the
servant accuses his master of being selfish, incon-
siderate, and unconcerned about his wife's peace of

mind. As if on cue, Mme Béverlei arrives, only to find a very depressing sight, a despondent Béverlei crouched on the dark stones of the deserted street.

The setting is magnificent in its symbolic meaning; while Béverlei wants the blackness of the night to swallow his existence, his wife shines a ray of light into the darkness, not only with her lantern but with the hope of her presence. Yet with his usual lack of sensitivity, the gambler tries to avoid her because he dreads having to explain the truth; he never fully understands her willingness to forgive, forget and start a new life. There might even be a mild sado-masochistic tendency in Béverlei, for he always hurts his loved ones and he always expects punishment for his actions; the problem is that his family never penalizes him. When Béverlei tells his wife that "De malédictions vous m'allez accabler" (act 4, sc. 5), she quickly retorts "Ah! mon coeur en est incapable:/ Il n'apprendra jamais qu'à bénir mon é-poux." (act 4, sc. 6) He insists, almost begs to be reprimanded: "Maudissez votre époux; il l'a bien mé-rité" (act 4, sc. 6); her noble soul only feels pity for the man.

In order to set the stage for the <u>désespoir</u> of the final act, the playwright presents the gambler in trouble also with the law; he is taken to jail for his failure to pay his debts. Neither his wife nor his servant has enough funds to buy his freedom. Act 5 takes place in a dark prison which matches the hope-lessness of the gambler's life; Tomi's appearance in the cell adds a new dramatic element. The young child sleeps peacefully because at last he has found his unfortunate and elusive father. Jarvis accompanies them, lamenting the evil effects of his master's gambling: "A quelle passion vous vous êtes livré!/ Que de vertus en vous un seul vice a détruites!" (act 5, sc. 1) Mme Béverlei enters then, already on the verge of despair; she feels incapable of helping her husband at a time when he most desperately needs assistance. She cannot calm his fears or boost his spirits:

Plongé dans un morne silence,
L'oeil fixe, il paroissoit ni n'entendre ni voir;
Et soudain, furieux jusques à la démence,
Poussant les cris du désespoir,
Il détestoit son existence.
                    (act 5, sc. 2)

Mme Béverlei realizes the seriousness of the
situation. Her husband cannot be left alone in such a
depressed state because he may try to put an end to
his problems, forever. She leaves Jarvis to look after the gambler while she settles some family matters:

> s'il s'éveille,
> Ne le laisse point seul: mène-lui son enfant,
> A l'aspect de son fils, à cette chère vue,
> D'un sentiment si doux un père a l'âme émue!
> (act 5, sc. 2)

Béverlei wakes with sinister plans which he feels he
must execute alone; pretending to need Leuson's
friendly advice, he sends Jarvis to find him (act 5,
sc. 4). After some hesitation, the loyal servant
obeys. The joueur has hastily reached a macabre decision: death, not only for himself, but for his son.
In his neurotic state of mind he feels he must "save"
Tomi while he sleeps peacefully.

The gambler considers suicide as the easy way
out. Not being a brave man, however, he fears the unknown, and therefore turns to religion. He prays
while pouring poison in a glass of water; he hopes
that his invocations to God will compensate for his
self-murder. The thought of death brings images of
peace to his mind; he longs to surrender, to stop
fighting for a futile life: "Je vais m'endormir dans
la tombe." (act 5, sc. 5) Still, the possibility of
eternal damnation frightens him:

> Si la mort, au lieu d'être un sommeil,
> Etoit un éternel et funeste réveil!
> Et si d'un Dieu vengeur ...
> (act 5, sc. 5)

He argues with his conscience which reminds him of his
duty to his family and of the fact that only the Crea-
tor has the right to end his days. He cannot cope
with the chaos which he has created, but he cannot
pray for his salvation, either; suicide might be the
easiest solution:

> Mourir, enfin, cent fois pour n'oser mourir une!
> ....
> On peut braver le sort
> Mais la honte! mais le remords!
> (act 5, sc. 5)

The neurotic _joueur_ faces the ultimate gamble and must make a choice: the stake is his life. Saurin has built up momentum for this dramatic scene by having Béverlei consider suicide on several occasions prior to act 5.[42] Béverlei hesitates briefly but his gambling spirit prompts him to tempt death:

Nature, tu frémis! ... Terreur d'un autre monde,
Abîme de l'éternité,
Obscurité vaste et profonde
....
Mais j'abhorre la vie, et mon destin l'emporte.
(act 5, sc. 5)

He takes the gamble and drinks the poison; always a loser, he has second thoughts about his hurried decision, but it is too late: "O réflexion trop tardive!" (act 5, sc. 5) Finding himself at the end of his life, he envies his son, uncorrupted by passions and just starting to live. Béverlei wishes he himself had a second chance to make a fresh start. His pessimism, however, almost turns him into a murderer. He perceives life as painful and wishes to spare his son from the suffering by killing him: "Mourir est un instant, vivre est un long supplice/ Qu'il passe, sans douleur, du sommeil à la mort." (act 5, sc. 5)

Fortunately, he remains lucid long enough for Tomi to wake up and move away; Mme Béverlei returns just in time to announce that the man responsible for her husband's imprisonment, i.e., Stukéli, is dead. Their fortune will be recovered and Béverlei will be freed. Ironically, it does not matter, for the _dupe_ is dying. In his despair, he realizes that he deserves his punishment: "J'ai violé les lois de la terre et du ciel." (act 5, sc. 8) As the end approaches, Béverlei finds some peace in prayer; for the first time since he started gambling, he humbly asks God to grant the well-being of his family:

Tu vois mes remords infinis:
S'ils ne peuvent, grand Dieu! désarmer ta vengence,
Ne l'étends pas, du moins, sur ma femme et mon
(act 5, sc. 8)   fils,

Saurin wanted his drama to have a moral, to teach a lesson about the evils of uncontrolled passion. He chose gambling because it was a leading cause of misfortune in his time; he wrote a tragedy

ecause he did not want his contemporaries to be mis-
ed, in a lighter play, by the glamor of the games. He
reated a main character who becomes the easy victim
f unscrupulous practices, in order to illustrate the
orruption that accompanies gambling. He allowed his
ambler to commit suicide as proof that there is no
ure for the neurosis; prevention is the only hope.
he tragedy ends on a tone of death, suffering, and a
arning to the young: "Si du jeu jamais vous sentez
es fureurs,/ Souvenez-vous de votre père." (act 5,
c. 8)

[1]Cailhava, p. 522.

[2]Edward Moore, The Gamester (Ann Arbor, Michigan: Edwards Brothers, 1948).

[3]Lancaster, French Tragedy, I, 327.

[4]Charles Cotton, The Compleat Gamester (London: George Routledge and Sons, 1674), pp. 1-2.

[5]Beaurepaire, p. 442.   [6]La Bruyère, p. 200.

[7]Ibid.

[8]Jean-François Regnard, La Satire contre les
maris, in Oeuvres de Regnard (Paris: Pierre Didot et
Firmin Didot, 1801), IV, 158-159. All subsequent
quotations will be taken from this edition and will be
indicated by page number following the citation.

[9]Bloch, p. 215.   [10]Ibid.

[11]Steinmetz, p. 103.   [12]Bloch, p. 216.

[13]Bernard Saurin, Oeuvres choisies de Saurin
(Paris: F. Didot l'ainé et F. Didot, 1812), p. 157.
Henceforth, all quotations from Béverlei will be taken
from this edition and will be indicated by act and
scene number.

[14]Halliday, p. 76.   [15]Bloch, p. 219.

[16]Edmund Bergler, The Psychology of Gambling
(London: International University Press, 1974), p.
234.

[17]Robert D. Herman, ed. Gambling (New York:
Harper and Row, 1967), p. 161.

[18]Reid, p. 58.   [19]La Bruyère, p. 105.

[20]Ibid.   [21]Marquiset, p. 9.

[22]Ibid.   [23]Bloch, p. 219.

[24]Fyodor Dostoevski, Great Short Works, intro.
Ronald Hingley, trans. Constance Garnett (New York:
Harper and Row, 1968), p. 393.

[25]Bergler, p. 234.   [26]Ibid., p. 229.

[27]Ibid., p. 23.   [28]Ibid.

[29]Ibid., p. 3.   [30]Ibid.

[31]Ibid., p. 23.   [32]Ibid., p. 26.

[33]Ibid.   [34]Ibid.

[35]Ibid., pp. 14-27.   [36]Bloch, p. 220.

[37]Cohen, p. 55.   [38]Bergler, pp. 4-5.

[39]Regnard, Satire, p. 159.

[40]Davis, p. 260.   [41]Herman, p. 162.

[43]Béverlei considers suicide in act 2, sc. 2;
act 4, scs. 1, 2, 3, 5, 6.

CHAPTER IV

RAYMOND POISSON

In order to illustrate the gambling mania in seventeenth-century French theatre, we have chosen a representative, but relatively unknown play by the author-actor Raymond Poisson. While we have described the phenomena and dramatization of games of chance in the previous chapters, we feel that our readers can grasp the present thesis better through direct contact with a primary souce supplemented by essential biographical details. It is our aim not only to promote the gambling motif in the Grand Siècle, but to make available to the reading public a previously inaccessible work which is not lacking in merit, only in availability.

There are many details missing in the biography of Raymond Poisson. We know little of his early life and can at best only guess at his origins and approximate his birthdate. Curtis believes that he was born between 1630 and 1633 into what one might consider a poor family. Although originally he intended to become a surgeon, it soon became apparent that he would become an actor. He entered the service of Duke François de Créqui for about three or four years,[1] but soon revealed his talents as "acteur comique du premier ordre," who would be admired even by his chief rival, Molière.[2] During his lifetime, Poisson was known by several noms de théâtre to include Tralage, Belleroche, and Crispin; the latter has endured to our day. Exactly where he spent his early years remains a mystery, but it seems safe to assume that he was associated with some traveling troupe of actors. In 1653 he married Victoire Guérin, who would become the mother of his children Charles, Pierre, Louise-Catherine, Paul, Marie, Jean-Raymond and Henri-Jules. In 1657 he was probably with Croisac's comedians and in 1659, according to a document cited by Curtis, he was authorized to set up a theatre and perform in Bordeaux; the context of the document implies that Poisson was then chief of the troupe. In 1678, after the death of his wife, he married a Catherine Le Roy.[3] Lemazurier gives us some detail of Poisson's physical description at about this time: "On trouve quelques plaisanteries relatives à cette grande bouche qui rendait la figure de Poisson plus comique, dans les pièces où il joua d'original."[4]

Although the critics Lyonnet and Fournel accept earlier dates, Curtis assigns the date 1660 as that of Poisson's first known association with the Hôtel de Bourgogne.[5] Shortly thereafter, he began his literary production: 1660 or 1661, Lubin ou le sot vengé, a success at the time, dedicated to an unknown noble; 1662, Le Baron de la Crasse, an initial success dedicated to the Duke de Créqui; 1663, Le Fou raisonable, a play dedicated to the Marquis d'Angély, Louis XIII's fou, and in which the role of Crispin was probably intended for Poisson; 1664-1665, L'Après-soupé des auberges, first performed in the Palais-Royal and in which Poisson probably played a role; 1666, Le Ballet des Muses, danced at Saint-Germain-en-Laye, and written in collaboration with Benserade and Lully; 1668, Le Poète basque, in which he played the role of the poet; 1668, Faux Moscovites, written to commemorate the visit of Peter Potemkin to Paris; 1671, Les Femmes coquettes, a successful play in which the author played Crispin; 1672, La Holande malade, a political play depicting international relations of the day between France and Holland. During the period of his writings, however, Poisson never lost interest in acting and continued his first profession until 1685.[6]

The playwright-actor was highly esteemed during his lifetime even by his rivals Molière, Quinault and Boursault, as evidenced by the fact that 1) he performed in Boursault's Les Nicandres in 1664 as Crispin (a role which Boursault specifically intended for Poisson) and later in his Comédie sans titre; 2) he played in Quinault's La Mère coquette; 3) while Molière attacks Boursault and other rivals in the Impromptu de Versailles, he never directs pejorative remarks to Poisson or his production. There is, moreover, no documented evidence that the latter ever partook in the Molière controversy. What is "known" about him unfortunately has been distorted by Joseph-Isidore Samson's play, La Famille Poisson (1846), which glorifies the author while taking considerable liberties with the historical facts. Nevertheless, some glory must be attached to him, since he acted in the productions of such famous authors as Pierre and Thomas Corneille, Montfleury and possibly Racine. His success as an actor greatly surpassed that as an author; Lancaster indicates that even Molière was envious of Poisson's acting ability since it was more "natural" than his own.[7] Although Poisson was disliked by Colbert, he remained in Louis XIV's favor and upon his retirement, the actor received a lump-sum payment of 4000 francs in addition to a 1000 franc per year lifetime pension. The King also assisted his protégé by ordering the reduction of a "pension" which Poisson had owed to a former member of his troupe, la Belle-rose.[8]

Poisson's influence on seventeenth-century French theatre is undeniable. We guess that he was a talented author, since he was accused of having been the hand that wrote Boursault's Mercure galant. We also know that he was a gifted actor, since many comic authors included Crispin parts in their plays, obviously intended for Poisson. When Boisrobert wrote La Jalouse d'elle même, he intended the role of Filipin for our actor, who eventually accepted it, but insisted that the name be changed to Crispin.[9] His roles were as varied as his plays, and he is credited for the success of numerous otherwise drab productions to include several by Scarron and Thomas Corneille. His talents were passed on to several of his descendants; his children and grandchildren entertained French audiences throughout the seventeenth and eighteenth centuries. Even after he ceased to write, he continued to perform until his retirement in 1685.

He was replaced as an actor by Jean-Baptiste de Rochemore who never had half of Poisson's success. Following retirement, he may have lived in Nantes or Charenton;[10] he died in Paris on May 9, 1690. Unlike Molière, Poisson was buried in the church without ecclesiastical problems. Since he was no longer acting, it was considered that he had repented the "error of his ways" and that he had been a playwright first, rather than an actor. Nevertheless, those in attendance at his funeral probably remembered his talents on stage, his ability to imitate Normans and Gascons, to give life to a variety of characters, and to make everyone laugh with him in the role of Crispin.

The Femmes coquettes will never be considered one of the best plays of the seventeenth century nor Poisson one of the greatest French playwrights. There were too many writers of greater talent in the spotlight of le Grand Siècle for our author to be well remembered. Lancaster mentions that he had helped to shape the work of the younger writers of the period 1680 to 1690,[11] and Curtis adds that he was important for the situation and development of the theatre rather than for actual roles.[12] Although none of his plays measures up to the chefs-d'oeuvre of Corneille,

Racine or Molière, some of their lesser works are on a par with Poisson's comedies. His chief contribution to literary history seems to be the creation of a stock type in the tradition of Scapin, Polichinelle, Arlequin, Briguella and Sganarelle: his Crispin. Probably based on the Crispinillo of Rojas Zorrilla's Obligados y ofendidos, dressed "de bottes et d'éperons," Crispin follows the stock type of the Spanish deserter which Regnard and Lesage would imitate after the author's death.[13]

Les Femmes coquettes was written in vers alexandrins either in 1670 or 1671 and its privilège dates from July 26, 1671. It was first performed in September of the same year at Versailles, but probably never appeared en province.[14] Lancaster observes that Poisson places several of his comrades on stage and that it shows numerous affinities with Molière's Ecole des femmes.[15] Curtis adds that there are several resemblances to the latter's George Dandin and Tartuffe, which we shall demonstrate in the notes.[16] Written in five acts, the comedy continues the tradition of the farce; it appears to be equally suited to one act as is Molière's Les Précieuses ridicules, traces of which can be found in Les Femmes coquettes. The pièce appears devoid of serious intent, careful structure and psychological development. We see it as a backdrop for a Crispin characterization to the detriment of general character study. According to Curtis, the stock character is a continuation of the écuyer in Lazarillo de Tormes, who demonstrates false pride and a major concern for appearances.[17] We may wonder whether Crispin was given such a predominant role because Poisson felt him essential to the intrigue or so that the great actor could demonstrate his varied talents. At any rate, the play was initially a success due to his ability to entertain; whether it would have been acclaimed as such with another actor is subject to conjecture, but we suspect that it would have received scant notice from contemporaries.

The other characters are down-played or outrightly neglected. Docile, the uncle, is a shallow imitation of Molière's Orgon and Mme Pernelle, and a vague echo of the stereotyped vieillard of the comic theatre.[18] Flavie and her accomplices show kinship to the Précieuses Cathos and Magdelon, but their vices are by far more serious than the préciosité affected by their predecessors. Flavio seems like the duped husband of the earlier farces and probably would be a

a cocu, if his wife were not so interested in gambling. Curtis comments in this respect:

> Poisson a négligé de faire de lui un vrai per-
> sonnage, mais il n'en est pas moins le meneur
> de jeu nécessaire à l'acteur. C'est sans
> doute le besoin de différer le dénouement, qui
> nous montre l'aboutissement de ses projets,
> qui a obligé Poisson à faire de Flavio un
> homme qui se réserve.[19]

If neither characterization nor plot are the main
strengths of this play, then what is? The significance of this comédie lies in the portrayal of an age
--that of Louis XIV. We have here a sociological
study of the times and people contemporary to Poisson,
but we also have proof of the gambling mania which we
have examined in the previous chapters and which has
become the focal point for the present study. Curtis
mentions that the gambling frenzy had taken hold in
the 1660's and all strata of society enjoyed it:

> Les fanatiques du jeu, soit qu'ils trichent,
> comme les chevaliers d'industrie, soit qu'ils
> jouent innocemment, comme Flavie, étaient tous
> atteints de cette rage de jouer. Les comédies
> en question montrent les effets de ce fléau
> sur la vie quotidienne et sur les caractères?[20]

Whether the reader examines this play for its sociological worth or merely seeks farcical humor, we trust
that he shall enjoy the Femmes coquettes. Rather than
bias the opinions of those who will read this play, we
shall refrain from further commentary and allow each
individual to decide for himself the merits of the
work. Let us conclude this chapter with Cailhava:

> Ridendo castigat mores: Elle corrige les
> moeurs en riant. Voilà quelle est la vérita-
> ble devise de la comédie. Faire rire et cor-
> riger les hommes est le double but que doit se
> proposer un Auteur comique.
> Les comédies qui réunissent le comique à une
> saine morale sont excellentes; celles qui ne
> font que comiques peuvent être bonnes; celles,
> dont la morale fait l'unique mérite, usurpent
> le titre de comédie; celles qui n'introduisent
> pas le spectateur et qui ne le font pas rire,
> sont des monstres dont on ne doit point
> parler.[21]

[1]A. Ross Curtis, _Crispin Ier: la vie et l'oeuvre de Raymond Poisson_ (Toronto and Buffalo: University of Toronto Press, 1972), pp. 4-6.

[2]Ibid., viii.　　　　　[3]Ibid., pp. 6-9.

[4]Pierre-David Lemazurier, _Galerie historique des acteurs du théâtre français depuis 1600 jusqu'à nos jours_ (Paris: J. Chaumerot, 1810), I, 444.

[5]Curtis, pp. 6-9.　　　　　[6]Ibid., pp. 26-27.

[7]Henry Carrington Lancaster, "Jean-Baptiste Raisin, _le Petit Molière_," in _Adventures of a Literary Historian_ (Freeport: Books for Libraries Press, 1968), p. 99.

[8]Ibid., p. 116.　　　　　[9]Curtis, pp. 56-67.

[10]Ibid., pp. 63-64.

[11]Lancaster, _History of French Dramatic Literature_, IV, part 2, 484.

[12]Curtis, p. 217.　　　　　[13]Ibid., p. 80.

[14]Ibid., pp. 229-230.

[15]Lancaster, _History of French Dramatic Literature_, III, part 3, 753-754.

[16]Curtis, pp. 212-216.　　　[17]Ibid., p. 85.

[18]Ibid., p. 214.　　　　　[19]Ibid., p. 213.

[20]Ibid., p. 227.　　　　　[21]Cailhava, p. 374.

CHAPTER V

<u>LES FEMMES COQUETTES</u>, Comédie de Raymond Poisson

ACTEURS

FLAVIO, mari de Flavie

FLAVIE, femme de Flavio

DOCILE, oncle de Flavie

AYMÉE, servante de Flavie et espione de Flavio

SAINTE HERMINE, coquette

SAINTE HELENE, coquette

AMINTHE, coquette

DU MANOIR, pipeur

DU BOCCAGE, pipeur

CRISPIN, valet de Flavio

COLIN, valet de Flavie

DAME ANNE, cuisiniere

La Scène est à Paris dans la salle de Flavio et de Flavie.

ACTE I

<u>Scène première</u>. FLAVIE, AYMÉE (<u>tenant Boccace</u>).

FLAVIE

Boccace apparemment te met de belle humeur?

AYMÉE

L'avez-vous lû?

FLAVIE
                   Boccace? hé, je le sçai par coeur.
Il t'emeut?

AYMÉE
          Oui, je sens que le rouge me monte.
La plûpart des maris en ont là pour leur compte;
Je vois pour les coëffer que l'on n'épargne rien.   5

FLAVIE

Ce sont des animaux qui le méritent bien.
A quelle heure est le bal?

AYMÉE
                      A dix heures, Madame.

FLAVIE

Aymée, hé que demain nous ayons cette Femme;
Rien n'est plus naturel que le blanc qu'elle fait;
C'est un éclat si grand....

AYMÉE
                      On le dit en effet....   10
Mais vendre dix Loüis chaque pot qu'elle porte...

FLAVIE

Qu'elle le vende vingt, Aymée, il ne m'importe.
Manquons-nous de Loüis quand mon oncle en a tant?
Qu'Aymée aille le voir, c'est de l'argent comptant.

AYMÉE

Ma foi, depuis un temps, lorsque j'y vais, je tremble.   15
Nous allons à la charge un peu dru, ce me semble;
Car dans ce dernier mois, je comptois aujourd'hui,
Que nous avons tiré deux mille francs de lui,
Qui ne nous ont duré que comme feu de paille;
De tout cet argent-là vous en faites gogaille;   20
Et l'ingenu dévot s'imagine souvent
Que vous voulez peut-être en fonder un Couvent,
Ou qu'aux pauvres honteux vous en faites largesse.

Comme il vous croit dévote, il a cette foiblesse.

FLAVIE

Dévote?

AYMÉE

    C'est par-là que j'ai sçu l'attraper.   25
(Nul ne croit que moi je puis bien le tromper,)   25A
Comme en tous mes discours il me croit véritable
Je vous dépeins un Ange, et votre époux un Diable,
Tout paisible qu'il est; car depuis quelque temps
Il est bien revenu de ses emportemens.

FLAVIE

Oui, quoiqu'Italien, il s'est fait à la mode.   30

AYMÉE

Il étoit malheureux s'il n'eût été commode.
Il ne brisera pas le conjugal lien:
Il souffre tout, voit tout, et ne se plaint de rien.

FLAVIE

Ce n'est plus le lien de l'amour qui le lie.

AYMÉE

Mais renvoyer exprès Crispin en Italie,   35
Pour tirer de sa mere un riche diamant,
Et pour vous le donner, c'est faire encore l'Amant.
Pour vous laisser plus libre il est à la campagne,
Où sans doute il bâtit des Châteaux en Espagne:
Et pour vous plaire enfin il baiseroit vos pas.   40
Il vous aime si fort....

FLAVIE
Moi, je ne l'aime pas.

AYMÉE

Je vous crois sans jurer.

FLAVIE
Ne m'en romps plus la tête;
Une femme peut-elle aimer son mari, bête?
Il faudrait être cruche,

AYMÉE (<u>ayant regardé</u>)
Hé, je le sçai fort bien.
Je parle aussi de lui par forme d'entretien.   45

FLAVIE (<u>étonnée</u>)
Mon oncle est l'homme seul qui nous est nécessaire.

99

AYMÉE

Pour attrapper son bien je fais ce qu'il faut faire.
Si quelqu'un l'intruisoit de nos déportemens,
Nous vérrions vous et moi d'étranges changemens;
Ou bien si quelque jour il venoit vous surprendre   50
Dans tout ce attirail, pour moi je m'irois pendre.
Car bien que vous soyez assez de qualité
Pour être du bel air, il croit en vérité,
Quand je parle de vous du ton dont je vous prône,
Que tout votre soin n'est que de faire l'aumône;   55
Que vous fuyez le monde, et ses dérèglemens;
Que tous vos habits sont de simples vêtemens.
Dans sa chambre il me tourne et devant et derriere.
Mais aussi je me mets tout comme une Touriere.
Vous, qu'il croit une sainte, au moins depuis quatre ans, 60
S'il vous voyoit des points, des mouches, des rubans,
Après s'être informé de toutes nos affaires,
Je serois tout au moins condamnée aux Galeres,
Vous entre quatre murs pour tous...frappe-t'on pas?

FLAVIE (ôtant ses cors et ses
mouches, se mettant un écharpe sur la tête.)
Regarde à la fenêtre, et vois qui c'est.

AYMÉE
                              Helas!   65
C'est votre oncle.

FLAVIE
La folle, avec sa baliverne!

AYMÉE
Point, Madame, c'est lui, je connois sa lanterne.

FLAVIE
Mon oncle?

AYMÉE
          Oui, c'est lui, je ne me raille pas.

FLAVIE
Qu'on n'ouvre pas si-tôt.

AYMÉE
              Mais Dame Anne est là-bas.
Elle a, je pense, ouvert.

FLAVIE
              Ma cappe donc: sois prompte.   70
Qui l'amene? et si tard, lui....

100

AYMÉE

Je l'entends qui monte.

Scène II. DOCILE, COLIN, FLAVIE, AYMÉE.

DOCILE

Bon soir, ma Niece.

FLAVIE

Helas! mon oncle, quel bonheur!
Quelle joie! Il m'en prend un battement de coeur.

AYMÉE

Monsieur Docile ici! Quelle réjouissance!

FLAVIE

Qui peut me procurer votre chere présence,   75
Mon bon oncle, et si tard?

DOCILE

Je vais à Saint Martin;
Et comme il est besoin que j'y sois du matin,
J'y couche cette nuit; et c'est pour une affaire,
Où quelqu'un a jugé que j'étois nécessaire.
Je me préparois bien à votre étonnement.   80

FLAVIE

Vous ne sortez jamais.

DOCILE

Je sors, mais rarement.
Hé bien! comment vous va? toujours dans la souffrance?

FLAVIE

Oui, mon oncle, toujours, mais je prends patience.

DOCILE

Le malheureux mari! dans vos afflictions
Redoublez, s'il se peut, vos bonnes actions.   85
Continuez-vous pas vos actes charitables?

FLAVIE

Autant que je le puis, j'ai soin des misérables.

DOCILE

C'est bien fait, vous sçavez que mon bien est pour vous,
Et que j'en veux frustrer votre fâcheux Epoux.

FLAVIE

Je le sçai; mais de bien, mon oncle, en ai-je affaire,   90
Que pour des malheureux soulager la misere?

DOCILE

Et l'argent d'avant-hier sert-il à les aider?

FLAVIE

Les mille francs qu'Aymée alla vous demander?

DOCILE

Oui.

FLAVIE

J'en ai fait, mon oncle, un heureux mariage.

AYMÉE

Un jour plus tard, la fille alloit faire naufrage.   95

DOCILE

En ces occasions n'épargne point mon bien;
Ce seroit négliger ton salut et le mien.
D'autres milles francs qu'en as-tu fait, ma fille?
Dis-moi?

FLAVIE

J'en revêtis une pauvre famille.

AYMÉE

Ils étoient treize.

FLAVIE

Aussi m'en coûta-t'il bien plus;   100
Tous nuds comme la main.

AYMÉE

Il faut couvrir les nuds.

DOCILE

Je m'inquiete peu de ce que font les autres,
Et je ne veux sçavoir d'affaires que les vôtres.
Aymée assez souvent vient m'informer aussi,
Et du bien et du mal qui se pratique ici.   105
Mais j'apprends a regret toujours plainte sur plainte.
Quel livre ai-je vû là.

FLAVIE (<u>en regardant Boccace</u>
<u>qui est sur la table</u>)
C'est Boc....

102

AYMÉE

             . C'est la Cour Sainte.

                    DOCILE
Montre.

                    AYMÉE
        On nous l'a prêtée, et depuis un moment,
On nous la redemande avec empressement,
Et je n'y songeois plus. Colin, qu'on la reporte.   110

Scène III. DOCILE, FLAVIE, DAME ANNE, FLAVIO, COLIN.

                    DOCILE
D'où vient que ce garçon est vêtu de la sorte?

                    FLAVIE
C'est un pauvre innocent qu'on a mis près de moi;
Le fils d'un Jardinier d'Aubervilliers, je croi,
Que mon mari connoît; c'est lui qui me le donne:
Il me suit en tous lieux; je crois qu'il m'espionne.   115

                    DOCILE
Je veux absolument parler à mon neveu.

                    FLAVIE
Ah! gardez-vous-en bien, c'est un Lion en feu,
Qui loin de s'adoucir tomberoit dans la rage.

                    AYMÉE
Vraiment il nous feroit un étrange ravage:
Le soir c'est un Démon dont nul ne vient à bout;   120
Porcelaine, miroir, pendule, il jette tout.

                    DOCILE
Toi, que fais-tu, pendant et qu'il brise, et qu'il casse?

                    FLAVIE
Moi, j'attends dans un coin que l'orage se passe.

                    DOCILE
Que je te plains!

                    FLAVIE
            Que faire à cet abandonné:

                    DOCILE
Qu'il est changé depuis que je te l'ai donné!   125
Est-il céans?

                    AYMÉE
            Hô non, depuis l'autre semaine
Il n'est pas revenu coucher.

                    FLAVIE
                Il se promene.

                    DOCILE
Mais si je lui parlois sur ces désordres-là?

                    FLAVIE
Il vous diroit que j'ai tous les vices qu'il a,
Que je mange son bien, que je suis trop joueuse,   130
Que je suis trop Coquette, et trop impérieuse....

                    DOCILE
Le malheureux!

                    FLAVIE
                Voilà comme il parle de moi.

                    AYMÉE
Et l'on croit ce qu'il dit comme article de foi.

                    FLAVIE
Plus on le croit, et plus mon ame est satisfaite.

                    DOCILE
Ah! c'est là ce qu'on nomme une vertu parfaite.   135

                    AYMÉE
Vraiment, Monsieur, ce sont ses moindres qualités:
Ses aumônes, son jeûne, et ses austérités....

                    FLAVIE
Hé ne la croyez pas: ne mentez point, Aymée.

                    AYMÉE
Voyez.

                    DOCILE
            Jamais vertu ne fut plus confirmée:
Je m'en vais: continue, et ne te lasse pas.   140
Sors-tu ce soir? j'ai vû ton carrosse là-bas.

                    FLAVIE
Oui, mon oncle.

                    DOCILE
            Si tard? l'affaire est donc pressante?

AYMÉE
C'est pour passer la nuit près d'une agonisante.

DOCILE
Ta conduite me charme; il est tard, je m'en vais.

FLAVIE
Quoi! nous quitter si-tôt?

DOCILE
Oui, tâche à vivre en paix.   145

FLAVIE
Hé, peut-on vivre en paix avecque la discorde?

AYMÉE
Les degrés sont glissans, tenez-vous à la corde.

FLAVIE
Adieu donc mon cher oncle.

DOCILE
Adieu: gagne le Ciel.

AYMÉE
Nous ne le nourrissons que de sucre et de miel.

Scène IV. FLAVIE, AYMÉE.

FLAVIE
C'est par-là qu'il en veut, il faut le satisfaire?.   150

AYMÉE
Hé, pour avoir son bien que ne doit-on pas faire?
Quand-il a demandé compte de son argent!

FLAVIE
Et bien n'ai-je pas eu l'esprit assez présent?

AYMÉE
Oui, la pauvre famille, et l'heureux mariage
Nous ont retiré là d'un dangereux passage.   155
Mais Boccace?

FLAVIE
Ah j'allois le nommer sottement.

AYMÉE
J'ai trouvé la Cour Sainte assez heureusement.

FLAVIE

Bien plus heureusement es-tu venue à dire,
Qu'il falloit promptement la rendre; il alloit lire.

AYMÉE

La demandoit-il pas?

FLAVIE

Vraiment, j'en ai tremblé.   160

AYMÉE

Vous étiez-là sans moi prise comme un blé.
N'avons-nous pas bien pris notre ton de bigotte?

FLAVIE

Que je m'en sçai bon gré, j'ai bien fait l'idiote.

AYMÉE

Mais moi, n'avois-je pas un air bien macéré,
Avec mes bras croisés et ma coëffe en carré!   165

FLAVIE

J'admire ton esprit.

AYMÉE

Hé, vous avoir instruite,
Pour attraper votre oncle, à faire l'hypocrite,
Il faut n'être pas bête: on ne l'attendoit pas.

FLAVIE

Hé, nous parlions de lui comme il heurtoit là-bas.

AYMÉE

On dit bien vrai, sût-il à plus d'une grand'lieu;   170
Quand on parle du loup que l'on en void la queue:
Il m'a bien fait trember, car en moins de trois ans
J'en ai tiré pour vous près de vingt mille francs.

FLAVIE

Je prétends bien t'en faire une ample récompense.

AYMÉE

A moi? Je n'aime pas tant l'argent que l'on pense,   175
Madame, il me suffit de votre affection.
Vous sçavez que le bien n'est pas ma passion,
Et que toujours l'argent me donne peu de joie,
S'il ne tombe en mes mains par une honnête voie.
Mais un présent de vous ne me fera qu'honneur.   180

FLAVIE

Non, non, viens m'habiller.

<u>Scène V.</u> COLIN, FLAVIE, AYMÉE.

COLIN (à Aymée)
Voici venir Monsieur:
Il monte avec un homme.

FLAVIE
Allons donc vite, Aymée.

<u>Scène VI.</u> FLAVIO, DOCILE.

DOCILE
Oui, de trop bonne part elle m'est confirmée:
Le chagrin que j'en ai ne peut être plus grand:
Mais vous entrez chez-vous d'un air qui me surprend.   185

FLAVIO
J'entre dans mon logis toujours de cette sorte:
J'ai le passe-par-tout dont j'ouvre chaque porte:
J'entre sans qu'on me voie, et je le fais exprès:
Lorsqu'on me croit fort loin, c'est lors que je suis près.
C'est mon foible, et chacun a le sien en ce monde: 190
Mais dites-moi sur quoi votre plainte se fonde?
Si dans votre retraite on vous donnoit avis,
De l'air dont vit ma femme, et de l'air dont je vis,
Vous ne la croiriez pas une Sainte peut-être.

DOCILE
Non, mais depuis long-temps elle travaille à l'être,   195
La voulant marier je lui parlai de vous:
L'obéissante fille avec un esprit doux,
Fort innocente alors sur un pareil mystère,
Tout ce qu'il vous plaira, dit-elle, il le faut faire.
Lui disant qu'il faloit un peu vous caresser,   200
Cette pauvre brebis courut vous embrasser.
Et depuis, de quel air a t-elle vécu femme?

FLAVIO
Oui, d'un air surprenant.

DOCILE
Ah! c'est une belle ame!

FLAVIO
Pour écrire sa vie on l'observe.

DOCILE
Hé tant mieux:

107

L'on n'y remarquera que des actes pieux: 205
Et cette nuit encor: Ah l'admirable femme!
Pour la traiter si mal il faut être sans ame.
Et si depuis quatre ans je ne vous ai point vû,
C'est que j'ai tout appris.

FLAVIO
Ah! l'on vous a déçu.
Oui, j'aimois votre niece, et l'ai trop bien traitée: 210
Mon trop d'amour pour elle est ce qui l'a gâtée:
Lorsque je dis gâtée, au moins entendez bien,
Que je ne veux toucher son honneur, ni le mien;
Mais elle est trop coquette, et trop impérieuse,
Donne de grands Cadaux, fait la grande joueuse,   215
Et tient Académie, elle qu'assurément
Le moins subtil au jeu tromperoit aisément.
Vous ne me croyez pas, couchez ici de grace;
Voyez l'échantillon de tout ce qui se passe,
Afin que par dehors vous voyez au dedans,   220
Ce que vous ignorez depuis trois ou quatre ans.
L'air dont elle me traite, et sa grande dépense
N'ont point encore pû lasser ma patience:
Ma douceur n'a rien fait sur ce volage esprit.

DOCILE
Le malheureux! Hélas! Elle me l'a bien dit.   225

FLAVIO
Sa compagnie encor, ce qui plus me chagrine,
Est d'une Sainte-Hélene, et d'une Sainte-Hermine,
Et deux Pipeurs qui font mille coups inouïs,
Qui prendroient ses Ecus pour des doubles Louïs.
N'est-elle pas, Monsieur, en une belle Ecole?   230
Si l'un mange mon bien, un autre me le vole.
Hé bien? Que dites-vous? Vous êtes étonné:

DOCILE
Ce que je dis, Monsieur? que vous êtes damné.

FLAVIO
Je vous croyois un Ange, et vous êtes un Diable.
Quoi, vous damnez les gens! rien n'est plus effroyable.   235
Observez votre niece avant que vous troubler.

DOCILE
Vous, chassez les Demons qui vous vont accabler.
Je sors.

FLAVIO
Sortez aussi de votre léthargie.

Qu'on vous éclaire au moins.

DOCILE
Non, non, j'ai ma bougie.

Allez, continuez votre déreglement.   240

FLAVIO
Vous, demeurez toujours dans votre aveuglement.

DOCILE (<u>à part</u>)
Cachons-nous, je n'ai point d'affaire plus pressante
Que celle de servir cette pauvre innocente.

FLAVIO (<u>seul</u>)
Qu'en quinze ans j'ai goûté de charmes dans ces lieux!
Mais que depuis cinq ans ils me sont odieux!   · 245
Je suis Italien, et me marie en France,
Je prends femme à Paris, O la haute imprudence
Que j'ai bien mérité ce dévorant souci!
Et que j'ai bien cherché ce que je trouve ici!
Crispin dans ce moment revenu d'Italie,   250
Va donner quelque treve à ma mélancolie:
S'il a pû de ma mere avoir le diamant,
Je pourrai me venger de ma femme aisément,
Et de ces deux Pipeurs qui se sont fait connoître,
En me volant mon bien, et pis encor peut-être.   255
Colin. Crispin, vient-il?

Scène VI. COLIN, FLAVIO.

COLIN
Il se débotte en bas.

FLAVIO
Qu'il monte tout botté.

COLIN
Monsieur, il ne peut pas,
Sa botte l'a blessé.

FLAVIO
Qu'il l'ôte donc, marouffle.

COLIN
Il l'ôte aussi, Monsieur, pour la mettre en pantouffle.

Scène VIII. CRISPIN, FLAVIO.

109

CRISPIN (boittant d'une botte à
un pied, une savatte à l'autre)

Peste! mon éperon m'a blessé diablement,   260
Monsieur?

FLAVIO
Hé bien Crispin, as-tu le diamant?

CRISPIN
Si je ne suis boiteux , il ne s'en faudra guere.

FLAVIO
Tu t'épouvantes trop. Et bien, que dit ma mere?

CRISPIN
Votre mere....Ouf; tenez, c'est-là sous mes deux doigts.

FLAVIO
Hé, tu me montreras ton mal une autrefois.   265
Dans mon impatience apprends-moi des nouvelles.

CRISPIN
Votre mere...Ah ce sont des angoisses mortelles.
Votre mere...Ah je vais me faire déchausser.

FLAVIO
Rends-moi réponse; et puis va te faire panser.
Que fait ma mere? Dis.

CRISPIN
                    Je m'en vais vous l'apprendre;   270
Elle a parlé deux jours, il m'a fallu l'entendre;
Et pour rendre, Monsieur, son esprit satisfait,
Il faut que je vous parle autant qu'elle m'a fait.

FLAVIO
Ma mere parleroit un mois sur un atome.

CRISPIN
Je m'en vais donc de tout vous faire un épitome.   275

FLAVIO
Tu me feras plaisir, abrege ce discours,
Car je n'ai pas le temps de t'entendre deux jours.

CRISPIN
Je commence d'abord d'un air fort amiable.
J'étois jeune autrefois, m'a-t-elle dit. Au diable,
Si j'ai trouvé sujet d'en douter un moment;   280
Elle est si jeune encor qu'elle est sans jugement.

FLAVIO

Ma mere jeune?

CRISPIN
Autant qu'elle a pû jamais l'être:
On diroit d'un enfant qui ne fait que de naître:
Car elle n'a ni dents, ni cheveux, non ma foi.

FLAVIO

Elle doit à son âge en avoir peu, je croi.   285
Finiras-tu bien-tôt?

CRISPIN
Oui, Monsieur, je l'espère.
Après, sur ses amours avec feu votre pere,
Elle m'a fait un conte.

FLAVIO
Il étoit fort nouveau.

CRISPIN

Un conte encor plus long que n'est le long-boyau:
Mais je le vais passer en poste.

FLAVIO
Hé pique, pique,   290

Fusses-tu déja loin.

CRISPIN
Bon, soyez colérique;
Car j'enrage, Monsieur, de voir depuis trois ans
Que l'on vous nomme ici le Job de notre temps.

FLAVIO

Fini, Crispin, ce bruit ne durera plus guere.

CRISPIN

Vous ne ressemblez pas à Monsieur votre pere.   295

FLAVIO

Pourquoi?

CRISPIN
Vraiment pourquoi? ce n'étoit pas un sot.

FLAVIO

Que veux-tu dire donc?

CRISPIN
Voyez, voyez ce mot:

Vous verrez en lisant cette lettre importante,
Que vous avez encor dix mille écus de rente;
Que Monsieur votre pere a fait tout son effort   300
Pour se voir opulent et riche après sa mort.
Comme il l'avoit prédit en homme fort habile
Qu'il seroit assommé dans la Guerre Civile,
Dessous le nom d'un autre il sçut mettre son bien.
Vous en croirez le sein de votre mere? Hé bien?   305

FLAVIO

Quoi, Crispin? J'ai ce bien encore en Italie?
Il faut y retourner.

CRISPIN
Si j'en fais la folie.....

FLAVIO

Quoi? tu n'y voudrois pas revenir avec moi?

CRISPIN

Non, ma foi.

FLAVIO
Pourquoi donc?

CRISPIN
Je sçai bien le pourquoi.

FLAVIO

C'est un si beau pays, Crispin.

CRISPIN
Qu'on m'écartelle,   310
Si j'y retourne; allez, je l'ai réchappé belle.
Ils sont Italiens, si j'avois sçu cela....
Un beau garçon, Monsieur, ne doit point aller là;
Et vous ne deviez pas m'exposer de la sorte.
Mais ç'en est fait enfin, n'en parlons plus, n'importe.   315
Mon voyage est heureux.

FLAVIO
Tu le seras aussi.

Le diamant l'as-tu?

CRISPIN
Vraiment oui, le voici.

FLAVIO

Il est fort beau.

CRISPIN

      Gardez que l'on ne vous le happe:
Il est ma foi flambé, si Madame l'attrape.
Elle a déja mangé votre bien et le sien;   320
Vous prenez patience, et vous n'en dites rien:
Toujours sa Sainte-Hermine, et cette Sainte-Helene
Le mange avec elle.

FLAVIO

      Elles ont cette peine.

CRISPIN

Vous devenez, Monsieur, aussi doux qu'un Oison.

FLAVIO

De tout ce que je fais, Crispin, j'ai ma raison.   325
Quelle est la tienne toi d'applaudir à ma femme,
Et d'être son flateur?

CRISPIN

      Moi, flateur de Madame!

FLAVIO

Tu la blâmes assez quand tu parles à moi:
Mais ce n'est plus cela quand elle est devant toi.

CRISPIN

Je voudrois avoir eu mille coups d'étriviere,   330
Et que tous les flateurs fussent dans la riviere.
Moi flateur! j'ai ma foi, le coeur un peu trop haut:
Je prends vos intérêts contre elle, et comme il faut.
Vous venez d'arriver?

FLAVIO

   Oui.

CRISPIN

      Dites moi, de grace,
Quelles gens vous gagez pour voir ce qui se passe.   335

FLAVIO

Aymée est espionne, et Colin l'est aussi.

CRISPIN

Dans cette charge Aymée a toujours réussi;
Mais Colin est un sot: pourquoi pas la Riviere,
Qui la sert à la Chambre!

FLAVIO

      Il est sur la litiere.

N'a-t-elle que Colin?

FLAVIO
Elle a ses deux laquais;   340
Mais, néant, dans sa chambre on ne les voit jamais.

CRISPIN
Elle souffre Colin?

FLAVIO
Elle? Elle en est bien aise.

CRISPIN
Oui, car le sot ne sçait ni le pair ne la praise.
Le fait-on habiller?

FLAVIO
Comme il suit tous ses pas,
Elle veut qu'on l'habille, et je ne le veux pas;   345
Car ce n'est pas mon fait, il a trop d'innocence
Pour faire le métier d'Espion.

CRISPIN
Je le pense:
Vous ne pouviez choisir un plus pauvre animal.

FLAVIO
Pourtant Aymée et lui ne s'entendent pas mal.

CRISPIN
Avez-vous appris d'eux déja quelque nouvelle?   350

FLAVIO
Non, je viens d'arriver; tous deux sont avec elle.
Je vais souper, tantôt nous le ferons jazer.

CRISPIN
C'est fort bien fait, pour moi je me vais reposer.

ACTE II

Scène première.   COLIN, AYMÉE

COLIN
Un Carrosse est là-bas qui demande Madame.

AYMÉE
Un Carrosse, innocent? Est-ce un homme? une femme?   355

                            AYMÉE
Non, on la vient querir pour le bal d'à-ce soir;
C'est Monsieur du Boccage et Monsieur du Manoir.

                            AYMÉE
Quoi, viennent-ils déja pour nous rompre la tête?
Ils n'ont qu'à s'en aller, Madame n'est pas prête.

Scène II. DU MANOIR, DU BOCCAGE, AYMÉE, COLIN.

                            AYMÉE
Vous venez justement pour me faire gronder.   360

                       DU BOCCAGE
Nous! pour quelle raison?

                            AYMÉE
                    Faut-il le demander?
Dès qu'elle vous verra, le chagrin la va prendre,
Car elle n'est pas prête.

                       DU MANOIR
                    Allons au Bal l'attendre.

                            AYMÉE
Hé! quelle heure est-il donc?

                       DU MANOIR
                         Il est l'heure du Bal,
A ma montre du moins.

                            AYMÉE
                    Votre montre va mal.   365

                       DU MANOIR
Le bal doit commencer à dix heures, Mamie.

                            AYMÉE
Oui-da, mais il n'est pas neuf heures et demie.

                       DU MANOIR
Il est dix heures, va, le Bal est commencé.

                            AYMÉE
Et bien, courez devant si vous êtes pressé.

                       COLIN (à du Manoir)
Monsieur, Monsieur est là, dans sa chambre ici proche.   370

                              115

DU MANOIR (à Boccage)

Ce sont trois cents Louis qui nous viennent en poche;
C'est lui qui paye tout.

DU BOCCAGE
De quand est-il ici?

DU MANOIR

Le veux-tu voir?

DU BOCCAGE
Nenni.

DU MANOIR
Sortons donc: le voici.

Scène III. FLAVIO, CRISPIN, COLIN.

FLAVIO

Colin, que fait ma femme?

COLIN
Hé, Monsieur, on l'habille.

FLAVIO

A dix heures du soir! Madame est bien gentille.   375
Et qu'a-t-elle donc fait? Répons donc: Es-tu sourd?

COLIN

Deux Monsieurs ont joué sur son lit tout le jour.

CRISPIN

Sur son lit.

FLAVIO
A quel jeu? Veux-tu me satisfaire?

COLIN

Ils ont joué tous trois à leur jeu d'ordinaire....

FLAVIO

Et quel est donc ce jeu?

COLIN
Ce jeu là me fait peur.   380

FLAVIO

A quel jeu donc, fripon?

COLIN
A la bête, Monsieur.

FLAVIO
Est-ce que tu cherchois le nom?

CRISPIN
Ah! respire.

COLIN
Non, je le sçavois bien, mais je ne l'osois dire.

FLAVIO
Diable soit de la bête et du sot animal.

CRISPIN
La bête vous a fait plus de peur que de mal.   385

FLAVIO
Quand ont-ils quitté jeu?

COLIN
Plutôt qu'à l'ordinaire,
A cause qu'à ce soir Madame avoit affaire.

FLAVIO
Sont-ils tous deux sortis?

COLIN
Oui, Monsieur, tristement;
Car Madame s'est fait donner un lavement,
Et tous deux y vouloient lui voir donner, je pense: 390
All' n'a jamais voulu le prendre en leur présence.

CRISPIN
Elle a tort.

COLIN
Ils vouloient lui donner tout de bon,
Car par force ils avoient déja pris le canon.

CRISPIN
La peste!

COLIN
All' s'est levée, all' s'est contre-eux fâchée,
All' les a fait sortir, après all' s'est couchée.   395

FLAVIO
L'a-t-elle pris enfin?

COLIN
                    Oui, Monsieur, et fort bien,
Jusqu'à la moindre goutte, on a répandu rien.

CRISPIN
Le voyois-tu donner?

COLIN
                    Oui, j'étois tout contre elle.

FLAVIO
Oui.

COLIN
          J'étois à genoux, je tenois la chandelle.

FLAVIO
Pourquoi ce lavement? se trouve-t-elle mal?   400

COLIN
Non, Dieu merci, Monsieur; c'est pour aller au Bal.

CRISPIN
Afin de n'avoir pas le teint brouillé.

FLAVIO
                              La folle!

COLIN
Les cousines le font.

FLAVIO
          Elle est en bonne Ecole.

CRISPIN
La courante à présent ne se danse pas mal,
Si chaque Dame porte un lavement au Bal.   405

COLIN
Aymée au moins, Monsieur, vient de dire à Madame:
Qu'ou venié d'arriver.

FLAVIO
          Hé bien, que dit ma femme?

COLIN
Alle dit...la voici.

FLAVIO (à Crispin)
          Cache-toi; tu verras

Son obligeant accueil, puis tu te montreras.

<u>Scène IV</u>.   FLAVIE, FLAVIO.

FLAVIE

La campagne vous plaît, Monsieur; j'en suis fort aise,   410
Et je souhaitterai toujours qu'elle vous plaise.
Mais me laisser six jours, et sans argent encor!

FLAVIO

Je vous avois laissé quatre cents Louïs d'or.

FLAVIE

C'est pour aller bien loin, vous êtes un brave homme.
Quatre cents Louïs d'or! c'est une belle somme: 415
Elle a duré deux jours, il faut vous l'avouer:
Ainsi j'allois rester quatre jours sans jouer.
Regardez quel affront; mais ce qui me console,
Les gens ont bien voulu jouer sur ma parole
Jusqu'à six cents Louïs.

FLAVIO
Les avez-vous perdus?   420

FLAVIE

J'en regagnai trois cents, et je dois le surplus:
Mais ce n'est pas encor ce que je vous veux dire.
Pourvû que l'on me joue, et que je donne à rire,
Vous êtes satisfait. Où sont ces chevaux gris,
Qu'avant votre départ vous m'aviez tant promis?   425

FLAVIO

Je n'avois point d'argent.

FLAVIE
Je n'y sçaurois que faire:
Et que n'en cherchiez-vous? Est-ce là mon affaire?
C'est à vous d'en trouver lorsque j'en ai besoin:
Cependant j'ai reçu par votre peu de soin
Dans le milieu du Cours la plus grand avenie.   430
Des Dames me voyant, c'est Madame Flavie;
Elle a, s'écria l'une, encor ses Chevaux noirs:
Jugez si j'étois lors dans de grands désespoirs.

FLAVIO

Vous en aurez, il faut laisser passer la Fête:
Ne sortez pas les soirs.

FLAVIE

119

                    Vraiment! vous êtes bête!
Je ne sortirois pas les matins ni les soirs,
Pour tous les biens du monde, avec des chevaux noirs.
Il me feroit beau voir! Ho bien faites en sorte
Que j'en aie au plutôt, car il faut que je sorte,
Et je sois au Cours en attelage gris.   440

Scène V. CRISPIN, FLAVIO, FLAVIE.

                         FLAVIE
Crispin est de retour?

                         CRISPIN
                    Ma foi vive Paris.
L'Italie....

                         FLAVIO
              Admirez la bonté de ma mere!
Voici ce beau dia....

                    CRISPIN (lui mettant la main
                         sur la bouche)
                 Monsieur, qu'allez-vous faire?

                         FLAVIE
Pourquoi donc empêcher ton Maître de parler?

                         CRISPIN
C'est un de ses cheveux qui l'alloit étrangler.   445

                         FLAVIO
Voilà mon diamant.

                         FLAVIE
                   Ah! que je suis heureuse.
De semblables Bijous je suis fort curieuse:
Je vais le mettre en gage.

                         CRISPIN
                   Hé bien! l'ai-je prédit?
Il est flambé, Monsieur, je vous l'avois bien dit.

                         FLAVIE
Il me faut dès demain trouver huit cents pistoles.   450

                         FLAVIO
Et bien, vous les aurez.

                         FLAVIE

                          120

                         Oui, j'aurai des paroles;
Je vous connois, Monsieur: demain absolument,
Je veux deux Chevaux gris, et je dois de l'argent.

                         FLAVIO
Hé pour l'argent du jeu rien ne presse: une excuse....

                         FLAVIE
C'est là le plus pressé; c'est ce qui vous abuse: 455
Des dettes l'on s'en rit; mais rien n'est plus constant.
Que pour l'argent du jeu l'on doit payer comptant:
Crispin, n'est-il pas vrai?

                         CRISPIN
                         Cela s'en va sans dire:
Pour de l'argent prêté l'on ne s'en fait que rire,
Comme Madame dit; mais pour l'argent du jeu,   460
Peste, un banqueroutier seroit digne du feu.

                         FLAVIE
Quelle honte de voir qu'un Valet vous confonde,
Et sçache mieux que vous comme on vit dans le monde!
Comptons. Trois cents Louïs qu'il faut rendre ce soir,
Deux cents pour les chevaux que je prétends avoir,   465
Ce sont cinq; et trois cents qu'il faut pour une affaire
Qui va faire grand bruit dans peu, mais qu'il faut taire,
Ce sont huit.

                         CRISPIN
           Il est vrai.

                         FLAVIE
                    Je compte nettement.   •
Ce sont huit cents Louïs qu'il me faut.

                         CRISPIN
                              Justement.

                         FLAVIE
Je vais au Bal; j'espère y voir un Gentil-homme,   470
Qui sur ce Diamant me prêtera ma somme.

                         CRISPIN
Comment! huit cents Louïs! je trouverai dessus,
Dès ce soir, si je veux, quatre ou cinq mille Ecus.

                         FLAVIE
Pourvû que dès demain j'aye ma somme entiere,
Gardez-moi le surplus, j'en puis avoir affaire.   475
Je vais au Bal, Monsieur; voilà le diamant.

                         121

Faites qu'à mon retour on m'ouvre promptement.
Veillez un peu.

FLAVIO
Je crains que le sommeil m'abatte.

FLAVIE
Hé, je veille bien moi, qui suis plus délicate.
Vous êtes fort à plaindre! Attendez-moi, sur tout.   480

Scène VI. FLAVIO, CRISPIN.

FLAVIO
Il faut patienter, Crispin jusques au bout.

CRISPIN
Vous avez depuis peu l'humeur bien patiente!

FLAVIO
Tout ce que veut ma femme il faut que j'y consente.

CRISPIN
Mais votre patience, est-ce un peu concerté?
Car vous êtes jaloux, vous êtes emporté;   485
Pardonnez, vous m'avez permis de vous tout dire,
Et même protesté de n'en faire que rire:
Cependant, plus Madame a de mépris pour vous,
Plus elle vous maltraite, et plus vous êtes doux.

FLAVIO
C'est pour mieux me venger; Oui, Crispin, je hazarde   490
A souffrir, s'il le faut, jusques à la nazarde:
Je vais plus que jamais, encor quelque moment,
Paroître à tous sans coeur, et sans ressentiment.
Mais dans peu tu verras de quel air je me venge.

CRISPIN (à part)
Il seroit un Cocu bien digne de louange!   495

FLAVIO
Tout ce que j'ai souffert sera même estimé,
Et l'on approuvera ce qu'on avoit blâmé.

CRISPIN
Si par-là vous avez beaucoup de renommée,
Je serai fort trompé, Monsieur.

Scène VII. AYMÉE, FLAVIO, CRISPIN.

122

FLAVIO

. Hé bien, Aymée,
Qu'a fait ici ma femme? Instruis-nous-en un peu.   500

AYMÉE

Elle a, par ma foi, fait grande chere et beau feu:
Elle a mis ses pendans et ses perles en gage;
Car Monsieur du Manoir et Monsieur du Boccage
Ont gagné son argent: Ce sont ces deux Joueurs:
L'on me dit l'autre Jour que c'étoient des Pipeurs,   505
Des gens qui font des tours de brelique et breloque:
Je l'ai dit à Madame, et Madame s'en moque.
Ils sont, dit-elle, heureux, mais ils n'ont pas de sens,
Et je n'ai jamais vû de pareils innocens:
Mon argent raquitté, j'aurois, je le proteste,   510
Honte de les gagner; c'est un vol manifeste:
Et presqu'à tous les Jeux ce ne sont que des sots,
Dit-elle: Elle a raison, ils disent de bons mots,
Quand ils sont hors du Jeu; mais au Jeu, je vous jure
Que rien n'est si plaisant que de voit leur figure.   515

FLAVIO

Ils gagnent cependant.

AYMÉE

Mais si grossierement,
Qu'il faut crever de rire en perdant son argent.

CRISPIN

Changent-ils fort souvent de Jeux de Carte?

AYMÉE

Voire,
Ils ne Joueroient que d'un si l'on les vouloit croire:
Madame voit cela, qui se tient les côtés,   520
Et rit de tout son coeur de voir ces hébétés.
Elle se plaît si fort à voir tant d'innocence,
Qu'elle a Joué dix fois d'un Jeu par complaisance.
Les cartes seulement ils ne les battent pas,
Et leurs grossieres mains les mettent en un tas.   525
Rien n'est si ridicule au Jeu que leur maniere;
Et pour les achever, ils sont courts de visiere:
Ils regardent tous deux les Cartes de si près,
Qu'il semble que pour rire ils le fassent exprès:
Les Cartes dans leurs mains sont d'abord corrompues;   530
Quand on vient à couper elles sont si bossues,
Que je crois qu'un bateau passeroit au milieu.
Cela fait comme un Pont.

CRISPIN

Quels aigres-fins! Tu-dieu!

AYMÉE

Je vous dis, rien n'est bon comme leur innocence.

CRISPIN

Madame rit donc bien?

· AYMÉE

Elle rit d'importance.   535

FLAVIO

Et perd-elle beaucoup avec ces innocens?

AYMÉE

Elle dit qu'elle perd plus de huit mille francs.

FLAVIO

Et n'ont-ils rien gagné que cela?

AYMÉE

Non sans doute.

C'est bien assez, je crois.

FLAVIO

M'entends-tu bien? Ecoute:

N'ont-ils point obtenu....

AYMÉE

Quoi donc?

FLAVIO

Quelque faveur?   540

Car je veux tout sçavoir.

AYMÉE

Expliquez-vous, Monsieur,

Je ne vous entends point.

CRISPIN

Tu ne le peus comprendre;

Monsieur voudroit sçavoir ce qu'il craint fort d'apprendre.

AYMÉE

Ha, ha, je vous entends. Ho, non, assurément,

Tous deux n'en ont jamais voulu qu'à son argent.   535 545

CRISPIN

Ah les honnêtes gens! qu'ils ont une belle ame!

Car ils n'en veulent point à l'honneur de Madame.

C'est bien justement qu'on va les soupçonner;
Ils n'ont autre dessin que de vous ruiner.
Voilà d'honnêtes gens!

AYMÉE

Madame Sainte-Hermine   550
Est, comme vous sçavez, son aimable cousine,
Qui vient souvent ici.

FLAVIO

N'y vient-il pas toujours,
L'autre soeur Sainte-Helene?

AYMÉE

Elle y vient tous les jours:
L'une est sa Favorite, et l'autre sa Fidelle.
Madame Amynthe y vient encor.

FLAVIO

Mais où va-t-elle?   555

AYMÉE

Dame, où va-t-elle? C'est ce que je ne sçai pas.
Colin, votre idiot, est toujours sur ses pas:
Je vois ce qu'elle fait ici, j'y suis présente;
Mais je n'y vois plus goutte alors qu'elle est absente.

FLAVIO

Je trouve en te payant tes soins bien épargnés.   560

AYMÉE

Ma foi! vos trois cents francs sont assez bien gagnés.

FLAVIO

Hé, que ne la suis-tu?

AYMÉE

Vous me la baillez belle!
Hé, veut-elle de moi ni de sa Demoiselle,
Pour la suivre jamais? Joint qu'elle n'a que moi:
Depuis tantôt un mois: vous le sçavez, je croi,   565
Je suis femme de Chambre, et je suis Demoiselle.
Parle-t-elle à quelqu'un, soit mâle, soit femelle,
J'écoute, et vois si c'est ou pour mal, ou pour bien:
Bref, je fais tout ici, j'ai du mal comme un chien;
Je passe sans manger les jours que j'espionne;   570
Et l'on me plaint encor trois cents francs qu'on donne!

FLAVIO

Je ne te les plains pas, va, tu les gagnes bien.

AYMÉE

Je crois, Dieu le sçait si je vous cele rien.

CRISPIN

Ne pleure point. Monsieur, Aymée est fort fidelle.

AYMÉE

Madame ne fait rien que je ne sois près d'elle.   575
Et Monsieur a grand tort de me traiter ainsi.(<u>Elle rentre</u>)

CRISPIN

Mais Colin l'a laissée au Bal, car le voici.

<u>Scène VIII</u>. COLIN, FLAVIO, CRISPIN.

FLAVIO

L'as tu laissée au Bal?

COLIN
                    Oui, Monsieur, alle danse.

FLAVIO

A-t-elle été souvent dehors en mon absence?

COLIN

All'a, je pense, été quatre ou cinq fois aux champs.   580

FLAVIO

Oui. Quels ont été là ses divertissemens?
Et qui sont tous les gens qui composent sa suite?

COLIN

Ses Joueurs, sa Fidelle, avec sa Favorite;
Et puis Madame Amynthe: Ils ne la quittent pas.

FLAVIO

Que font-ils tous aux champs?

CRISPIN
                         Ce sont des fins merles;   585
On ne t'éloignoit pas pour enfiler des perles?

COLIN

Hô non, car son colier on l'avoit renfilé
D'une corde à boyau, mais il s'en est allé;
Un Cuisinier le garde, alle l'a mis en gage,
Avec ses Pend'oreilles; all'en a de Iouange.   590

FLAVIO

Ma femme découcher! Demandons s'il sçait bien....

CRISPIN
Vous en sçavez que trop, ne demandez plus rien.

FLAVIO
Quel jour étoit-ce encor?

COLIN
C'étoit l'autre semaine.

CRISPIN
Hô, pour le jour, Monsieur, n'en soyez point en peine;   595
Si Madame a poussé les affaires à bout,
Vous en devez avoir senti le contre-coup.

FLAVIO
Méchant bouffon, tais-toi. Dis-nous quel jour ma femme.....

CRISPIN
Vous l'avez sçû, Monsieur, aussi-tôt que Madame;
Et si les cornes font, comme on le peut penser,   600
Plus de mal à sortir que les dents à percer,
Sans doute vous devez, sans faire d'autre enquête,
Avoir eu ce jour-là grande douleur de tête.

FLAVIO
Mais Crispin, cesse un peu, l'on est chagrin à moins.
De ce qu'elle fait là, n'aurai-je aucuns témoins?
Étoit-ce son Carrosse?

COLIN
Hô non, c'étoit un Fiacre.   605

FLAVIO
Comment étoit vêtu le Cocher?

COLIN
Comme un poacre.

CRISPIN
Comme ils sont tous.

FLAVIO
Quoi! seule en ce Carrosse?

COLIN
Non.

On la vint prendre.

FLAVIO
Qui?

COLIN
Madame Lisimon.

FLAVIO
Madame Lisimon est vertueuse et sage,
Et j'aurois tort, Crispin, d'en prendre aucun ombrage: 610
Son amour pour ma femme est plein d'honnêteté.

CRISPIN
L'honneur de femme à femme est fort en sûreté.

FLAVIO
Le Bal va-t-il finir?

COLIN
Hé, Monsieur! il commence.

FLAVIO
Ma femme viendra donc fort tard?

COLIN
Hô, je le pense.

FLAVIO
Va l'attendre.

CRISPIN
Il pourra l'attendre jusqu'au jour.   615

FLAVIO
Crispin, allons dormir attendant son retour.

ACTE III

Scène première. FLAVIO, CRISPIN.

FLAVIO
Tu vois bien qu'en dormant, Crispin, la nuit se passe,

CRISPIN
Je sens de plus, Monsieur, que le sommeil délasse.

FLAVIO
Ma femme n'être pas encore de retour!

CRISPIN

L'on court en ce temps-ci le Bal jusques au jour.   620

FLAVIO
Mais que faire ici donc attendant qu'elle vienne?

CRISPIN
Vous souffrirez, Monsieur, que je vous entretienne:
Si jusqu'à son retour il faut attendre ici,
Qu'y faire que causer? Causons donc.

FLAVIO
                            Qu'est-ce-ci?
Elle, courir le Bal! Ce n'est pas-là la cause.   625

CRISPIN
Par ma foi, Monsieur, elle court autre chose;
Et je me doute ici de ce que l'on peut voir.

FLAVIO
De quoi te doutes-tu? Dis, je le veux sçavoir;
Et devant qu'il soit nuit, quelque prix qu'il m'en coûte;

CRISPIN
Ne vous doutez-vous point de ce que je me doute?   630

FLAVIO
Non.

CRISPIN
    Non; Madame joue! elle a joué si bien,
Qu'elle a, ma foi, joué votre honneur et le sien.

FLAVIO
Ah!

CRISPIN
    Ah! je le veux bien, Monsieur, elle est fort sage;
Mais si je l'entreprends avecque mon visage,
Quelques Louïs en main, et l'habit d'un Marquis,   635
Je suis fort assuré que son coeur m'est acquis.

FLAVIO
Tu prétends donc, Crispin, lui donner dans la vûe?

CRISPIN
Je passe pour avoir moins d'esprit qu'une grue;
Mais je vais vous montrer d'un art ingénieux,
Qu'elle se prend par l'or, et non pas par les yeux.   640

FLAVIO

Je te fournirai l'or.

CRISPIN

                    Bon; vous lui ferez rendre;
Car je suis assuré que je lui ferai prendre:
Après que j'aurai fait ce que font les Amans,
C'est à dire, poussé tous les beaux sentimens,
Je toucherai tout franc dessus la grosse corde;   645
Et si je fais si bien, Monsieur, qu'elle m'accorde....
Enfin.....vous m'entendez, qu'elle m'accorde tout,
Je ne pousserai point les affaires à bout.
Ne craignez rien.

FLAVIO

          Hô non.

CRISPIN

                    Ce sont biens qui sont vôtres:
Je n'ai garde d'aller faire comme les autres: 650
J'ai pour ces choses-là plus de respect pour vous.
Je lui veux envoyer d'abord un billet doux;
Après, la Fripperie est un lieu fort commode,
Pour trouver promptement un habit à la mode.

FLAVIO

L'on les donnoit jadis tous aux Comédiens.   655

CRISPIN

Bon! C'étoit donc du temps des Négromantiens.

FLAVIO

Du temps de Modory, du temps de Bellerose.

CRISPIN

Fi, c'étoit du vieux temps. Ah! c'est bien autre chose!
Paris est tout changé, la langue l'est aussi.
Vous sçavez bien qu'on a retranché grand-merci,   660
Et je vous remercie.

FLAVIO

          On ne s'en sert plus guere.

CRISPIN

Ce sont cinq ou six mots dont on n'a plus que faire.

FLAVIO

Quand on donne pourtant, ces mots-là servent bien.

CRISPIN

Mais ils ne servent plus, car on ne donne rien.

Dans Paris à présent, qu'on donne ou qu'on demande,   665
Ou l'on est prisonnier, où l'on paye l'amende.
Sans cet ordre chacun ne faisoit que donner;
Les petits et les grands s'alloient tous ruiner.

FLAVIO

La police à Paris est belle, je l'avoue.

CRISPIN

L'on n'y voit plus ni duels, ni vols, ni gueux, ni boue,   670
Mais je pense, selon mon petit jugement,
Que cela ne s'est fait que par enchantement:
L'on va même, dit-on, empêcher qu'il n'y pleuve.

FLAVIO

Bon, bon.

CRISPIN
L'Hyver prochain vous en verrez l'épreuve.

FLAVIO

Quoi! l'on peut empêcher qu'il ne pleuve à Paris?   675

CRISPIN

Un diable ingénieur l'a, dit-on, entrepris.
C'est qu'on veut retrancher les choses inutiles:
De quoi diable sert-il qu'il pleuve dans les Villes!
On veut rendre Paris propre et ces en tout temps,
Et faire quant il pleut qu'il ne pleuve qu'aux champs.   680

FLAVIO

Si nous voyons cela nous verrons un prodige.

CRISPIN

Avant qu'il soit un an vous le verrez, vous dis-je.

FLAVIO

Cela ne se peut pas.

CRISPIN
Non?

FLAVIO
Assurément.

CRISPIN
Non!
Moi qui vous parle, moi, j'ai vû dans Trianon,
Quand le froid rendoit l'eau plus dure que le marbre,   685
Les parterres fleuris, et les fruits dessus l'arbre.

131

Un diable Jardinier et goutteux, en tous temps,
Des plus rudes hyvers faisoit-la des printemps.

FLAVIO
Comment parer le vent, et la pluie, et la grêle?

CRISPIN
Tout ne se peut-il pas quand le diable s'en mêle?   690
Mais Versailles, le Louvre, et ces grands bâtimens,
Tout cela ne se fait que par enchantemens.
Croyez-vous que ce soit de véritable pierre?
De la pierre qui vient du ventre de la terre?

FLAVIO
Oui, qu'on polit en marbre, et que l'on adoucit.   695

CRISPIN
Ce n'est que du carton que le diable endurcit:
Verroit-on en trois ans une ville bâtie,
Si les démons n'étoient un peu de la partie?

FLAVIO
Il est vrai que jamais on n'a vû rien d'égal.

CRISPIN
Un démon Architecte a fait l'Arc Triomphal.   700
N'avez-vous point entré dans la Salle enchantée,
Qui fut l'hyver passé des démons habitée?

FLAVIO
La Salle des Balets? Elle charme en effet.

CRISPIN
Ce n'est rien, il faut voir ce que le Diable y fait:
Je vis....

FLAVIO
Tes visions sont toujours de la sorte.   705

CRISPIN
Si ce sont visions que le Diable m'emporte.
J'y vis sans m'effrayer le Ciel et les Enfers,
Les Diables, et les Dieux, et les Monts et les Mers,
Des Palais enchantés, des Déserts effroyables:
J'y vis faire aux Démons des postures de Diables: 710
Dix millions de gens en furent tous charmés;
Et je n'ai jamais vû des Diables plus aimés.
Puis après, chaque Dieu qui venoit à la ronde,
Avoit dedans le ciel le plus beau train du monde.

132

Tais-toi.

CRISPIN

Votre chagrin la fera-t-il venir?   715
Je fais ce que je puis pour vous entretenir.
Monsieur, parlons encor de Paris, je vous prie.
Paris, je suis badaut, Monsieur, c'est ma patrie.
Ces lanternes, le soir mises de pas en pas,
Font qu'en marchant nos yeux ne servent presque pas,   720
Tant il fait jour la nuit dans la plus noire rue:
L'on n'entend plus crier, aux voleurs, tue, tue.

Scène II. DAME ANNE (effrayée), AYMÉE (toute éperdue),
            FLAVIO, CRISPIN.

DAME ANNE
Miséricorde, hélas! aux voleurs, aux voleurs!

AYMÉE
Aux voleurs. Qu'est-ce donc, Dame Anne?

DAME ANNE
                              Je me meurs.
Le malheureux Crispin assassine son Maître.   725

CRISPIN
Qui, moi?

AYMÉE
      Fermez la porte, il faut prendre le traître:
Au voleur.

CRISPIN (se mocquant d'elle)
        Au voleur.

DAME ANNE
        Hélas! secourez-nous.

CRISPIN
A qui diable en ont donc ces folles et ces fous?

FLAVIO
Mais qui provoque donc toute cette crierie?

AYMÉE
Pour moi, je n'en sçai rien, c'est Dame Anne qui crie.   7300

DAME ANNE

Moi! quand j'ai vû Crispin, et crier au voleur,
J'ai crû sincerement qu'il égorgeoit Monsieur.

CRISPIN

Pourquoi croire cela, chienne de cuisiniere?
Je faisoit un récit.

FLAVIO (les renvoyant)
Sortez.

CRISPIN
Ah la sorciere!
La carogne a, je crois, perdu le jugement.   735

FLAVIO

Ton récit se pouvoit faire plus doucement.
Ma femme ne peut plus guere tarder, je pense.

CRISPIN

L'on se divertit plus ici qu'en lieu de France.

FLAVIO

Paris est le séjour des jeux et des amours;
Mais les femmes, Crispin, y font d'étranges tours.   740

CRISPIN

Oui, la votre sur tout.

FLAVIO
Je n'en fais point de doute;
Quand un homme est bien fait je crois qu'elle l'écoute.
Mais....

CRISPIN
Mais vous allez voir par mon déguisement,
Qu'elle écoute un magot quand il a de l'argent.

FLAVIO

Elle te connoîtra.

CRISPIN
Comme je prétends être,   745
Je le donne à ma mere à me pouvoir connoître.
Vous nous observez; mais ne vous montrez pas:
Je mettrai sa fierté furieusement bas.
Pour en venir à bout je mets tout en pratique,
Et je vais déployer toute ma Rhétorique.   750
Elle succombera, mais ne vous effrayez
Qu'alors que vous verrez votre tête à vos pieds;

134

Que lors que vous verrez comme une chose claire,
Qu'il tient plus qu'à moi de conclure l'affaire.

FLAVIO

Je consens à goûter ce divertissement,   755
Pour te faire sortir de ton aveuglement,
Et pour te faire voir par ton expérience,
Que ma femme est coquette, et que c'est tout, je pense.
(on frappe)

CRISPIN

Vous verrez, vous verrez, Monsieur, je ne dis mot;
Je crois qu'un de nous deux fera ce soir bien sot.   760

FLAVIO

On frappe assurément, voici notre coureuse,
Regarde.

CRISPIN

Oui, c'est elle, et sa bande joyeuse;
Les cousines y sont, et les Pipeurs, je croi.
Ils sont en bonne humeur.

FLAVIO

Tant mieux: retire toi.
Ils croiront être seuls, ne parois point pour cause.   765
Moi feignant de dormir, j'apprendrai quelque chose.

(Flavio se va asseoir sur un siege, où il fait semblant
de dormir)

Scène III.   FLAVIE, SAINTE HERMINE, SAINTE HELENE, AMINTHE,
DU MANOIR, DU BOCCAGE, FLAVIO.

FLAVIE

Ah, la sotte guenon que la Reine du Bal!

AMINTHE

Et son grand mal-bâti d'Amant?

SAINTE HERMINE
Ah! l'animal!

SAINTE HELENE

Quel est-il?

FLAVIE
Je n'ai pas l'honneur de le connoître.

SAINTE HERMINE

Il a l'air d'un laquais dans l'habit de son Maître.   770

FLAVIE

Ma Fidelle a raison, elle le peint fort bien;
Un Laquais revêtu.

SAINTE HELENE
                    Mais vous ne dites rien,
De cette noire peau dedans son habit jaune?
Et tout son ruban jaune encor large d'un aune?

FLAVIE

La raupe se croyoit la mieux mise du Bal.   775

SAINTE HELENE

Et la plus belle aussi.

FLAVIE
                    La jaune lui va mal:
Quand je vis tout ce jaune à la noire Coquette,
Je crus voir un charbon dedans un aumelette.

DU BOCCAGE (entendant ronfler Flavio)
Mais, s'il vous plaît, quel est cet honnête ronflant?

FLAVIE

C'est Monsieur mon mari qui dort en m'attendant.   780

DU MANOIR

Il faut que le bon homme ait peu de feux dans l'ame,
Pour dormir attendant une si belle femme.

FLAVIE

Mon mari me viendroit caresser! son abord
M'est une vision qui me blesse si fort,
Que je n'en conçois point qui me soit plus horrible.   785

SAINTE HELENE
Elle est fort dégoûtante.

FLAVIE
                    Enfin elle est terrible.

SAINTE HELENE
Cependant, hier Nison disoit, j'en ai bien ri,
Qu'elle fut amoureuse un mois de son mari.

FLAVIE
Tout de bon? Vous raillez.

AMINTHE
Ha! rien n'est plus étrange.

DU MANOIR
Mais un mari bien fait encore?

FLAVIE
Fût-ce un Ange,   790
Un Narcisse en beauté, je soutiendrai toujours
Qu'on ne peut pas aimer son mari quinze jours.

SAINTE HELENE
Vraiment, c'est tout au plus.

SAINTE HERMINE
Quinze jours! que je meure
Si j'ai jamais aimé mon mari plus d!une heure.

DU BOCCAGE
C'est assez.

DU MANOIR
Celui-ci ronfle comme un cheval: 795
Madame, un Camouflet nous seroit un régal.

Scène IV. CRISPIN, SAINTE HELENE, FLAVIE, SAINTE HERMINE,
AMINTHE, DU BOCCAGE, DU MANOIR, FLAVIO.

FLAVIE
Crispin.

CRISPIN
Madame.

FLAVIE
Hé bien l'affaire est-elle faite?

CRISPIN
Oui, Madame, et dans peu vous serez satisfaite.(il rentre)

FLAVIE
C'est assez.

DU BOCCAGE
Ce garçon paroît fort ingénu:
Je l'ai vû quelque part.

FLAVIE
Il vous est inconnu.   800

137

Quel est-il?

FLAVIE
    C'est Crispin, un rare personage,
Un flatteur éternel, un complaisant à gage:
Je change exprès d'avis dix fois en un moment,
Et dix fois le flateur est de mon sentiment.
En voulez-vous avoir le plaisir tout-à-l'heure?   805

DU MANOIR
Volontiers, rappellez-le. Est-ce ici qu'il demeure?

FLAVIE
Il est à mon mari: c'est son sur-Intendant,
Son conseil, et son tout, mais un fou cependant
Qui s'empresse pour rien, et fait le nécessaire.
Crispin.

DU BOCCAGE
    Il n'entend pas.

FLAVIE
        Il vient, laissez-moi faire.   810

Scène V.   CRISPIN, FLAVIE, SAINTE HERMINE, SAINTE HELENE,
        AMINTHE, DU BOCCAGE, DU MANOIR, FLAVIO, DOCILE.

FLAVIE
Vois-tu ton Maître-là qui dort comme un Valet.
Mériteroit-il pas, Crispin, un camouflet?

CRISPIN
Oui, ma foi.

FLAVIE
    Par plaisir je veux que l'on lui donne;
Divertissons-nous-en.

CRISPIN
        La piece sera bonne.

FLAVIE
Lui-même il en rira, je crois, comme un perdu.   815

CRISPIN
S'il n'en rit le premier je veux être pendu.

FLAVIE

138

Non, ne lui donnons point, je crains qu'il ne s'emporte.

CRISPIN
On souffre rarement un affront de la sorte.

FLAVIE
Sans doute: et j'essuierois d'abord tout son courroux.

CRISPIN
Il réveilleroit enragé contre vous.   820

FLAVIE
Je rêve; mon mari n'a point l'ame assez basse,
Pour prendre un camouflet de si mauvaise grace.

DU BOCCAGE
Ce n'est qu'une fumée, et qui ne dure pas.

FLAVIE
Il n'est rien plus galant.

CRISPIN
Sur tout dans les jours gras.

FLAVIE
Il en rira, Crispin, donnons-lui sans scrupule.   825

CRISPIN
S'il n'en crevoit de rire il seroit ridicule.

DU MANOIR
Ce papier-ci, je crois, ne sera pas mauvais.

SAINTE HERMINE
Les sçavez-vous donner?

DU MANOIR
J'en donne à mes Laquais.

FLAVIE
Cachons donc les Flambeaux, il ne verra personne,
S'il s'éveille du moins, ni celui qui lui donne.   830

SAINTE HELENE
Que chacun gagne au pied.

DU BOCCAGE
L'on se retirera.

SAINTE HERMINE

Nous lui verrons donner, et puis chacun fuira.

                         FLAVIE
Ma Favorite, au moins, à ce soir la partie:
Ma Fidelle le sçait.

                    SAINTE HELENE
              Oui, j'en suis avertie.

                         FLAVIE
Ma bonne le sçait.

                         AMINTE
           Oui.

                         FLAVIE
               Donnez le Camoufflet.   835

                    DU MANOIR (donnant un soufflet
                    à Flavio)
Cachez donc le Flambeau.   La peste, quel soufflet!

Scène VI. FLAVIE, FLAVIO, CRISPIN, AYMÉE.

                         FLAVIE
Vous dormiez.

                         FLAVIO
           Je dormois, et de la bonne sorte.

                         FLAVIE
Qui s'attendroit à vous coucheroit à la porte.

                         FLAVIO
Le sommeil a vaincu mon assiduité.

                         FLAVIE
C'est bien dit. Mon argent me l'a-t-on apporté?   840

                         FLAVIO
Dans une heure il sera dessus votre Toilette.

                         FLAVIE
Que l'on n'y manque pas qu moins.

                         FLAVIO
                    La chose est faite.

                         FLAVIE

                         140

Car je ne veux dormir que jusques à midi.
J'ai des affaires.

FLAVIO

Bien.

FLAVIE
Mais n'est-il pas Jeudi?

FLAVIO

Oui.

FLAVIE
Que l'on se retire, allons donc, qu'on me couche.   845

Scène VII. FLAVIO, CRISPIN.

CRISPIN
Vous en venez d'avoir une assez rude touche.

FLAVIO
J'ai, je l'avoue, été surpris du camouflet.

CRISPIN
Le souffleur en remporte un assez grand soufflet.

FLAVIO
Je ne sçai pas comment j'ai retenu ma rage.

CRISPIN
Il est vrai qu'on ne peut en souffrir davantage.   850

FLAVIO
Je me vengerai: songe à ton déguisement.

CRISPIN
Je vais pousser Madame, et vigoureusement.

FLAVIO
Elle est impertinente, et coquette, et joueuse:
Avec tous ces défauts, je la crois vertueuse.
Mais je veux des Pipeurs r'avoir tout mon argent: 855
Si ma Femme vouloit, dessus son diamant
Elle en emprunteroit sept ou huit cents pistoles,
Pour jouer avec eux, et je prendrois mes drôles.
J'irai tantôt la voir exprès pour ce sujet,
Et ferai, si je puis, réussir mon projet.   860

CRISPIN

141

Pour avoir des Pipeurs son argent, ou le vôtre,
Ce piège est bien grossier.

FLAVIO
                    J'en retiendrai quelque autre,
Où quelques fins qu'ils soient ils tomberont, je croi.
Quand tu seras vêtu, Crispin, avertis-moi.

CRISPIN (<u>seul</u>)
Il faut un billet doux: comment diable le faire?   865
Le plus court est, je crois, d'aller chez un Notaire.
Mais on dit que l'amour fait avoir de l'esprit;
Si j'étois amoureux, je ferois cet écrit:
Que je le sois ou non, allons, je le veux faire;
Je le ferai peut-être aussi-bien qu'un Notaire.   870
Pour l'habit, s'il est riche, on me louera bien.
Habillons-nous de deuil, cela ne coûte rien.
Le Crêpe neuf est cher, il iroit trop du nôtre:
Le Crêpe repassé bousse encor plus que l'autre:
Je ferai mieux, allons mettre ce noir atour,   875
Et comme un galant homme allons faire l'amour.

ACTE IV.

<u>Scène première</u>. AYMÉE, FLAVIO.

AYMÉE
C'étoit, ce disiez-vous, des frippons, et des gueux:
Madame a toujours eu bonne opinion d'eux.

FLAVIO
Leur procédé, sans doute, est tout-à-fait honnête,
Va le dire à ma femme, afin qu'elle s'apprête,   880
Puisqu'il viennent jouer, à les bien recevoir:
Et moi, de mon coté, je ferai mon devoir.

<u>Scène II</u>. COLIN, FLAVIO.

COLIN
Tous ces porteux sont-là, Monsieur, avec leur corde
Pour lié les Joueurs, et sans miséricorde.

FLAVIO
Ils n'exécuteront que mon commandement.   885

COLIN
Quoi! parce qu'ils vouloient donner ce lavement
Hier au soir à Madame, êtes-vous en colere?

142

Si Madame est fâchée, all' ne l'est, pargué, guere,
Car ils s'en vont venir.

FLAVIO
Paix, les voici déja.

COLIN
Ils viennent pour jouer, mais ils ne joueront ja.   890

Scène III. DU BOCCAGE, DU MANOIR, FLAVIO.

DU MANOIR
Ah! Seigneur Flavio!

FLAVIO
Du meilleur de mon ame
Je vous suis.....

DU MANOIR
Nous venons divertir votre femme.
Le voulez-vous pas bien?

FLAVIO
Ah: Messieurs! trop d'honneur:
Je ne suis rien ici que votre serviteur;
Et comme moi, ma femme est fort votre servante.   895

DU BOCCAGE
Nous lui jouons beau jeu, du moins.

FLAVIO
Elle est contente.

DU MANOIR
Mais elle nous attend pour jouer avec nous.

FLAVIO
Je suis de la partie.

DU BOCCAGE
Oui?

FLAVIO
Je vais avec vous.

Scène IV. FLAVIE, AYMÉE.

FLAVIE

143

Ce sont eux.

AYMÉE
Direz-vous qu'ils n'ont que des paroles?

FLAVIE
Ils ont pris devant toi chacun huit cents pistoles.   900

AYMÉE
Oui, Madame, et n'ayant rendu le diamant,
Ta Maîtresse devoit en user autrement,
M'ont-ils dit en riant; elle nous doit connoître.
Elle prétend par-là nous éprouver, peut-être.
Dis-lui que nous jouerons contre elle incessamment;   905
Que sa parole vaut plus que son diamant;
Que nous ne sommes pas gens à prêter sur gage;
Que nous ne voulons pas retarder davantage,
Et que dans ce moment tous deux allons partir,
Avec dessein formé de la bien divertir,   910
Et lui faire offre encor de seize cents pistoles.
Ce sont-là des effets, et non pas les paroles.
Vous les venez de voir entrer présentement.

FLAVIE
Je m'en vais les trouver dans un petit moment.
Viens-t'en me r'attacher les rubans de ma tête.   915

AYMÉE
Le cheval de Monsieur n'est pourtant qu'un bête,
Madame.

FLAVIE
Il va crever d'un si beau procédé.

AYMÉE
Tantôt en parlant d'eux, si je n'avois cédé,
Je crois qu'il m'eût battue à la fin.

FLAVIE
                              Quelle joie
J'aurai de le confondre! Il faut que je le voie,   920
Pour lui chanter sa game; et devant ces Messieurs,
Qu'il a toujours traités de Filoux, de Pipeurs,
Il en aura l'affront.

AYMÉE
                 Mais tout du long de l'aune:
Madame, il faut un peu lui montrer son bec-jaune.
J'entends quelqu'un venir.

144

FLAVIE

Sans doute ce sont eux;   925

Ils me cherchent: viens donc me r'attacher mes noeuds.
Je reviens sur mes pas ici leur rendre grace,
Et jouer avec eux.

AYMÉE

N'en êtes-vous point lasse?

Scène V.   COLIN, DAME ANNE.

DAME ANNE

Hé, qu'ont-ils donc tant fait ces deux pauvres Monsieux,
Colin?

COLIN

Ils n'ont rien fait, c'est qu'ils font des voleux.   930

DAME ANNE

Voleux? De quoi?

COLIN

D'argent, mais on leur a fait rendre,
Et je crois que Monsieu ne les fera point pendre.

DAME ANNE

Ah! que j'en suis fâchée! y sont si bonnes gens.

COLIN

Monsieu leu va bien-tôt donné la clef des champs;
Par tant bien qu'ils seroient pendus par la Justice,   935
Car y sont entachés d'un autre maléfice:
Madame ne croit pas qu'y soient des voleux.

DAME ANNE

Non, all' les aime bien on dit qu'y sont Pipeux.

COLIN

Y pipent donc chez eux: ni moi, ni Dame Aymée
N'avons vû ni tabac, ni pipe, ni fumée.   940

DAME ANNE

Monsieu s'en va venir, allons rire là-bas:
Veux-tu, Colin?

COLIN

Hô non, ma mere ne veut pas:
Laisse-moi-là, si donc.

145

DAME ANNE

Mais t'as si bonne mine.

COLIN (la rebuttant)

Allons donc.

DAME ANNE

Monsieu vient.

Scène VI. FLAVIO, COLIN, DAME ANNE.

FLAVIO (les faisant rentrer)
Est-ce ici ta Cuisine?
Allons. Tout mon dessein a très-bien réussi,   945
Je tiens et mes Pipeurs et mon argent aussi.
Ils vont dans un moment sortir de la derriere,
Fort tremblans de la peur que je leur viens de faire.

Scène VII. FLAVIE, AYMÉE, FLAVIO.

AYMÉE (apercevant Flavio)
C'est Monsieur.

FLAVIE (à Flavio)
Je suis dupe, et j'abonde en mon sens!
Je n'eus jamais le don de me connoître en gens!   950
Et Monsieur du Manoir, et Monsieur de Boccage
Enfin n'étoient pas à leur apprentissage.
Ce n'étoient que des gueux, des fourbes, des Pipeurs!
Vous deviez dire encor que c'étoient de Voleurs:
C'est tout ce qui manquoit à votre calomnie.   955
C'est être prévenu d'une étrange manie!
De prendre deux hommes d'honneur, s'il en est sous le Ciel:
Charger sans fondement et d'opprobre et de blâme.
D'honnêtes gens à qui l'on donneroit son ame;   960
Des gens que vous voyez qui me donnent leur bien
Sans vouloir assurance, écrit, gage, ni rien.
Dites-moi, s'il vous plaît, quel Démon vous inspire?

FLAVIO
J'ai tort, je le confesse, et je n'ai rien à dire.

FLAVIE
Se confesser coupable est quelque chose encor.   965
Le diamant?

FLAVIO
Je l'ai.

146

FLAVIE
Les huit cents Louïs d'or?

FLAVIO
Ils sont sous le tapis de la table où l'on joue.

FLAVIE
Un procédé pareil me charme, je l'avoue.

FLAVIO
On ne peut trop louer de si beaux sentimens.
Madame, faites-leur mille remercimens.   970
Ils ont le coeur grand, et l'ame bien placée,
Et tous deux ont agi bien loin de ma pensée.

FLAVIE
En jouant avec eux je vais les en louer.

FLAVIO
Je pense qu'ils n'ont pas le loisir de jouer.
Les voici.

Scène VIII. DU BOCCAGE, FLAVIO, FLAVIE.

FLAVIE
Je ne sçai comment je pourrai faire   975
Pour vous remercier.

DU BOCCAGE (s'en allant)
Il n'est pas nécessaire.

FLAVIE
Cet homme a tout l'honneur que l'on sçauroit avoir.

FLAVIO
Vous n'en verrez pas moins à Monsieur du Manoir.

Scène IX. DU MANOIR, FLAVIO, FLAVIE.

FLAVIE
Je ne sçai de quel air, Monsieur, on peut répondre
A vos civilités.

DU MANOIR (s'en allant)
C'est vouloir nous confondre.   980

FLAVIE
A-t-on jamais agi plus généreusement?

147

S'enfuir pour m'épargner jusqu'au remerciment!
Hé tout cela, Monsieur, fait votre bévue,
Et tous vos jugemens faits à la boulle-vue.
Nous avons leurs Louïs.

FLAVIO

Oui, je vais les compter;   985
Et Crispin aussi-tôt vient vous les apporter.

FLAVIE

Mais, vous allez sortir.

FLAVIO

Mais, avant que je sorte,
Vous les allez voir.

Scène X. AYMÉE, FLAVIE.

FLAVIE

Qu'est-ce qu'Aymée apporte?

AYMÉE (tenant une large Lettre
cachetée de noir)

Ce n'est pas un poulet, c'est un cocq d'Inde noir
D'un Vicomte, je crois, qui va vous venir voir.   990

FLAVIE (lisant le dessus)
A la belle Flavie,
Que j'aime plus que ma vie.

La déclaration est belle en cet endroit!
Et ce large poulet marque un galant adroit.

AYMÉE

Je doute fort qu'aux lieux où l'on vend la volaille,   995
Il se trouve un poulet d'une aussi belle taille.

FLAVIE

Il est même plié tout à fait galamment.

AYMÉE

Et sa lugubre soie est mise largement.

FLAVIE

Voyons donc le dedans d'un dehors si funeste.
C'est un volume que ceci.   1000

AYMÉE

Tredame, on peut bien dire ici,
Le porteur vous dira le reste.

148

FLAVIE (lit)

Ce n'est point par mon nom, ni par ce billet doux,
Que vous pourrez me reconnoître;
Mais s'il vous ressouvient d'avoir reçu chez vous   1005
L'homme le mieux taillé qu'aucun homme puisse être;
C'est moi qui maintenant dessous un fort grand deuil,
Pour avoir trop été de l'humeur d'Alexandre,
Ne porte plus qu'un bras, qu'une jambe, et qu'un oeil:
Les trois membres pareils sont demeurés en Flandre.   1010

AYMÉE

Trois membres! Quel malheur!

FLAVIE

Il est grand en effet.
(Elle continue.)

Je suis pourtant encore assez bien fait.
Si cinq cents Louis d'or peuvent faire une somme,
Qui vous fasse répondre à l'ardeur de mon feu,
Vous pourrez bien dire dans peu   1015
Que vous avez trouvé votre homme.
J'ai voué cet argent à vos charmans appas:
Si cette somme vous agrée,
J'avance, ne reculez pas.
Faites trêve à la simagrée:
Je suis prompt, vous verrez dans une heure en plus tard,
Le Vicomte de Beauregard
Mais souffrez cependant que d'une ame enflammée
Je vous baise, et Madame Aymée.

AYMÉE

Les Vicomtes sont donc fortement amoureux?   1025
Madame, il prétend donc nous aimer toutes deux.

FLAVIE

Aymée, il prétendra ce qu'il voudra prétendre,
Pour moi, je ne prétends que le voir et l'entendre:
Par sa lettre je vois qu'il n'a pas son égal;
Que de corps, et d'esprit il est original.   1030

AYMÉE

Je vois bien comme vous que ce n'est qu'une buze;
Mais il offre, Madame, et qui refuse muze;
Fût-il le plus grand sot qui soit dans l'Univers,
Il faut le recevoir tantôt à bras ouverts.

FLAVIE

Comment! à bras ouverts recevoir une bête?   1035

AYMÉE

Ma foi, son compliment est pourtant fort honnête:
Si vous l'examinez, vous trouverez toujours
Qu'offrit cinq cents Louïs est un fort beau discours.

FLAVIE

Je ne le connais pas.

AYMÉE
Pouvez-vous méprendre?

Et puisqu'il a laissé dans la bataille en Flandre,   1040
A ce qu'il mande au moins, l'oeil, la jambe et le bras,
Marqué de la façon le connoîtrez-vous pas?

FLAVIE

Sans doute. Ce n'est donc que la moitié d'un homme!

AYMÉE

Mais sa somme est entiere, et c'est tout que la somme.
Et qu'importe pour lui, qu'il soit entier ou non?   1045

FLAVIE

Il faut qu'il soit bâti d'une étrange façon.

AYMÉE

Il est encor trop bon pour ce qu'on en veut faire:
Qu'il soit comme il pourra, ce n'est pas-là l'affaire.
Mais Dame Anne paroît.

Scène XI. DAME ANNE, FLAVIE, AYMÉE.

DAME ANNE
Un Monsieur est là-bas.

AYMÉE

Son nom?

DAME ANNE
Il est manchot d'une jambe et d'un bras.   1050

Et borgne encor d'un oeil.

AYMÉE
Vraiment, c'est le Vicomte.

DAME ANNE

Il se peigne là-bas, mais je l'entends qui monte;
J'ai r'oublié son nom; c'est un laid Marcassin.
Il est noir comme un Diable, et blond comme un bassin.

150

Monsieur de Beauregard est un fort honnête homme;   1055
Dame Anne taisez-vous.

DAME ANNE
C'est ainsi qu'il se nomme:

Scène XII.   FLAVIE, AYMÉE, CRISPIN (Déguisé sous le nom de
              Vicomte de Beauregard, manchot, borgne, une jambe
              de bois, et en grand deuil.

CRISPIN
J'entre sans bruit, Madame; en ces lieux-ci jamais
Je ne mene Cocher, Carrosse, ni Laquais:
On peut voir là-bas de train qui ne déplaise.
Coucherai-je céans? J'en renvoierois ma chaise.   1060

FLAVIE
Non, s'il vous plaît, Monsieur, ne la renvoyez pas,
Elle peut demeurer sans scandale là-bas?

CRISPIN
Ma chaise là-bas?

FLAVIE
           Oui.

CRISPIN
              Non, le peste me tue,
Mon chiffre rend un peu ma chaise trop connue:
Si jamais on l'y voit je veux être tondu: 1065
Elle est dans l'autre rue où je suis descendu;
Et quand je vais à pied la glissade est à craindre.

FLAVIE
En cet état, Monsieur, que vous êtes à plaindre.

CRISPIN
Fructus belli, Madame: éloigné de vos yeux,
Que j'ai cent fois nommés, et mes Rois, et mes Dieux,   1070
Les Favoris de Mars sont traités de la sorte.
Fructus belli. Voilà tout ce qu'on en rapporte.
Tel porte au Camp de Mars des jambes et des bras,
Qui, comme vou voyez, ne les rapporte pas.
Une jambe de bois, un moignon, l'oeil de verre;   1075
Fructus belli. Ce sont tous les fruits de la Guerre.
Que l'amour est puissant, et que des yeux si doux.....
Mais dites franchement, me reconnoissez-vous?
Tout trouvé que je suis vous me cherchez peut-être.

AYMÉE

Seyez-vous donc.

FLAVIE

J'ai peine à vous bien reconnoître.   1080

AYMÉE

Vous ne remettez pas Monsieur de Beauregard?

CRISPIN

Vous n'aviez pas douze ans que j'étois goguenard,
Et que j'étois bien fait, amoureux comme un diable.

FLAVIE

On connoît peu l'amour dans un âge semblable.

CRISPIN

Vous n'alliez pas alors vous chauffer à son feu.   1085

AYMÉE

Vous commenciez pourtant à vous sentir un peu,
Et preniez grand plaisir à lire dans l'Astrée.

CRISPIN

Pour ce sujet aussi, Madame fut cloîtrée;
Votre oncle vous voyant y lire si souvent,
Le scrupuleux bigot vous mit dans un Couvent.   1090

AYMÉE

Oui, Monsieur le Vicomte a fort bonne mémoire.

CRISPIN

Hô diable! je crains peu que l'on m'en fasse accroire.
Qu'il a passé depuis d'eau dessous le Pont-neuf!

FLAVIE

Vous parlez de vingt ans.

CRISPIN

Avec encore neuf.

FLAVIE

Je n'ai pas encore trente, je vous assure.   1095

CRISPIN

Vous en avez quarante à fort bonne mesure.

FLAVIE

Quarante! C'est piquer les gens au dernier point.

                              AYMÉE
Monsieur de Beauregard rêve.

                         CRISPIN
                      Il ne rêve point.

                         AYMÉE
Ce sont contes.

                         CRISPIN
                 Ce sont des vérités certaines.
Jean de Vuerth étoit lors prisonnier à Vincennes: 1100
Ce Vaudeville-ci, je pense, étoit nouveau;
Il ne me souvient pas des mots, mais l'air est beau.

La, la, la, la, le
La, la, la, la, la,
Et leur redit encore   1105
De dans son 'aussement.
Be, be tout est frelore,
La Duché de Milan.

Que les airs bégayés étoient lors agréables!
Ceux qu'on fait aujourd'hui sont tous si pitoyables: 1110
Ah! les Musiciens que l'on avoit aussi
Etoient en ce temps-là bien autres que ceux-ci.
Mais il n'est pas ici question de Musique,
Ni d'âge encore moins, puisque cela vous pique.
Je vous vois de quoi faire un Arsenal d'appas,   1115
Et quatre magazins de ceux qu'on ne voit pas,
Les attraits de vos yeux....et mon coeur....dans mon ame....
L'amour que j'ai....l'argent....quand d'une ardente flamme....
Voilà cinq cents Louïs que j'apporte en un mot,
Car je ne sçai point tant tourner au tour du pot: 1120
Sans de propos d'amours vous faire une légende,
Ne voyez-vous pas bien ce que je vous demande?
Et que mon pauvre coeur qui vient de s'enflammer
Veut....enfin ce qu'il veut on ne le peut nommer:
Le devinez-vous pas?

                         FLAVIE
                 Comment, vous m'osez dire,   1125
Connoissant ma vertu....

                         CRISPIN
                    Vous me faites bien rire.
Votre vertu tiendroit contre cinq cents Louïs!
Non, Madame, ce sont de ces coups inouïs,
Qu'on voit fort rarement arriver dans le monde.

                              153

Oui, Monsieur. Ramassez votre perruque blonde.   1130
C'est Crispin, ne dis mot, je veux m'en divertir.

CRISPIN
Cinq cents Louïs sont beaux.

FLAVIE
Mais peut-on consentir
A des choses qui sont d'une telle importance!
Tout d'un coup s'entr'aimer sans faire connoissance!

CRISPIN
Et l'avons-nous pas faite?

FLAVIE
Il est vrai, mais encor   1135
Faut-il....

CRISPIN
Il ne faut rien que se connoître en or:
Prenez-le.

FLAVIE
Je le prends, mais c'est vous seul que j'aime,
L'or ne m'est rien.

CRISPIN
Cedez à mon ardeur extrême.

FLAVIE
Vous êtes le plus fort, et des termes si doux....

CRISPIN
Si je suis le plus fort, je veux porter les coups.   1140

AYMÉE
Cela se pourra bien.

CRISPIN
C'en est fait, je succombe,
Vos yeux font dans mon coeur le fracas d'une bombe.
Ah! quel embrazement! je brûle, il faut périr,
Hé vite! nul que vous ne me peut secourir.

FLAVIE
Mais vous vous tourmentez comme une ame damnée.   1145

CRISPIN
Ah! si le feu prenoit à votre cheminée,

Ou que votre maison fût en flamme, ma foi,
Vous vous tourmenteriez bien autrement que moi.
Tu sçais guérir les gens, mon Ange, sois moins fiere.

FLAVIE

Oui, je les sçais guérir de la bonne maniere;   1150
Et sur tout quand ils sont malades comme vous.
Qu'on appelle Crispin, pour lui donner cent coups.

CRISPIN

Moi, battu d'un Faquin!

FLAVIE
            C'est tout ce que mérite
Un homme comme vous.

AYMEE
            Vous n'en serez pas quitte
Pour vos cinq cents Louïs, Monsieur Fructus belli.   1155

FLAVIE

Qu'on me donne un bâton. Je vous trouve joli.

CRISPIN

Ah! Madame, tout beau, vous frappez un Vicomte.

AYMEE

Monsieur de Beauregard, n'avez-vous point de honte?
De tenter par argent une femme d'honneur?

CRISPIN

Tu fais la prude aussi, servante de malheur.   1160

AYMEE (le bâtonne)
Comment? servante!

CRISPIN
            A moi Laquais, Laquais, hé Page.

AYMEE
Fais venir tout ton train, et tout ton équipage,
Fructus belli. Tu dois recevoir tour à tour.
Et des fruits de la guerre, et des fruits de l'amour.

Scène XIII. FLAVIE, AYMEE.

FLAVIE

Ce maraut de Crispin, Aymée!

                    AYMÉE
                              Il se faut taire;   1165
Ce déguisement-là cache quelque mystere,
Mais l'effronté Coquin!

                    FLAVIE
                    Mais qu'il est ingénu!
Car le sot ne croit pas avoir été connu.

                    AYMÉE
Sa perruque est tombée heureusement, Madame;
Car cinq cents Louïs d'or ébranlent bien une ame: 1170
Là, dites franchement qu'eussiez-vous fait enfin,
Si ce Vicomte-là n'eût point été Crispin?

                    FLAVIE
Il auroit remporté son argent; mais écoute,
Comme celui-ci vient de mon mari, sans doute,
Qu'il a crû me tenter par-là, je te promets   1175
Qu'il se peut assurer de ne le voir jamais.
Il ne pouvoit venir plus à propos, je meure,
Il sert fort au Cadau qu'on verra dans une heure.

                    AYMÉE
Et qui fera grand bruit dans le monde, je croi.

                    FLAVIE
Je prétends bien aussi faire parler de moi.   1180
Mais c'est trop discourir, rentrons, que je m'apprête:
A terminer ce jour par cette belle fête.

                    ACTE V

Scène première. FLAVIO, CRISPIN.

                    FLAVIO
Pour tes coups de bâton, j'en ai de la douleur.

                    CRISPIN
Hé, les coups de bâton ne me sont rien, Monsieur.

                    FLAVIO
Mais l'affront?

                    CRISPIN
                    Encor moins, c'est une bagatelle.   1185

                    FLAVIO
Tu n'avois pas assez bonne opinion d'elle:

                         156

Elle étoit peu d'humeur à suivre ton desir;
Et tu t'es allé là faire battre à plaisir.

CRISPIN

Jamais place pourtant ne fut mieux attaquée:
Je ne sçai quelle mouche, ou quel ton l'a piquée.   1190
Quand elle prit l'argent, vous vîtes bien, je croi,
L'amour désordonné qu'elle sentit pour moi;
Que d'abord son ardeur alla jusqu'à l'extrême,
Et qu'elle me donna de l'amour à moi-même,
Si fort que je doutai, comme elle m'avoit mis,   1195
De pouvoir vous tenir ce que j'avois promis.

FLAVIO

C'étoit pour attraper ton argent, pauvre buse.

CRISPIN

Elle en tenoit, Monsieur, je vous demande excuse;
Elle faisoit des yeux de Merlan, par ma foi;
Elle étoit devenue amoureuse de moi: 1200
De quoi diable sert-il de déguiser l'affaire?

FLAVIO

Mais l'argent?

CRISPIN

                    Hô l'argent! je n'y sçaurois que faire.

FLAVIO

Tu sçais bien qu'elle et moi nous avons arrêté,
Que je la laisserois ce soir en liberté,
Et que nous coucherions peut-être chez mon frere.   1205

CRISPIN

Oui, vous lui dites, mais vous ferez le contraire.

FLAVIO

Tu l'as dit: je veux voir ce qu'on voit rarement;
Des femmes en débauche, et qui fort librement
Se disent leurs secrets, et qui n'ont nulle honte
De dire de bons mots, et de faire un bon conte.   1210
Je vais pour ce sujet m'emparer tout ce soir
D'un lieu d'où je pourrai tout entendre et tout voir.

CRISPIN

Leur débauche, je crois, sera divertissante.

FLAVIO

Mais la conclusion n'en sera pas plaisante.

CRISPIN

Elle dauberont-là le prochain assez bien.   1215
Monsieur.

FLAVIO

Malheur sur qui tombera l'entretien.

Scène II. DOCILE, FLAVIO, CRISPIN.

DOCILE (<u>paroissant tout ému</u>)

Ha!

FLAVIO

D'où sortez-vous donc effrayé de la sorte?

CRISPIN (<u>tombant de frayeur</u>)

Monsieur, que de bon coeur le diable vous emporte.

DOCILE

Ah, mon neveu! je suis un homme confondu.

FLAVIO

Comment!

DOCILE

Mon oeil a vû, mon oreille entendu: 1220
Mais enfin je ne crois mon oeil, ni mon oreille:
Je ne sçai si je dors, je ne sçai si je veille;
Ma niece est un démon: j'ai vû la vérité:
J'ai vû votre innocence, et sa mechanceté,
Lorsque j'espérois bien voir de quoi vous confondre.   1225

FLAVIO

Où vous étiez-vous mis?

DOCILE

Je ne puis vous répondre.

J'étois caché.

FLAVIO

Mais où? ne le puis-je sçavoir?

DOCILE

Dans ce lieu, d'où j'ai pû tout entendre et tout voir.

FLAVIO

Vous l'avez observée enfin, vous l'avez vûe;
Votre pauvre brebis.

158

DOCILE

Ah! c'est une perdue: 1230
Aymée est un Serpent dont le Démon se sert,
Et toutes deux enfin se damnent de concert.
J'ai crû par son rapport, et sa pitié feinte,
Que ma niece vivoit comme vit une Sainte.
Que d'argent elles m'ont consommé toutes deux 1235
Sous ombre d'en aider de pauvres malheureux!

FLAVIO

Souhaitez-vous du bien?

DOCILE

Non, je suis assez riche.

FLAVIO

Ma femme vient ici; rentrez dans votre niche:
Je vous y joins, allez.

Scène III. FLAVIE, AYMÉE, FLAVIO, CRISPIN.

FLAVIE

Que veut dire ceci?
Comment! Crispin et vous êtes encor ici! 1240
Si vous ne me laissez en liberté, je meure.....

FLAVIO

Sans courroux, s'il vous plaît, nous sortons tout à l'heure,
Vous ne nous rencontrez ici que par hazard.

FLAVIE

Soupez chez votre frere, et revenez fort tard,
Nous serons tout au moins jusqu'à minuit ensemble, 1245
Mes cousines et moi: même encore il me semble
Que quand elle voudroient coucher ici, je croi
Que l'on ne chasse pas le monde de chez soi.

FLAVIO

Nous allons donc souper, et coucher chez mon frere.

FLAVIE

Allez, Monsieur, allez, vous ne sçaurez mieux faire. 1250

FLAVIO

Divertissez-vous bien.

FLAVIE

Nous le ferons aussi:
Vous n'avez seulement qu'à n'être pas ici.

N'avez-vous point ce soir besoin de moi, Madame?

FLAVIE

Non, va te promener.

CRISPIN
J'y vais.

Scène IV. FLAVIE, AYMÉE.

AYMÉE
Ah la bonne ame!
Je viens de préparer votre mets surprenant   1255
Dedans un grand bassin.

FLAVIE
Fort bien; mais cependant
Je ne crois pas, Aymée, être encore à te dire,
Que nous voulons un peu goinfrer, chanter et rire,
Et qu'il falloit avoir quelques petits ragoûts
Qui nous fissent du moins boire deux ou trois coups.   1260
Qu'as-tu donc préparé?

AYMÉE
D'un vin de Bar-sur-Aube,
Et du vrai Saint Thierri, d'un Dindon à la daube,
Avec les pieds de Porc à la Sainte Menehou,
Un Saucisson. Mais où voulez-vous manger?

FLAVIE
Où?
En ce lieu même, Aymée; et vous ferez en sorte,   1265
Qu'on ne fasse qu'un plat, et que l'on nous apporte
La table toute prête, et verre et vin dessus:
Qu'on ressorte aussi-tôt, et qu'on ne rentre plus;
Afin que nous puissions librement et sans peine,
Si le coeur nous en dit, parler de nos fredaines.   1270
Pour le plat que tu sçai, qui s'en va les ravir,
Quand je t'appellerai tu viendras le servir,
Avec l'hypocras, les eaux, la limonade;
Mais comme je t'ai dit sans buffet ni parade.
Il est tard, toutes trois devroient bien être ici.   1275

AYMÉE
J'entends quelqu'un là-bas, je crois que les voici.

FLAVIE

Dame Anne ouvre à chacun.

AYMÉE
Elle n'a garde, diantre.

FLAVIE
Mais redis-lui sur tout que qui quesce soit n'entre,
Les voici, laisse-nous.

Scène V. SAINTE HERMINE, SAINTE HELENE, AMINTHE, FLAVIE,
          FLAVIO (caché avec) DOCILE et CRISPIN.

FLAVIE
Je brûlois de vous voir.

AMINTHE
Enfin vous voulez donc nous régaler ce soir?   1280

FLAVIE
Je n'ai pas entrepris de vous faire grand chere,
Mais nous rirons du moins si nous ne mangeons guere.
Chacun est libre ici, car j'ai pris de grands soins
Pour nous y voir ce soir seules, et sans témoins.

SAINTE HELENE
Vous avez fort bien fait.

SAINTE HERMINE
              Oui, seules, on respire,   1285
Et l'on peut hardiment dire le mot pour rire.

FLAVIE
Nous nous divertirons toutes quatre assez bien.
Avant hier, que fis-tu?

AMINTHE
              Qui, moi? je ne fis rien.

FLAVIE
Toi, je ne te vis point Dimanche, ma Fidelle.
Nison voulut l'avoir?

SAINTE HERMINE
              Oui, je soupai chez elle,   1290
Et l'on joua le soir à mille petits jeux.
A la comparaison, aux couleurs.

AMINTHE
              Ils sont vieux.

SAINTE HERMINE

Oui, ceux-là le sont tous, mais je m'en vais vous dire
Un jeu qui nous plut fort, et qui nous fit bien rire.
Un homme, qui sans doute en sçaivoit de nouveaux,
Nous fit toutes jouer au jeu des Animaux.   1295
L'on en prend trois fâcheux, ou bien trois agréables;
Chacun nomme les siens, et les plus raisonnables
Montrent là leur esprit parlant contre ou pour eux:
Comme chacun nommoit trois animaux fâcheux,
De tous les animaux les plus fâcheux, je pense,   1300
Et les trois qui le plus font perdre patience,
Qui sur les plus fâcheux, dis-je, emportent le prix,
Ce sont les oncles.

                         CRISPIN (bas)
              Bon.

                         SAINTE HERMINE
                    Les peres, les maris;
Mais les maris sur tout, car le plus agréable
Devient bien l'animal le plus insupportable.   1305

                         CRISPIN (bas)
A vous le dé, Monsieur.

                         SAINTE HELENE
                    Vous rencontrâtes bien.

                         SAINTE HERMINE
Si bien que les maris servirent d'entretien,
Qu'on quitta tous les jeux, et que cette matiere
Servit à les dauber d'une étrange maniere.

                         SAINTE HELENE
Quand on prend un mari ce n'est pas pour l'aimer.   1310

                         FLAVIE
Vraiment non, l'on le prend pour se faire estimer
Dessous ce nom de femme, et faire nos affaires;
Pour nous fournir enfin cent choses nécessaires,
Et nous donner l'argent dont nous avons besoin.

                         AMINTHE
On ne prend un mari que pour avoir ce soin.   1315

                         FLAVIE
Mon mari pour cela vaut bien autant qu'un autre.

                         SAINTE HERMINE
Nos maris ne sont pas bâtis comme le vôtre.

FLAVIE

Le mien pour une buze est des mieux façonnez.

CRISPIN (bas)

Monsieur.

FLAVIE

Je puis par tout le mener par le nez.

AMINTHE

Pour peu que les Galans se rendent agréables,   1320
Les maris les mieux faits sont tous insupportables.

SAINTE HELENE

Hé ma foi! sans avoir Galant ni Favori
Le plus méchant régal du monde est un mari.

FLAVIE

C'est que loin de chercher les moyens de nous plaire
Par quelques petits soins, ils sont tout le contraire.   1325
Faites à la traverse un ami là-dessus,
Ils deviennent si sots qu'on ne les aime plus.

CRISPIN (bas)

Monsieur.

FLAVIE

Ce sont les soins des Galans qui me touche;
C'est pour eux seuls qu'ici l'on doit ouvrir la bouche.

SAINTE HERMINE

Il est vrai qu'ils nous font goûter tous les plaisirs;   1330
Ils vont même souvent au-devant des desirs.
Le Bal, les Violons, le Cadeau, la Musique:
Nous les voyons enfin mettre tout en pratique;
Pousser à nos genoux des soupirs tout de feu.
Le moyen lors qu'un coeur ne s'attendrisse un peu!   1335
Qu'il puisse être de glace au milieu de leur flamme!
Ils ont un air touchant, un abord qui prend l'ame:
Enfin ce n'est que soins, que transports et qu'ardeur.

FLAVIE

Demeurons donc d'accord qu'un Galant touche au coeur,
Et qu'en tous lieux ils sont tellement en usage,   1340
Qu'un mari fait par tout un fort sot personnage.

CRISPIN (bas)

Monsieur.

SAINTE HELENE

Les pauvres gens! C'est fait d'eux; car enfin
Les femmes à présent ont toutes le goût fin.

FLAVIE

Mais à propos de goût, mes cousines, je pense
Qu'il est temps de manger: qu'on serve en diligence.   1345

SAINTE HERMINE

Les cornets suffiront avec de l'hypocras;
Car la viande me suit.

SAINTE HELENE
L'on n'en mangeroit pas.

Scène VI.   AYMÉE, FLAVIE, SAINTE HELENE, SAINTE HERMINE,
            AMINTHE, FLAVIO (caché), DOCILE, CRISPIN.

FLAVIE

Il faut nous réjoüir, que nous allez-vous dire?

SAINTE HERMINE

Nous ne laisserons pas de chanter et de rire.

FLAVIE

Sers-nous donc les cornets avecque l'hypocras.   1350

AYMÉE

Et quand servir la viande?

FLAVIE
Elles n'en veulent pas.

AYMÉE

Vraiment nous voilà bien: tout est prêt, on se tue,
Il est Jeudi, voilà de la viande perdue.

AMINTHE

Aymée est en colere.

AYMÉE
On prend aussi des soins

Pour vous bien régaler.....

AMINTHE
L'on n'en tira pas moins.   1355

FLAVIE

Apporte-nous ici ce que l'on te demande,
Et va pleurer plus loin la perte de la viande.

164

Est-ce que toutes deux vous vous mocquez de moi?

AMINTHE
Elles crevent de rire, et je ne sçai de quoi.

SAINTE HELENE
Je ris de son chagrin, elle se désespere.   1360

SAINTE HERMINE
Moi, je ris du discours qu'elle lui vient de faire.

Scène VII. AYMÉE et DAME ANNE (apportant une table), SAINTE
            HERMINE, FLAVIE, SAINTE HELENE, AMINTHE, FLA-
            VIO (caché), DOCILE, CRISPIN.

AYMÉE
Là, voilà vos cornets avec vos hypocras.

AMINTHE
Il ne faut que cela.

FLAVIE
Va-t'en.

AYMÉE
Le beau repas
Pour faire tant d'apprêts!

SAINTE HERMINE
Elle ne se peut taire.

FLAVIE
Allons, approchons-nous.

AMINTHE
Voici bien mon affaire.   1365

FLAVIE
Aimes-tu l'hypocras, ma Bonne?

AMINTHE
Et qui le hait?

FLAVIE
Ce n'est pas moi.

SAINTE HELENE
Ni moi.

SAINTE HERMINE
J'en bois comme du lait.

AMINTHE
Nos Argus à présent sçavent-ils où nous sommes?

FLAVIE
Qu'ils le sçachent ou non, laissons ces vilains hommes:
Un si long entretien ne peut qu'être ennuyeux.   1370

SAINTE HERMINE
A moins que de chanter quelque chanson contr'eux:
Ah, ma foi! je le veux, puisque le sujet s'offre,
J'en vais dire une, moi qui chante comme un coffre:

C H A N S O N
A quoi servent les maris
Quand on a des favoris?   1375
Chantons toutes à la ronde
Pour ne nous pas ennuyer;
Le meilleur mari du monde
N'est jamais bon qu'a noyer.

CRISPIN (bas)
Monsieur.

SAINTE HELENE
Elle a raison.

AMINTHE
Faites-nous donc paroître   1380
Ce mets si surprenant.

SAINTE HERMINE
Qu'est-ce que ce peut-être?

FLAVIE
Servez les abricots, et le mets surprenant.
On va vous le servir, mais chantons cependant.

C H A N S O N
Les Galans touchent au coeur
Bien mieux que cette liqueur: 1385
Leurs petits soins prennent l'ame;
C'est toujours régal nouveau;
Et jamais homme à sa femme
Ne donna bal ni cadeau.

Scène VIII. FLAVIE, AYMÉE, SAINTE HERMINE, HELENE,

AMINTHE, **FLAVIO** (<u>caché</u>), DOCILE, CRISPIN.

(<u>Aymée apporte un bassin plein de Louïs d'or.</u>)

FLAVIE
Mesdames, ce mets-là peut-il vous satisfaire?   1390

SAINTE HERMINE
Est-ce un enchantement?

AMINTHE
Quoi! des Louïs, ma chere!

SAINTE HERMINE
Vous aviez bien raison de nous vanter ce plat.

SAINTE HELENE
Il attache la vûe.

AMINTHE
Ah! le charmant éclat!

SAINTE HELENE
Ha que sa vision est un heureux présage!

SAINTE HERMINE
Pour en avoir un peu l'on met tout en usage.   .1395

AMINTHE
Il n'est rien avec lui dont on ne vienne à bout.

SAINTE HELENE
Rien ne résiste à l'or, c'est un passe-par-tout.

SAINTE HERMINE
C'est un métal charmant, mais il est si farouche,
Qu'on ne peut le toucher.

FLAVIE
Hô, celui-ci se touche,
Et s'empoche de plus.

AMINTHE
S'il est de moi touché...   1400

FLAVIE
Mais on ne l'a servi que pour être empoché.
Je sçai que vos maris ne vous en donnent guere,
Et qu'enfin toutes trois vous en avez affaire.
Ma Favorite, allons.

SAINTE HELENE
Je ne touche point là.

FLAVIE
Ma Fidelle, ma Bonne, à quoi sert tout cela?   1405
Ma Favorite, allons, cela me désoblige.
Prenez donc.

SAINTE HELENE
Prendrons-nous?

FLAVIE
Oui, prenez-tout, vous dis-je;
S'il en reste, je crains qu'après un tel repas...

Scène IX. FLAVIO, DOCILE, CRISPIN, FLAVIE, SAINTE
HERMINE, SAINTE HELENE, AMINTHE, AYMEE.

FLAVIO (prenant le bassin de Louïs)
Non, non, ne craignez rien, il n'en restera pas.

FLAVIE
A quoi bon, s'il vous plaît, cette entrée insolente?   1410

FLAVIO
On va vous l'expliquer, Madame l'impudente.

FLAVIE
Helas! je suis trahie: ah, qu'est-ce que je voi?
Mon oncle?

DOCILE
Oui, serpent.

FLAVIO (rentrant avec les Louïs)
Ces Louïs sont à moi.

DOCILE
Oui, tout est découvert, Tison d'enfer, perdue.
Esclave du démon, te voilà confondue.   1415
A quoi donc t'ont servi vingt mille francs? A quoi?
Dis.

AYMEE
Le vent du bateau n'est pas trop bon pour moi.
Comme j'avois ce soir droit de goûter aux sausses,
J'ai pris de la meilleure, il faut tirer nos chausses.

DOCILE

L'on en a retiré huit mille des Pipeurs   1420
Qui vont être pendus comme fameux voleurs.

                        CRISPIN (à Aymée qui rentre)
Voilà du changement, ma pauvre Agonizante:
Si j'en suis crû, ta mort ne sera pas si lente.

Scène dernière. FLAVIO, DOCILE, CRISPIN, AMINTHE, HE-
               LENE, FLAVIE, SAINTE HERMINE.

                            FLAVIO
Mesdames, descendez, vous pouvez désormais
Vous dire toutes quatre un adieux pour jamais: 1425
Vos maris sont là-bas.

                     SAINTE HERMINE
                 Hé quelle est leur envie.

                            DOCILE
De vous faire, je crois, mener une autre vie,
Si loin d'eux, qu'ils n'iront ajamais vous ennuyer.

                            FLAVIO
La plûpart des maris ne sont bons qu'à noyer.

                            DOCILE
Vous pouvez dire adieu, mes honnêtes parentes,   1430
A la débauche, aux jeux, aux chansons, aux courantes:
                                        (à Flavie)
Pour vous, votre mari va faire son devoir.

                    SAINTE HERMINE (à Flavie)
Où nous vont-ils mener?

                            FLAVIE
                  Hé, qui peut le sçavoir!

                        CRISPIN (chantant)
Repondez à vos cousines,
Qu'elles vont, qu'elles vont aux Feuillantinet.

                        SAINTE HERMINE
Hélas!

                        SAINTE HELENE
        Hélas!

                            AMINTHE
                Hélas!

FLAVIE
Hélas, quel traitement?

FLAVIO   1435
Ce n'est que pour changer de divertissement:
On chante là les airs tout d'un autre maniere.

SAINTE HERMINE
Quelle colation!

SAINTE HELENE
Ah! qu'elle est singuliere!

AMINTHE (à Flavio et à Docile)
Ah! quel malheur pour nous si vous n'êtes touchés.

CRISPIN
Ah! quel bonheur pour vous de pleurer vos péchés.

SAINTE HERMINE
Un Cloître!

DOCILE
Il faut montrer une ame plus constante.   1440

CRISPIN
La Scene des mouchoirs n'est pas la moins plaisante.

DOCILE
Allons, c'est assez rire et pleurer dans ce lieu.

SAINTE HERMINE
Adieu, chere cousine.

SAINTE HELENE
Adieu, cousine.

AMINTHE (Elles s'en vont)
Adieu.

FLAVIO
Vous prendrez dès demain le chemin d'Italie.

FLAVIE
Moi?

FLAVIO
C'est où je prétends guérir votre folie.   1445

FLAVIE

170

Que je sois à Paris dans un Cloître plutôt,
Mon coeur.

CRISPIN
Ce n'est pas-là la chanson de tantôt.

FLAVIE
Faut-il aller si loin languir dans la souffrance.

CRISPIN
Monsieur vous pourra-là prêter sa patience.

FLAVIE
Ah! vous avez été le meilleur des maris.   1450

CRISPIN
Oui.

FLAVIE
Pour vous contenter je veux bien à Paris
Etre entre quatre murs.

CRISPIN
Mais c'est une folie;
Quatre murs à Paris, ou quatre en Italie,
C'est toujours quatre murs.

FLAVIE
Oui, mais l'éloignement...

FLAVIO
Allons, Madame, allons, plus de raisonnement.   1455

CRISPIN (seul)
Bon, bon, point de quartier; voilà comme il faut être:
A cet emportement je reconnois mon Maître;
Oui, c'est être homme là, que de n'écouter rien.
Il se vange un peu tard, mais il se vange bien.
Toutefois je demande à tous tant que vous êtes   1460
Grace pour les Pipeurs et les Femmes Coquettes.

F I N

All notes are indicated by the line of the play to which they refer. Throughout the text, we have maintained with only slight modifications the original orthography of Poisson's play. The inconsistencies of spelling and usage are therefore those of the author.

1 - Boccace: Italian Renaissance writer, author of the Decameron, whose influence was widespread in French literature. Poisson mentions this name because of its similarity to that of the Pipeur du Boccage.

4 - maris en ont là: in the Decameron, there are numerous tales of cuckholds and deceived husbands.

8 - hé que: archaic usage similar to the Spanish ojala.

11 - Louïs: monetary unit of the seventeenth century. Will Durant and Ariel Durant, in The Age of Louis XIV (New York: Simon and Schuster, 1963), ix, equate this amount with $50.00 US (1962 value). The unit was worth 20 Francs of the seventeenth century. Ten Louis would therefore be a considerable sum for the times.

21 - l'ingénu dévot: Docile.

24 - dévote: non-pejorative sense of devout.

36 - diamant: this precious stone is found frequently in the seventeenth-century French theatre, often with variable symbolism. Cf. Edme Boursault, Marie Stuard, in The Fallen Crown: Three French Mary Stuart Plays of the Seventeenth Century, ed. Michael G. Paulson (Washington, DC: University Press of America, 1980).

59 - Touriere: non-cloistered member of a religious order in charge of overseeing the entry of any item from the outside to the religious community. By extension and degeneration, this type of person often permitted unauthorized visits within.

63 - Galères: as late as the seventeenth century, criminals were often condemned to varying sentences in the galleys of the French navy. In Racine's Les Plaideurs, the line "aux galères" shows the frequency of this punishment.

76 - Saint Martin: various possibilities. Perhaps la
Porte St. Martin in Paris. The reference is ironic
since St. Martin, like Docile, was noted for his generosity and charity toward the poor and unfortunate.

107 - Boccace: in order to turn suspicion from herself, Flavie should avoid references to Boccaccio
whose stories might be considered licentious owing to
the number of adulterous subjects.

Scène III - Although the name FLAVIO is listed among
the characters, he does not appear in this scene.

162 - bigotte: one who demonstrates excessive and
narrow outward religious devotion and zeal.

186 - Flavio here resembles Molière's victimized
George Dandin.

203 - une belle âme: Cf. Molière's Tartuffe, "le
pauvre homme."

216 - Académie: "un lieu où l'on donne publiquement à
jouer." Cf. Gaston Cayrou, Le Français classique
(Paris: Didier, 1948), p. 6.

228 - Pipeurs: cheats. From piper, "tromper adroite-
ment," (Cayrou, p. 663).

229 - Ecus: French coin with the shield of France in-
scribed upon it; each was worth approximately 5 Francs

246 - Italien: Flavio feels punished for marrying
outside of his nationality much as does George Dandin
for marrying above his social class.

Scène VIII - this is the number indicated in all editions, although there is no scene VII.

274 - one of the stereotypes of Italians in the seventeenth century is that of extremely talkative people.

293 - Job: biblical character known for his patience.

303 - Guerre Civile: the context can be understood to
be with regard to one of the Frondes or to one of the
many Italian civil wars.

312 - Un beau garçon: reference to the widespread
practice of homosexuality in Italy in the sixteenth

and seventeenth centuries. Gossips of the age believed that Henry III was corrupted by the Italians
during his visit to Venice and that he had inherited
a susceptibility to this "disease" through his mother,
Catherine de Medici.

324 - Oison: small goose, by extension a foolish person.

356 - querir: chercher.

366 - Mamie: archaic form of mon amie.

372 - De quand: depuis quand.

391 - All': Elle. Colin follows the tradition of the
comédiens italiens by speaking with an Italian accent.

400 - lavement: the use of lavements was frequent in
the seventeenth century and is often found in Molière's
theatre.

450 - pistole: ancient French coin worth ten Francs.

518 - Voire: vrai.

656 - Négromantiens: nécromanciens, practitioners of
the black arts.

657 - Mondory/Bellerose: famous actors of the seventeenth century; the latter was associated for a time
with Poisson's troupe.

665-670 - reference to the vain efforts in Paris to
suppress gambling, an impossible task since the most
affluent and influential were the chief offenders.
Contrary to Crispin's indications, dueling was not
completely stopped, even though the more stringent enforcement of the anti-dueling edicts did abate their
frequency.

676 - diable ingénieur: efforts were made at this
time to facilitate sanitation and to eliminate the mud
in the Parisian streets.

686 - diable Jardinier: Le Nôtre, who designed the
gardens of Versailles.

691 - reference to the wonders of Versailles, the
Louvre and their attractive gardens. Cf. Christopher

Hibbert, <u>Versailles</u> (New York: Newsweek, 1972), pp.
14-48, for details of construction and engineering.

700 - Arc Triomphal: Arc de Triomphe du Caroussel,
which still stands today near the Louvre.

796 - Camouflet: originally, smoke blown in someone's
face or nose, but by extension, any humiliating affront.

1053 - Marcassin: young boar.

1057 - Scene inspired from Molière's <u>Précieuses ridi-
cules</u>.

1071 - favoris de Mars: soldiers. Mars is the Roman
god of war.

1087 - Astrée: pastoral novel by Honoré d'Urfé, which
was very much in vogue during the seventeenth century.

1093 - Pont Neuf: bridge on the Seine in Paris built
during the reign of Henry IV.

1100 - Jean de Vuerth: obscure reference, perhaps a
fictitious name.

1131 - This line is obviously delivered to Aymée.

1353 - Jeudi: Thursday night was the last occasion
they would have to eat meat, Friday being a day of
fasting (until 1965).

1368 - Argus: creature from mythology who had one
hundred eyes, half of which always remained open in
order to watch over his charge.

BIBLIOGRAPHY

I. Primary Souces.

Dancourt. _Théâtre choisi_. Paris: Librairie Garnier Frères, n.d.

Fournel, François V. _Les Contemporains de Molière_. Paris: Firmin-Didot et Cie., 1876.

Poisson, Raymond. _Les Oeuvres de Poisson_. 2 vols. Paris: Compagnie des Libraires Associés, 1743.

Regnard, Jean-François. _Oeuvres de Regnard_. 5 vols. Paris: Pierre Didot et Firmin Didot, 1801.

Saurin, Bernard. _Oeuvres choisies de Saurin_. Paris: F. Didot l'aîne et F. Didot, 1812.

II. General Works.

Adam, Antoine. _Histoire de la littérature française au XVIIe siècle_. 5 vols. Paris: Del Duca, 1949-1956.

Allen, David. _The Nature of Gambling_. New York: Coward-McCann, Inc., 1952.

Alvarez-Detrell, Tamara. "The Aristocratic Young Gambler in the Society of _Le Joueur_ and _Il giorno_." _The USF Language Quarterly_, 18, no. 3-4 (1980), 21-24.

_____. "From Chaos to Harmony: Regnard's _Le Joueur_ and Goldoni's _Il giuocattore_." Tallahassee, Florida: Paper presented at the Florida State University Comparative Literature Symposium, January 26, 1979.

_____. "Saints and Monsters in _The Gamester_ and _Béverlei_." Tallahassee, Florida: Paper presented at the Florida State University Comparative Literature Symposium, January 22, 1981.

Ashton, John. _The History of Gambling in England_. New York: Franklin, 1968.

177

Beaurepaire, Edmond. "Les Maisons de jeu au Grand
    Siècle." Mercure de France, 83 (1910),
    440-448.

Bergler, Edmund. The Psychology of Gambling. London:
    International University Press, 1974.

Bloch, Herbert A. "The Sociology of Gambling." Amer-
    ican Journal of Sociology, 57, no. 3 (1952),
    215-221.

Boileau, Nicolas. Oeuvres poétiques. Paris: Flam-
    marion, 1903.

Cailhava, M. de. De L'Art de la comédie. 4 vols.
    Paris: Didot, 1772.

Calamé, Alexandre. Regnard: sa vie et son oeuvre.
    Paris: Presses Universitaires de France,
    1960.

Cayrou, Gaston. Le Français classique. Paris:
    Didier, 1948.

Charaux, A. "Molière et Regnard." Etudes Francis-
    caines, 26 (1911), 511-549.

Choisy, François Timoléon de. Mémoires pour servir à
    l'histoire de Louis XIV. Paris: Mercure de
    France, 1966.

Cohen, John. Behaviour in Uncertainty and Its Social
    Implications. New York: Basic Books, Inc.,
    1964.

_____. Chance, Skill and Luck. N.p.: Longmans
    Green, 1960.

_____. Risk and Gambling. N.p.: Longmans Green,
    1956.

Cotton, Charles. The Compleat Gamester. London:
    George Routledge and Sons, 1674.

Courcillon, Philippe de, Marquis de Dangeau. Abrégé
    des mémoires. 4 vols. Paris: Treutel et
    Würtz, 1817.

Curtis, A. Ross. Crispin Ier: la vie et l'oeuvre de

Raymond Poisson. Toronto and Buffalo: University of Toronto Press, 1972.

Davis, Clyde. Something for Nothing. Philadelphia: J.B. Lippincott Company, 1956.

Des Granges, Charles-M. Le Théâtre au XVIIIe siècle. Paris: Hatier, 1962.

Dostoevsky, Fyodor. Great Short Works of Fyodor Dostoevsky. Introduction by Ronald Hingley. Translated by Constance Garnett. New York: Harper and Row, 1968.

Dufresny, Charles. Amusements sérieux et comiques. Paris: Editions Bossard, 1721.

Durant, Will and Ariel Durant. The Age of Louis XIV. New York: Simon and Schuster, 1963.

Forkey, Leo. The Role of Money in French Comedy During the Reign of Louis XIV. Baltimore: The Johns Hopkins Press, 1947.

France, Clemens. "The Gambling Impulse." The Psychology of Gambling. New York: Harper and Row, 115-156, 1974.

Gaxotte, Pierre. The Age of Louis XIV. New York: Macmillan, 1970.

Halliday, John. The Psychology of Gambling. New York: Harper and Row, 1974.

Herman, Robert D., ed. Gambling. New York: Harper and Row, 1967.

Hibbert, Christopher. Versailles. New York: Newsweek, 1972.

Huizinga, Johan. Homo Ludens: A Study of the Play-Element in Culture. New York: Roy Publishers, 1950.

Jamati, Georges. La Querelle du Joueur: Regnard et Dufresny. Paris: Messein, 1936.

Kunstler, Charles. La Vie quotidienne sous la Régence. Paris: Librairie Hachette, 1960.

La Bruyère, Jean de. Les Caractères. Paris: Editions Garnier Frères, n.d.

Lancaster, Henry Carrington. Adventures of a Literary Historian. Freeport: Books for Libraries Press, 1968.

_____. French Tragedy in the Time of Louis XV and Voltaire. 2 vols. Baltimore: The Johns Hopkins Press, 1950.

_____. A History of French Dramatic Literature in the Seventeenth Century. 9 vols. Baltimore: The Johns Hopkins Press, 1936-1940.

_____. Sunset: A History of Parisian Drama in the Last Years of Louis XIV: 1701-1715. Baltimore: The Johns Hopkins Press, 1945.

Lemazurier, Pierre-David. Galerie historique des acteurs du théâtre français depuis 1600 jusqu'à nos jours. 2 vols. Paris: J. Chaumerot, 1810.

Lenient, Charles F. La Comédie en France au XVIIIe siècle. Paris: Hachette, 1888.

Levron, Jacques. La Vie quotidienne à la cour de Versailles. Paris: Hachette, 1965.

Linder, Robert M. "The Psychodynamics of Gambling." Annals of the American Academy of Political and Social Science, 269 (1950), 93-107.

Marquiset, Alfred. Jeux et joueurs d'autrefois. Paris: Emile-Paul Frères, 1759.

Mitford, Nancy. The Sun King: Louis XIV at Versailles. New York: Harper and Row, 1966.

Mongrédien, Georges. La Vie de société aux 17e et 18e siècles. Paris: Hachette, 1950.

_____. La Vie quotidienne sous Louis XIV. Paris: Hachette, 1948.

Moore, Edward. The Gamester. Ann Arbor, Michigan: Edwards Brothers, 1948.

Newman, Otto. Gambling, Hazard and Reward. London: Athalon Press, 1972.

Norman, Hilda Laura. *Swindlers and Rogues in French Drama*. Chicago: The University of Chicago Press, 1928.

Paulson, Michael G. *The Fallen Crown: Three French Mary Stuart Plays of the Seventeenth Century*. Washington: University Press of America, 1980.

Perkins, Ernest B. *Gambling in English Life*. London: The Epworth Press, 1950.

Reid, Ed. *The Green Felt Jungle*. New York: Trident Press, 1963.

Sévigné, Madame de. *Lettres*. 3 vols. Paris: Bibliothèque de la Pléiade, 1960-1963.

Steinmetz, Andrew. *The Gaming Table: Its Votaries and Victims*. 2 vols. New Jersey: Patterson Smith, 1969.

Tilley, Arthur. *The Decline of the Age of Louis XIV*. New York: Barnes and Noble, Inc., 1968.

LEGAL ETHICS IN THE PRACTICE OF LAW

Third Edition

TEACHER'S MANUAL

Richard Zitrin
Adjunct Professor of Law
University of California, Hastings College of the Law

Carol M. Langford
Adjunct Professor of Law
University of San Francisco School of Law

Nina W. Tarr
Professor of Law
University of Illinois College of Law

NOTE TO USERS
To ensure that you are using the latest materials available in this area, please be sure to periodically check the LexisNexis Law School web site for downloadable updates and supplements at www.lexisnexis.com/lawschool

---

Editorial Offices
744 Broad Street, Newark, NJ 07102 (973) 820-2000
201 Mission St., San Francisco, CA 94105-1831 (415) 908-3200
701 East Water Street, Charlottesville, VA 22902-7587 (434) 972-7600
www.lexis.com

(Pub.3083)

TABLE OF CONTENTS

OVERVIEW, ORGANIZATION AND SUGGESTED SYLLABI

AN INTRODUCTORY THOUGHT

We are convinced that legal ethics can be one of the most enjoyable and rewarding courses in the law school curriculum. Although ethics teachers have often complained about the lack of motivation among their students, particularly because the course is required in most places, we have found that where the material is made *accessible* to the students, so that they can understand how ethical issues apply in "real life" lawyering situations, not only do the students thoroughly enjoy the class, but we do too. Perhaps more importantly, students seem to learn something in the process both about the black-letter ethical rules and about *themselves* and their own sense of ethical and moral behavior. Best of all for us, we find that with each class we teach, *we* learn something important about *ourselves*.

We wrote *Legal Ethics in the Practice of Law* largely to be able to share this exciting experience with others. The book has been designed for use as a general text for legal ethics and professional responsibility courses from seminar size up through large class sections, and in clinical programs that are responsible for their students' legal ethics education. We focus in this teacher's manual on the approaches that have worked successfully for us and our students. We don't expect that any teacher will agree with all these approaches. Nor do we expect that everyone will agree with all our opinions on how to resolve the ethical dilemmas described in the book. But we see this manual as the opportunity to give you our own two cents' worth — to describe what's worked well for us over the years. There is nothing magical in this approach; we hope you will combine these ideas with your own as you develop these materials for your own course.

OVERVIEW OF THE MANUAL

We believe that the best use of the problem-driven approach we have adopted comes when the problems are discussed among the students and teacher in an interactive format because students have the opportunity for a wide-ranging substantive discussion about each problem selected. Understandably, we prefer a seminar format with student-led discussions, whether as a stand-alone course or in conjunction with a clinical program. The ideal physical setting is where the students and teacher can face each other around a large table or group of tables. We understand, though, that many teachers do not have this luxury. Large class sizes (and few credit units) continue to be a fact of life at many law schools. We have made a conscious effort to ensure that these materials are equally valuable in large sections. Some teachers may divide larger class sections into smaller, more workable groups, or mini-law firms. Others may prefer to use the problems as a framework for a more traditional large class Socratic approach.

1

We believe that teaching legal ethics, whatever the setting, is best done when analysis takes place in a practical context. Basic ethical black-letter precepts must be taught and understood. But because most ethical issues arise out of the "real life" crucible of actual practice, we believe that learning to recognize ethical issues is a skill closer to trying a law suit or interviewing a client than it is to a traditional casebook analysis of contract or tort law. At the same time, there is inevitably a strong relationship between ethical precepts and personal morality, one that we want to encourage each student to evaluate for himself or herself.

Given our point of view, and to make the discipline accessible to students, we have chosen to include many readings from the popular and legal press in addition to law review and case excerpts. Accordingly, which readings have more application to the individual teacher, and which questions in the problem have more appeal, will likely depend on that teacher's goals.

In our own instruction, we take an approach which tilts heavily to student-teacher interaction and free-flowing discussion. Role playing by both students and teachers is strongly encouraged. We also encourage the students to use their creativity, by performing skits, using videos, or using their initiative in other ways. Teachers should also role play and act as devil's advocate; these are valuable means of helping to focus discussion. This manual offers numerous suggestions for teacher role play and devil's advocacy.

We suggest that teachers carefully review the Introduction of the text, which sets forth the basic philosophy of our book. We believe that while some ethical problems have clear "black letter" answers, many do not. This book emphasizes those places where clearly established ethical precepts appear to conflict. These ethical gray areas, dilemmas, and quandaries are less susceptible to clear-cut answers, and present situations where it may not be clear what "doing the right thing" means. We believe that this is the best way to get students truly to understand legal ethics.

We have also learned from long experience that it is best to avoid teaching this subject matter by taking strong stands on the "right" and "wrong" answers. We try to withhold our own views and analysis until near the end of the discussion. We have found that this path encourages debate and discussion — and legitimate, honestly held differences of opinion.

Since the "right answers" are often elusive, *recognizing the problem and discussing alternative approaches to solving it often becomes more important than the precise solution reached.* When "black letter" rules conflict, we try to reassure students that the absence of a specific "answer" is not cause for alarm. The students should also be encouraged to "take chances" in classroom discussion, without fear that their answers will be criticized as "wrong." But it is equally important for teachers to clearly state their own views before the

discussion ends. Students look to us for our views, and they should hear them, and hear them clearly.

ORGANIZATION OF THE MANUAL

The defining organizational subdivision in this book is the Problem rather than the Chapter. This is done to focus attention on the problem approach to this course. Accordingly, we also divide up this manual into Problems rather than Chapters.

Outside of reading our introductory remarks **(THE POINT BEHIND THE PROBLEM)** and perhaps the list of **APPLICABLE RULES**, we strongly suggest that the teacher read the particular problem and accompanying readings before turning to the **DISCUSSION** section in the Teacher's Manual. These sections, which form the bulk of the manual, presume that the teacher is already familiar with the problem and readings.

For ease of organization, and hopefully to make the manual clearer to you, the text of the manual has been broken into six segments for each problem. They are:

(a) The Point Behind the Problem:

A relatively brief section of about three paragraphs explaining the general purpose behind the particular problem. We try here also to describe any particularly difficult points, significant issues or subtleties that we are trying to convey through the problem.

(b) Applicable Rules:

A list of sections of both the 1983 (as amended) and 2002-2003 American Bar Association Model Rules of Professional Conduct (we will use the abbreviation **MR**), the American Bar Association Model Code of Professional Responsibility (Model Code) both ethical considerations (**EC**) and disciplinary rules (**DR**), and, since California is the only state whose rules are neither Rules-based nor Code-based, the California Rules of Professional Conduct (**CA**) and Business & Professions Code (**CA B&P**), which are applicable to all or part of a problem. We leave it to the teacher, assisted by the discussion section of the manual, to determine which rules are applicable to which parts of the problem.

Since as of this writing (December 2006), many states have not adopted the 2002 version of the Model Rules, we include references to both 1983 and 2002-3 sets of rules. We have also decided to retain our references to the Model Code for one more edition, even though use of the Code has been almost entirely superseded. This decision is consistent with what we have done with our companion volume, the 2007 edition of Zitrin, Langford & Mohr, *Legal Ethics: Rules, Statutes, and Comparisons*.

Should you wish, we can provide you with a separate document presenting all of the **APPLICABLE RULES** sections together, for those who wish to distribute this rules guide to students. Although we prefer to emulate "real world" practice by presenting the practice problem and requiring the students to research what rules apply, we understand that other teachers prefer to provide the rules to the students. Just write, phone, or e-mail us or your LexisNexis representative.

(c) Suggested Questions to Ask:

We add questions we think are interesting to raise but which, for a variety of reasons, we did not include in the problem itself. We believe these questions are better used when raised by the teacher during the class discussion. Sometimes we have held these questions out of the text because we don't want to give away too much of the game in the problem itself, or because how well they serve as devil's advocacy may depend on the direction in-class discussion takes. Many of these questions also appear in the **Discussion**.

(d) Suggested Role Plays:

We find role plays to be an important part of the course. They are both enjoyable and an excellent instructional tool. We list some of the role plays we have successfully used in our courses in this section of the manual. We also often refer to them in the longer **Discussion** section.

During the life of the first edition, several teachers asked us to amplify what we mean by "role plays." We mean a direct interactive experience between teacher and student, or among students, in which each person plays the role of a lawyer, a client or the like. Sometimes, explaining why a particular strategy will "work" or "not work" in the "real world" is not nearly as effective as playing out that strategy in words and actions in front of the entire class. For example, students tend to take overly idealistic positions about how they would deal with particular ethical situations; these simply may not work in practice.

This can be most easily demonstrated when the positions taken by these students are played out in actual role plays. *These role plays need not be either complicated or lengthy*; brief, simple dialogue will frequently make the point.

To provide an illustration about how such role plays work in our class, we have drafted the dialogue from one example, and reproduced it below. We have chosen the "Penknife scenario" posited by Professor Monroe Freedman, which we have incorporated into **Problem 15** at **page 399** of the text, and which is further described in the text at **pages 422-3**. The Teacher's Manual contains a brief description of how we use the Penknife Scenario; you might wish to read that before reading further here.

We find the penknife role play particularly effective with students who evaluate the situation and conclude that when they advise their client, they will avoid giving the "right answer." These students wish to avoid explaining to the client why it is important whether the defendant carries the penknife with him all or most of the time. By playing out the roles of client and lawyer, it becomes increasingly clear that it is difficult, if not impossible, for the student/lawyers to avoid directly answering the defendant's questions in an actual interview.

This is how the dialogue of this role play might go:

Student/Attorney: (Quoting Freedman's scenario) Do you regularly carry the penknife in your pocket? Do you carry it frequently or infrequently, or did you take it with you only on that particular occasion?

Teacher/Client: Why do you ask me a question like that?

Student/Attorney: Well, it could be important to your case.

Teacher/Client: How do you mean, important?

Student/Attorney: Well, how often you carry the knife could be a factor in how the case stacks up against you. (At this point, we invite students to try various ways of avoiding acknowledging the actual significance of the frequency of carrying the penknife, in whatever set of words they may choose.)

Teacher/Client: Yeah, but how is it important?

Student/Attorney: I'll tell you after you tell me how often you carry the penknife.

Teacher/Client: You mean you're not gonna tell me why it's important? What are you here for? I need your advice.

[or]

Man, you must be kidding! You're supposed to be my lawyer!

Student/Attorney:	I am your lawyer. Just trust me. I'll tell you why it's important, but you have to answer me first.
Teacher/Client:	(Thought bubble): Why isn't this damn lawyer answering my question? I got to be missing something here. I mean, I carry this knife every day. But man, if I carry it all the time, it's gonna look like I do violent stuff. I don't want to get into that. I'm just gonna give him the answer she [or he] wants to hear.
	(Spoken out loud): I only carry it once in a long long while.

From here, the teacher can go on to explain the flaws of not fully advising the client, even if that advice might lead to the client lying as a result, using this role play as an example.

Role plays can be very simple, as this one is, and still have the desired effect of getting a point across that might take far more time and far more debate than the few minutes devoted to the role play itself. Again, as we said in the Teacher's Manual, we find role plays a continuing source of illumination of many of the points we wish the students to appreciate. We encourage their widespread use. Any teacher using these materials who would like to discuss role plays with us is more than welcome to call or e-mail us; we look forward to the opportunity of talking with you.

(e) Suggested Video Clips:

Many professors enjoy using video clips from movies and television to enhance the learning experience and explore the book's problems from a slightly different angle. For this Third Edition, with the help of our friend and colleague Rob Waring, who has taught both Legal Ethics and courses on law, culture and society and law and film, we are including suggested video segments for most of the problems in the text. These are optional, of course, and we're sure that there are other movie and TV segments that could serve equally well. (If you have your own favorites, we hope you will let us know.) We are in the process of investigating whether we will be permitted to compile these suggested video segments on a DVD to make it available to all who request it — whether or not they adopt our text — to enjoy and use.

(f) The Discussion:

This section forms the bulk of the manual's contents. It serves as an analysis of the issues and major points which might be raised in discussing each particular problem, and the relevant readings and source materials. Where we refer to specific readings from the text, we highlight the reference by using the bold-faced word **Readings**, and a bold-faced reference to the **Section #** where

the particular reading is found in the text. Except as noted, references in the discussion sections are to the 1983 ABA Rules as amended.

Note that many problems have a large number of questions accompanying them. Not all these questions are of equal importance; some may only be asked rhetorically. Because individual teachers will choose to emphasize different questions asked in each problem, we often orient our discussion towards the underlying points to be raised in the problem, rather than a strict question-by-question analysis.

In the Discussion sections, we will share with you our perspectives on how the difficult issues presented by the problems might best be resolved. These conclusions are our personal views, and are intended to provide some closure about our perspective. We do *not* consider them "right" answers, and we recognize that reasonable minds will differ about many of these issues. Where we ourselves become two or three reasonable minds who differ, we try to provide something of our separate perspectives.

There are, however, recurring themes that appear throughout this manual and in the course book itself. Some are of central importance, others of more practical application. We will see all more than a few times. We list several here:

- the tension between the needs of the client and those of society;

- the extent of the difference between legal ethics and ordinary morality, and the tension between the two;

- the importance of making full disclosure to clients;

- the difficulties facing young lawyers in practice, particularly associates in large firms;

- the importance of malpractice issues, and the interrelationship between malpractice, the rules of ethics, and other norms;

- the significance of racial and gender diversity of the profession *and*, at least in some common circumstances, the presence of bias;

- the difference between the rules of evidence and the rules of ethics, especially the distinction between privilege and confidentiality;

- the significance of semantic distinctions—a "critical distinction" according to one ABA comment—so that how we say what we say may be of great importance.

FIRST ASSIGNMENT AND FIRST CLASS

For pre-class reading, we assign the book's **Introduction** and **Chapter One**, a total of 34 pages. We spend part of the first class going over our course "ground rules" and describing the nature of the rules of legal ethics. In discussing our "ground rules," we discuss the way we intend to teach the course, and as specifically as possible what we intend to require from each student. It is especially important to explain the in-class participation which we expect. We discuss the grading elements at length, including our preference for basing our grades in significant part on students' in-class discussion presentations of problems.

We also discuss the nature of the papers or open-book essay examinations we require at the end of the semester, and explain our preference for these types of examinations, consistent with our desire to replicate actual practice situations. (For those who may be interested, we explain in greater detail our in-class methodology and final exam preferences below, under section (C) of "Suggested Syllabi and Course Approaches," which we've called "How We Teach Our Course.")

Whenever possible (and we try to make sure it's always possible), we take some time to go around the room, to ask students what kind of law they are thinking of practicing and what their law-related work experience has been. By describing the experiences they have had in the past, the kind of law firms in which they have worked and the kind of work they have done, and by telling us the kind of law they intend to practice, the students provide us with diverse backgrounds and experiences which help us in our discussions and role plays. We also tell the students about our own backgrounds and experiences, so that they may appreciate the particular perspectives — and perhaps the particular biases — that we bring to the classroom.

We then review for the students the rules relevant to determining ethical behavior, explaining the history of the transition from the ABA Code to the Rules, and on to the changes made in 2002 and 2003 based on the work of the Ethics 2000 Commission. We go over the different organizational schemes used by the Code and the Rules, all of which is set forth in the book's Introduction in section (C). Although the Code's organizational scheme and the majority of its substance is fading from states' usage, we still include it, as we continue to do for the moment in our annually-updated Rules book. Some teachers also use the first class as an opportunity to review the basic concepts, including admission to practice and discipline, contained in Chapter **13**. Those teachers may also wish to assign that last chapter as pre-class reading. We prefer to leave this chapter for a later date as time allows.

Instead, we move forward to discuss the historical perspective of the law as an elite profession, and evaluate the slow development of a more modern egalitarian perspective, matters described in the Introduction in the segment

from Jerold Auerbach's still-vibrant book. (See **Readings**, page 9.). We use the last part of the first class to engage the students in an interactive, substantive discussion of the readings in **Chapter One**. See the separate section that follows.

SUGGESTED SYLLABI AND COURSE APPROACHES

(a) A Course Overview

The organization of the subject matter of the text is quite traditional. We begin with the undertaking of a case, and move through getting a fee, confidentiality, and conflicts of interest to the interrelationship between the ethical obligations to the client and those owed the legal system. While we feel we have chosen a sensible chronology for the course, there is nothing sacrosanct about the order of the problems. Each problem is self-contained and may be taken out of order; each teacher should evaluate his or her individual preferences.

The text contains a total of 31 problems. As a practical matter, however, where the course is taught for only two units and/or where the class sections are large lecture hall size, it may be impossible to cover all the problems. Complete coverage of all 31 is not necessary for a thorough course in legal ethics. In our attempt to make the coverage of the text as complete as possible, add new topics to keep current, and satisfy different professors in diverse teaching settings, we have been somewhat overinclusive. Even in our three-unit seminar courses, we limit student-led discussions to between 22 and 26 problems. We prefer to mix the problems in with visiting guests of varying perspectives (DAs, public defenders, big firm partners and associates, judges), film and TV clips, and so on.

(b) Suggested Syllabi

If a limited curriculum is necessary, we suggest the following 14 to 17 problems set forth under "**Short Course**" below, in addition to as many "practice-specific" problems that the instructor has time to fit in. Which of these practice-specific problems to choose might well depend on where students are likely to wind up after graduation. For a longer course — we ourselves consider 26 problems to be a difficult-to-attain maximum — we would either add several that appeal to us personally or, as we often do, allow the students to choose the last four or five from a list of seven or eight possibilities. Our long course might look something like that described below. Here are our suggested Short Course and Long Course syllabi (and remember, they're just suggestions):

Short Course	Long Course
Problems 1 &/or 3, 4, 7, 8, 12 or 13, 14 &/or 15, 17, 18 &/or 19, two of 24-26, 27, 28, 29, 31; & practice-specific problems as time allows	**Problems 1, 3, 4-8, 11, 12, 14, 15, 17-19, 23-29, 31 and student choice of <u>two</u> or <u>three</u> of the below problems**
<u>Practice-Specific Problems:</u> **10 (law firms and disqualification)** **11 (class action, insurance defense)** **21 (mediation)** **22 (prosecutors)** **23 (government attorneys)**	**2 (the despicable client)** **9 (lawyers' interests conflicts)** **10 (law firms and disqualification)** **13 (multi-cultural lawyering)** **16 (Rule 11 and candor to court)** **20 (civility, contempt, publicity)** **21 (mediation)** **22 (prosecutors)**

(c) How We Teach Our Course

For the benefit of those who may find it helpful, we describe below the way we teach our courses. While these methods have worked for us with these materials, we recognize that there are undoubtedly many other ways to use these materials as effectively or more effectively. Our purpose here is hardly to suggest that this is *the* way to do it, but rather that this is an approach to the ethics class that has worked well for us.

We have the luxury of teaching most often in seminars and small sections of from 20 to 40 students. We focus here on our seminar classes as opposed to teaching an integrated ethical component within a student clinical experience, since these clinical settings vary so widely. We have also taught large sections; while no large section can accomplish quite as much as a seminar, or quite match the interaction and student participation possible in smaller classes, we nevertheless find that the same methodology we use in classes of 20 to 40 students is workable and successful with a larger class size of 75 or even 100.

Our course, like our book, is problem-driven. We assign two or three students each, depending on class size, to prepare a presentation on each problem. In large sections, some professors like to create "law firms" of eight or ten students, and find various ways of ensuring that all participate. A presentation generally evolves into a discussion of the problem participatory. We see the teacher's role largely as that of a facilitator, allowing the presenters to make their points, and then guiding the student discussion by asking questions, playing devil's advocate, taking student "straw polls" to see how the class stands on tough issues, role playing various parts, both lawyers and

clients, and, if necessary, making sure that all of the principal issues and significant ethics rules have been addressed.

We liken our role to the captain of a ship who keeps a hand on the tiller while the students work to sail the ship, learning about the wind and currents along the way. If the students get off course, a light hand on the tiller, in the form of a question asked, a little devil's advocacy or a brief role play, will generally right the course quickly.

However, before we leave a particular problem, we make sure that we express clearly our own opinions about the answers to the principal questions we have raised. We try to emphasize that these may not always be the "right" answers, but they reflect our best efforts at resolving the ethical dilemmas in question. And while we try not to be too dogmatic about most of these conclusions (there are a few issues where we admit we express our conclusions more dogmatically), we have learned the importance to our students of our expressing our conclusions clearly.

We tell our student presenters to feel free to be innovative in the way they make their presentations. Some students do role plays and skits, others do point-counterpoint arguments, and a few use visual props and even engage the entire class in a role play. Many students simply present their thoughts about the problem in a more traditional way. We believe that this freedom of approach helps engage these students — and the entire class — in the problem at hand. In the early weeks of the semester, we work closely with the student presenters to explain how they might approach their task.

We believe that a great deal of the learning in legal ethics can and should take place in the classroom — and, of course, in the courtroom, interview room, or other setting where students in clinical programs get to try their hands at practicing law. Accordingly, in the first class, we make as clear as possible to the students the importance of participating in the class discussion. We tell them that not only will their student colleagues learn more if they are heard from, but that we will learn more too. We stress this participation, because the ethical concepts and dilemmas that form the substance of our course are best understood when they are argued about and fought over. Participation includes listening as well as talking, and so we require attendance in our classes to the extent permitted by our administrations. For example, while we always excuse an absence for a clinical program necessity, we do not excuse absences for on-campus interviews.

To the extent allowed by the particular school administration, we make class participation a significant element of the final grade in the course. We grade the class presentations heavily, if possible giving them as much weight as the final paper or examination.

Speaking of grades, again to the extent allowed, we prefer to give our students take-home papers, or if they are not allowed, then open-book essay

examinations. We do recommend strongly against using any form of short-answer final examination. An example of a final exam/paper topic might be asking students to write a law firm opinion letter about one or another ethical dilemma, or asking the students to take the role as staff counsel to a state ethics committee which has been asked to draft a new rule or ethics opinion.

We know that teachers who use these materials will find many other successful ways of teaching legal ethics. We would be happy to discuss our methodology further with you. We are also eager to learn what worked for you in teaching this exciting subject. Please feel free to contact any of us. Richard Zitrin can be reached at (415) 956-4030 or zitrinr@usfca.edu while Carol Langford can be reached at (925) 938-3870 or langford@usfca.edu and Nina Tarr can be reached at (217) 333-2065 or ntarr@law.uiuc.edu. We are happy to share our thoughts and experiences, and look forward to having you share yours with us.

CHAPTER ONE

Initial Reflections on Ethics, Morality, and Justice
in an Adversary System

(a) Two Basic Focuses and an Interactive Discussion

The readings in **Chapter One** set forth two of the most basic focuses of the book. The preliminary discussion of these issues — concentrating on raising questions without trying to answer them, in an effort to whet students' appetites — serves to preview many of the problems that serve as the book's defining organization.

The first focus, delineated by the Mellinkoff and Washington *Post* excerpts **(Readings, Sections 2** and **3)**, sets forth in historical perspective the difficult task of zealously representing a client, especially an "unworthy" one, when our society cries out for protection of its greater good. The concept of "zealous" representation raises the issue that perhaps most clearly bothers today's public. But it is also one that has long been seen as a basic tenet of the practice of law.

We begin with a discussion of the laudable motives ascribed by Prof. Mellinkoff to those who, like Charles Phillips and Lord Brougham, were willing to put their clients' interests above all else. Then, we contrast that with the perspective of today's average citizen, as reflected in the *Post* article. Has the laudable, courageous stand of 19th century English barristers been superseded by a higher duty for lawyers to protect society? Another issue we want to introduce to students is the extent to which a lawyer is justified in acting as the client's judge, rather than "merely" as an advocate. This is a theme which will recur throughout the course.

The second focus of **Chapter One** centers on the meaning of "ethics," and "legal ethics," and how these terms relate to both group and individual morality.

(b) Defining the Term "Ethical"

We like to take this opportunity to parallel the readings by discussing what is meant by the term "ethical." We do this to help students define this term for their own personal use. Black letter ethics rules, we have learned, don't cover everything. Between the gaps, we find we have to work with our own sense of right and wrong.

We often frame the discussion by suggesting two disparate definitions: (1) an ethical lawyer is one who abides by the ethical rules, as defined by the four corners of rules of professional conduct in a particular jurisdiction and the law relating to those rules; vs. (2) an ethical lawyer is one about whom another lawyer might say "There goes a highly ethical attorney." There are obviously more definitions than these, and more erudite ways of defining the term

"ethical." But these two definitions are based in actual practice; lawyers say these things about other lawyers. Accordingly, we start there.

In this discussion we make particular reference to the Postema article in **Section 4** of the **Readings**, and to our own comments in **Section 5**. We also point out the dichotomy between people who believe in a constant moral component in one's lawyering vs. those who see lawyers in the traditional role of an advocate without a particular moral imperative.

Some of the issues we raise with our students are these:

- Whether students feel that ethics rules at their inception had a moral basis, or whether their basis was entirely legal in nature;

- Whether a definition of "ethical" that looks to the four corners of the rules of ethics is more of a *legal* standard than one based on any moral sense;

- Whether "ethical" should ever mean what you can "get away with";

- Whether the students can accept the idea of a moral component to their lawyering, and as we argue in **Section 5** of the **Readings**, a moral component to ethical behavior. (Our own view, which we readily realize is not for everyone, is that lawyers work most successfully as integrated ethical and moral beings when they are able to merge their sense of morality with their sense of ethics. This helps them understand their ethical selves — perhaps even as advocates — as being morally justified within the context of their profession, as we suggest in the readings.);

- Whether having different perspectives of what must be done "ethically" and what must be done "morally" can be viewed, as we suggest, as a *moral dilemma*; and

- Whether a standard of conduct which takes morality into account is a *higher* standard, or whether it is merely a *different* standard, not higher but parallel. For example, the ethical requirement to maintain inviolate the confidence of the murderer who has buried bodies is a very difficult standard to meet. Can it be argued that this is a "higher" standard than the straightforward moral standard to which most non-lawyers could easily adhere? The point we try to make here is that a moral component to one's behavior does not necessarily mean that you are acting "better" than someone who adheres to a "strictly ethical" standard.

The McCoy article (**Readings, Section 6**) is one of our personal favorites — a compelling statement about how one man learned the limits of his own and others' abilities to "do the right thing." McCoy's lesson about the sadhu holy man, not written about legal ethics at all, can be used to get all of us thinking about squaring living our lives with our responsibilities to others. McCoy argues for a new look at *group* ethical behavior, something which is of

increasing interest and importance to law firms. In our own thoughts in the next section of readings, we look at a related issue — how cultural differences may affect our views of ethical lawyering. We introduce the torture memorandum to illustrate our meaning; we return to both the cultural issue and the torture memos again later in the volume.

Cultural bases for ethical and/or moral behavior — or as McCoy witnessed, its absence — are not an excuse. The article about the bar-taking good Samaritan (**Readings, Section 8**) speaks loudly for not relying solely on the group ethic, and for a place for *individual* principles of morality.

The observations about group and individual morality can be tied to the issue of zealous advocacy by returning to the actions of Charles Phillips in Courvoisier's case, as described by David Mellinkoff. In representing a known guilty client 150 years ago in England, Phillips, after all, had to do so without much support from his peers before the bar. Today, however, the lawyer who represents an "unworthy" client has far more support from the organized bar, and from the "culture" of the profession. We ask if it is time for that group ethic or culture to change. Should we more closely follow the views of a society where people complain about the modern roles of lawyers? Or does our job remain putting the representation of our clients first?

(c) "The Whole Nine Yards"

Finally, lest the first class have students in a state of distress, we present (**Readings, Section 9**) first the perspective of a lawyer who "represents the client, not the case," providing a holistic concept of lawyering. This is followed by the extraordinary and heartwarming story of Julius Berger and his lawyer and adopted grandson Ronald Pohl, who helps the elderly composer hear his own music played in concert. This section of readings illustrates a point we maintain throughout our course — it is possible to be an excellent lawyer without losing one's humanity. Margolick's article parallels our own thoughts about "going the whole nine yards."

Without being paternalistic, lawyers can and do go the extra mile for their clients in ways that serve their clients in a profound and fundamental way. We believe that a client's best interests are often best served when the lawyer moves beyond a traditional role of handling the case and focuses on the person instead. The quoted "lawyer of our acquaintance" — throughout this volume, such "lawyers" generally reflect our own views — says that he often gets emotionally involved in his clients' lives, something attorney Ronald Pohl certainly did on behalf of his musician client.

(d) Keeping a Handle on the Discussion

The discussion we suggest can be lengthy or quite brief. It is important for the teacher to keep a handle on it, since the discussion is so abstract. Students

tend to enjoy the subjective "philosophizing" that this discussion allows, so it is important for the teacher to keep an eye on the ball by not letting it get too abstract and unfocused. We believe the focus should be on how lawyers (and law students) see themselves as professionals, and see their role in society, together with some thoughts about how the society as a whole views us. But if the conversation stays focused, we feel the discussion of the moral component of lawyering is a very important one, indeed one which flows throughout the course of this volume.

PROBLEM 1

Hanging Out Your Shingle

THE POINT BEHIND THE PROBLEM:

The goal here is to provide students with a relatively easy, straightforward problem that begins at the beginning — undertaking a case — and which also covers a lot of territory. Generally speaking, after students go through the process of discussing the issues involved, many, and probably most, will conclude that Arthur Hunnicut may take the case, and that the newly-minted lawyer in Part II may also take at least the incorporation case, and at least under the rules may take the domestic case as well. The point is that if a lawyer is able to *become competent* during the course of the representation, the ethical requirement of competence will be met.

We use Problem 1 to raise three other recurring issues that will be important throughout the course. First, in **Section 8** of the **Readings**, we introduce the concept of *fiduciary duty*. This most fundamental duty of lawyers, the obligation to put the client's interests ahead of our own, is ever-present, and we refer to it throughout the course. It is important for students to understand from the outset of this course the significant interrelationship between ethical rules and other methods of judging behavior, such as negligence standards. But it is also important that they appreciate the differences.

Both "competence" and "fiduciary duty" have dual meanings, which are similar but distinguishable, as both ethical and negligence standards. We discuss each. (See **Readings, Section 7** on competence.) This discussion — both the significance of malpractice and negligence in today's practice *and* the distinction between malpractice and ethics — is our second recurring theme. From time to time during the semester, we will look at relevant standards other than ethical rules, including negligence, rules of evidence (e.g., privilege), discovery sanctions and other judicial sanctions such as contempt. In short, we want students to appreciate that ethics cannot be understood in a vacuum, and that the ethics rules are only a start.

Problem 1 also introduces a third recurring theme: the concept of making full disclosure to the client. Those students who decide to undertake the incorporation or the domestic relations case will have to decide whether and to what extent they will let the prospective client know of their inexperience. As we will throughout this course, we argue the beauty of full and candid disclosure. We believe that this serves the interests of the clients, and thereby, in the long run, serves the lawyers as well.

Finally, Problem 1 discusses the use of referral fees. While the Model Rules allow the limited use of referral fees, both lawyers and the public continue to debate whether they are ethical. Students must understand that except under

17

the more liberal California rule a division of fees must be made "in proportion to the services performed and responsibility assumed by each," or where both lawyers assume full responsibility for the matter.

APPLICABLE RULES:

Model Rules: MRs 1.1; 1.2; 1.3; 1.4; 1.5, especially 1.5(e).
Model Code: DRs 2-103; 2-106; 2-107; 6-101(A); 7-101; EC 7-8.
CA Rules: 2-200; 3-110; 3-500.
CA B&P: 6068(m).

SUGGESTED QUESTIONS TO ASK:

- If you were an average person, how would you go about finding a lawyer? What would you look for in a lawyer?

- How do you define "competence?"

- Is it likely that the economic realities of Arthur's practice allow him to turn down a financially rewarding case that he is competent to handle, though inexperienced?

- If you don't take either of the cases offered you, how will you ever be able to take your first case?

- When does a lawyer's fiduciary duty begin? Can it begin before the representation actually commences?

- Is "hand holding" a legitimate reason for a lawyer to remain associated in a case?

- May a lawyer charge for the time spent reaching a threshold level of competence?

SUGGESTED ROLE PLAYS:

- Play the role of the client who is considering hiring a newly-admitted lawyer and wants to make sure that the lawyer is the right one.

- Play the role of Ann Wilson, who still wants Arthur as her lawyer despite his inexperience, to show the importance of trust.

- Role play the part of a newly-minted attorney. Make that lawyer's speech to the prospective client about why, despite inexperience, the client will be well-served by hiring you.

SUGGESTED VIDEOS:

- Incompetence and its consequences: *Body Heat*, DVD chap. 18, 1:05:48 — 1:10:09.

- The ethics of referrals: *Erin Brockovich* DVD chap. 32, 1:30:30 — 1:32:20. Also see binding arbitration at chaps. 34-36, 1:34:23 — 1:42:14.

DISCUSSION:

If time is limited or you prefer to concentrate on one fact pattern, Part II may be the better choice. It involves less sophisticated facts, and also gets students directly involved, since some of them will be hanging out their shingle within a year or two.

(a)   Competence:

The most important issue raised in this problem is competence. We begin our discussion by asking students how they would find a lawyer if they were in the shoes of Martin Haines (**Readings, Section 1**). What would they want in their lawyer? We then invite students to define "competence." They usually do quite well, as well as many of the courts that have attempted to define this term (see **Readings, Section 7**). We make sure we tell them how well they have done, in order to raise both their feelings of competence and their confidence. **MR 1.1** and its comment list factors that affect competence. We compare these to the definitions of both the courts and our students.

We point out the interrelationship between competence as a term of *ethics* and competence as a standard for *negligence* in malpractice cases. This distinction between legal standards (malpractice and negligence) and ethical ones is important, because it will recur throughout the course. Students must be able to distinguish among ethical and other standards. Some, such as one law professor whose views are expressed in **Section 7**, argues that malpractice liability is more likely to be a check on lawyers' behavior than discipline.

(b)   Should Arthur Take the Railroad Case?

We try to deal with Arthur and the newly-minted lawyer together as to whether they should take the cases they have been offered.

Students will differ widely on whether Arthur can take the personal injury case, and differ even more widely as to whether they, in Part II, can take either of the two cases, especially the family law matter. They will see Arthur as having at least some litigation experience, and although they recognize that he has neither Fred nor Mary's experience, most students conclude that Arthur would provide *competent* representation. We agree. But many students also feel that Fred or Mary would do a much better job. Thus, while they conclude it may be *ethical* for Arthur to keep the case, they often prefer he would not. We are somewhat more comfortable with Arthur taking the case; we point out to the students that there is always a better lawyer somewhere, or at least one with much more experience.

We assist the students in working through the alternatives facing Arthur. We ask whether the economic realities of his practice allow him to turn down a case that may be financially rewarding merely because he is not expert in the field.

Some students feel that Ann Wilson's faith in Arthur makes a difference, but many feel that it does not. We believe that Ann's faith in Arthur is a positive factor should Arthur decide to take the case. We remind students of our discussion about what they look for in an attorney — that one of the most important components is trust. That is what Ann has for Arthur. "Yes," some students will reply, "but that is because Ann would expect Arthur to do the right thing rather than undertake a case he doesn't know how to handle." This is a valid point. But our own experiences teach us that the importance of our client's faith in our doing the case ourselves, while understanding our level of experience, cannot be underestimated.

Before we discuss Question 3 in Part I, on referring the case, we like to turn to the student who has hung out a shingle. If you prefer, of course, you can complete the discussion of Arthur before moving on.

(c) Taking on Your First Cases:

Students will be most reluctant, understandably, to take the domestic relations case. They may have reluctance to take the incorporation as well. They generally feel that the incorporation is at least a quantifiable task on which Arthur has volunteered assistance. While they appreciate that ethics rules allow them to take the divorce, most of them feel personally uncomfortable doing this.

We express sympathy for this point of view. We appreciate that students understand they are permitted under the rules to take even the divorce case, so long as they can *become* competent while doing it. We also appreciate their reluctance, because this domestic relations matter is serious, and even involves children (though without any indication of a dispute over them).

At the same time, however, we find ourselves encouraging them to at least consider whether they could take the divorce case and do a competent job. We do this for three reasons. First, we believe that many newly-minted lawyers, with time on their hands to do the job right, can do as good a job as many experienced attorneys. Second, some clients may find access to the legal system difficult other than through the services of less-experienced — and thus less expensive — lawyers. Third, everybody in every profession must have his or her first case. Fourth, we want to evaluate along with the students what provisos and protections would be necessary if they decide to undertake the domestic case. In other words, how could they ensure that they'd do a good job? The article on "client screening" in **Section 2** is key here. Whether a

student's first case will work out well may have more to do with choosing the right client than anything else.

The idea of becoming competent during the course of the representation is one worthy of significant discussion. On one hand, it sounds like a "legal fiction" created to allow lawyers to represent clients in unfamiliar areas. On the other, the alternative is to preclude lawyers from representing clients in any fields with which they are not familiar.

The mentoring article (**Readings, Section 5**) provides a clear clue to our perspective. We discuss with the students how they could take the incorporation and even the domestic case while getting enough help to be competent, and even good. We believe that part of the answer is to network with one's colleagues, and to call for help as loudly and as often as necessary. We tell our students that our profession is a collegial one, where lawyers are often genuinely happy to provide assistance or to help teach another how to handle a case. Many bar associations now have formal mentoring programs that assist young lawyers in honing their skills.

(d) Law School Education:

This discussion seems inevitably to lead us to a discussion about law school education, and whether students feel it has prepared them for the practice of law. Students are often eager to talk about the role law school education has played, particularly if they are now working in law firms and seeing how it is in the "real world."

We point to Judge Posner's article and the **Readings** in **Sections 4** and **6** on clinics, internships, and continuing education. We like to ask whether taking torts and getting a good grade is more or less helpful to handling a personal injury case than having participated in a legal clinic. Students usually overwhelmingly vote for the clinic. Teachers may find it worthwhile to discuss the MacCrate report, in which the ABA suggested law school education should be more practically based. (A more recent perspective from Robert MacCrate is cited in the **Supplemental Readings**, **#3**, at the end of the Problem.) If the states where your students usually practice have performance exams or programs such as the Illinois' Basic Skills course (**Section 6**) a discussion of these programs can enrich the class.

This subject matter is somewhat tangential and not necessary to an understanding of Problem 1. But we consider it an important piece of the discussion, in part because students find it interesting, and also because it seems to relax them and encourages them to "open up" in a lively debate. We have found that when the first discussion has widespread and enthusiastic student participation, it sets a tone for future discussions, sometimes for the entire semester. This widespread participation will inevitably make the class more successful.

(e) Disclosure:

Let's assume that the new attorney decides to take the domestic case. What must the lawyer disclose to the prospective client about his or her inexperience? This question turns in part on the issue of fiduciary duty, which we raise in the **Readings** in **Section 8**. One significant issue is when fiduciary duty begins. Does it start *before* the representation begins? Or is it "every man (or woman) for himself" until the representation starts?

Most students will feel that some kind of disclosure of their limitations is necessary, but will be afraid that "too much disclosure" will result in the client fleeing out the door, with the result that they'll never get to do that first case. We don't agree. We think candid disclosure can be combined with a little salesmanship. This is a good opportunity for role playing the parts of both the client and the attorney. As the client, the teacher may invite a student to give his or her speech about experience and background, asking enough questions along the way to point out why a limited disclosure doesn't give the client enough information.

We like to role play the speech of the new attorney. This is an excellent opportunity for teachers to use their own practical experience. We like to tell our prospective "clients" something like this:

> "I've never done an incorporation and have never represented anybody on a domestic relations case before. But I promise I will make you the single most important client I have. I'm smart, I'm willing to learn, and I'll work hard for a reasonable fee. And your case will be my absolute highest priority."

Some students who are more comfortable taking the incorporation than the domestic relations case are encouraged by this disclosure statement to at least consider the possibility of taking the domestic case as well. One can suggest to the students that such a speech can even be used as a public relations tool to make the young inexperienced lawyer more attractive, while still being honest with the client.

(f) Referral Fees:

We left Arthur before addressing the question of referral fees. Is Arthur's receiving a referral fee justified if he is merely "holding Ann Wilson's hand"? The difference between a referral fee (for which no work is done) and a fee for actually participating in the case as associate counsel should be discussed briefly. Many students may see this distinction as another legal fiction. But there are legitimate differences between these two roles, and legitimate roles for associate counsel. Is hand holding a legitimate role? We think that in some cases (Ann's may be one, given her trust in Arthur), it is.

The question of whether Arthur can choose Fred rather than Mary because Fred will give Arthur a referral fee is an interesting one. While we generally

do not find ourselves with much time for discussion of this collateral point, we are particularly interested in it because it turns not just on the issue of the propriety of referral fees, but also on the question of when Arthur's fiduciary duty to Ann begins. If he owes her no duty before taking the case, he has no duty to refer her to the *best* lawyer as opposed to another good one. Since Fred is good at his job and will give Arthur a referral fee, such a referral would be appropriate.

But we ask what would happen if Arthur had been representing Ann for a while and decided he needed to bring in a more experienced lawyer. As we will see more fully in **Problem 9** and **Problem 27**, a lawyer has a fiduciary duty to the client which includes putting the client's financial interests ahead of the lawyer's own.

The other issue raised here is whether the referral fee is appropriate at all if Arthur retains no involvement in the case. Prof. Hazard's article in **Section 9** provides a perspective to which the instructor can provide a counterpoint in a classroom discussion.

(g) Fee Arrangements:

If possible, the teacher may want some brief discussion with students about fee agreements, since they are entered into at the beginning of representation. However, we will revisit this issue more thoroughly in **Problem 3**. A related issue is whether the lawyer should charge for the time it takes to become competent. Since a lawyer may undertake a representation and become competent during the course of the representation, should the attorney charge for the time spent to reach a threshold level of competence? Students will have differing views, and there is no bright-line test.

While we come down on the side of not charging for this time, we believe that disclosure, again, is the key. What has the new lawyer advised the client? After the new lawyer has made the speech about how the client will be his or her "most important one," what has the lawyer said about the intent to charge for time learning things that anyone competent in that field would already know? Though we'd prefer a different course, we would agree that *if* proper disclosure were made that "learning time" will be charged (and presumably reduced rates were being charged due to the lawyer's inexperience), the lawyer could bill for this time.

PROBLEM 2

Must We Take This Case?

THE POINT BEHIND THE PROBLEM:

The focus of this problem is to evaluate how far a lawyer must go in putting aside personal feelings or personal advancement in agreeing to undertake a case. The problem attempts to answer whether there is a duty on the part of lawyers to represent unwanted or unpleasant clients where comparable legal services may not otherwise be available. We personally believe strongly in pro bono work (**Problem 31** presents the issue, and our perspective). But we ultimately conclude here that lawyers simply need not *ever* set aside their personal feelings in determining whether to undertake a *particular* case, nor must they set aside their own economic goals, personal advancement or political agendas. Once the case is taken, however, the story is very different, and they owe their clients all the fiduciary duties described in the previous problem.

Despite our ultimate conclusion, we find the discussion of these issues a fruitful one. It serves as a counterpoint to the first problem by emphasizing that the decision to undertake a case may turn on a lawyer's — or a law firm's — practical, personal, political, and economic perspectives.

APPLICABLE RULES:

Model Rules:	MRs 1.2; 1.7; 1.16; 6.1, especially (b)(3); 6.2
Model Code:	DR 2-109; 5-101; ECs 1-1; 2-1; 2-26; 2-27; 2-28; 2-30; 7-1
CA B&P:	6068(h)

SUGGESTED QUESTIONS TO ASK:

- How useful are the ethical rules in dealing with this problem?

- Don't law students argue both sides of moot court questions? Shouldn't lawyers be able to represent divergent views with which they do not agree?

- Isn't it necessary for lawyers to represent people espousing unpopular causes, in order to ensure that all are able to find representation?

- Have you as students had any experiences where you were asked to help provide legal services to someone whom you found more than a little distasteful?

- Would any student here say "I will *never* represent anyone whose cause I don't believe in?"

- Can you be competent and sufficiently zealous on behalf of someone whose ideas you abhor?

- Suppose one of your law firm's stated purposes is to provide representation for those who speak out, regardless of the content of their speech; would that change your mind about taking on Hemp's case?

- would it change your mind if the John firm were the only firm in the area capable of handling a free speech case like Hemp's?

- Can you justify the firm's willingness to represent Prof. Jerrold while refusing to represent Hemp?

- As an associate, how would you go about objecting to a new firm client?

- Would your decision to protest a new client depend on how you think you'd fare in your next evaluation?

- What would happen where no representation can be found for an individual, such as in the *Mallard* case? How would you deal with this situation?

SUGGESTED ROLE PLAYS:

- The teacher and students together role play a partnership meeting of the John law firm.

- Role play a law firm partner who advocates taking the case for reasons of free speech, *or* because the economic factors can be dealt with, *or* because the John law firm is the only available firm in the area, and so on; see if you can persuade the students (your law firm "partners") that Hemp's case must be taken on.

- Role play a Jewish or African-American partner who says "I'll resign if you take this case."

- Role play associate telling a partner "I will not work on this case."

SUGGESTED VIDEOS:

- Client unpopular in the community: *To Kill a Mockingbird* — Atticus explaining his defense of Tom Robinson to the victim's father. DVD Chap. 9, 22:30 — 23:42.

- Representing a challenging client: *I Am Sam* — "My lawyer thinks I am retarded." DVD Chap. 11, 1:00:08 - 01:22.

DISCUSSION:

(a) Overview:

This problem will simply not be answered concretely by black-letter rules. We discuss the rules and their limited utility in **Section 1** of the **Readings**. Even the language of the California State Bar Act ("never to reject for any [personal considerations] ... the cause of the defenseless or the oppressed") may not apply to Hemp because she is more likely to be seen as the oppressor than the oppressed, and a university professor is unlikely to be viewed as defenseless.

The rules tell us of the importance of providing legal assistance to those who might not otherwise gain adequate representation. But the unpleasant nature of this representation will be a lot for many students to swallow. We find, however, that many other students tend to bend over backwards to overcome their personal feelings, even when they are doing this because they think the "right answer" is to take Hemp's case.

We often begin discussion of this problem by suggesting role playing a partnership meeting of the John law firm. We often have students list on the blackboard the reasons given in the problem for turning down the case and evaluate the adequacy of each, either in turn or in combination.

Generally, the students find themselves caught between their personal instincts not to take Prof. Hemp's case and their concern that there may be some ethical obligation to do it. Once they have evaluated all of the reasons not to take the case, it is easier for them to feel "OK" about simply saying no to representing Prof. Hemp. Students sometimes feel in the beginning of the discussion that they are choosing between the "ethical" thing to do and practical realities, such as the economics of their law practice. For example, one student recently asked whether his consideration of economic concerns meant that he was ignoring the ethical issues.

Before we end our discussion, we want to make sure we have reassured these students that turning down Hemp is *not* unethical. Rather, we emphasize how discussing the pros and cons of representing her can itself be an ethical process, by helping us understand how our motives relate to our decision.

(b) Representing Clients Whose Views You Hate:

The students may point out (the teacher can if they don't) that traditional law school curricula involve students arguing both sides of the same moot court problem, and the like. Should lawyers represent views that disagree with their own? Is this a laudable goal since it ensures widespread representation?

Ask students about their own experiences helping people whom they found distasteful. They will generally be eager to discuss this. They can be asked whether any of them would claim "I never represent anyone whose cause I

don't believe in." Even those who feel most strongly about coordinating one's beliefs with one's clients may acknowledge the fact of life that from time to time, they will have to represent people in whose causes they do not believe. This is an opportunity to discuss large law firm practice, where associates cannot control their clientele and are asked to work on cases as required by their partners.

When it comes to someone as abhorrent to many as Prof. Hemp, some students will raise the issue of whether they can be sufficiently competent and "zealous" on her behalf, given that the views she espouses are anathema to their own beliefs. But begging off from representing someone like Prof. Hemp on this basis may dodge the main issue of whether the law firm is going to exercise its "personal right" to refuse the case. Students who press this point should be tested on it, such as by asking whether they can conceive of a situation in which they "have to" represent somebody reprehensible or at least very unlikable, and whether they can put their personal feelings aside to do it. Most will admit they probably can. (We'll revisit this issue in **Problem 14**.)

(c) Why Turn Down Hemp's Case:

The problem suggests several reasons for turning down Prof. Hemp's case. Among them are: (1) her political views themselves, and the firm members' distaste for them; (2) the political aspirations of Dean John; (3) the danger of losing other valuable clients of the firm; (4) the problem in recruiting top-level students, particularly minority students; (5) the strong objections of one Jewish partner; (6) the general image of the firm in the legal community. Aligned against this is the firm's apparent commitment to free speech and Dean John's close relationship with the teachers' union. These last factors may not be enough, even if coupled with what the students perceive as a generalized ethical obligation, to persuade the students that Hemp must be represented.

(d) Playing Devil's Advocate and Re-Balancing the Scales:

The teacher can play devil's advocate, role play a partner who is pressing the point of why the case should be taken, or add factors in favor of taking the case, to re-balance the scales. Among the factors the teacher can add are what the firm stands for — that is, the sign over the firm's door, whether symbolic or otherwise, that says this firm represents those who speak out, regardless of the content of that speech.

Another factor to pose to students is that if the John firm, noted for the taking of these cases, turns down Prof. Hemp, no one in town is likely to represent her; thus, she may be denied representation completely. We like to ask the students what would happen if this is the only firm in the area capable of giving Hemp adequate representation.

Since students may focus on the harm to Dean John's political career, you may want to tweak the hypothetical by making John Badou handle the case, and not Dean.

If students raise the economic damage to the firm from the case, the teacher can suggest that the firm's senior partners are confident they can persuade the confection company of the value of protecting free speech and thus talk them out of leaving, and persuade their Jewish clients to stick it out with them regardless of the representation of Hemp. Use the Credit Suisse example (see **Readings, Section 5**) to demonstrate the various approaches a law firm can use when deciding whether to take a case.

The teacher can also point out the inequity between the firm's past willingness to represent the equally repugnant African-American Professor Jerrold and now refusing to represent Hemp. The only apparent material difference between these two is that Hemp is white. Finally, we ask the students to change the university's location to a rural county, where the John firm may be the *only* possible source of representation for Hemp.

All this may persuade a few students that perhaps the representation *must* be undertaken. Students are particularly affected by the lack of other available counsel. But the real point is to demonstrate that *even if* all these factors are present, the law firm still has no obligation to undertake the representation.

(e) Happy, Healthy?:

Law students get their first taste of life as a big firm associate through the first of two excerpts of Prof. Schiltz's excellent 1999 *Happy, Healthy* article (**Readings, Section 6**). Our hope is that they will come to understand how difficult it can be to work within a large firm, here to try to persuade the firm not to take a client that is guaranteed to bring in big billings. Students can debate various ways of approaching a firm's management committee. A discussion of salary, life-style, and their willingness to take a moral stand should be included.

(f) What then Should the John Firm Do?

There is much, including the example of such lawyers as Michael Tigar and Anthony Griffin (see **Sections 2 and 3** of the **Readings**), and the language of ethical considerations and such statutes as the California Business and Professions Code cited in the **Readings, Section 1**, which argue in favor of taking the case of even the most reprehensible of clients. But where an Anthony Griffin agrees to represent a client he abhors, he nevertheless has sensible personal and professional reasons for doing so, such as the vital importance of protecting free speech or academic freedom. Many criminal defense lawyers refer to their representation of unpleasant and violent criminal defendants as their effort to uphold the Fifth and Sixth Amendments to the Constitution, as we'll see further in **Problem 14**. The brief **Section 4** in the

Readings offers the example of lawyers representing suspected terrorists or, in the case of Lynne Stewart, the "blind sheikh." The instructor might lead a discussion of the consequences to those who represent the extreme in unpopular clients.

We believe that where a law firm undertakes to represent Prof. Hemp, it does so because the goals involved (upholding free speech and academic freedom) outweigh the detriments. Whatever Lynne Stewart's unethical actions, she made a choice to represent the sheik, the same choice made by Tigar and Griffin. But where a firm believes that the detriments (loss of political advantage, economic considerations, etc.) outweigh the benefits, that firm is perfectly within its right to decline the representation, and will likely do so.

Our own belief is that *any* reason proffered by a lawyer for not being willing to take a *particular* case (as opposed to all cases of a particular type, or all pro bono cases) is sufficient. We all have the right to maintain the freedom to choose whether a particular individual or entity will become our client. In so doing, we are entitled to choose based on any reasons which appeal to us, including such subjective matters as our impression of the individual as a person.

(g) Court Appointed Pro Bono Work:

The teacher may want to touch on the enforced pro bono issue that takes the last several pages of the **Readings (Sections 7** and **8**). What happens when no representation can be found may be what occurred in the *Mallard* case. We use this as a preview of **Problem 31**, which directly discusses whether pro bono work should be required of all attorneys.

PROBLEM 3

Getting a Client and Getting Paid

THE POINT BEHIND THE PROBLEM:

Problem 3 creates a relatively straightforward situation involving undertaking a case. This problem builds on **Problem 1** by focusing on three essential elements of most cases — the inception of a lawyer-client relationship; paying fees; and the scope of representation.

Part I of the problem evaluates to what extent a lawyer may find herself with an unwanted, even surprise client. Students will have to parse carefully the details of the conversation between Tennant and her old classmate to determine *whether* an attorney-client relationship existed, the consequences of that relationship including malpractice implications, and the course(s) Tennant might have taken to avoid this sticky situation.

In Part II, there is no question about the attorney-client relationship, but many questions about the *scope* of the engagement. While Part I foreshadows the issue of the scope of representation if Tennant has gotten herself a client, what is the breadth of her responsibility? Part II deals with this issue directly. The two paragraphs that constitute **Question 3** of **Part II** focuses directly on the scope of representation and how a vaguely-worded scope is likely to inure to the benefit of the client and the detriment of the lawyer.

The other portions of **Part II** directly address ways in which lawyers may (or may not) obtain a fee. As indicated by the order of the Readings, we tend to discuss the scope of representation issue first, and then look at various aspects of collecting a fee. The fees suggested by the problem come in several "modern" forms: a hybrid hourly fee and percentage interest in the corporation, a different twist on contingent fees, and the ambiguity that may exist when fee agreements are not explicitly clear.

Explicit clarity is one overriding principle to be learned here. Part of any lawyer's duty, particularly at the beginning of the case, is to communicate clearly. When the scope of representation or the fee arrangement are not explicitly clear, there is both an excellent chance that some clients will not understand these matters, and a good chance that, whether they understand or not, certain clients will use any ethical ambiguity as grounds for an advantage, including a malpractice claim.

APPLICABLE RULES:

Model Rules: MRs 1.1; 1.2; 1.4; 1.5; 1.8, especially (a), (e), and (i).
Model Code: DRs 2-103; 2-106; 2-107; 5-101(A); 5-103; 5-104(A); 7-101; ECs 5-1, 5-3, 5-5, 5-7, 5-8, and 7-8.

CA Rules: 3-110; 3-300; 3-500; 4-100; 4-200; 4-210
CA B&P: 6068(m); 6147; 6148; 6149

SUGGESTED QUESTIONS TO ASK:

- If Olive really became Alice Tennant's client, what was it exactly that Alice was obligated to do?

- Does what Tennant told Olive rise to the level of "legal advice"? Or is it merely the friendly imparting of legal information?

- Was there a better – or at least a safer – way for Alice to give Olive a little friendly advice?

- Does this story convince you that you should never give any advice to anyone at a cocktail party or in another off-the-cuff situation? Being realistic, do you really think you can live up to this standard?

- Was Tennant's real mistake not following up with Olive when Olive didn't make an appointment? Or had Alice already created a problem for herself?

- Is the Martini/Tennant scenario primarily about poor ethics, poor malpractice avoidances, or both?

- Would Olive have as good an argument that she had gotten legal advice from Alice if Tennant had advised the audience generally in her speech that it is always important to make sure that there is adequate insurance coverage?

- Did Joan Goebel's contract provide too broad a scope of representation? Has Joan been incompetent, merely negligent, or neither?

- How could Goebel have narrowed the scope of her engagement? Should she have added "Services to be rendered" that she was not going to ensure transfer of the liquor license at boat and jet ski titles? Would this have been enough?

- Is it ethical for Joan to receive as much as 10% of Jerry's company's stock as payment for her work?

- Is this ethical even if Joan continues to receive a $50/hour fee as well? Or a contingency fee? Is there an ethical difference between these two?

- What, if anything, should or must Joan do before agreeing to take stock in Jerry's company?

- What, if anything, should or must Joan do before agreeing to change part of her fee to a contingency?

- If she strongly suspects that it will work to her significant economic advantage, may Joan agree to a contingency fee without advising Jerry of this advantage?

- Given that Goebel only spent sixty hours on the marina matter, does Hamilton have a good argument that the fee charged is excessive?

- What did you think of the fees in the *Brobeck* and *Fordham* cases? Do you agree with the decisions? Which fee did you consider more excessive? Too excessive?

SUGGESTED ROLE PLAYS:

- Play the role of Olive as someone who is attempting to draw out Alice Tennant to get free legal advice.

- Role play the part of Olive as someone who innocently asks a question and has no hidden agenda.

- Play the part of a friend of one of your students who at a social function asks, "Say, Georg[e][ina], you go to law school; what do you think about ...." in order to see how the student handles the answer.

- Play the part of Jerry Hamilton suggesting that Goebel take a percentage of stock, and see how the student handles Goebel's role.

- Play the part of Jerry Hamilton explaining to Joan Goebel after the fact why he considers the problem with title to the boats to be Goebel's fault.

SUGGESTED VIDEOS:

- Insider stock holdings: *The Insider* DVD chap. 20, 1:43:23 - 48:15

DISCUSSION:

There should be enough time to handle both aspects of this problem. We suggest beginning with the issue of whether the attorney-client relationship exists, move on to the scope of representation in both **Part I** and **Part II**, and then discuss the attorneys' fees and stock issues in the second scenario. We also try to be mindful about distinguishing between ethical behavior and potential malpractice.

(a) The Inception of an Attorney-Client Relationship:

Can it really be that just by asking a couple of questions at the end of a speech, Olive Martini has become Alice Tennant's client? Is it possible that Tennant's suggestion to make sure to avoid being underinsured rises to the level of giving legal advice? Students may tend to doubt these propositions, but we think that — at least as the problem is drafted — the best answer to

both these questions is "yes." The **Readings, Sections 1, 3,** and **4** (in **Section 4** we particularly address duties to those who may not be clients), and the famous *Togstad* case cited in the **Supplementary Readings**, support this thesis.

We also believe that the actual transaction between Olive and Alice, in contrast, involves legal advice. Alice gives no admonishment or warning about the inadequacy of her advice; while she tells Olive to call her on Monday, this was not a prerequisite to giving information to Olive. This is particularly true since Alice provides the information in response to a relatively detailed set of specific facts described by Olive. These specifics distinguish this advice from the general "get enough insurance" advice Tennant may have suggested in her speech. Alice has not been sufficiently circumspect, and her comments do not, in our view, protect her from having obtained a new client or claiming not to have imparted advice rather than information.

A few more specific points: First, there is a narrow line between advice and information. If everything said about the law were legal advice, we would all be practicing law every day. But pointing out the speed limit in a school zone is imparting legal *information*, not advice. Matters are more likely to rise to the level of advice when a specific legal circumstance is involved, and the question asks for knowledge beyond the ken of most nonlawyers. Here, as **Question 4** of the problem suggests, the effect on a *known* pre-existing condition has legal implications for Olive.

Second, the Internet and the nature of legal services for the poor have turned far more scrutiny on limited scope of representation issues. The **Readings, Section 4** introduce the website client and "unbundled" legal services, concepts we'll return to at length in **Problem 6** on technology, and **Problem 31** on pro bono work. But this is a good time for a brief discussion, or at least mention, of these two emerging issues.

(b) A Client for Purposes of Confidentiality:

A third point concerns the issue of a client "for purposes of confidentiality," which we discuss in the **Readings, Section 2** and again briefly in **Section 4**. Two subpoints here: first, as we intimate in this Problem and discuss more fully in **Problem 4**, students must recognize that even if there is *no* attorney-client relationship, the lawyer may owe the putative client the duty of confidentiality; second, we raise the issue of whether there is any difference between getting a new client and imparting legal advice.

While the terminology is different, and there are certainly clients for purposes of confidentiality, here we see Olive's "clienthood" and Alice's giving legal advice as a whole, essentially two sides of the same coin. While the **Readings, Section 4** contain a discussion of non-client beneficiaries of legal services, we see Olive as a client in the more traditional sense. The

question is what is the scope of Tennant's representation and her duties to Olive?

(c) Malpractice Liability:

The third point concerns the difference between ethics and malpractice issues, a recurring theme we emphasized in **Problem 1**. While we have come to believe that malpractice is an intrinsically significant portion of a full-coverage course in legal ethics or professional responsibility, it is important to distinguish between Tennant's possible "mere" negligence and the ethical standard of competence. If Alice is to be held liable for malpractice, it does not mean she has acted unethically.

Is Alice likely to be found liable for malpractice? Under the facts as given, we think it is substantially more likely than not. Once the issue of "clienthood" is resolved, evaluating the advice itself is somewhat easier: Alice ignored information available to her in giving advice to avoid being underinsured, did no research — hardly possible under the circumstances, our students will point out, but absent nonetheless, and did nothing to qualify her advice until the anticipated office meeting.

Is this a harsh result? Yes, undoubtedly, particularly if Olive set up her old friend to do exactly what she did. (In teaching this scenario to lawyers, we often added that Olive had, not so coincidentally, brought the lease with her.) Students, who undoubtedly will acknowledge that they too have given cocktail-party legal advice — which, incidentally is, strictly speaking, also the unauthorized practice of law — may say that they will never say anything off-the-cuff again other than "I don't give advice. I'll see you in my office." We believe that this is unrealistic, for lawyers and students alike like to talk, even show off. In fact, the point here, as in **Part I** of **Problem 5**, is not to say "Don't do it," but to suggest realistic protections.

(d) What Could Alice Have Done?:

Is there any way for Alice to avoid this harsh result? It may come down to semantics and record-keeping. The importance of semantics — a recurring theme in this book — should not be underestimated. Alice has done little to qualify her advice or to define it as non-legal. This is a good opportunity to role-play Olive and see how our students could do a better job.

Some ideas that come to mind: (1) Alice might specifically warn that she cannot give legal advice over a post-speech cocktail, and while *generally* anyone must be careful to have insurance, Olive would have to come to Tennant's office to get actual legal advice; (2) After the disclaimer, Alice might say something about what *she* might do in similar circumstances, but again emphasize that legal advice can only occur in the office; (3) We have heard lawyers emphasize that the information Olive is getting is worth exactly what Olive is paying for it.

Perhaps more important is the necessity to follow up the meeting with a letter. We don't generally believe in so-called "CYA letters," believing that actually protecting the client works to the best advantage of the lawyer. However, this is one instance where the protection of the lawyer's interest is as important a reason to write a follow-up letter as protecting the client's interests. A letter from Tennant saying that Olive did not call for an appointment as planned, that Tennant provided only offhand "seat of the pants" *information* during a friendly cocktail hour, and that Olive should not rely on such information as advice will go a long way towards protecting Alice. It also helps *Olive*, who will be informed that merely following Alice's suggestion about insurance may not be enough to protect her.

It is of more than passing moment that **ABA MR 1.4**, governing communicating with clients, underwent wholesale changes in 2002 that increase the duties of lawyers to communicate clearly with clients. Some instructors may find it valuable to have students examine a redlined copy of the two versions of the rule to see how the ABA's thinking has changed. **MR 1.2**, on the scope of representation, also underwent significant recent changes.

(e) Fee Agreements Generally:

Before evaluating Goebel's fee agreement specifically, it is useful to ask a more general question: what are the essential elements of any fee agreement? Students usually do a rather good job in defining these elements, including the rate of compensation, the manner and means of payment (such as a contingency fee), and even the payment of costs. Another component, somewhat more difficult for students but at least as important, is defining the scope of representation, discussed below.

It is also valuable to have a brief discussion of the wisdom of putting fee agreements in writing. One of the major (and relatively few) defeats the Ethics 2000 Commission suffered was the attempt to require written fee contracts. (They are required under **MR 1.5** for contingency cases.) Nevertheless, it seems foolhardy to us for a lawyer not to memorialize a fee contract in writing for her *own* protection.

(f) Scope of Representation:

We begin our discussion of Joan Goebel's fee agreement with the issue of "scope of representation." Remember that the ABA rule, **MR 1.2**, changed significantly in 2002.

What did Joan sign on to do? It was clear between her and Hamilton that he was going to take care of title to the boats and jet skis. Yet the written agreement makes no mention of this limitation. (Note that while we point out, in **Readings, Section 5**, that many states still do not require written fee agreements, verbal agreements will likely do little to protect the lawyer against a client claiming a broader scope of representation. Juries and other finders of

fact are far more likely to point to the failure of the lawyer to make things clear in writing.)

It is worth noting a parallel between the scope of representation here and in Part I of the Problem. There, assuming Olive became a client, the scope of representation is obviously very narrow and transitory. Narrow though it may be, it still exists, for the purpose of giving advice on a single occasion.

How should Goebel have defined the scope of the engagement? Most students — and most lawyers we've presented with this problem — will be satisfied if the instructor presents them with a phrase such as "Lawyer shall *not* be responsible for obtaining title to boats, jet skis, or other water vehicles." But this is *not* necessarily sufficient, either to apprise the client of the limits of responsibility or to protect against a malpractice suit. A far better alternative is language that also excludes Goebel from being involved in any way regarding the water vehicles, including *giving any advice* to Hamilton about *how* he should go about obtaining title. Only in this way is it clear that the *entire* responsibility falls on him — doing the work and figuring out how to accomplish the work.

Such limitations of scope are necessary both to fully apprise the client and to protect the lawyer. They frequently come in situations where clients are trying to shave costs, an understandable goal. It is laudable for lawyers to cooperate with this goal, but it is of vital importance for fee agreements to be detail-oriented, so that they carefully circumscribe the extent of the representation.

(g) Stock for Services?:

The **Readings**, **Section 9**, especially the Ringel article and the **Notes** immediately preceding it, specifically address this issue. Receiving stock (or options) for services is worrisome, but increasingly becoming a reality, even a necessity. Where a "start-up" does not have the cash flow to be able to pay for legal services in the ordinary way, it couldn't exist without some alternate form of payment. We have far less difficulty with taking stock at the commencement of a company's operation than later on in the process. Obviously, the rules of professional conduct regarding doing business with a client (**MR 1.8(a)**, especially the newly-revised language of **1.8(a)(3)**, **Cal. Rule 3-300**, etc.) must be scrupulously followed. Notice in our companion **Rules Book's Rules Comparison Section** the differences between these rules are noted.

The hybrid nature of the fees charged by Goebel does not provide any additional reason to give us pause. Such arrangements at the start-up stage may be necessary in order to create the entity at all. Again, we are far more troubled with post-start-up stock arrangements. Those relationships that cannot be justified by necessity to the client seem to serve the interests of the lawyers rather than those of the clients. They are not unlawful or unethical, but we

prefer to advise against engaging in them. The danger for the kinds of conflicts of interest we discuss in **Problem 9** are simply too great.

(h) Contingency Fees:

As the **Readings, Section 6** indicate, there are many criticisms of contingency fees, but few actual limitations. In fact, our tort system would not exist in its current form without them. Moreover, in our view, poor and modest-means individuals would face enormous obstacles in gaining access to the legal system. Hybrid contingent/hourly or contingent/flat fees are becoming increasingly common. We see no inherent prohibition in a hybrid stock/contingency fee, although it will be subject to closer scrutiny because it *twice* involves the issue of doing business with a client (although, as the first paragraph of **Section 6** states, contingent fees are generally considered exempt from this rule.)

Still, assuming the pitfalls described in the Readings can be avoided, we have little doubt a hybrid stock/contingency fee would be upheld in the Hamilton matter. This is more likely to be true since Hamilton proposed the contingency fee arrangement. See the **Readings** following **Section 7**, and particularly the *Raymark* case.

(i) Excessive Fees?:

A brief review of both cases excerpted in **Section 7** is worthwhile. In the *Brobeck* case, Moses Lasky received his $1 million fee because he had performed as promised, complete with the use of his then-illustrious reputation. In the interesting *Fordham* decision, the fees were deemed excessive despite an excellent result. The notes after *Fordham* attempt to articulate the reasons for the different decisions, and the **Readings** in **Section 8** provide further information on the more specific issue of the relationship between value of the case and value of the fees. We are not convinced that the *Fordham* case is likely to be widely followed.

We strongly suspect that sophistication of the client — present in *Brobeck* but not in Fordham — is a significant factor. Further, given Fordham's excellent result and his forthright notice to his client's father, the fee payor, about both his billing method and his inexperience, it appears that what put Fordham over the top for disciplinary purposes was his billing for learning-curve time, a point made by the *Fordham* court, and discussed by us in **Problem 1**.

PROBLEM 4

Roger Earl Receives Some Evidence

THE POINT BEHIND THE PROBLEM:

The principal purpose of this problem is to introduce the attorney-client confidential relationship in a dramatic context. The context — the presentation and possible secretion of evidence — is used as a vehicle to show that there are some limits on attorney-client confidences, and to examine where these outer boundaries should be drawn. This problem also highlights the complexity of the attorney-client confidential relationship.

Some teachers may prefer to begin the discussion of confidentiality with **Problem 5** rather than **Problem 4**. **Problem 5** deals with confidentiality in a somewhat more straightforward context, using three different examples of when confidentiality becomes an issue. We prefer to begin with **Problem 4** because its high dramatic content engages the students' interest. But in this problem, the discussion of confidentiality has the complicating factor that it flows from the revelation of evidence disclosed by the client to the lawyer.

Students will quickly realize that the issue of confidential communication is far more complicated than it may initially appear. Some specific points raised in this problem are rather clearly defined by rules and case law. But many major issues are not susceptible to facile analysis, including the problem's principal issue: What should the lawyers do with evidence proffered by the client during a confidential communication? Students should debate how lawyers balance their duties to maintain client confidences with the duty not to assist in the client's commission of a crime or suppression of evidence.

Finally, through the *Garrow* case (**Readings, Section 1**), in which Garrow's lawyers maintained his confidences by not revealing where two bodies were buried, the students will perceive, for the first of many times during the course, the tension between their duty to one's client, and what they would ordinarily believe is the "morally right" thing to do.

APPLICABLE RULES:

Model Rules:	MRs 1.2, especially (d) and 2002 Comment paragraphs 9 and 10 (1983 Comment (6) and (7)); 1.6; 3.3; 4.1. (Note significant changes to MR 1.6, and to MR 1.2, Comment, paragraphs (6) and (7).)
Model Code:	DRs 1-102; 4-101, especially (C); 7-102; ECs 4-1; 4-2; 4-4; 7-1; 7-5; 7-8.
CA Rules:	3-100, 5-220.
CA B&P:	6068(e)(1) and (e)(2).

SUGGESTED QUESTIONS TO ASK:

- What would you have done if you were Garrow's lawyers? Would you have been *able* to do what they did?

- What would you do if you were in the position of the lawyer whose client will not tell his partner that he has contracted AIDS? Do you agree with how Delaware dealt with this issue?

- What would you do if you were the lawyer in Zacharias' hypothetical #3 where your defense doctor discovers a life-threatening aneurysm in plaintiff?

- What constitutes possession of the gun? Is it sufficiently under Earl's control when sitting on the desk? Or must he take it or at least touch it in some way?

- Once Earl has the gun on his desk, how can he justify allowing Adams to take it back, even if Earl has not so much as touched it?

- If Earl feels obligated to turn the gun over to the police, is he obligated to first tell Adams what he is going to do?

- Isn't Earl's telling Adams what he will do with the gun tantamount to advising Adams to get rid of it himself?

- If the gun or money bag must be turned over, in what form must it be? Must Earl identify himself and whose gun or bag it is?

- Could Earl mail the gun or money to the D.A. in a plain brown paper bag, and let them figure out to which case it belongs?

- Would the court treat intangible evidence (where the witness saw something, for example) differently from tangible evidence? Fruits and instrumentalities of a crime versus mere evidence?

- Would Earl's withdrawal from the case do any good? Why, or why not?

SUGGESTED ROLE PLAYS:

- Play the part of Adams giving Earl the gun and asking what to do, to emphasize the drama and immediacy of the situation.

- Play the part of Earl advising Adams; change the import of his advice not so much by what he says, but by the way in which he says it. You can use the *exact* same words but vary your tone of voice to leave a clearly different impression of your meaning.

- Play the part of Earl and/or a judge examining Earl if Earl turns the gun over to the D.A. anonymously, without indicating where it came from.

- Role play Carlton seeking advice from Earl though he has not previously been Earl's client: or play Earl as if he believes that he has no

responsibility to maintain Carlton's confidences, to underscore Carlton's reasonable expectation of confidentiality.

SUGGESTED VIDEOS:

- The buried bodies case: *Ethics on Trial*, WETA Washington D.C. Public Television, 1986, first segment, interview of attorney Frank Armani by Fred Graham (11 minutes).

- What to do with evidence discovered at the crime scene: *Primal Fear*, DVD Chap. 16, 1:09:09 — 1:11:10.

- Transmitting evidence to the prosecution: *Primal Fear*, DVD chap. 19, 1:24:02 - 28:04.

- The meaning of confidentiality explained: *The Firm* — Confidentiality turned on its head to save a lawyer — Tom Cruise explains to the "clients" why he can never say anything bad about them because "I am your lawyer," DVD chap. To Be Identified

- Confidentiality of documents: *The Rainmaker* — confidential documents from an ex-employee, DVD chap. 26, 1:43:46 — 1:45:10.

THE DISCUSSION:

(a) Overview:

The problem has been designed with Adams as the primary focus of discussion, with reference as needed to Baker. Between these two clients, they cover the range of general issues on the subject of confidentiality. There is no significant difference between Adams' bringing the gun to Earl and Baker's telling Earl where the money is hidden except that the gun on the desk presents a far more difficult and immediate problem. Nor does it actually matter much that Carlton is not a client when he walks in, because he is a client for purposes of confidences, as we discuss in **Section 8**. Carlton is included to make that point, and Dunn is included because he is planning a crime *in the future*, which Earl may not be involved in assisting.

Both Adams and Baker involve the client's confidential presentation not merely of evidence, but of the fruits or instrumentalities of a crime. The differences between Baker and Adams are three: While both cases involve more than mere evidence, Baker's case involves the fruits rather than the instrumentality of a crime; Baker's evidence is located outside the lawyer's office, rather than physically presented to the lawyer; and without Baker's evidence the DA's case is weak. We don't believe these differences significantly change the analysis.

The presentation and disclosure of evidence by Roger Earl's clients makes his situation analogous to both the *Ryder* and *Meredith* cases (**Readings,**

Sections 3, 4, and 5). We recommend that these two cases and the readings analyzing them be discussed thoroughly by the students.

(b)   The Issue of Confidentiality Itself:

Roger Earl is such a wonderful opportunity for role play that students may launch into Adams' presentation of the gun, and what to do with the gun, before stopping to evaluate the basic issue of confidentiality itself. We find it useful to turn as soon as possible after the beginning of the discussion to examine the principle of confidentiality directly. The series of readings in **Section 1** about the famous case of the lawyers who discover two buried bodies in upstate New York form an excellent basis for this discussion. Students find these readings particularly interesting, even compelling. We couple them with a showing of the 11-minute segment of video of Frank Armani, referred to in the **SUGGESTED VIDEOS** section above. Although the video is now 20 years old, the poignancy and difficulty of the situation, as Armani saw it, gives it our vote as the most compelling video we use.

In reading what Garrow's two lawyers did — and did not do — students are often torn between the obligation many perceive, to maintain the confidences of their clients, and their inability to remain silent in the face of the horrors of a body buried in a mine shaft. Some draw an "ethical/moral" distinction between what the rules might require and how they would feel compelled to act. This provides another opportunity to discuss briefly the interrelationship of the rules of ethics and one's own sense of morality.

Beyond mere rumination, however, students should examine the Garrow case in the light of other information. Of particular value are the confidentiality exceptions suggested by Prof. Zacharias in **Section 11** of the **Readings**, and the insoluble dilemma confronting a lawyer concerned about the transmission of AIDS (**Readings, Section 9**). We have now incorporated Zacharias' hypotheticals into the problem. Particularly compelling is his third hypothetical, familiar to us as *Spaulding v. Zimmerman*.

Regarding the rules, it is useful to ask students how they should evaluate the exceptions to confidentiality set forth in the two versions of **MR 1.6**, as well as **DR 4-101(C)**. Here the differences between the 1983 Rules, as amended, and the 2002 Rules are substantial and important. The 2002 version eliminates three qualifiers: that the act be criminal, imminent, or committed by the client. A majority of states already had a rule with more exceptions than "old" **MR 1.6**.

For those in California, since our last edition California has ceased to become the only state in which no exceptions to confidentiality existed in the ethics rules. After several failed attempts by bar groups to convince California's Supreme Court to add an ABA-style rule, the legislature, which has joint responsibility for lawyers' ethics, amended **CA B&P Code 6068(e)** to add **(e)(2)**, a narrow, ABA-1983-version exception to confidentiality.

While most states' rules no longer require imminence or a client's crime, it remains useful to briefly discuss whether such rules can or will ever be applied literally. That is, even if their state's ethics rule allows only a narrow exception, will the students really maintain their clients' confidentiality in the face of imminent AIDS transmittal, or where the defense doctor finds a life-threatening aneurysm in plaintiff? And what about the buried bodies? Even the 2002 ABA Rules have no grounds for revealing information there. (We revisit the issue of confidentiality in the face of corporate product danger, similar to Zacharias' hypotheticals 4 and 13, in **Problem 25**.)

(c) The Gun:

Students will have differing views on what Roger Earl should do with the gun. The potential solutions cover a broad range: turn the gun over to the police; turn it over but only anonymously; refuse to take possession of the weapon in the first place, thereby hoping to avoid the necessity of turning it over; take possession of the gun but without turning it over.

Little in this range can clearly be ruled out as a reasonable alternative except the last, which seems to be in direct conflict with *Ryder*. If students express the belief that they can take possession of the gun and not turn it over, they should be confronted more directly with the *Ryder* and *Meredith* cases, which strongly argue the impropriety of any active participation on the part of the lawyer in concealing the fruits or instrumentalities of crimes.

The teacher will be valuable in acting as devil's advocate here, to underscore the tension between the duty to maintain confidences and the need to avoid assisting in the client's criminal activity. If the students conclude that the gun has to be turned over to the police, the teacher might emphasize these questions: What about the oath of confidentiality all lawyers are sworn to follow? How can violating a confidence be justified? On the other hand, some students may argue that Earl should refuse possession of the gun and leave it — and the decision about what to do with it — to Adams. Here, the teacher might inquire how the students plan to inform Adams of this news. If they reply that they would tell Adams that if they take the gun they must turn it over, the teacher can ask whether turning the gun over and abandoning the client's interests is any different from telling the client that one is about to do so.

We see the key issue as being whether Earl has *actively* participated in the concealment or possessed the concealed item, whether gun or money. We believe it would be appropriate to decline to take the gun so long as Earl has done nothing at all with it. More clearly, we see no obligation at all on the part of Earl to dig up the money. We believe that Earl may advise his clients that if he does take the gun or the money, he is obligated to turn either over to the appropriate authorities. But the ramifications of that disclosure can be significant, as we see below.

(d) What Should the Client Be Told?

As we have just seen, the question of what to do with the gun will necessarily include the issue of what the client will be told. Adams and Baker will want to know what's going to happen. Clients are, after all, entitled to candid communications from their attorneys. If Earl feels obligated to turn over the gun to the police, is he equally obligated to inform Adams of his intentions? The teacher should help students to appreciate the irony that the very act of informing the client what Earl will do with the gun may color what *Adams himself* will actually do. Thus, if Earl says that if he keeps the gun he will have to turn it in, that may well have the effect of telling even a modestly sophisticated Adams to grab the gun back and find a way to destroy it himself.

Role playing is particularly valuable in discussing this issue, and student discussion leaders who choose to act out the roles of Adams and Earl are often both enlightening and entertaining. The teacher will also serve a valuable function by playing these roles with a perspective that differs from the students'.

The particular value of role playing in this problem is that it serves to point out that "real life" is not like a transcript, and that conversations between lawyer and client are dynamic ones, with emotional content to the words. Phrasing, manner of presentation and nonverbal cues can make all the difference in the world. For example, if Earl tells Adams "you should turn the gun in," he may mean "you should *turn it in*," or "you *should* turn it in (but) ....," or a number of other shadings, each conveying different — even opposite — meanings.

Interesting insights occur when role playing a conversation in which Earl tells Adams that if the lawyer keeps the gun, he will have to turn it over to the authorities. Adams may well pick the gun back up and head for the nearest bridge, from which to toss the weapon. If this occurs, some students will see the lawyer as responsible for Adams' suppression of evidence. On the other hand, if Earl declines to tell Adams what the alternatives are, he may be failing in his duty to give Adams the very advice which brought the client to Earl's office that day.

Toward the end of this discussion, the teacher may want to emphasize **paragraph 9** of the Comment to **MR 1.2 (paragraph 6** in the **1983 Rules** as amended). The new (and significantly different) version of this comment says that a lawyer is not precluded from "giving an honest opinion about the actual consequences" even if the client uses that opinion in a criminal or fraudulent way. "There is a critical distinction," concludes this comment in language that remains unchanged and which we find particularly useful, "between presenting an analysis of legal aspects of questionable conduct and recommending the means by which a crime or fraud might be committed with impunity."

Students may feel that what Earl tells Adams is nothing more than a semantic dance around telling Adams directly how to conceal his own weapon. We disagree; while it may seem like mere semantics to our students, it is here that we find the "critical distinction" between thoroughly advising the client on the one hand, and pointing the way to fraud on the other. This is our first encounter with a theme that will run throughout the course of this book — whether the way lawyers say things are mere semantic distinctions, or differences in the substance of how lawyers should perform their roles. (We will see this issue often, including in **Problems 15, 19, 20, 24** and **26.**)

We believe that in addition to advising his clients that he must turn over the gun (or money) if he takes it, Earl should advise them that they may not themselves suppress the evidence. We appreciate that this advice may be ineffectual, and may not prevent Adams, for example, from destroying the gun. But we do not believe that the advice Earl gives while declining possession of the gun, if objectively presented, makes him responsible for his client's later illegal act. Telling the client what conduct is illegal is a simple matter of giving complete advice.

(e) After the Lawyer Takes Possession:

If a consensus is reached that once he takes possession of the gun, Earl has an obligation to turn the evidence in, several additional questions are raised. The first is, what is possession? Earl doesn't possess Baker's bag full of money, but what about the gun? Is the gun sitting on Earl's desk sufficient? Must he take it or at least touch it in some way? May Adams still take it back at that point? Or is that a facile way for Earl to dodge responsibility?

Second, if it is agreed that Earl takes possession of the weapon so that he has complete dominion and control, and thus must turn it over to the authorities, how does he accomplish this? It seems relatively straightforward to conclude that if not turning over the gun is suppressing evidence, wiping off fingerprints would be also. But in what form must the gun be turned over? Must Earl identify himself and whose gun it is? May he mail the gun to the D.A. in a plain brown paper bag, and let them figure out to which case it belongs? Is there a course of conduct in between these relative extremes? Again, the teacher can play valuable roles both as devil's advocate and in role playing Earl or a judge or prosecutor examining Earl's conduct after the fact.

If Earl does take possession, we believe he has an obligation to turn it over to the D.A. Moreover, the character of the evidence — fingerprints, original container, etc. — may not be altered, for that would constitute the destruction of evidence. We do not necessarily believe, however, that Earl must provide the D.A. with a "road map."

The delivery of the gun to the D.A. without the means of tracing the weapon back to Earl — e.g., hand delivered in a brown paper wrapper — provides

what is for us the most challenging question in this problem, one which can be answered either way with ample justification. We believe that the anonymous transfer may strike the best balance between the obligation to maintain confidences and the duty to avoid assisting in fraud or concealment of evidence. Others will argue, however, that under *Meredith*, the prosecution no longer has the opportunity to discover the gun as it existed when the lawyer came into possession of it, and therefore Earl must disclose at least that he has sent the D.A. the weapon.

(f)   Ethics vs. Evidence:

In discussing these last issues, it is most valuable to point out a distinction between *Ryder* and *Meredith*, and the earlier California case of *People v. Lee* (cited in the Silverman article in **Section 5** of the **Readings**), which cites *Ryder* and is the progenitor of *Meredith*. Neither *Meredith* nor *Lee* is a case that turns on ethics issues. Both are *evidence* cases that center on the issue of attorney-client privilege. This is important for two reasons.

First, it provides an excellent opportunity early in the semester to point out that ethical concepts, such as confidentiality, and evidentiary concepts, such as privilege, are similar, but are by no means the same thing. More generally, this means that the rules of ethics should be separated from substantive disciplines for purposes of evaluating the ethical issues involved. The same point may be made about the *Tarasoff* case (**Readings, Section 6**), since the failure to reveal a confidence in that case resulted not in discipline of the doctor, but rather a finding of *tort* liability. See also the *Purcell* case in the **Readings, Section 8.**

As with evidence issues, cases finding liability in tort must be distinguished from cases setting a standard of *ethical* behavior, a point which we raised in **Problem 3**. The teacher may raise the question of whether *Tarasoff requires* a lawyer to act in a particular way, in the sense that ethical rules *require* certain behavior, or whether *Tarasoff* merely means that one *may get sued successfully* by failing to reveal information when a life may be at stake.

Secondly, as we read *Meredith*, since it is an evidentiary privilege case, it does not tell us what a lawyer must *necessarily* do. It tells us, rather, that when the lawyer acts as the attorney in *Meredith* did, the privilege will fall. We do *not* believe *Meredith* says that had the lawyer acted differently, such actions would be wrong. Seen in this light, it means that the universe of acceptable conduct for Roger Earl is best seen as circumscribed by *Ryder* and the aftermath of the Garrow murder case, both disciplinary matters, rather than by *Meredith*.

Teachers may also inquire into whether there is a significant difference between treating the fruits and instrumentalities of the crime, on the one hand, and mere evidence on the other. The answer to this is not clear, although none of the cases included in the readings deal with mere evidence.

(g) Carlton, Dunn & Withdrawal:

Carlton's case is included primarily to raise the specific point that confidentiality begins as soon as an individual with a reasonable expectation of speaking confidentially begins to speak, even if that person is not ultimately taken as a client. As we saw in **Problem 1**, such would-be clients are sometimes called "clients for purposes of confidentiality." A brief role play can demonstrate why Carlton has a reasonable expectation of confidentiality.

Dunn's case is included primarily to raise the issue of whether the client's intended commission of a future crime is confidential. The related issue is the comparison between advising Dunn and advising Adams and Baker. **MR 1.2(d)** helps illuminate the distinction between advising about future crimes and advising in a manner which may lead to a crime or concealment. **Paragraphs 9 and 10** of the **Comment** to **Rule 1.2** are particularly valuable. (Under the **1983 Rules** these paragraphs are enumerated **6 and 7**, and have significant substantive differences from the 2002 language.)

Finally, the issue of withdrawal of counsel should be discussed. While withdrawal is always a possible result, we believe it is rarely a remedy. Too often, it merely "passes the buck" to the next attorney, who is likely to be more ignorant of the circumstances than the first lawyer. Here, if disclosure of evidence is mandated, withdrawal will not protect Earl from having to do it. Moreover, as a practical matter, permissive withdrawal is often difficult to obtain, particularly in a criminal case approaching a trial date. Here, withdrawal does not directly relate to the "real" issue: whether confidences should be revealed and evidence turned over, and how. But if it appears that as a result of a disclosure to a particular authority, the attorney will be subpoenaed as a witness, withdrawal may be required.

(h) Professor Zacharias' Hypotheticals:

Professor Zacharias' hypotheticals in **Section 11** of the **Readings** illustrate the tension between the lawyer's duty of confidentiality and the lawyer's duty, if any, to the public. The hypotheticals we have excerpted all pose tough cases where the lawyer's moral imperative will be to reveal the confidence even where the Rules do not create an exception. We believe that ultimately most State Bar disciplinary authorities would not prosecute a lawyer who, for example, revealed to a judge that his client was plotting to kill him. But the issue gets murkier where, for example, a financial fraud is involved as in hypothetical number six. You will not be able to address all of Zacharias' hypotheticals, and you may not even be able to discuss three. We suggest doing number three, as it raises the *Spaulding* case cited within the hypothetical. The point is to demonstrate how hard it can be to uphold our duty of confidentiality.

(i) Confidentiality and Terrorist Suspects:

No discussion of confidentiality in the post-9/11 world would be entirely complete with at least a reference to the effects of national security issues on confidentiality. The **Readings** in **Section 10** focus on this issue, with a mid-2006 article on taping attorney-client conversations being the centerpiece. By and large, our students enjoy discussing these issues, and we find that the circumstances, while politicized, form a good basis for bringing home the meaning of confidentiality in a real-world setting. Each instructor, of course, will make a determination about the extent to which hybrid ethical and political issues in a post-9/11 world should be discussed in class, and the tenor of that discussion.

PROBLEM 5

When Does A Lawyer Talk Too Much?

THE POINT BEHIND THE PROBLEM:

This problem looks at the basic concept of attorney-client confidentiality from three different perspectives. In this way, we follow up the more dramatic — but unusual — scenario in **Problem 4** with a practical survey of some typical ways in which the issue of confidentiality arises. The important lesson here is to remind students to "keep their eye on the ball" by ensuring that the confidences of their clients are protected. To do this, lawyers must remain vigilant to the need to protect these confidences at all times.

Part I is designed to show how easy it is for lawyers to let down their guards and allow confidences or secrets to slip out in ordinary discourse among friends, or other everyday settings. By emphasizing the client's general unpleasantness, **Part I** also emphasizes that *secrets*, variously defined as anything relating to the representation, or matters learned during representation that might be embarrassing or detrimental to the client, must be protected just like confidences themselves.

Part II emphasizes the difference between consulting another lawyer *on behalf of the client* and consulting one *on the lawyer's own behalf*. While the article and other material in **Section 2** of the **Readings** are obviously important to an understanding of this subject, the most important point is the change in the ABA's Model Rule 1.6 explicitly permitting such consultations. In addition to the *de jure* status of the rules, it is important for students to consider the reasons (1) lawyers need the ability to consult confidentially with their own counsel about a client's conduct; and (2) clients would not want this done. This tension governs this portion of the problem.

Part III deals with the specific issue of client identity, and the widely disparate series of cases and ethics opinions on the issue of whether a client's identity can be confidential. **Parts I, III and III** are quite distinct and raise separate issues relating to confidentiality. We suggest that each be dealt with separately. We tend to spend more time on **Parts I and II** than on **Part III**.

APPLICABLE RULES:

Model Rules:	MRs 1.6, 4.4 (<u>Note</u> important revisions to 1.6 in 2002.)
Model Code:	DRs 4-101; 7-101
CA B&P:	6068(e).

SUGGESTED QUESTIONS TO ASK:

- What if Matt Gold's revelations were more substantively negative, such as calling his client a liar, or his case meritless?

- How does a lawyer decide what is OK to reveal in a conversation with the lawyer's friends? What if the lawyer thinks (incorrectly) that the revelation would not be detrimental or embarrassing to the client?

- Can a lawyer use a "rule of reason" in balancing concerns about confidentiality with practical reality?

- Is negotiating an agreement to resolve the client's case favorably a situation where revealing a secret during the course of that negotiation is presumptively approved by the client? Even if the information revealed is "embarrassing" to the client?

- What duties, if any, does the consulted attorney have to the consulting attorney? To the consulting attorney's client?

- If a client insists on going to trial, should the rules about keeping the identity of the client confidential suddenly change? If identity has to be revealed at trial, is Professor Wolfram right that it should not be considered confidential at all?

- Should the evidentiary privilege or the ethical rules about confidentiality govern when a client wants his or her identity kept confidential?

SUGGESTED ROLE PLAYS:

- Play the role of client Anthony Verdi when he finds out what his lawyer said about him on Thursday evening.

- With a few students, play the role of a group of attorneys sitting around "talking shop" and *not* disclosing any confidences or secrets, a surprisingly difficult thing to do.

- Play the role of a lawyer consulting with an expert on ethics who is trying to avoid revealing confidential client information.

- Have students engage in the same role play with you in the part of the consulted lawyer, who insists on knowing enough information to adequately provide the help you need.

- Play the part of a client who learns that the student — his or her lawyer — has revealed his secrets to another lawyer without the client's permission.

- Have a student role play Attorney Grey explaining to Varady under what circumstances Varady's identity will or will not be confidential. Play the

part of Varady seeking advice from Attorney Grey about how to deal with this circumstance.

▪ Play the part of the court clerk at Varady's arraignment, who calls the case and then asks, "Armand Varady, is that your true name?"

SUGGESTED VIDEOS:

▪ Keeping client confidentiality: *Legally Blonde* — The Alibi, DVD chap. 21

▪ Divulging client confidences with permission: *The Firm* — Meeting with the mob, DVD chap. *17*, 2:17:43 — 2:22:40

DISCUSSION:

(a) Part I — Do Loose Lips Sink Ships?

Attorney Gold's conversation with his colleagues about client Verdi is typical of what lawyers say at such cocktail-hour conversations. Students who have worked at law firms may have had the opportunity to participate in such sessions. Lawyers are inclined to talk, and schmoozing in the manner of Matt and his friends is a very common occurrence. But the effect on confidentiality is clear: Unless the lawyers are all from the same firm, where the umbrella of confidentiality applies, confidences have been breached.

Some law students may feel that discussions about a client's predilections and predispositions, as opposed to what the client has told the lawyer, really are not breaches of confidentiality. But the rules of every jurisdiction have traditionally included the protection of confidences *and secrets*, meaning anything learned during the representation, the disclosure of which could be embarrassing or detrimental to the client. Under ABA **MR 1.6**, this is no longer expressed as secrets, but as anything "relating to the representation of a client." This broad but vague language keeps the definition of confidentiality wide open. Many states have retained the "secrets" concept, while some have adopted the newer, broad MR 1.6 definition.

It is important for students to understand the significance of such matter-of-course disclosures. The fact that they are done as a matter of course does not make them appropriate. It is for this reason that we include in **Section 1** of the **Readings** the statements of the lawyer for Polly Klaas' alleged killer. The students should also be asked to review the text of the rules on secrets. In that way, the point can be made that such indiscretions are impermissible across the board, and that it is highly inappropriate for the lawyer to decide what is all right to reveal, and what is not. Some students may argue that if Gold refers to Verdi anonymously, the disclosures he makes are acceptable. That may be true, so long as nobody can trace whom Gold is talking about. But Matt speaks at his own peril; if anyone does learn who the client really is, he could be held accountable for his "loose lips."

If the students are not convinced of the impropriety of the revelations made by Matt Gold, the teacher can suggest more extreme examples to test the students' views. For instance, suppose Gold said that Verdi was a "lying son of a gun," or "couldn't tell the truth to his own mother." Or that Gold believed Verdi had been concealing assets in an off-shore bank account.

The negotiation situation raises other issues, such as whether the goals of negotiation justify disclosures to opposing counsel that are inappropriate if made to somebody else. Again, recourse to the rules may be best. The students should examine what they say regarding when the revelation of confidences or secrets is permissible. Is negotiating an agreement beneficial to the client an instance where the revelation is presumptively approved by the client? This is a closer question, but we think the answer is "no" absent client approval.

Prof. Abbe Smith's piece in **Section 1** serves as a strong reminder of just how broad confidentiality is, at least in the eyes of a "confidentiality absolutist." Prof. Smith's examples of when she would be torn but still maintain confidentiality are useful particularly in how they translate into a broadly defined core concept of "inviolate" communications.

(b) Part II — Lawyer-to-Lawyer Consultations:

Sometimes, such as in **Part II** of this Problem, a lawyer feels the need for her own counsel, *not* on behalf of her client but to assist her in defining her own duties. This might relate to fraud or other illegal or even dangerous conduct of a client, a budding conflict between the lawyer and client, or myriad other reasons. The Moss-Bridge article in **Section 2** is valuable in addressing an overview of this situation, and ABA Opinion, 98-411. While helpful, though, it hardly provides a definitive solution to the issue.

Under the **2002 Model Rule 1.6**, the ABA has specifically permitted such communications (with new language underlined):

(b) A lawyer may reveal ~~such~~ information <u>relating to the representation of a client</u> to the extent the lawyer reasonably believes necessary

(2) <u>to secure legal advice about the lawyer's compliance with these Rules;</u>

This is hardly the last word on the issue either, of course. The questions posed in **Part II** attempt to take the issues surrounding confidentiality a few steps further. Anonymous advisements may be permitted but at the peril of the lawyer making the disclosure (see our discussion in **Part I**), and, according to **MR 1.6, comment 4 (2002 edition)**, "so long as there is no reasonable likelihood that the listener will be able to ascertain the identity of the client or the situation involved."

New **Rule 1.6(b)(2)** does not specifically authorize an attorney-client relationship between the consulting and consulted attorney, but seems to imply

that it is permitted where the consulting lawyer's compliance with ethics rules is at stake. **Comment 7** of the new rule adds little; while saying that disclosing information is permitted even if not "impliedly authorized" to carry out the representation — the older standard — it does not say that the consult*ed* lawyer becomes counsel to the consult*ing* lawyer.

However, that is the conclusion that makes the most sense to us. Clearly, a confidential communication may now exist between the consulting and consulted lawyer, and the consulted lawyer may give advice to the consulting attorney about the proper ethical course. This clearly creates an attorney-client relationship. Answering this question first helps resolve the answers to some of the problem's other questions. Seen in this light, the possible conflicts of interest facing McGuire, and his duties to maintain the confidences of Redfern, should be seen as governing McGuire's further involvement in the case. While the course book has not reached conflict of interest issues yet, it appears that McGuire must be loyal now only to Redfern.

But *Redfern*, able to consult only because of MR 1.6(B)(2) exception, would herself seem obligated to make the *least possible disclosure* necessary to discern her ethical duties, and to place the greatest possible restriction on dissemination of such disclosures. It seems wrong — not to mention counterintuitive — to suggest that McGuire would be able to use the confidences imparted by Redfern, unless another exception to the rule of confidentiality — danger to others, for example — were involved.

This portion of the new version of Rule 1.6 is an important edition to assist lawyer to do the right thing. While the change seems straightforward enough, on careful examination there are a number of subtleties that make some significant discussion in class worthwhile. Only time will tell how these issues are eventually resolved.

(c) Confidentiality and "Unbundled" Services

The **Readings, Section 4** do not directly relate to any of the three parts of the Problem itself, but they raise an increasingly important issue, one that is far broader than the specific example in the Readings. In the new millennium, where multi-disciplinary entities are a reality — and for many poor people, like those described in the Bruston article, the *only* possible reality — how can lawyers successfully maintain confidentiality, serve the needs of their client, and be true to the entity for which they work? Instructors who find this an interesting subject will likely find students willing to engage in a discussion of this important issue.

(d) Part III — Can the Identity of the Client Be Confidential?

The readings in this area present very different views: one lawyer who went to jail rather than reveal a name (**Readings, Section 5**); one noted ethics expert, Charles Wolfram, who believes that identity is never confidential

(**Section 6**); and cases and ethics opinions that go in varying directions (**Section 6 Notes** following the Wolfram reading, and the cases cited in the **Supplemental Readings**). A few important issues should be highlighted.

One is the interrelationship between confidentiality and privilege, as the note following the Wolfram reading points out. There is a clear distinction between an ethical duty to protect confidences and the evidentiary rule of privilege. But law students and experienced practitioners alike are often tempted to confuse these two concepts.

The client identity issue is particularly interesting as it relates to this privilege/ confidentiality distinction. To the extent that it is learned *during the course* of the attorney-client relationship, identity may be, if not a confidence, a *secret*. Nevertheless, many cases have held it to be not *privileged*. All this presents an interesting dilemma for attorney Grey. The North Carolina opinion cited in the readings, for example, holds that he may not reveal his client's identity until the time of trial. But, we might ask, if the client insists on going to trial, do the rules suddenly change? Does evidentiary privilege rather than ethical requirements suddenly govern his conduct? If this is so, then why is there authority allowing for the protection of the identity *up until* the time of trial if that identity has to be revealed *at trial*? You may want to include the *Burns* and *Cesena* cases from the **Supplemental Readings** in your discussion.

As the **Notes** in **Section 6** suggest, there are "few safe harbors" here. While it is difficult to provide a definitive answer, it is possible to provide reasonable guidance, first by looking at the confidence/privilege distinction, second by understanding that protection of information relates not only to confidences but to secrets as well, and third by pointing out that the line may be drawn when the issue includes making misrepresentations to the court. The students may be tempted to use withdrawal as an answer to this issue, but, as in **Problem 4**, it simply passes the buck.

We believe that the identity of a client can be and sometimes is confidential. We disagree with those who take the position espoused by Prof. Wolfram. If the identity issue is examined from the point of view of its being a "secret," it is easier to understand this position. Nevertheless, we are troubled by the effect of potentially misleading the court; this may limit the extent to which confidentiality of identity may be maintained. Some of our students point out, however, that people are entitled to be called by whatever name they choose. Still, we do not know how much this helps when the lawyer as the client swears under oath to his name.

If you have time, you may want to return to some of Zacharias' hypotheticals in **Problem 4** and discuss how you could reveal the confidences raised by the hypotheticals without revealing the client's identity. Note that most of the identification issues seem to arise in civil rather than criminal cases.

(e) Confidentiality Surviving Death:

We believe that *Swidler v. Berlin*, so widely reported and discussed — and excerpted in **Section 7**, merits discussion here. Its inclusion serves more than a current events purpose. *Swidler* explains an important component of confidentiality: the expectations of the client that the information be held inviolate no matter what — even after death.

(f) The True Meaning of Confidentiality:

We believe that the last reading in the Problem, in **Section 8**, presents a powerful statement of what confidentiality in its true sense is all about. The brief of ethics-associated lawyers on representing Guantánamo detainees and the near impossibility of a confidential attorney-client relationship is a clear and compelling review of the basic principles necessary to the most unusual and special interaction between lawyer and client. While some instructors might prefer a less political topic, we have found that its immediacy engages students in a way that helps bring the point — about confidentiality, not politics — home

.

PROBLEM 6

Technology + Confidentiality = Trouble

THE POINT BEHIND THE PROBLEM:

The point behind **Part I** is to emphasize the effect of new technology on traditional notions of confidentiality, and other traditional ethical concepts. As the legal landscape changes into a virtual world of electronically-sophisticated communications, it would be impossible to see no effects on ordinary principles of legal ethics. Despite the enormous changes of recent years, especially in the way in which we communicate, the first part of this problem does not require a particularly challenging or sophisticated analysis. Indeed, the same basic tenets that guide us through the other problems relating to confidentiality serve us equally well here.

Part II examines the inadvertent transmission of confidential information, evaluating both the duties of lawyers on the both ends of the transmission. We focus mostly on the receiving end and the conflicting duties to either make use of information inadvertently disclosed or to refrain from using it when the lawyer knows it was intended to be confidential.

The importance of this problem stems in significant part from the central role that modern electronic communications hold in the firmament of today's law firms, and especially — even more than the professors teaching the subject — the lives of our students. While the answers, at least in **Part I**, may not be particularly complex, a course without this problem or similar material would in our view be incomplete. We remind students that they need to be acutely aware that more changes will come, and quickly, as this is a fluid area that requires us all to stay alert.

APPLICABLE RULES:

Model Rules:	MR 1.6, 1.7, 4.4
Model Code:	DR 4-101, 7-101
CA Rules:	3-310
CA B&P:	6068(e)

SUGGESTED QUESTIONS TO ASK:

- Is communicating confidentially by e-mail, cell phone or portable telephone worth the risk? Why or why not?

- List the ways of communicating with a client and evaluate their relative safety or risk.

- Does the use of a cell phone in a public area vitiate the privilege and confidentiality? Does sending an e-mail from a university library

computer room or an Internet cafe? What other uses of communication devices might create similar issues?

- How central to confidentiality and privilege is the question of the client's reasonable expectation of privacy? The lawyer's expectations?

- What kinds of communications may result in loss of confidentiality *and* waiver of the attorney-client privilege?

- Is the practical reality that voicemail and fax transmissions will inevitable be reviewed by the opposing side? Or documents with prior edits and comments? Would having an ethical rule prohibiting such review change a lawyer's actual behavior?

- What kinds of further regulations would be helpful in dealing with inadvertently-disclosed confidential material?

SUGGESTED ROLE PLAYS:

- Play the role of a managing partner in a law firm listening to — and playing devil's advocate with — Tecchi's pitch for more technologically advanced methods.

- Play the role of a lawyer contacting the client from home on a portable phone.

- Play the part of a client who has *not* been fully informed of the ramifications on confidentiality of a communication and is now finding out there may be a problem.

- Role play a "client" who believes that based on the information s/he obtained on the Internet (1) the student's firm represents her; and (2) she got advice that did not solve her problems.

- Play the role of Bluestone's client when she learns that her lawyer had a valuable voicemail transmission that he destroyed rather than listen to, or a document with embedded data that Bluestone himself stripped of all but the current text.

SUGGESTED VIDEOS:

- Internet issues: *The Net*, DVD chap. To Be Identified.

DISCUSSION:

(a) E-Mails:

The issue of the security and confidentiality of e-mails provides an excellent case study of what happens when lawyers (and ethics experts) are

too quick to react to technological changes. As the **Readings** in **Sections 1 and 2** describe, the majority rule on confidentiality of e-mails has already changed twice. The current prevailing wisdom — that they are *safer* than other means of communication — makes sense to us. E-mails are not perfectly safe; however. For example, copies are far more difficult to destroy than shredding a letter. Moreover, with new subpoenas and discovery that includes hard drives, "unscrubbed" e-mails are increasingly hard to destroy.

We believe that it is equally important to mention the potential malpractice ramifications of an intercepted e-mail (and for that matter, of intercepted cell phone communications), since the veil of confidentiality only goes so far and, as **Section 2** indicates, malpractice is the most likely venue for those who hedge about the acceptability of e-mail confidentiality when discussing "sensitive" information.

(b) Telephone Communications:

Again, the analysis of this question is rather straightforward, laid out in the **Readings, Section 3**. Prof. Hricik, who has specialized in such matters, provides an excellent overall template from which to discuss the difference between the kinds of telephone communications, the extent of their security and thus their confidentiality, and the possibilities for the future. (Although this reading is "old" by hi-tech standards, its analysis still has currency.) Notice the ALAS warning at the end of the **Section 3** in the **Notes**. It is important to note than an issue central to both e-mails and phone communications is the participants' reasonable expectation of privacy — with an emphasis on "reasonable."

(c) Websites and Other Internet Issues:

These issues are a bit more complex. Websites, of course, are not merely means of communicating, but may be the situs of advertising, solicitation, giving legal advice, and even obtaining a client. Most of the time devoted to **Part I** of this problem may be best spent here, both with respect to the excellent survey provided by the Hanna article in **Section 4** and with regard to other Internet issues, modernized since the last edition, discussed in **Section 5**. It is here where our young partner Tecchi is likely to run into real trouble.

The most important issue for students to grasp is that they must look beyond the surface use of a website or other Internet mechanism in two distinct respects. First, the actual technology being used is of paramount importance. The security of information cannot be understood without a firm understanding of the technology. For instance, if a disclaimer button provides an admonition that no legal advice is being given, but that button appears on a website's *inside page* rather than its *home page*, it may be far less likely to be seen by the visitor, and thus more open to attack. Similarly, a website that

allows a browser to skip accepting an agreement about the site's limits is far more subject to criticism than one that *requires* a response from the user. And if individual lawyers can be e-mailed from a law firm website, certainly a convenience, there may be an expectation of a response.

Second, it is equally important to understand how the technology interrelates with ethics issues. Parsing through the ethics issues, as we have done for the rest of the problems on confidentiality, is still absolutely necessary. Recognizing when a lawyer or firm may be engaged in the practice of law is also of particular importance. The Hanna article and the additional material in **Section 5** should be read thoroughly and understood fully. As lawyers network, leave their LANs on all night long, and use open DSL lines, the "firewalls" they need to build to prevent anyone from outside accessing their client information must be higher and stronger. We continue to believe that the best firewall is one that at day's end shuts down the system so it is impenetrable from the outside, but this costs the convenience of access.

Another area of particular concern and worthy of both mention and discussion is the effect of the availability of e-mail transmissions directly to lawyers from a law firm website. This is certainly a convenience, but one that comes at the cost of possibly creating a duty to respond on the part of the e-mailed lawyer.

Other issues, such as how to replicate shredding documents by permanently destroying electronic information, are also worthy of discussion, though — as our daily headlines tell us — these are rapidly evolving technologies. Privacy issues also abound. "Cookies" come in different "flavors." Some memorize passwords and other identifying data, such as credit card information. You may want to ask students if they have ever been welcomed back to a site by name (most have), and whether they have considered this in light of their own privacy.

These areas of the law are obviously works in progress and under great flux. Jett Hanna has continued to update revisions of his article on a periodic basis as the issues change; while we have left the original piece intact and added our own **Section 5** materials, those interested can get other versions of his work directly from him at the Texas Lawyers' Insurance Exchange. One of the professor's goals might be to emphasize that students will have to keep current on these matters in a vastly expanding and exponentially escalating electronic age.

(d) Part I — Part II Transition — "Metadata" and Embedded Data:

We have revised the fact pattern in this part of the problem, changing it from an inadvertently recorded phone call to a more cutting-edge issue —

"metadata" and embedded data. We feel this more technologically sophisticated — and increasingly worrisome — fact pattern provides a good transition between **Parts I** and **II** of the Problem. The analysis of lawyers' duties regarding inadvertently disclosed information (below, Part (e)), is largely unaffected by the change in the facts, but how to deal with embedded data itself is causing quite a stir.

Section 6 of the **Readings**, a new section of the text, addresses the issue of what some, call "metadata," but which we more properly (according to Prof. Hricik's advice to us) term "embedded data." The focus on the two New York opinions, one on receipt of this data, the other on disclosing it, points to the double-edged nature of this issue. The use of the data turns on the propriety of using inadvertently disclosed information, but the second New York opinion charges the lawyer who does not "scrub" the document of its "tracked changes" and other embedded information with an affirmative duty. As the text notes, we see the two opinions as at least somewhat contradictory, as do others. But reasonable minds will differ even on this issue.

One rather fine point: Successive drafts of a document may be and often are materially different than lawyers' comments embedded in the margins of the documents. We think it likely that the more revealing the information — many lawyers like to think out loud in their comments to their colleagues embedded in documents in progress — the more likely lawyers will be charged with a duty to scrub the document. It is less clear, as least intuitively, that a more revealing disclosure would create a different standard for the *receiving* lawyer.

(e) Part II — Reading and Using Inadvertently Received Confidential Information:

Part of the purpose of **Part II** is to point out that indiscretions can occur anytime or anyplace. Teachers should resort to their own practice experience for examples of indiscrete or simply sloppy revelations of confidences and secrets. Conversations in the courthouse elevator are a prime example, as are whispered washroom consultations, and confidential conversations at lunch or on airplanes. Our perspective: if the information transmittal is not viewed as Browning's fault, it soon will be. But what should Bluestone do?

Whether attorney Bluestone may view the document's "tracked changes" and comments, or read the fax transmission, raises difficult questions without clear answers. The New York opinions give us only one perspective. Others are addressed by the *Aerojet* case (**Readings, Sections 7**), post-*Aerojet* litigation in California and elsewhere, described in **Section 9**, the changing view of the ABA as reflected in two opinions 12 years apart with different results (**Section 8**), and our analysis of the state of the law, at least as of mid-2006, as set forth in **Section 10**. While ethicists debate this issue, students

will generally find it somewhat difficult to avoid the temptation to review easily available embedded data, and even more difficult to not read embedded data that comes to Bluestone already disclosed in the document. Most students will also find the fax transmission very difficult to avoid reading.

Students often see the issue of reading the inadvertently transmitted materials as a rather simple question of "zealous" advocacy in the face of the other side's error. The *Aerojet* court's dicta agree with this perspective. This may simply be reflecting reality that as a practical matter, attorneys will feel compelled to read the fax. The law, of course, is not so clear.

The *WPS* case (**Section 9** of the **Readings**) presents a more recent view than *Aerojet*, but the *Rico* case referred to in this section still has not been decided. There is a wide factual gulf between *WPS* — documents not covered by discovery and clearly marked as confidential — and *Aerojet*, in which the witness' name *should already have been turned over* in discovery. While there are other indications beyond *WPS* of a movement away from *Aerojet* (**Readings, Section 10**), as yet there is no clear consensus on this issue.

What of the fact that the fax described in the problem contains the cover sheet with the clear admonition that it is intended to be confidential? Most law firms now routinely send this admonition on their fax cover sheets, and an increasing number put a similar alert on their e-mails. But many firms have used such notices injudiciously — sending the cover sheets to their tailor, child's school, or even more inappropriately, to opposing counsel. Such communications are hardly confidential. When opposing counsel gets the admonitions in routine faxes and e-mails about scheduling, in our view it would be reasonable for counsel to simply *ignore* future warnings completely. We recommend *two* sets of fax cover sheets and e-mail signature, one containing the warning, and one without it.

(f)   A Clearer Issue — Notice:

As we state in the text in **Section 9**, the one issue that seems rather clear is that a lawyer who receives inadvertently disclosed information should give notice to the other side of the receipt of the transmission. Although the law is still not settled on this issue either, we would be quite surprised if future cases did not require notice, regardless of how they treat the issue of viewing and/or using the inadvertently disclosed documents. The *Rico* case now pending before the California Supreme Court focused on the notice issue below and is likely to enlighten us further on this point when decided.

(g)   Inadvertent Interceptions — Ethics and Morals

Time allowing, it is worthwhile to discuss one of the recurring themes in this court: the interrelationship between the practical application of the rules

of legal ethics and a lawyer's own sense of right and wrong. Here, however, there may be something of a role reversal of these two concepts, with students arguing for the need to help a client, even if they know the other side did not intend to disclose the information.

We find this a close question. We lean towards the view that when an edited document, fax, or confidential voicemail (our fact pattern in the first two editions) is received that is clearly intended not to be revealed to the other side, the other side best deals with this problem by taking the high road and not reviewing the material *once its secret nature is discovered*. We understand the practical difficulty this creates, and must temper this conclusion with the observation that if the matter inadvertently transmitted is material we should have been entitled to — as in *Aerojet* — the practical reality is that the temptation to use the material might be too great. We also recognize that some, even considerable, reading is often required to determine whether the transmittal was indeed confidential.

We also look at this circumstance from the point of view of the attorney who has made the inadvertent disclosure (and the client of that lawyer). Our views are closely reflected in the statement of the lawyer of our acquaintance in **Section 8** of the **Readings**. (As usual, the lawyer of our acquaintance reflects our own views.) We believe, however, that for lawyers to refrain from reviewing such inadvertently-disclosed material, more regulation and clearer guidance in regulation are absolutely necessary.

PROBLEM 7

When Are Two Clients Too Many?

THE POINT BEHIND THE PROBLEM:

Conflicts of interest are perhaps the most common ethical issue confronting the average lawyer in day-to-day practice. **Problem 7** serves to introduce the concept of conflicts of interest in several uncomplicated situations. We begin this section of the course book emphasizing *concurrent* conflicts. Some of the subtleties of conflicts of interest are then dealt with in **Problems 8, 9, 10 and 11**.

The purpose of **Problem 7** is to assist students in spotting potential conflict of interest situations whenever they occur, and in understanding the breadth of these situations. To do this, we focus on the concept of "loyalty" rather than "conflicts of interest" and the difficult distinction between "potential" and "actual" conflicts. We like to track **MR 1.7**'s approach by asking whether there is anything which "materially limits" a lawyer's loyalty to a particular client. We find the term "conflict of interest" something of a misnomer, since it implies *adversity*, which we find confuses more than illuminates the issue.

The second purpose of the problem is to point out that, through candid communication with clients, many routine conflicts of interest such as those described in this problem are waivable. Indeed, we believe some probably *should* be waived for the convenience of the parties themselves, such as the husband and wife in the car accident who will only want one lawyer.

APPLICABLE RULES:

Model Rules:	MRs 1.4; 1.7 (and see 1983 comments 4 and 5 and 2002 comments 5, 8, and 14-20); 2.4 (2002 Rules), 2.2 (1983 Rules).
Model Code:	DR 5-105; ECs 5-18; 5-24.
CA Rules:	3-600.

SUGGESTED QUESTIONS TO ASK:

- Do conflicts of interest exist only where adversity exists?

- Are there situations where it is clearly in the clients' best interests that conflicts between them be waived?

- Is Healy representing both parties to the divorce, only one, or neither? Does it matter?

- Does the dissolution of the graphics business involve an adversarial situation? Does it involve clearly differing interests?

- Would *formation* of a graphics business between two or more partners involve adversity? Differing interests?

- May a lawyer remain silent about what the law actually is in the face of clients who misunderstand that law?

- Should the lawyer ever act solely as a "scrivener," merely memorializing the agreement between parties?

- If students feel there is an imbalance of power in either the divorce or the graphics business dissolution, is it possible they have interpreted the balance of power the wrong way?

- In deciding whether to undertake representation of two clients, how important is it that the clients want only one lawyer?

- What concerns should you take into account in memorializing an agreement to represent more than one client?

- What if you receive confidential information from one party that is important for the other party to know? May you tell? If you do, do you violate a confidence? If you don't, do you violate your duty of zealous advocacy?

- What if, in the personal injury case, one spouse was driving and partially negligent, or the car was owned by one and not the other?

- What if, in the personal injury case, one spouse wants badly to go to trial right away or have the case settled while the other spouse is still in treatment, making it difficult to ascertain the gravity of her injuries?

SUGGESTED ROLE PLAYS:

- With a student who believes that Plevin should not represent both Tom and Emerald in the dissolution of the business, role play Tom and/or Emerald explaining to Plevin why they really only want one lawyer, in order to demonstrate why sometimes it is more appropriate to waive a conflict than to force clients to have separate counsel.

- Role play a client and have a student explain the conflicts of interest or limitations on loyalty the client will waive upon signing a disclosure and waiver.

- Role play the part of defense counsel offering a lump sum settlement to both husband and wife in the personal injury case. Refuse to divide up the amount between husband and wife, telling plaintiff's counsel "That's your problem."

- Play the part of a district attorney who offers co-defendants Billy and Joe a "package deal" and will not budge on either defendant.
- Role play the Vandivers (injury case) as the student attempts to explain the possible conflict of interest.

DISCUSSION:

(a) An Overview of Problem 7:

In this problem, like some others, we have provided intentionally sketchy fact scenarios to allow the students to explore the potential conflicts of interest. Our purpose has been to leave most of the slate blank, to allow for the students and teacher to explore the question of impaired loyalty (or the potential conflict of interest), rather than spelling out the conflicts in a way which would make it too obvious. We suggest an approach that deals with each of the four parts in turn, though some teachers may prefer to skip Part IV in the interests of time.

We also suggest an approach which includes the witness scenario set forth in **Section 4** of the **Readings**. This scenario, particularly when discussed near the end of the class, is designed to drive home the point about impaired loyalties. Since the two individuals involved in that scenario are not in the position of traditionally adverse or conflicting clients, our point is to emphasize the impairment of the lawyer's loyalty when such a circumstance (or any other similar circumstance) appears.

The first three readings in the problem, on F. Lee Bailey and by Profs. Dubin and Zitrin (**Readings, Sections 1 and 2**), are designed to illustrate basic conflict issues. **Section 3** is designed to show why confidentiality and loyalty are so closely and intrinsically related. The reading about Billy Joel's lawyers (**Section 5**) is designed to show what a tangled web can be woven when lawyers are oblivious to impairments of their loyalty. In analyzing conflicts issues, we find the Comments to **MR 1.7** particularly helpful.

We suggest starting with **Part I** but moving quickly to **Parts II** and **III** to compare the three scenarios. We generally discuss the conflicts of interest in both **Parts I** and **II** before discussing whether there is an adequate way of disclosing and waiving such conflicts. We then go on to **Part III** to see what we have learned and apply it to a new fact situation, and then conclude with a brief review of **Part IV**, a criminal case and thus considerably different from the other three. Throughout, we use frequent "straw polls" to gauge whether students are comfortable taking on the joint representation and to ask whether they feel the clients in question are adverse to each other.

(b) The Divorce Case:

Some students may recognize this situation as being very similar to a divorce mediation. For this reason, it may be useful to briefly review **1983**

MR 2.2 on intermediaries and see how that rule (especially the **Comment, Para. 6**) views the receipt of confidential information. This rule, however, was deleted by the **2002** rules revision, and a new general rule covering all neutrals, **MR 2.4**, inserted. This may not be the best time to get too sidetracked on this issue. For those who will use **Problem 21** on mediation later in the semester, that is another and likely better opportunity for this rules comparison.

The students may wish to discuss whether Healy is a lawyer engaged in traditional representation of both parties, or an attorney acting as an intermediary. But it is important that here too, the discussion not bog down in this area. The bottom line is that she *is* an attorney, and must be held to the standards of an attorney, with respect to both conflicts of interest and receipt of confidences.

Nevertheless, it is useful to spend a few moments discussing whether Healy is representing both parties to the divorce, or representing only one with the other going along for the ride. The **Supplemental Readings** cite to *Klemm*, the best known case on representing both sides in a family law matter, and references to sources dealing with family law, estate planning, real estate, and patent conflicts that may be of assistance to students leading a discussion on this issue. Here, ultimately, our view is that the issue of who is being represented begs the question, because Healy has clearly taken on a responsibility to both husband and wife.

The Hammonds' situation presents a clear conflict of interest. Irma and Sam are literally on opposite sides of the same case. While this does not preclude joint representation in many states, the point here is that the conflict — or material limitation on loyalty — must be acknowledged first, before the issue of what to do about it may be addressed.

Many students will feel that it is inappropriate for Healy to represent both parties in any circumstance. They will point to the issues raised in **Questions 2, 3 and 4** as reasons for this. They are right about this, at least for themselves. We would never push anyone to represent both parties in a domestic relations case. Before completing the analysis, however, we prefer to wait until we have evaluated the dissolution of the graphics business in **Part II**, because that scenario has many similarities to (and some differences from) the divorce case.

(c)   The Graphics Business:

Students will readily see a comparison between the divorce situation and the graphics business, and will generally feel that the latter situation is less adversarial. But this is not necessarily the case. We use Quan Huen Graphics to illustrate the inherent direct adversity between somebody selling a business and somebody purchasing the same business. One dollar more in price is inevitably one dollar more spent by the other side. Nevertheless, students — and, in fact, practicing lawyers as well — often find it much easier to represent both parties to the graphics business negotiation than the divorce case.

To illustrate why we prefer to talk about limitations on a lawyer's loyalty rather than use the more traditional term "conflicts of interest," we take three straw polls with out students as we begin a discussion of the sale of the graphics business. First, we ask them whether they believe that the plan for Emerald to sell out to Tom constitutes an "adversarial situation." Most students feel that it does not. Next, we ask whether Tom and Emerald have a conflict of interest between them. Again, many students answer "no."

Finally, we ask whether Tom and Emerald have *adverse interests*. We often define that term for the sake of clarity to include differing economic interests. Almost all the students believe that these two friends *do* have adverse and differing interests. Now, when we return to the question of whether a conflict of interest exists, and put it in the context of whether attorney Plevin's loyalty towards either client is limited by his obligations to the other, almost all students agree that this is the case.

To further clarify the point, we suggest changing the scenario from the dissolution of a business to the formation of a partnership. Many lawyers routinely represent several partners in putting a deal together without having carefully thought through the potential for conflicts of interest. They have not appreciated the impairment to their loyalty in representing more than one prospective partner. Indeed, in our experience, this has been a frequent source of malpractice complaints. We particularly like to cite to the first sentence in the **fourth paragraph** of the **Comment** to the **1983** version of **MR 1.7** (similar to **paragraph 8** of the **Comment** to the **2002** Rule): "Loyalty to a client is also impaired when a lawyer cannot consider, recommend or carry out an appropriate course of action for the client because of the lawyer's other responsibilities or interests."

In this part of the problem, we have intentionally not included the "what if" questions that we did for the divorce case. We want to get the students themselves to raise these concerns. If they do not, they should be added by the teacher. For example, what if the agreement proposed by Emerald and Tom is badly skewed in Tom's favor? Should you remain silent? What if there is a basic misunderstanding about tax law, for example, or the way in which assets are evaluated? Or what if one party is a passive owner with little knowledge of the day-to-day running of the business?

The similarities between the divorce and the graphics business can then be evaluated. Both involve people who trust the single lawyer's judgment. Both apparently involve situations where the clients only *want* one lawyer. Both also involve situations where there may be unequal bargaining power between the two parties, a fact to which many of the students may be sensitized. (By the same token, however, when this comes up, we note that it is not necessarily Tom who will work the deal to his advantage. If students worry about Emerald's "weakness," the teacher may wish to play devil's advocate and point out that perhaps that it is *Emerald*, who has done the books for 27 years, who actually knows the value of the business, whereas Tom, the graphics designer, has little business sense. Power imbalances can cut both ways.)

The discussion can now refocus on whether one lawyer is appropriate in both **Parts I and II**. The students should be asked how important it is that the clients only want one lawyer. There is an enormous economic consequence in having a second lawyer, particularly where the parties now agree, and where two lawyers may drive them apart unnecessarily. On the other hand, their individual rights and remedies are more clearly taken care of with two lawyers. Ultimately, whether Healy represents both the Hammonds, or Plevin represents Tom and Emerald, are personal choices to be decided by each prospective attorney. The key point is that such dual representation is possible only if appropriate disclosures and waivers are made.

(d)   When and How Can Conflicts Be Disclosed and Waived?

We return here to look more closely at the issues raised by **Questions 2** and **3 in Part I**. If any students would undertake to represent both the Hammonds, or both Tom and Emerald, they should be asked what concerns they would have to take care of before engaging in such joint representation. These important issues should be part of this discussion: (1) What should be done about confidential communications; (2) How much should the lawyer advise the two clients about the law, and what the lawyer thinks is the best or fairest thing to do; (3) When should the lawyer withdraw if things don't go well; and (4) When is it simply not possible to ask clients to waive conflicts of interest?

Confidences: We have longed believed that a key to conflicts of interest is the receipt of confidential information. Where a lawyer receives confidences from one or another party and must keep them from the second party, the lawyer sets up a situation where the conflict of interest is irresolvable. This is because the lawyer may eventually have to choose between refusing to reveal the confidence, on the one hand, and zealously representing the other party on the other hand.

For example, what if Sam advises Healy that he secretly sequestered money in a hidden account? If Healy tells Irma, she violates a confidence; if she doesn't, she's not zealously representing Irma since she fails to provide an

important piece of information. Or, what if you know a secret about *Emerald*, such as that she is in dire financial straits? To avoid this situation, we believe that if joint representation is going to take place, there must be a clear agreement among the clients to waive any rights to communicate all confidential information, that is, everything Mr. Healy tells will be disclosed to Mrs., and vice versa.

This proposition has an interesting effect on students. To some, it will make them more comfortable about undertaking the joint representation of either the Hammonds or Tom and Emerald. To others however, it will cause them to conclude that they will never undertake such representation. It can also have a side effect on the representation. If Mr. or Mrs. insists on making a confidential statement to the lawyer notwithstanding their agreement not to, it is unclear whether that previous agreement is binding. A lawyer in this situation may well be forced to withdraw (see below).

Advising the Clients: Should the lawyer act solely as a scrivener, merely memorializing what the agreement is between the parties? Some students may see this as a way around the conflict, because it is facially neutral to all. Other students will object that there may be power imbalances between the clients that are perpetuated and even exacerbated by the lawyer's failure to give legal advice. Our view is that part of the very job of being a lawyer is to give such advice, and the lawyer should not lightly abandon that responsibility. But how can this be done in the joint representation setting?

Students will differ on how to solve this problem. We believe that the clients should be informed about the law. If after being informed, they decide to agree in a way that does not fully comport with what a court might order, or what the law would require, that's fine, because it is their *informed* choice. They have been given the baseline advice from which to work. If, on the other hand, the lawyer refuses to give advice to anyone, the clients are abandoned to what may be their own misunderstandings and ignorance of the law.

Withdrawal: If the parties cannot agree and wind up in a dispute, withdrawal from the entire case as to both parties may be inevitable. It is worth some discussion to consider how much the lawyer may persuade the two parties to reach a meeting of the minds before withdrawing. Would pushing too much in effect be favoring the lawyer's own interests in remaining in the case as opposed as to what the clients may need — separate counsel?

(e)   The Conflict Waiver Letter:

All these matters should be addressed in a document in which the clients are informed of and consent to waive any conflicts of interest, that is, any impairment of loyalty on the part of the lawyer. The potential dangers should be "front-loaded" as ground rules, so that when the clients consent to joint representation they do more than merely consent to having a lawyer with impaired loyalty. They should consent in addition to having a lawyer who, for

example, will not receive any confidences from one without telling the other, who will provide objective advice to all about the law as he or she understands it, and who will withdraw in the event a dispute between the two parties arises. Note that the **2002** version of **MR 1.7** now requires "informed consent, confirmed in writing."

Any other ramifications of joint represent should also be included in this letter. We enclose below a copy of a letter we have used as a conflicts waiver letter which may be useful to the teacher to explain what we mean. One of the key ingredients of this letter is that it is written in *English*, not in legalese, an important point to make to students.

November 3, 2007

Mary Jones
xxxx xxxxxxx Lane
Somewhere, CA 99999

Maxine Smith
xxxxx xxxxx Street
Elsewhere, CA 99999

RE: Jones & Smith v. Employer

Dear Mary and Maxine:

This is the letter I said I'd write about our representation of you in this case. It will be necessarily long, for which I apologize in advance. But most, and hopefully all, of this we have already discussed. Some might consider a letter like this unusually informal. However, I believe strongly — since you both wish me to represent you — that it is vital to anticipate as much as possible what might happen in the future. To compensate for this letter's length, I'll try to write it as much as possible in English, rather than legal "mumbo jumbo."

Please read this letter in conjunction with the fee agreement enclosed. Consider this letter part of that agreement. Again, as I told you both by phone when we last spoke, I would prefer that you call me to discuss this letter and the fee agreement before you sign it, even if you agree to everything here.

The purpose of this letter is to discuss the effect of our representing both of you, and the potential "conflicts of interest" between you.

As we have discussed, there are some advantages and potential disadvantages to our representing both of you.

Among the advantages: There is a certain strength in numbers. Your cases are so similar — you both held the same type position, maintained similar levels of performance, received similar work evaluations, and were given the same "reasons for firing" in your personnel files.

One person making a claim could be seen as a swearing contest. Two people with almost identical claims begin to show a pattern of conduct that we believe was both

unfair and discriminatory. While you can always testify for each other, there's something about being in it together that we all feel would appeal to a jury.

Joint representation might also help us convince defendants that we are to be taken seriously, thus helping settlement. Also, doing the case is likely to be significantly less expensive. Given the complexity of your "high tech" jobs, substantial discovery and a large number of depositions will have to be taken and at least two expert witnesses hired. Consolidating the case means you don't each have to pay for each deposition, or your own expert witnesses. It is true, however, that a consolidated case with separate lawyers for each of you would accomplish many of these cost savings.

However, there are some potential disadvantages of joint representation. First, among the two of you and your lawyers there can be no confidential communications. Everything that one of you says is shared by all of us (though it's confidential to any "outsider"). This means making a commitment to candor and to working together.

Second, although your cases are very similar, there are always differences personal to your own experiences. This is especially true here about the search for new employment. The two of you simply will not experience the same thing. This means that ultimately, if a settlement is in the offing, it may well not be the same for each of you, nor should it be. The same is true for argument to the jury at trial; your cases won't be identical.

In rare instances — it's a nasty trick, but it's been done — defense counsel will try to drive a wedge between two parties, perhaps by offering to settle reasonably with one and not the other. Other unforeseeable things relating to life situations can happen, causing one of you to, for instance, need a continuance while the other is ready to go to trial. These matters — literally too numerous to try to catalogue — can turn the potential for conflicts of interest into an actual conflict.

In these events, we'd have to evaluate whether the potential conflict of interest has turned into a real conflict. It's possible, for example, to go ahead and settle one person's case and not another's, without conflict. But if there's an insoluble or irreconcilable conflict, if necessary we would withdraw from the case of one or, very likely, both of you, when it becomes apparent we can't represent both of you to our fullest extent.

It's really this last point that's the key. We — attorneys and clients alike — need to feel confident that we can represent you in such a way that our loyalty to one of you, and our efforts, are not in any way interfering with our loyalty and efforts to the other.

Having said all this, we wouldn't even consider representing you both if we didn't think that the chances are high that the advantages outweigh the disadvantages. But it's a very important thing to consider, and not to be undertaken lightly.

Again, please give me a call to discuss any or all of this, before signing below that you agree to this joint representation.

Cordially yours,

Leslie Q. Lawyer

[Consents]

(f)   Sometimes You Just Can't Waive A Conflict:

While we take the view that many conflicts can be waived if they are bolstered by an appropriate waiver letter, we want to be careful to avoid going overboard in this regard. Many conflicts simply cannot be waived. We like citing to **paragraph 5** of the **Comment** to the **1983** version of **MR 1.7**, which limits the extent of acceptable waivers in ways that are most sensible. See also **Comment paragraphs 14-19** to the **2002 Rules**, discussing "nonconsentable" conflicts. First, no lawyer should ask for a conflict to be waived "when a disinterested lawyer would conclude that the client should not agree to the representation under the circumstances." Second, there may be situations, as described in that paragraph, where it is not possible to disclose sufficient information to obtain *informed* consent. That is the problem raised by the witness scenario set forth in **Section 4** of the **Readings**.

(g)   The Personal Injury Case:

We save the case of Mr. and Mrs. Vandiver to recap what the students have learned. Even after the discussion about impairment of loyalty, some students will still see conflicts of interest as a matter of adversity, and will believe that there is no conflict of interest in the husband and wife personal injury case because there is no present adversity. This is an appropriate time to underscore the many subtle ways that a lawyer's loyalty may be compromised.

For example, the Vandivers received very different injuries, Mrs. Vandiver's being very much more severe. Additional potential conflicts may be suggested by the teacher: perhaps one or the other was driving, and driving negligently; perhaps one or the other but not both owned the car; perhaps one of them wishes to go to trial as soon as possible while the other one would prefer to wait, a seemingly minor issue which nevertheless results in *some* small impairment of loyalty.

Students often see the issues of settlement and the Vandivers' divorce differently. The divorce is a relatively clear situation of traditional conflict. The settlement offer is not always seen that way. The teacher can help the students appreciate that any aggregate settlement offer given by the defendants will mean that any dollar going to Mrs. is not going to Mr. and vice versa. It is frequently beneficial and fun to role play the settlement negotiation between teacher as defense counsel and student as attorney for both husband and wife, to show the impairment of loyalty facing the student "attorney." "Defense Counsel" can put a lump sum on the table and refuse to divide it between husband and wife. That requires the Vandivers to either play tug-of-war with the settlement or work it out another way.

(h)   Prospective Waivers:

We include this issue because the use of prospective waivers has become more common. Since the rules require informed consent to waive a conflict, in

our view prospective waivers will rarely suffice unless the client signing is a sophisticated client who is savvy about legal services. Nonetheless, the students should know that they have been used and upheld on a limited basis. See **Readings**, **Section 6**.

A related issue is that even valid waivers may no longer be sufficient once circumstances change. It is useful to briefly return to the second and third scenarios to see how changed circumstances — timing or money issues — or new facts — discovery of an additional bank account for the graphics business or a comparative negligence issue in the accident case — could require a second conflicts waiver.

(i) The Criminal Case:

Here, as the readings in **Sections 7** and **8** suggest, there may be conflicts of interest even where the defendants are willing to consent. Students who are having difficulty seeing the potential impairment of loyalty should again consider the settlement conference example, here a plea bargain where the district attorney insists on more time for Joe but will allow charges against Billy to be dropped. The two brothers may also have different prior records, drug histories, and numerous other matters which can create conflicts of interest between them.

In criminal cases, as the case authority in the last several pages of the readings notes, courts have used much stricter standards before allowing joint representation even with informed consent of all involved. We concur; we seriously question whether even with waivers, joint representation in criminal matters is in the clients' best interests.

(j) Wrapping Up:

As the readings in **Section 9** note, there are myriad potential conflicts situations — or, more descriptively, impairments of loyalty — that exist throughout the practice of law. Some of these are addressed in the Supplemental Readings. Before passing on to the other specific problems in this chapter, it is worth reiterating the breadth and significance of this issue.

PROBLEM 8

Who Is My Client?

THE POINT BEHIND THE PROBLEM:

If the issue in this problem were literally just "who is the client," the answer would be simple: it is the entity itself, the partnership, corporation or union. But lawyers who represent organizations, whether they are corporations or other organizations such as partnerships, have among the most difficult of tasks: determining not just who their client is, but the corollary issues — with whom may they maintain confidential communications; and what individuals speak on behalf of the client. The principal objective of this problem is to delineate the complexities of these issues, and to provide some foundational guidance for law students who might find themselves in such circumstances.

This is not an easy task; it is very difficult to come up with a definitive understanding about such situations. Rather, we set more modest goals: first to explore the problem; second to point out the need for awareness at the inception of representation of the possibility that such issues will arise; and finally to explore the possibility of dealing with these issues when the lawyer first undertakes representation. One last issue of significance: the recurring problem of the difference between privilege and confidentiality, as demonstrated by the excerpted cases.

APPLICABLE RULES:

Model Rules:	MRs 1.7, 1983 Comments, paragraphs 8 and 14, 2002 Comments, paragraphs 34 and 35; 1.13.
Model Code:	DR 5-105; ECs 5-18; 5-24.
CA Rules:	3-600.

SUGGESTED QUESTIONS TO ASK:

- How can Esperanza Dejos abide by the requirements of MR 1.13 and take her concerns about the partnership to the highest level of the partnership, when that "highest level" is Lavin himself?

- How can Dejos justify continuing to consider Lavin the representative of her client when it appears he is stealing from the limited partners?

- How sure does Dejos have to be about the truth of Andy's suspicions before she discloses what's happening to the limited partners?

- As a practical matter, how can a lawyer work with a managing general partner if some level of confidences cannot be maintained?

- What other alternatives exist for Dejos other than taking the matter to Lavin and disclosing the situation to all limited partners?

- Is it reasonable to disclose the situation to the other general partners and not to the limiteds based on an analysis of who is the client? Or is such disclosure justified because the other general partners can more directly control the business?

- What if Dejos confronts Lavin and Lavin fires her on the spot? Does he still have that authority?

- What if Lavin demands that Dejos immediately return all partnership papers and files to him? Should she comply?

- What if Dejos discloses to the other general partners, and they say "so what," or *they* fire her?

- What if Lavin himself has made the disclosures to Dejos? What if he prefaces these disclosures by telling her that what he is about to say should be held in strictest confidence?

- What if Lavin is an individual client of Dejos? What if he is Dejos' *largest* client, through Dejos' representation of half a dozen of his limited partnerships? Would he not be, in any practical sense, the actual client?

- Is the *Garner* case an ethics case? What about *Upjohn* and *Payton*?

- How does Dejos determine what is in the "best interests" of the organization in the first place?

- Can you think of any possible solutions to Dejos' dilemma, if she had to start all over again? Does it make sense in terms of setting "ground rules" as we did in Problem 7?

SUGGESTED ROLE PLAYS:

- Play the role of Dejos hearing what the accountant has to say, to evaluate whether she is sure enough of the information he is providing.

- Play the role of Lavin being confronted by Dejos; assume that Dejos represents other limited partnerships of Lavin's.

- Play the part of Lavin approaching Dejos and asking to discuss something with her in strictest confidence.

- Role play Eddie O'Neill calling Dejos and quizzing her about what to do, if the student playing Dejos is not sure she should reveal the information to O'Neill. (O'Neill will ask probing questions that make it very difficult for Dejos to refuse to answer.)

- Play the part of a lawyer setting up a partnership and trying to define not only the roles of the relevant partners, but also her role as partnership counsel, so as to avoid getting in Dejos' situation.

DISCUSSION:

(a)   A Difficult Problem with Less Than Clear Solutions:

We believe it is necessary from the outset to explain to our students how difficult a problem this is. Otherwise, it is easy for them to get frustrated with the concept of representing an entity, which of course can only speak through its constituent representatives. Understanding that the lawyer represents the entire entity is, in itself, important. But that's the easy part.

The real questions are, who speaks for that entity, and with whom are confidences maintained? These issues are complicated by the partnership setting. The law and ethical code interpretations, described in **Section 10** of the **Readings**, are very uncertain on the last issue of whether the individual partners are clients. Thus, **Problem 8** as it is constructed raises many issues not easily answered — issues which would be as frustrating for attorney Dejos as they are for the students evaluating the problem.

(b)   What Should Dejos Do with the Knowledge She Has Learned?

Students will readily conclude that Dejos owes her obligation to the partnership as an entity. Again, the problem is in deciding what this means. If Lavin speaks for the partnership, students may feel that Dejos must keep this information between herself and Lavin. This is particularly true if they interpret the potential fraud as one being committed by the *partnership itself,* since the money is still in partnership accounts.

Many other students will sense that all the limited partners are entitled to know what Dejos has learned. They have support for this view in those authorities (see **Section 10**) that indicate that all partners of a partnership are clients. Those who evaluate this carefully may understand that, as with joint representation in **Problem 7**, this means in effect that there can be *no confidences* as among these different partners. They may then conclude that it is appropriate to disclose to O'Neill and the other limited partners.

When students have either of these clear points of view, we like to ask some pointed questions as devil's advocate. To those students who believe that the partnership speaks through Lavin, we ask how Dejos can continue to talk only to him when it appears that he is stealing from the limited partners. To those students who want Dejos no longer to answer to Lavin, we point out that **MR 1.13** advises a lawyer for an entity who is concerned about the welfare of the entity to take the matter to the highest authority within that entity. Here, isn't that Lavin?

To students who feel that Dejos should reveal what is going on to all of the limited partners, we ask how certain she has to be that the accountant's suspicions are correct. We also ask how it is possible as a practical matter for a lawyer working directly with the managing general partner to have to disclose everything between them to all of the limited partners.

(c) Other Possible Solutions to Dejos' Quandary:

There may be a middle ground between the two extremes suggested above. It is that Dejos' duty is to the partnership, and that that duty is best served by not committing a fraud, particularly on the individual limited partners. Students who take this view may reason that Lavin does not speak for the partnership itself, since it appears that what he is doing is inimical to the interests of the partnership, at least in the long run. We think this last analysis is quite solid. The teacher can point out the consequences of what would happen should Dejos only disclose the situation to Lavin as if Lavin alone speaks for the partnership.

On the other hand, immediate disclosure to all the limited partners should also be closely scrutinized. For example, Dejos may not even know all their names or whereabouts since she is not general counsel for the partnership and may not be privy to that information. Under those circumstances, how could she even accomplish disclosing to the limited partners? Students may say that Dejos should look to the partnership agreement. Certainly that would help if the agreement addresses this issue. We have not stated the terms of the agreement purposely to get the students to discuss the issues where there is no agreement on the issue or where the agreement is vague.

We ask what other alternatives exist for Dejos besides taking the matter to Lavin or disclosing the situation to all limited partners? One is further investigation of the accountant's allegations; certainly, this is understandable. But at some point, when she is convinced of the harm being done to the partnership, she should act.

Dejos might decide to disclose the situation to the other general partners; students sometimes suggest this solution. The teacher might ask if it is reasonable to disclose the situation to the other general partners and not to the limiteds based on an analysis of who is the client? Or because the other general partners can more directly control the business?

(d) Making a Tough Situation Even Tougher:

In actual practice, things seldom go as planned. So we raise some questions which can make Esperanza's task even more difficult. For example, what if she confronts Lavin and Lavin fires her on the spot? Does he still have that authority? What if Lavin demands that Dejos immediately return all partnership papers and files to him? Should she comply? What if Dejos

discloses to the other general partners, and they say "so what" or "just keep quiet"? Or *they* fire her? These questions point out the very real, possibly insoluble, difficulties that Dejos may find herself facing.

Another question we explore is what would happen if Lavin himself admitted stealing to Dejos, perhaps prefacing his remarks by asking her to hold what he said in strictest confidence. This directly raises the question of whether Lavin is entitled to communicate confidentially with Dejos. This confidentiality conundrum is a central issue in settings such as those in this problem. See **Readings, Sections 7** and **10**.

Note the difficult issue of "*Upjohn* waivers" as it relates to Lavin, much less the employees described in the King-Formherz article in **Section 7**. That article correctly, in our view, points out that limited or vague waivers are likely to be construed against the attorney requesting them, even though the lawyer and corporate entity survived scrutiny in the case King and Formherz analyzed. Cohen's somewhat tongue-in-cheek suggestions that attorneys should give their corporate officers *Miranda* warnings before listening to what they have to say presages the Enron situation we will examine in depth in **Problems 24 and 25**.

But the Cohen article in particular also articulates the real problem faced by organization counsel who have working relationships with certain members within the organization who consider themselves to be clients, whether they are or not. For example, Lavin may have five other limited partnerships which Dejos represents, in effect being Dejos' biggest "client." Moreover, most states' ethics rules allow lawyers to represent both the partnership and the partners themselves as individuals (see **Readings, Section 10**). We ask what would happen here if Lavin, independently of the partnership, was an individual client of Dejos?

The students must consider the practical reality facing lawyers in Dejos' situation. Even if Lavin is not being personally represented by Dejos, Dejos may be representing six of his limited partnerships, and in any practical sense, this may make Lavin not only her "client" but perhaps even her largest "client." If none of the other partnerships have anything wrong with them, it will present any lawyer, even one with considerable skills, with an extremely difficult dilemma.

(e) Disclosure to O'Neill:

More students will be sympathetic to disclosing to O'Neill if O'Neill directly asks Dejos a question about the partnership assets. This is natural, since it is difficult to imagine an attorney simply ignoring the reality of a situation and not telling O'Neill she can be of no assistance. But it is unclear that Dejos' obligations to O'Neill actually change when O'Neill asks Dejos for advice. There is nothing in the asking for advice per se which elevates O'Neill's status as client beyond where it had been a moment before; besides,

O'Neill arguably is speaking as an individual, and not as a limited partner. This situation can be used to explore the possibility that Dejos has some ongoing obligation to the limited partners where she sees a fraud being committed.

(f) The Frustration of *Garner*, *Upjohn* and *Payton*:

The *Garner* and *Upjohn* cases (**Readings, Sections 3 and 4**) are important both for what they do say and what they do not say. Both these cases focus on the issue of privilege, though from different points of view. Neither of them, however, goes terribly far in solving the dilemma faced by Esperanza Dejos. Specifically, the conclusion in *Garner*, to remand the case to determine the privilege issue consistent with the factors set forth in the opinion, is particularly disturbing to us. The court, having developed a case-by-case factor analysis, then begs the question by remanding rather than applying it.

We believe that a discussion of the *Garner* and *Upjohn* cases, as well as the *Payton* case excerpted in **Section 5**, is important to show what these opinions do deal with, but also to show how much is left *unresolved* for the attorney in Dejos' uncomfortable situation. Moreover, we see these cases not as ethics cases at all, but as evidentiary cases, turning on the issue of privilege. Indeed, *Garner* is primarily a *discovery* case, the issue being whether the shareholders' rights to discover certain information overcomes the privilege, and *Payton* involves a public agency, and not a corporation.

(g) A Rules Discussion and Comparison:

We also encourage the students to express their frustration about the inadequacy of the ethical rules on this subject. We share some of this frustration. Clearly, under the **1983 ABA Rules, MR 1.13**'s suggestion to appeal to the organization's higher authorities is totally ineffectual here. But in 2003, **Rule 1.13** was modified significantly. It is especially valuable to discuss the effect of the new rule, especially 1.13.(c) and (d), that — like Sarbanes-Oxley — allows going outside the entity if necessary to protect the entity. Examine what this really means. If going outside the partnership to disclose HiFly's malfeasance would *destroy* HiFly, may the lawyer do it? And is contacting the limited partners covered by the revised 1.13? (We would argue that this is not at all clear and that the whistleblowing now permitted by new 1.13 is similarly not clear until courts and other authorities have had their say.)

It is also worth mentioning to our students the history of the development of **MR 1.13**, which as originally drafted by the Kutak Commission, would have allowed "whistleblowing" for corporate counsel in certain circumstances. The rule which was eventually passed is a far cry from what the commission originally envisioned.

Finally, we make mention of **CA 3-600**, particularly the last paragraph of the discussion section. There, the rules-makers acknowledge that organizational lawyers sometimes have "difficulty in perceiving their correct

duty." But instead of telling us what to do, the discussion ends with this sentence: "In resolving such multiple relationships, members must rely on case law." We get no more satisfaction from this than we get from the conclusion in *Garner*.

(h) Subsidiaries and Change of Organizational Control:

Although subsidiaries are not involved in the Problem, they are an important issue that should not be overlooked. They also are a complicated issue to follow, but brief discussion is merited here. For example, to what extent should subsidiaries be evaluated by law firms conducting a conflicts analysis? The **Readings** in **Section 6** address the ABA Ethics Opinion on subsidiaries. While an attorney is not necessarily barred from representing a parent company while suing an affiliate, we believe that a lawyer would best refrain from doing so, given the downsides: loss of a client, a disqualification motion, and potential civil liability.

Where a change in organizational control occurs, such as a hostile takeover, whether the attorney-client relationship, and hence the attorney's duties and privilege attach to the new entity can be a complex question that depends on the legal status of the old and new entity. the *Tekni-Plex* case (see **Readings Section 8**) is indicative of the kind of analysis that takes place when organizational control is in question. While the case ties ethics concepts to evidentiary terms like privilege, this creates some confusion as to how to analyze these situations. The court essentially says that since the old entity did not "die," the new entity has an attorney-client relationship with the lawyer. This analysis seems too facile to us, but it may be the simplest solution to a thorny conundrum.

(i)   The Union:

The analysis of the union situation is really very similar to that of the general partnership. Here, the **Readings** in **Section 9** do little to clarify the circumstances of union counsel any further than those concerning partnership counsel. Indeed, the cases seem to have trouble with the issue of "control" that was endorsed in *Tekni-Plex*. Time permitting, we encourage students to go through an organizational analysis similar to what they have done with partnerships. Given the complexity of the partnership issues, however, there is not always time in class to do this.

We do try to mention how the unusual and dramatic United Mine Workers litigation demonstrated how "the best interests of the organization," in this case the UMW, could change over a period of time. Similarly, the "best interests" of other organizations, such as Tekni-Plex or HiFly, may also change depending on circumstances.

(j)   What Solutions Can Be Offered?

The problem does not directly call for solving this problem should it come up again, but such a discussion can be most worthwhile. The teacher might ask, if Dejos had it to do all over again, what she could have done to avoid this situation. Our idea here is to discuss the possibility, as seen in **Problem 7**, of "front-loading" solutions by having "ground rules" understood by everybody as representation begins. Perhaps these ground rules can be put into the partnership agreement.

These ground rules may work rather imperfectly in the organizational setting, particularly compared to the examples in **Problem 7**. But it our view that they will work better than no solution at all. For example, if there is a clear understanding about who may impart confidences to the lawyer and who may not, or who speaks on behalf of the partnership and who does not, much of the solution to Esperanza Dejos' problems will have been decided before the problems occur.

Some students suggest that Dejos' best solution to her problems is to resign as the organization's counsel. This may possibly help *her* problems, but does little or nothing to help the partnership. All it does is "pass the buck" to some other possibly unsuspecting lawyer. The issue of withdrawal comes up frequently during the course of the semester. We generally find it a "solution" which creates more problems than it solves. As we felt in **Problem 4**, when Roger Earl is presented with a gun, we would rather see the able attorney in our hypothetical handle the situation than pass it on to someone else who is likely to have less information and less ability to solve the problem.

Finally, students may raise the specter of an audit letter by Andy Arthursen that reveals the accounting irregularities. We discuss this issue more fully in **Problems 24 and 25**.

PROBLEM 9

What Happens When Your Personal Interests Get in the Way?

THE POINT BEHIND THE PROBLEM:

This problem's purpose is to bring home an idea we have discussed in several earlier problems — that the lawyer's personal interests in a matter will often diverge from the client's, and that it is important for the lawyer to be aware of this.

We harken back to **Problems 1** through **3**, where the lawyer's own interests can easily diverge from those of the client, and where we introduced the concept of fiduciary duty (see **Problem 1, Section 8**), the obligation to put the client's interests ahead of the one's own. That concept is the essential idea here. In other words, conflicts between a lawyer's interests and those of the client must always be resolved in favor of the client.

Nowhere is the conflict between a lawyer's interests and those of the client more clear than on economic issues, especially the lawyer's receipt of a fee. The Ewing article in **Section 1** shows the extent to which self-interest can go. The Zitrin article in **Section 3** quotes the California Supreme Court as saying "almost any fee arrangement between attorney and client may give rise to a 'conflict'," and the recent Illinois survey discussed in **Section 2** seems to prove this point. **Part I** is designed to bring these points home to students, and the collateral point that lawyers retain a fiduciary duty to give their clients their best efforts under the circumstances regardless of fee issues, unless and until they are out of the case. It also focuses on the delicate problem presented by withdrawing from a case without harming the client.

Part II focuses on conflicts that are not fees-based — economic and "relationship" issues. **Part III** returns to the fees issue from another angle — here, the impropriety of a quick-fix settlement that saves the lawyer *time*.

APPLICABLE RULES:

Model Rules:	MRs 1.5, including Comment, paragraphs 1, 2, 3 and 5; 1.7, Comment, paragraph 5 (1983) or paragraphs 8, 10, 11 and 12 (2002); 1.8; 1.16, especially (b)(5) and (6) and (d), and Comment, paragraph 8.
Model Code:	DRs 5-101; 5-103; 5-104; 5-107; ECs 1-32; 5-1 through 5-7.
CA Rules:	3-120; 3-300; 3-310(B); 3-700(A)(2), (C)(1), (F); 4-200.

SUGGESTED QUESTIONS TO ASK:

- Can William effectively waive any conflict over the lawyer receiving a fee by agreeing to plead guilty?

- Should William's agreement to plead guilty under these circumstances be evaluated by the standards in MR 1.7, that the waiver of any conflict be reasonable to the objective attorney? Would William's guilty plea be truly voluntary?

- Would it be reasonable of the lawyer to require William's entire fee before beginning the case?

- What, if at the beginning of the representation, the lawyer and William decide to "split the difference" between a case that goes to trial and a plea bargain case? Would a $5,000 fee, win or lose, plea bargain or jury trial, be reasonable?

- How far does William's lawyer have to go to provide competent representation, in the event the lawyer is not being paid for trial?

- Posit three identical criminal defendants, one paying a substantial hourly sum, one paying a flat fee, one where the lawyer is being paid at reduced court-appointment rates. To which case should the lawyer devote the most time? The least?

- How does a lawyer consider the level of duty owed to a client based on the amount and mode of payment? Is each client entitled to "competent" representation, or to a lawyer's very best efforts?

- Are the efforts owed by the lawyer to Lola Lipp the same as those owed to William Simons?

- If the lawyer withdraws from representing Lola, wouldn't that materially adversely affect her case?

- What if Cameron simply can't afford to pay Lola's additional costs, even though they appear absolutely necessary?

- What may Cameron say in her motion and supporting declaration to withdraw?

- What if Arnie only had two shares of Globie stock? Would disclosure still be necessary? Would it be advisable?

- What should be the test of whether Arnie must disclose a personal relationship with someone connected with Globie?

- What if Arnie's aunt worked in Globie's machine shop? Is this a circumstance Arnie has to disclose?

- Have Prager's clients truly given their informed consent to his two-hour minimum court appearance? To his billing three clients at the same time?

- Can't Sam Shade consider his own fees as well as what's best for the client in advising Bentley about his p.i. case?

- In your work experience, have you seen any examples of lawyers who "churn" files by spending too much time on them? Have you seen other billing horror stories?

SUGGESTED ROLE PLAYS:

- Play the part of William discussing the plea bargain with his lawyer, where William says "I simply can't afford to go to trial; I guess I'd better plead guilty."

- Play the role of a lawyer discussing expenses with Lola Lipp, and asking her to make choices about what work should and should not be done. Conversely, take the part of Lola.

- Role play the judge hearing Cameron's motion to withdraw.

- Play the part of Arnie disclosing to the airline pilots seemingly trivial matters such as two shares of stock or his aunt working for Globie. How then do the students, as the pilots, react?

- Then play the part of the pilots learning, after the fact, of these minor relationships: what is the attitude of the pilots then about Arnie? ("If it was so insignificant, why didn't you tell us about it?")

- Play the part of the client in quizzing a lawyer about how counsel can spent one hour in the air and bill two separate clients for the entire hour.

- Play Billy Shears attempting to justify to the client the half-hour bill for two phone messages.

- Role play a lawyer explaining to the client why the client will receive good "value" for billing greater than the lawyer's hourly rate, because of the lawyer's particular expertise on the complex antitrust matter in question.

DISCUSSION:

(a) William Simons and Fiduciary Duty:

We spend somewhat more time on William Simons than on Lola Lipp, and more time on **Part I** of the problem than on **Part II**.

Criminal defendant Simons has simply run out of money and is unable to perform his part of the fee agreement. The lawyer has done absolutely nothing wrong. Some students will feel that under these circumstances, where the

lawyer is blameless, William's acceptance of the plea bargain is okay. Others will feel that the lawyer should withdraw from representation. Some will not see the conflict of interest between lawyer and client. But a discussion of the actual effect that his inability to pay has on William's case will generally bring the point home.

If the lawyer allows the plea bargain, whether recommending it or not, the attorney essentially permits it *only because* there has been no full payment of fees. The problem states that the plea bargain is "far too stiff." With full fee payment, it wouldn't be considered. While students may wish to talk about the risks of trial, this begs the question. Here, we are told that no lawyer would argue for this plea bargain under ordinary circumstances. This places the lawyer's fees in conflict with the best interests of William, going to the very essence of fiduciary duty.

If students have difficulty with this concept, the teacher might analogize to the waiver provisions discussed in **paragraphs 14 - 19** of the **Comments** to **Model Rule 1.7** and similar language. We have seen that this language requires that all waivers of conflict of interest must be reasonable to the reasonably objective attorney. (The **2002 Rules** now use the phrase "consentable.") The teacher might also ask whether a guilty plea based on William's inability to pay his lawyer is truly voluntary as required by law (e.g. the United States Supreme Court decision in *Boykin v. Alabama*). Is it reasonable to conclude that if William pleads guilty, his guilty plea is coerced by his inability to pay his attorney? Playing the part of William discussing the deal with his lawyer, or agreeing to plead guilty, may also prove fruitful in explaining this issue.

(b)   Charging William Fees, and Withdrawal:

Interestingly, **paragraphs 1, 2 and 5** of the **Comment** to **Model Rule 1.5** discuss the situation where more fees are required of the client during the course of the litigation. The teacher and students may wish to explore how these paragraphs apply to William's case.

We raise the issue of whether the lawyer would be better off having William pay the entirety of the fee before the case begins. Many criminal defense lawyers charge a flat fee for many legal services. We like to ask students to suppose that the lawyer charged William a flat $5,000 fee. This would split the difference between the $2,500 short-of-trial and $7,500 through-trial fees. If the case went to trial under these circumstances, the lawyer would lose out, because the trial would have to be completed. On the other hand, if William pled guilty, the lawyer would make out favorably because the case would not have to be tried.

Most students readily see the conflict of interest in charging fees this way. They appreciate that some lawyers — or at least unscrupulous ones — might persuade William to plead guilty because they will get more income. They

also understand that the lawyer might not try as hard in trial. But we suggest this fee-paying method simply to point out that it does not solve the conflicts *inherent* in any fee-charging arrangements. It merely changes the nature of the conflict.

Withdrawal is an option that students will discuss and consider, although in many states it would be difficult to accomplish, particularly close to trial. The students should then evaluate what the lawyer does next. Most will eventually come to the conclusion that the lawyer is "stuck" in the case and must competently represent William, and learn from the experience for the next time.

As we have pointed out before, we don't generally favor withdrawal as a solution to ethical problems, because it merely passes the buck to another lawyer, and sometimes compounds the problem. Here, a new privately retained lawyer would also cost money, and any new lawyer would have to start the case from scratch. If the students too readily agree that the lawyer is "stuck" representing William no matter what, the teacher might play devil's advocate, emphasizing that the attorney did nothing wrong, and that it is William who is breaking the fee contract. But we agree that ultimately, the lawyer is "stuck" with the trial.

(c)   How Good a Job Must the Lawyer Do in Representing William?

Students will generally agree that the lawyer must represent William *competently*. But how far does this go? We like to suggest a scenario to the students, and do some brief role plays regarding it. We posit two or three roughly identical cases, for example a murder case with one eyewitness, a good deal of circumstantial evidence, and some evidence of motive. We ask the students to play the role of defense counsel. The first client retains the lawyer at $300 an hour; a second client retains the lawyer for a $25,000 flat fee. During the course of the cases, however, it appears to the lawyer that it will take more time than originally anticipated. We ask the students on whose case they will work harder.

To our surprise, some students said they would work harder on the $300-per-hour case than on the flat fee case. They reasoned that since lawyers are operating in a "service industry" where the value for services reflects the service received, you essentially get what you pay for. Students agree that the flat fee client is entitled to "competent" representation, but not necessarily the best representation, such as filing every possible winning motion or briefing every significant evidentiary point.

We then posit a third case with the same underlying facts. In this case, however, the lawyer is appointed by the court at a rate of $60 per hour. We again ask the students on which case they would spend more effort. Again, while many say they would expend the same effort for both cases, a surprising number of students say they would work harder on the $300-per-hour case.

We take strong issue with this view. It is our abiding belief that a lawyer owes the client the best job that lawyer can possibly do under the circumstances. In other words, the lawyer does what has to be done on the case. To illustrate our point, we write the letters A, B and C on the blackboard, and next to them write the fee arrangements for those three clients. Then, after we have "undertaken" the three cases, we return to the blackboard and erase the fee information. To our mind, what fee we are being paid is no longer relevant; what is relevant is what the case requires.

(d) Lola Lipp — The Civil Case:

We do not contend in our three defendants example above that all those defendants will be able to afford the same *ancillary* services — out of state DNA experts, jury focus groups and the like. These kinds of ancillary services are what differentiate Lola's case — at least in part (a) — from William's. In Lola's case, the lack of money relates to costs and thus the ability to do additional investigation and line up expensive experts. That is different from a criminal case, where a DNA expert could prove innocence. Moreover, Lola's case is civil; the constitutional requirements of due process and effective assistance of counsel are not at issue here. Finally, the possibility of withdrawal is more realistic.

The point here is that while the same conflicts between the ability to spend money and the goals of the case still exist, they need not always result in lawyer self-sacrifice. Civil cases are run on budgets all the time; here, Ms. Lipp must tighten her budget more than was originally anticipated. She was notified in a letter that her costs could increase, although the lawyer told her this was "unlikely."

Many students will see the letter as providing inadequate notice, but we do not. Some discussion of this is useful, because it emphasizes a central theme about all conflict of interest problems (and many other ethical problems) — notice and disclosure to the client. But the lawyer has said that nothing can be guaranteed; indeed, that was part of the point of the letter. Reasonable disclosure does not have to be perfect or predict the future correctly. We feel this notice was clearly sufficient; it's just that the "unlikely" event of higher costs came to pass.

People make choices all the time about what discovery and investigation they can afford. The teacher may wish to cite examples from experience of where clients in civil cases have asked a lawyer *not* to spend more than X dollars, or not to engage in a particular form of discovery. We also ask our students if they have seen the lawyers they work for do this.

Given our view, students will want to know how Lola's lawyer is giving his or her "best efforts" to Lola in the way we insist on doing for William, regardless of whether he pays the rest of the fee, and for the three murder

defendants regardless of the fees they paid. We answer this way: we said that the criminal defendants were owed the lawyer's "best efforts under the circumstances." Just as the richest defendant may be able to afford a jury consultant while William may not, Lola's lawyer has to pick and choose how expenditures are made. But in terms of *the lawyer's own efforts*, we believe that, as with William, the lawyer is required to give the best representation possible. The term "under the circumstances" in effect relates to ancillary matters other than the lawyer's individual effort.

(e) Contingency Fees:

As **Sections 2** and **4** of the **Readings** discuss, contingency fees have particularly strong inherent conflicts of interest. But just as with hourly or flat fees, the fact that such an inherent conflict is created does not mean that the fees are inappropriate. A lawyer still owes the client the best possible effort. While some commentators, including "tort reform" advocates, now argue for the abolition of contingency fees, our view is that overall they serve to provide access to the courts, and do not create any more of a conflict than fees such as the two-level payment scheme for William Simons.

As **Section 5** of the **Readings** implies, William Simons' fee in effect may be contingent since his second payment depended on his need to go to trial. This is not, however, a contingency fee in the traditional sense. The *Fee* case **(Section 4)** raises the issue of opposing counsel creating a conflict by offering a structured settlement or makes a separate offer of attorney's fees. Ultimately, the lawyer has a fiduciary duty to put his client's interests above his own — even his interest in getting a fee. The *Fee* case is also relevant to **Part III**.

(f) Withdrawal and Practical Reality:

May, or should, Cameron withdraw from representing Lipp? The rules on withdrawal can be complicated and difficult to understand. The teacher and students should look particularly at **MR 1.16(b)(6)** and **paragraph 8** of the **Comment**. The overriding requirement is that any withdrawal be accomplished without harm to the client's case. (See **MR 1.16(d)**.) The Pallasch article and other material in **Readings, Sections 6 and 7**, squarely address this issue.

The teacher should discuss with the students the practical realities of getting out of a case: filing a noticed motion; notice to the other side, done in a way that protects the client's rights while still informing the court of the nature of the request, so as to avoid "material adverse effect" to the client; and/or finding another attorney to take Lola's case. If no new lawyer can be found, this may mean Lola representing herself *pro se*. But wouldn't that clearly materially adversely affect her case? Withdrawal where liability begins to look "iffy," as in **Question I(2)(b)**, may violate the lawyer's fiduciary duty to the client. A review of the **MR 1.16** factors should be undertaken to evaluate this.

This is a perilous reason for withdrawal. Our perspective is that she signed on for the case of her own free will, and should not withdraw on this basis. Many states (including California) agree, at least to the extent that a withdrawal in a contingency matter will generally be grounds for voiding not only the contingency fee but any quantum meruit recovery.

As a practical matter, attorney and client may choose to continue the representation but curtail it. We find this an appropriate time to bring some closure to the issue of a lawyer's "best efforts," by discussing the reality of making a living from the practice of law, and having to choose among cases and sometimes even to set priorities among them.

Not all cases will necessarily get the same amount of attention; this is the reality of law practice. Here, if the attorney and Lola choose to curtail the discovery in the case, Lola's case may get less attention by virtue of their arrangement, but the lawyer will still do the best job possible under the circumstances. The lawyer may be wise to memorialize the agreement to curtail discovery — and some of its dangers — in a writing between attorney and client. This also has an important malpractice-protection advantage.

However, where Cameron cannot afford to do work *necessary* to present Lola's case adequately, she may be required to withdraw on competence ground. This presents an enormous problem if no new lawyer can be found; Cameron is between a rock and a hard place. Withdrawing may be seen in a future malpractice case as abandoning the client.

Whether the lawyer has withdrawn or been fired, it is now rather clear (see **Readings**, **Section 8**) that the client "owns" the file, including most work product. We believe the file should be turned over and swiftly. (We have seen a breach of fiduciary duty cause of action added to a malpractice case when this hasn't happened.) If the lawyer wants a copy of the file, it should be copied at *her* expense, absent a provision in the fee agreement to the contrary.

The direct economic interest that lawyers have in their cases is important to recognize, because it is a reality which cannot be ignored while evaluating what is the "ethically right" thing to do. While fiduciary duties require lawyers to put the needs of their client ahead of their own, it would be foolish to ignore that lawyers have needs as well, and that if they don't make sufficient money they cannot continue to do what they do.

(g) Part II — Arnie Berkowitz and His Stock:

Economically-based conflict between lawyer and client does not have to relate to fees. Here it is the stock portfolio of the lawyer. Arnie's interests in having his stocks appreciate in value is directly in conflict with what he is being told by the Airlines Pilots Association. To us, there is a clear conflict of interest. You might bring in **MR 1.7 Comment 5 (1983)** or Comments **8-11 (2002)** and discuss the concept of impaired loyalty. We try to move quickly

beyond this threshold issue to the question of what to do about the conflict. That addresses our second point: this conflict can be cured if full disclosure is made to the prospective clients, and that full disclosure is done in the manner discussed in **Problem 7**. Perhaps, for example, the pilots would require Arnie to sell his shares in Globie.

We like to ask students what Arnie should do if he had, for example, only two shares of "Globie" given to him by his grandmother for his bar mitzvah. Some students argue that this is too trivial to worry about. But we argue strongly for disclosure. The pilots are very unlikely to be bothered by this, whereas failure to disclose could create problems for Arnie later on, particularly malpractice claims if the case does not go well. Our point should now be getting familiar: disclosure "up front," of even "technical" conflicts, almost always will serve the best interests of the client, and thereby ultimately serve the lawyer as well. This is true from both an ethical and malpractice perspective.

(h)   Arnie's Case — Personal Relationships:

Question 2, Arnie's golfing buddy CFO, is included here to point out that the interpersonal relationships of lawyers are just as important — perhaps more important — in determining conflicts as financial considerations. This kind of relationship is one which the pilots would reasonably want to know about. In our view, it is a conflict of interest, or, put a better way, an *impairment of loyalty*, and Arnie must disclose it. Indeed, depending on how close they are, it may be a more difficult conflict for Arnie to set aside. Arnie's CFO friend serves as a reminder that the principle of loyalty may be a more understandable concept than "conflict of interest."

The teacher may want to ask about other personal relationships more attenuated than the one suggested in Question 2. For example, "What if Arnie's aunt worked in Globie's machine shop?" Just as with the two shares of stock, the answer should be the same: disclose the information to the client. Either the client will consider it trivial and not care at all, or the client will consider it significant and appreciate the disclosure.

In any event, it is the client who should be able to make this call, not the lawyer. A client's perception of what may constitute an impairment of loyalty may be different than the lawyer's. Arnie may know in his heart that his aunt working for Globie makes no difference to him, or that he can deal with his good buddy CFO friend even if negotiations break down. But that is no guarantee that the pilots will see it the same way.

In short, there is no "down-side risk" to making such disclosures; the worst that can happen is that the client will feel there is too great a conflict of interest, and look elsewhere for counsel, something the client has an absolute right to decide. More likely, in our experience, the client will appreciate the disclosure and waive any conflict of interest.

(i)   Sam Shade's Personal Injury Case:

Students differ widely on their attitude toward Sam Shade's handling of Bentley's personal injury case. Many feel that Bentley does quite well, since he gets some money right away, and doesn't have to put himself through the anguish (or the expenditure of time) of going to trial or up to the date of trial.

The issue for us is different. Shade's own focus is on his anticipated fees and how much time he will have to spend in the event of a quick settlement versus a possible trial. You might recall the **Readings, Section 2**, and the lawyers' self-interest described there. This concern about Spade's own financial rewards is, to our thinking, a clear breach of his fiduciary duty to his client. He is putting his own self-interests ahead of his client's case. We believe that his fee really should not be considered at all in determining how to advise his client about settlement or trial. Shade's financial gamble, after all, is undertaken at the time the case is accepted, which is the reason for his taking a contingency fee.

Students may argue that strategically, Shade's suggestion of a quick settlement makes sense. But this begs the question. Interposing strategic concerns does not affect the fact that Shade is improperly considering which way he will make more money per hour. An apt analogy, which some students may be able to identify from their work-related experience, is the "churning" of files by some counsel, for example, insurance defense counsel. This is the opposite of Shade's situation; lawyers will work unnecessary hours on a file and keep the case open without settling in order to bill more hours out.

(j)   Other Issues Raised in the Readings:

The teacher may want to have some discussion about the other issues raised in the readings not directly covered by the problem. See **Sections 9, 10, and 11**. Again, it comes down to the fundamental fiduciary relationship between lawyer and client, which gives the lawyer relative power over the client. In the case of a sexual relationship with a client (**Readings, Section 10**), it becomes a question — not dissimilar from the business transaction — of whether the lawyer has improperly used his or her position of authority over the client to abuse the fiduciary relationship for personal motives. Some commentators cite competence as the main issue, but we think this misses the point.

Lawyers' personal and political agendas (see **Section 11** of the **Readings**) are included to round out the discussion of how lawyers' and clients' needs and goals differ materially. Time allowing, we like to discuss the issue of how a lawyer's personal or political agenda can affect performance on a case. Ulterior motives will, if present, often get in the way of doing what is right for the individual client, even if these motives are altruistic. Most clients, whatever concern they may have for the good of society, are more concerned about the success of their individual cases. We like to say that personal and political agendas are fine, but that lawyers must take as much care to exclude

these from the way in which a client is represented as they would with any financial issue.

Lastly, a word about "positional" conflicts. While this merits only a paragraph in **Section 11** of the text, it is an issue that is garnering increasing scrutiny in recent years. While we predict that "outlawing" positional conflicts in this day and age of relaxed conflicts rules and increasing screening (see **Problem 10** immediately below) is highly unlikely, it will continue increasingly to be the subject of debate and scholarly analysis.

PROBLEM 10

Conflicts of Interest and the Business of Being a Profession

THE POINT BEHIND THE PROBLEM:

This problem concerns an increasingly frequent occurrence; a law firm considering merger or the addition of several new attorneys from another firm, and the consequences to the law firm's practice. There are several principal points in this problem. First and foremost is that the timing of the conflict — whether it involves adverse representation of *current* adverse clients — will likely govern the analysis. Second and equally important is that evaluating conflicts of interest in this setting requires a complicated and rather technical analysis of several factors, particularly where the conflict is with a *former* client. The purpose of this analysis is to determine the extent to which the law firm may be precluded from undertaking or continuing representation.

The second purpose of this problem is to explain to the students the basic elements of this conflict analysis: (1) whether the conflict relates to a former or current client; (2) law firm imputation, or the rule that a law firm is generally treated exactly like one single lawyer when analyzing conflicts of interest; and (3) that the analysis is further complicated by the need to evaluate whether a conflict exists because of the former and current clients of the *firm's new lawyers*, or the former and current clients of *the new lawyers' old firm*. This last issue also brings up the question of whether some lawyers in the firm may be "screened" off from information about cases in order to cure the conflict, as suggested in **Part II** of the problem.

APPLICABLE RULES:

Model Rules:	MRs 1.2; 1.7; 1.9, including Comment, paras. 3-9.; 1.10; 1.11; 1.16, especially (d).
Model Code:	DRs 2-210; 5-101; ECs 2-21; 4-5; 4-6; 5-13 through 5-20.
CA Rules:	3-310; 3-500; 3-700.
CA B&P:	6068(m).

SUGGESTED QUESTIONS TO ASK:

- How would Royster feel getting sued by his own attorneys, even if those attorneys are representing it on unrelated matters?

- Is there a "substantial relationship" between the *Hoosier v. Royster* case and Meeker, Reynolds' former representation of Royster?

- Suppose Meeker only represented Royster in a series of landlord-tenant cases against companies that had failed to pay Royster for space they had

leased? Would this allow Markovich to bring the Hoosier case with him to Meeker?

- Does it make sense to require the disqualification of a lawyer's *new* firm when that lawyer, while at the old firm, never worked for the client now being sued by the new firm? Does it matter that the new lawyer has nothing to do with this case at the new firm?

- What are the justifications for requiring complete law firm imputation, even where the particular lawyers in question never worked on the cases in question? Or even for the clients in question?

- If the litigators leave B&B and move to Meeker, Reynolds without the Hoosier case, turning it over to other B&B lawyers, is the representation "current' or "former" as concerns Meeker and its new (former B&B) lawyers? Can they argue that their *imputed* representation is a *former* imputed representation?

- If a law firm is to be considered as one lawyer when it works to the firm's client's advantage, how can it not be considered one lawyer for all purposes?

- How would you set up an effective ethical screen for your law firm? Do you think it would work in actual practice?

- How would your answers to the problem or to the questions above differ if the persons changing firms were paralegals? Law students? Secretaries?

SUGGESTED ROLE PLAYS:

- Play out the conversation between a lawyer looking to make a "lateral move" from one firm to another, and the incoming firm's partner who is concerned about conflicts of interest.

- Play the role of a client who finds that her former attorney, or a member of her former lawyer's firm, is now working on the other side of a case against her.

- Role play with the class the partnership meeting at Meeker, Reynolds when the issue of the new B&B litigators is being decided.

DISCUSSION:

(a)   The Root of the Problem:

The complexities of this problem have caused us to draw more of a complete road map in the **Readings** (especially **Section 4**) than we do in most problems. Nevertheless, students who lead a discussion of this problem may still require a substantial amount of help from the teacher. It is necessary to carefully isolate issues, and is often helpful to diagram the interrelationships of

various attorneys and parties on a blackboard. We often find ourselves lecturing more in this problem than in many of the others combined. We find it helpful to work through the rules of imputation, substantial relationships, and screening as we go along, applying them directly to the questions in the problem segment by segment, and including other twists on the facts of the problem to complete the picture.

The basic issues can be divided into five component parts: (1) the general rule of law firm imputation; (2) whether the matters involve current clients or one party that is a former client; (3) if there is a *former* client, whether there is a substantial relationship between the *former* representation of that client and the *current* representation of the ongoing client against the former client; (4) if there is a *former* client *and* there is such a substantial relationship, whether the disqualification of the law firm should be mandated by the involvement of that firm's *new lawyers' former firm* or whether it should require involvement of the *new lawyers themselves*; and (5) whether there is a legitimate way of screening the new lawyers if there is such a substantial relationship.

The **Readings** in **Section 1** are designed to help grasp the basics. The first piece explains what happens when a conflict is simply "missed," while the second article shows both the strict construction used when the conflict is considered concurrent, and (as the **Note** after the article states), introduces several key concepts: imputation; substantial relationship; the "hot potato" doctrine; and screening. More about each follow in the later readings.

(b) Imputation and Hot Potatoes:

Before we get to more complicated concepts, we explore two straightforward and relatively intuitive ones. First, law firm imputation simply relates to the rule, as set forth in **MR 1.9** and elsewhere, that for purposes of conflict of interest, *any* conflict that applies to one particular lawyer is imputed to *all* the lawyers in that attorney's law firm. A discussion of the parameters of this rule is important if students are to understand it fully. We suggest that the teacher take the students through the analysis step by step to make sure it is understood, using the guides in **Readings** in **Section 1**, on Pettit and Martin's "technical" conflict, in **Section 2** — our own explanation of law firm imputation and the excerpt from the *Cinema 5* case — and the reference in the Notes to the *Picker* case in **Section 3** of the **Readings**.

Understanding imputation from Meeker, Reynolds' perspective is relatively easy: Meeker's clients, and the conflicts they create, are imputed to the entire firm. Understanding the effect of conflicts once lawyers start moving from one place to another is considerably more complicated. If Royster were a current client of Meeker, the first part of this answer would be easy: The duty of loyalty would prevent anyone in the firm from suing its own client, and no one coming over from B&B could be involved in such a suit, *or* bring the case against Royster over to Meeker from B&B.

As for the so-called "hot potato" doctrine, discussed in **Section 3**, *Picker* and the other "hot potato" cases we cite, especially the Duane Morris case included in **Section 1**, say that a law firm cannot turn a current client into a former client simply by withdrawing. The importance of the distinction between "current" and "former," which we've already noted is key, is discussed further in Part (c). If law firm imputation and the hot potato doctrine are taken together to their logical extreme, one would think that individual lawyers in a law firm would not be able to make a "hot potato" lateral transfer with any more success than the firm as a whole could obtain. Keep this in the back of your mind as you analyze the substantial relationship test with your students.

(c)   Current or Former Representation:

As we've noted, in many, perhaps most, jurisdictions, conflicts and disqualification analysis turns on whether Royster is a past or present client of B&B. For example, suppose Meeker, Reynolds still represents Royster, but only on a series of landlord tenant cases against companies that had failed to pay Royster for space they had leased — completely unrelated to the *Hoosier v. Royster* matter at B&B. The law in most states — and the *Cinema 5* case — is clear: If Royster is a current client of Meeker, imputation will be extended to *all* lawyers throughout the firm, whether or not they are working on cases for that client. This would apply to any lawyer arriving from B&B. (If you are looking for a contrary view, see Prof. Tom Morgan's 1997 article cited in the **Supplemental Readings** to **Problem 7**.)

Some students ask why the substantial relationship test (discussed below) can't be used in situations of concurrent representation. After all, they reason, if the ongoing Royster representation concerns" deadbeat" lessees, that has nothing at all to do with the Hoosier litigation. Indeed, the matters might involve two different offices in two different cities — or on two different *continents*. We point out to these students that the "substantial relationship" test doesn't apply because the test focuses not on confidentiality and potential harm, but on the simpler concept of *loyalty*. We ask students to look at it from the point of view of the client: How would Royster feel getting sued by its own attorneys, even if the particular attorneys are a continent away?

Students sometimes ask a more difficult question that ties together the two issues of law firm imputation and concurrent representation: If the litigators leave B&B and move to Meeker, Reynolds, and leave the *Hoosier* case behind, allowing other B&B lawyers to continue to represent Royster, is the representation "current" or "former" as to Meeker, Reynolds and its new (former B&B) lawyers? This is the first issue addressed by the question of whether the conflict "runs" with the old law firm or the "lateral transfers," the former lawyers of that firm.

The answer to this question is not clear, and there are reasonable arguments on both sides. On one hand, the B&B representation is ongoing. On the other hand, the former B&B lawyers are no longer there and Meeker's representation has ceased. Can they successfully argue that any *imputed* representation of Royster by the former B&B attorneys has become a "former" imputed representation? We are not sure what courts would decide. Here's where the hot potato concept, applied to the entire law firm, may impact the former vs. current issue.

(d) The "Substantial Relationship Test":

We now must address the central question in the problem: What happens if Meeker, Reynolds' representation of Royster has been entirely completed? Could they, as Royster's former lawyers, undertake representation against their *former* client? Could new partner Markovich bring the *Hoosier* case with him?

Since Meeker, Reynolds does not currently represent Royster, the issue becomes whether there is a substantial relationship between Meeker's *former* representation of Royster and Meeker's impending *current* representation of Hoosier *against* Royster. The students should follow the analysis in **Section 4** of the **Readings**. Though we have drafted with a careful eye on a readable step-by-step approach, this can still be somewhat heavy going, and the close guidance of the teacher is advised. Of particular importance are **paragraphs 3** et seq. of the Comments to **MR 1.9** (and **paragraph 3** of the new **2002 Rules**), which deal extensively with rules that relate to lawyers moving between firms.

The broader view, articulated in the *Trone* case in the **Readings, page 275**, is that more than the underlying facts of the representation is in issue. Anything that was learned during the course of the former representation that now can be used against the former client — the way the CEO scowls or giggles in deposition, and what counsel knows those expressions mean — can create this substantial relationship. The personal relationships formed between lawyer and client may be the basis of a disqualifying conflict of interest. The several California cases cited with *Trone* both depart from and lend support to this analysis.

We recognize, of course, there are other views than those in California. The ABA opinion cited on **page 275** limits the significance of a former client's strategies and policies, and the Restatement criticizes the "playbook" theory. (We note that this colloquialism, apparently based on football, involves something of a misunderstanding of the issue, which we believe is better described by the "poker tell" phrase we suggest.)

The **2002** edition of the **Model Rules, Comment 3**, lends support to both broad and narrow perspectives. It says that "a lawyer who has represented a businessperson and learned extensive private financial information … may not

then represent that person's spouse in seeking a divorce." On the other hand, this same paragraph states: "In the case of an organizational client, general knowledge of the client's policies and practices ordinarily will not preclude a subsequent representation." There remains a large gap between these two examples. Does a substantial relationship exist under the facts in the problem? We wanted to make this a close question, but on balance, given the financial details, we think the answer is "yes."

Whatever their positions, students may well have difficulty with the idea that lawyers unassociated with Royster who happen to be in the same firm with lawyers who worked for Royster would be unable to change firms without causing disqualification. While this may seem unfair, it is important to note the reasons for such a rule. They relate directly to the nature of the attorney-client relationship itself, and to the way in which confidential communications are held, that is, collectively within the law firm. Put in this context, the reasons for such a broad rules interpretation will at least be explained to the students even if they don't agree.

(e) Whether Disqualification Turns on the Involvement of the Law Firm or of Particular Lawyers:

If there is a substantial relationship between the current representation of Hoosier by B&B and Meeker's former representation of Royster, *and* B&B's representation involved work done by any of the former B&B lawyers (such as Markovich) who have since moved to Meeker, then Meeker, Reynolds will be disqualified. But here, for illustrative purposes, we want to change the facts of the problem. You may choose to do the same with your students.

What if Meeker, Reynolds was suing *Hoosier*? Further, what if the new Meeker lawyers *had no significant involvement* in the B&B representation of Hoosier? Generally, the clients of each B&B's lawyers would be the clients of all other B&B attorneys, and the confidences those clients impart would be imputed to all at the firm. Applied here, Meeker, Reynolds would presumably argue that the lawyers they want to hire never worked on the Hoosier matter at B&B. But those lawyers *were* at B&B while *other* lawyers worked on the Hoosier case.

This attenuated imputation bothers many students (and indeed many attorneys) for two reasons. First, the B&B litigators may never have had anything to do with opposing Meeker's client at their old firm. Second, these litigators could move to Meeker, Reynolds and never have anything to do with the former B&B client. Indeed, largely because of such arguments, the law in many jurisdictions has changed. Since *Silver Chrysler*, described at **page 276** of the text, this restrictive rule has been liberalized in many states in this narrow "double imputation" situation. As the text indicates, this liberalization gains support from **MR 1.9(b).**

If these authorities are followed, imputation that would be automatic in the case of concurrent representation would not be so in the case of a former representation. Thus, Meeker, Reynolds would not be disqualified if it could show that *none of the new lawyers from B&B* had any involvement in the former representation such that confidences were imparted *to them*, even if they are presumed to have been imparted to their former firm. While many may disagree with us, we have trouble with this rule for the reasons expressed on **page 277**, and prefer the District of Columbia/Nebraska approach. The readings on **pages 276-8** are particularly important in understanding this issue.

We note, finally, that **2002 MR 1.9, Comment 4 (Comment 3** in its **1983** incarnation), which evaluates whether lawyers moving firms have imputed conflicts, states that "the rule should not unreasonably hamper lawyers from forming new associations . . . . If the concept of imputation were applied with unqualified rigor, the result would be radical curtailment of the opportunity of lawyers to move from one practice setting to another. . . ." But this makes this rule one that is designed to protect lawyers and not clients — in our view anathema to the primary goal of the ethics rules.

(f) Screening:

Ultimately, since there are many situations when conflicts sufficient to disqualify will exist, whether they are permitted will more and more often rest on the issue of "screening." As we discuss in **Sections 5 and 6**, despite the obvious "common sense" solution that ethical screens would provide, screens are disfavored in most jurisdictions, except as they relate to government lawyers. As of this writing, over 30 states still have an absolute bar on private lawyer screening (see the **Readings** at **pages 282-3**), and the "Ethics 2000" Commission's attempts to broaden screening were defeated in the ABA House of Delegates. Many students are troubled by this, since screening seems to make such good practical sense.

We commend the teacher's attention to the last paragraph in **Section 5**, at **page 279**. We do believe that jurisdictions that take a broad view of the substantial relationship test may tend to take a broad view on screening as well, and vice versa. This makes some intuitive sense in that broad law firm disqualification would tend to support screening in those occasional exceptions, whereas narrower disqualification would seem to argue against screening where disqualification would be warranted. However, this is a generalization and hardly uniform. California, for instance, is relatively broad on the substantial relationship test and narrow as to screening.

We personally share many of the reservations expressed in this problem about creating screens. After all, if a law firm is to be considered as one lawyer when it works to the firm's and client's advantage, how can it not be considered one lawyer for all purposes? **Section 6's** Romshek and Hamilton and Coan "dialogue" states the cases pro and con thoroughly and thoughtfully.

(g) Party "Interests," Sharing Space, Nonlawyer Migration, and Withdrawal:

While they are not part of the facts set forth in the beginning of the problem, these issues are – and will become – of increasing importance. They are undoubtedly worthy of discussion, and only time and volume of material — and not importance — relegate them to the end of this Problem. The *Morrison-Knudsen* case in **Readings**, **Section 7** goes farther than most, but we include it because we believe that this court's analysis, careful and logical, has much to recommend it. The court's eye remains fixed on what we see as this issue's most important factor: the true benefit — and more importantly, the *detriment* — to the client.

Section 8 of the **Readings** summarizes the state of the law on the second and third issues mentioned above. No doubt by the time you read this, the law will have changed. These important issues will remain in flux for some time. Our purpose here is to alert students to these issues so that they may be aware of the problems when they occur. Finally, we take time in **Section 9** to round out the discussion of withdrawing from a case that we addressed in part in **Problem 9**.

PROBLEM 11

A Day In The Life Of Lynch, Dahl & Wong

THE POINT BEHIND THE PROBLEM:

This problem — our fifth and last on conflicts of interest — raises two separate and distinct situations that frequently occur in actual practice and both cause frequent problems with conflicting loyalties. Significantly, as the introductory paragraph of the problem notes, these are two areas where the rules of professional conduct have not kept up with the realities of everyday practice. The principal points of **Part I**, the attorney acting as insurance defense counsel, are simply to familiarize students with the "tripartite" relationship and to underscore that whenever the lawyer's loyalties conflict, her duty is owed to the insured client, not to the insurance carrier. This is true even where that carrier has an ongoing relationship with the lawyer and her law firm. We also want students to examine the "legal fiction" of dual representation of insureds and insurers.

Part II concerns the increasingly complex world of class action litigation. Again, the main purpose of this part is to familiarize students with the territory, some of the ethical conundrums inherent in class action practice, and some of the legal fictions inherent in this area of practice. Particularly acute are the questions plaintiffs' lawyers face about who their clients are, how subparts of a class, even if certified, may conflict with other subparts, and how the temptations inherent in this under-regulated field increase the danger of attorneys putting their own interests before their clients'.

APPLICABLE RULES:

> Model Rules: MRs 1.2; 1.4; 1.6(a); 1.7, including 2002 Comment, para. 25; 1.8(b)(c) and (f), including 2002 para. 11; 1.16; 2.3; 5.4(c); 5.5; 7.2; 7.3.
>
> Model Code: DRs 2-210; 4-101(A), (B); 5-101; 5-105; ECs 2-21; 4-5; 4-6; 5-13 through 5-20.
>
> CA Rules: 1-300; 1-400 and relevant standards; 3-310, especially (F)(1); 3-700.
>
> CA B&P: 6068(e).

SUGGESTED QUESTIONS TO ASK:

- Does Dahl's "reassuring" Midge about telling the truth increase Dahl's need to not reveal what Midge says?

- May Midge's confidences still be maintained by Dahl?

- May Dahl send a copy of Midge's transcript to the insurance carrier?

105

- May Dahl urge the insurance carrier to settle the lawsuit quickly after learning who was really driving?

- Why do we allow the "legal fiction" of insurance defense counsel's dual role?

- Should insurance companies be permitted to have "captive" in-house defense counsel? Why or why not?

- Does a class action lawyer represent the class, the class representatives, or *all* the class members?

- Does the answer to the previous question change depending on whether the class is pre- or post-certification?

- How can a lawyer protect sub-classes with different needs, such as the "remote store" purchasers in Nyala's class?

SUGGESTED ROLE PLAYS:

- Play the part of an insurance claims adjustor who is quizzing Dahl (played by a student) about Midge's case.

- Turn this role play around; play the role of Dahl trying to avoid revealing Midge's confidences to a claims adjustor.

- With a student, play the roles of Nyala and Wong as they grapple with and argue about the potential conflict in **Question 2**.

- Play class action defense attorney guaranteeing Nyala a large fee for a quick settlement.

SUGGESTED VIDEOS:

- Settling with client: *A Civil Action* — DVD chapter — closing scenes

- *Erin Brockovich* — DVD chapter To Be Identified — Hinkley meeting scene

DISCUSSION:

(a) The Insurance Defense Case:

The students should feel free to discuss aspects of Dahl's representation of Midge, but the answers should wind up being the same: Dahl may not tell Secured anything that would jeopardize Midge's case, *even if* this occurs in deposition. Clearly, what Midge tells Dahl directly is a confidence. What Dahl learns at deposition is learned during the course of her representation of Midge, and should, therefore, probably be considered a secret (see **Problems 4 and 5**). This raises the question of whether Dahl can even send the transcript of Midge's deposition to the carrier. We feel that she can if this is her ordinary practice. We do not think, however, that she can highlight Midge's confession.

But clearly by this time, Dahl is between a rock and a hard place about how to deal with Midge.

If in Dahl's opinion Midge is perpetrating a fraud on the carrier, Dahl may have to withdraw from further representation. If she determines she must do this, she is obligated to do it in a way which does not jeopardize Midge's interests, something which can prove difficult since the carrier will want to know why Dahl is withdrawing, and in any event may be able to venture a pretty accurate guess.

(b) Dual Representation?:

We believe it is beneficial to allow students sufficient time to explore the relationship between insurance defense counsel, the insurance carrier, and the insured client. This relationship is a common one, but one that is partially artificial, since the insured "client" is in some respects a third-party beneficiary, but is deemed the "client" so that her interests are adequately protected. To many, the "real" client from the practical point of view is the carrier, but the carrier is not the "client" from the ethical point of view, at least once an overt difference in interests occurs (see the cases in **Sections 1** and **2** of the **Readings**, especially the Clifford article, added in this edition, highlighting and arguing for broad adoption of a client's bill of rights.)

Students must understand that, as with **Problems 7** and **8**, a key to the conflict of interest Dahl now faces is confidentiality. When this confidentiality diverges from the ordinary duties of defense counsel, Dahl has a problem. In insurance cases, there is a second important conflict inherent in the representation: the independence of professional judgment to be exercised on Midge's behalf, as required by **MR 1.8(f)**. Oddly, the rules continue to offer little guidance for the insurance defense lawyer in this situation. Yet, one thing is clear: Midge has no voice in determining whether to settle the lawsuit. By contract, only the insurer decides, independence of professional judgment notwithstanding.

The insurance industry employs many lawyers; the odds are that more than one student in the class will be doing insurance defense work five years from today. So it is particularly important that students grapple with the question of why we allow the Danielle Dahls of the legal world to be placed between the rock and the hard place described here. As we point out in **Section 3** of the **Readings**, calling Dahl's role "dual representation" is an unconvincing legal fiction. We have long liked the Michigan Supreme Court's opinion in *Atlanta International Insurance* (**Readings, Section 3, page 301**) for its down-to-earth explanation of the unique relationship between insurance defense counsel and the lawyer's two masters.

Why do we allow insurance defense counsel to do what they do? Because insurance as we know it would simply not exist otherwise. This is the only

way we have developed to have the carrier provide legal representation to the insured — a lawyer whose job is to protect the insured's interests. In our view, therefore, we have a practical reality and a legal fiction that impact a lawyer's ethical responsibilities.

(c)   Captive Law Firms and Outside Auditors:

The **Readings, Section 4 and 5** are valuable to discuss, as they raise four discrete issues at one: breach of confidentiality to third-party auditors, the unauthorized practice of law by "captive" law firms, the conflict of interest that can arise more directly when the insurer is also the *employer*, and, once again — and perhaps most significantly — the insurance defense counsel's exercise of independent professional judgment. We see the UPL issue as somewhat less significant than the others. The conflicts issue is an important one. It governs the Montana decision, where the court answered the "who is the client" question first before moving on. But while acknowledged by the Kentucky Supreme Court, the conflict of interest issue was not necessary to the majority's holding. On the other hand, the problem of exercising independent professional judgment relates to both captive law firms *and* audit overseers, whose reports to the carrier may temper what the carrier "permits" counsel to do.

Can counsel adequately represent the insured in these circumstances? Audits are increasingly criticized and seem to be on the wane, but the Kentucky view, while we agree with it, is as of this date definitely a minority opinion. Though in 2002 courts in two major states, Texas and California, have been examining the issue, more and more insurers are tempted by the in-house solution as a way to keep down costs.

(d)   Class Actions Generally and Solicitation:

If anything, there are fewer rules and cases addressing the ethical issues facing class action counsel than there are in the world of insurance defense. Yet the issues, including identifying the client, are considerably more complex. Mass tort cases and complex multijurisdictional litigation only make these issues more difficult.

We ordinarily begin our discussion with a *brief* look at solicitation of class representatives. We don't dwell on this — **Problem 30** covers that topic thoroughly — and the students generally see the basic issue at once. We focus the discussion on the unusual nature of class actions generally, and the reality, discussed in the **Readings, Section 6**, that lawyers often organize and define the class themselves, and have far more power over ultimate case determination than attorneys in most traditional litigation. (Note, however, the 2006 Milberg Weiss indictments referred to in the **Note** at the end of **Section 6**, which could have important ramifications for plaintiffs' class action lawyers down the road.)

(e)   Who Are the Clients of Class Action Lawyers?:

Clearly, the principal client, at least after class certification, is the class as a whole. But surely the clients include the class representatives; case law makes this uniformly clear. Yet, as the strange story of Charles Chalmers in **Section 6** ("Huh, *I'm* the Lead Plaintiff?") describes, the participation of class representatives in settlement discussions — or even their knowledge of settlement issues — is considered by many class action attorneys to be an "annoyance."

The **Readings** in **Section 7** describe what we see as a more difficult and, indeed, problematic issue: whether passive class members are considered clients once the class is certified. Clearly, many courts conclude they are "clients," yet bear few of the normal indicia of "clienthood," and have no say in settlement except the ability to object at a "fairness hearing" or to opt out if dissatisfied. More problematic is that some classes (the airline price-fixing class several years ago comes to mind) have millions of class members, many of whom never become known to class counsel. (In *Amchem*, **Readings**, **Section 8**, the attempt at settlement had included persons as yet unknown and even unborn.) This leads us to a question that the courts we cite seem to have largely ignored: How can a lawyer or law firm take another case with any confidence that the firm does not *concurrently* (thus unethically") represent and oppose one of its "clients" in a massive class action? For that matter, how can the firm possibly run a conflicts check **Question 2** of **Part 2** of the problem addresses this issue. Nyala *knows* the conflict, which gives her a leg up on many, but we tend to the view that no conflict should exist in her firm's representation against a *passive* class member. We consider this an impossible standard to meet.

These issues of clienthood are most troubling, particularly the lack of rigorous law and other regulation. Since the class *representatives* have been singled out as representing the entire class or at least a discrete segment or subclass, and since they have fiduciary duties to the class under **Fed. R. Civ. Proc. 23**, we believe they *must* be treated as clients. On the other hand, we do not understand how *passive class members* can be considered clients in the usual sense. Then what are they — or what should they be? We think the best analysis is one, adopted in some jurisdictions, that see passive class members as less than clients, but rather persons to whom the class lawyers still owe a fiduciary duty. Is this a legal fiction? Perhaps, although less of what we have come to accept with policies of insurance.

(f)   Conflicts Among Class Members:

Classes are not one-dimensional. Even more than corporations, they are multi-faceted, with often disparate interests thrown together for the sake of the whole. As the **Readings**, **Section 8** discuss, including the important Supreme

Court decision in *Amchem*, subclasses may have very differing interests, particularly when it comes to deciding the terms of settlement. Given the control that class action counsel have over the settlement process, lawyers must assiduously guard against choosing one class segment over another.

This is the problem that confronts Nyala in **Question 3** of the Problem, and it's not one that is easily answered. Nevertheless, our view is that in many class actions there should be more subclasses, each protected by its own class representatives, than now commonly exist. Without these subclasses, each of which would be entitled to a reasonable settlement, there is too much pressure — and too much incentive in the form of attorneys' fees — to expect class counsel to protect all subclasses simultaneously, even though this is clearly their sworn duty. Indeed, we have seen the rather routine settlement of class actions that clearly benefit one segment of the class, while doing little — or even harming — another. The Bank of Boston case referred to in **Section 9** is perhaps the most egregious example.

(g) Class Action Horror Stories:

Sections 9 and **10** of the **Readings** focus on the underbelly of the class action world — plaintiff's lawyers taking large fees while class members get little or nothing of value; defendants' counsel who know that settling with the class will be facilitated by settling with the plaintiffs' counsel for fees; coupon settlements that aren't worth the paper the coupons are written on; and frivolous class actions designed to do little more than enrich attorneys. These stories are true, and all too common. What they indicate — and the purpose of their inclusion here — is the need for more regulation in this important area of law, especially a serious effort to address class action issues under the rules governing professional conduct.

(h) The Importance of This Problem in the "Real World" of Practicing Lawyers:

It is important for students to understand how often such problems, relating to both insurance defense and class actions, come up in actual practice. Thousands of lawyers work tens of thousands of insurance defense cases a day. Common law and the rules of ethics have fashioned a relatively straightforward solution to their dilemma. The problems raised in **Part 2** are less widespread, but increasingly common, though they remain quite complex.

Again, we urge our students to look at this from the client's perspective. For example, many of our students point out that we seem to accept "legal fictions" in the insurance defense situation in and class action law. While this may be true of necessity, it remains the case that our fiduciary responsibilities as lawyers are to put the needs of our clients ahead of business considerations which may support our own goals, whether they be continued work from an

insurance carrier or a large class action fee at the expense of some or all the class.

PROBLEM 12

Is the Lawyer the Client's Savior or His Mouthpiece?

THE POINT BEHIND THE PROBLEM:

This problem raises one of the most challenging dilemmas a lawyer can face — what to do when the client wants to act in a way that the lawyer is convinced is not in the client's best interests, and indeed may harm the client. Here, the situation is exacerbated by the client being an immature 14-year-old with psychological difficulties.

The analysis of this problem breaks down into three parts: (1) in giving advice, how strongly can the lawyer persuade, even arm-twist, the client to do what the lawyer thinks best; (2) to what extent may the lawyer make the actual decision for the client; and (3) how does the lawyer's authority to make a decision change when the client is not a mature, unimpaired adult?

The overriding purpose of this problem is to confront and evaluate many students' natural inclinations to act in the "best interests" of their client — or, more accurately, what the students *believe* is in the client's best interests — regardless of the client's own wishes. The discussion should allow students the opportunity to balance what they "know" is the right decision for the client with the danger of "playing God" by deciding for the client. It should force them to consider both the danger of inserting their own views for those of the client, or those of parent, and the danger of acting merely as a mouthpiece even if by most objective standards the client is harmed as a result.

It will be very important to point out in conclusion that the teacher's questions are merely devil's advocacy. The students' arguments should be validated by pointing out the extremely difficult and delicate issues presented. We concentrate on **Part I**, while **Part II** incorporates the interesting death penalty readings. The class may also benefit from a discussion of the three hypotheticals on **page 326**. But one could easily concentrate on **Part II** as well. These serve to remind students that this issue comes up in a variety of contexts outside of juvenile law.

Note, finally, that the battered woman section of this problem has been moved into **Problem 13**. This problem, new to this edition, enables us to focus specifically on the multicultural issues that often face today's lawyers. Those instructors who choose to use only one of these two problems may find that classes will benefit from some discussion of the battered woman problem and the special issues it presents.

APPLICABLE RULES:

Model Rules: MRs 1.2; 1.14; 1.16; 2.1.
Model Code: DRs 5-107(B); 7-101; ECs 7-1; 7-7; 7-8; 7-11; 7-12.
CA Rules: 3-310(F); 3-500; 3-510.

SUGGESTED QUESTIONS TO ASK:

- How hard can you push if you know that Joe, alienated from his parents but trusting of you, relies on your advice and is likely to do what you say? Must you back off a little with someone this dependent?

- Is laying out the factors pro and con ever enough for a client? Especially one like Joe?

- What is the role of the parents in your efforts to persuade Joe? Should their capabilities be taken into account? Their own wishes? How important are these wishes?

- Does the advice we give depend on our own evaluation of the parental home? How subjective can our evaluation be?

- How can you justify merely being a "mouthpiece" when you know it's not best for Joe? Doesn't that call into question whether you are really representing Joe to the best of your ability?

- On the other hand, if you don't reflect Joe's views, then who speaks for him? Who expresses *his* desires, *his* fears, *his* perceptions and concerns if it's not his duly authorized representative?

- Is the lawyer who is so sure of what's in Joe's interests "playing God" with Joe's life? How can any of us be so sure of what is in Joe's best interests?

- How would you approach representing the death penalty client in the *Deere* case?

- Would you come to the same balance of decisionmaking in **Parts I and II**? Why?

- How does Joe's disability or youth affect the lawyer's behavior?

- How do you determine the lawyer's conduct when the disability is less clear or less extreme than in the *Bolden* case?

- How young a child would you allow to effectively tell you what to do?

- How would you handle the scenarios on **page 326**?

SUGGESTED ROLE PLAYS:

- Play the role of the lawyer who finds that Joe uncritically accepts the advice offered without close questioning or close scrutiny; determine how

hard you want to push Joe, or whether you want to just objectively lay out the factors pro and con.

- Play the part of the lawyer after Joe says he has definitely made up his mind, that he wants to go to the Youth Authority, and that he does not want to hear other alternatives. Or have the student play the lawyer's role, while you play the role of Joe, confused, immature, but with a mind firmly made up.

- Play the part of Joe's parent while the student plays Joe's lawyer.

- If a student proposes to refuse to follow the advice of the client in *Deere*, play the role of the defendant.

- With a student as the lawyer, play the role of our former client "Chuck," described below in the Discussion, who wants his lawyer to argue on behalf of his wife rather than himself.

SUGGESTED VIDEOS:

- "You guys are all the same": *The Verdict*, DVD chap. 12, 48:44 - 51:11.

- The impaired client: *I Am Sam*, DVD chap. 11, 1:00:08 - 1:01:22.

THE DISCUSSION:

(a) Using Powers of Persuasion:

A successful discussion could closely track the questions in the problem. The first issue raised is the "easy" question: how far may the lawyer go, acting as Joe's advisor, in pushing the youth to accept the lawyer's vision of what's best? In this discussion, some students may argue that we should limit ourselves to merely defining the alternatives for Joe in the most objective way possible, then letting him make his own decision. But with this particular client, many students will be inclined to take a much more aggressive stance in trying to persuade Joe.

This "easy" question, though, has some hidden pitfalls. We ask some of the following questions to help the students explore these pitfalls: Can you push as hard if you know that Joe, alienated from his parents but trusting of you, relied on your advice and is likely to do what you say? Or would this kind of dependency make you back off a little in how strongly you state your position? Is it fairer to push harder on, say, a sophisticated adult business client than a weaker client like Joe? Or is pushing the business client unnecessary? These questions are designed to show how the will of a weak, unempowered client can easily be overborne by a seemingly all-knowing lawyer. Most also presage

Problem 13. While students may still decide to use all powers of persuasion with Joe, they will hopefully do it with their eyes open.

The role of the parents should be acknowledged and discussed. Some questions which the teacher might ask include: What is the role of the parents in this effort at persuasion? Should their capabilities be taken into account? Does our advice depend on our own evaluation of the parental home? Or on the parents' own wishes, and if so, how important are those wishes? The issue of identifying the client should be revisited here, since often it is the parents of the juvenile who are paying for the lawyer's services. Even if they are not paying, there is a natural tendency to accept the views of reasonable and capable parents. It is most important not to lose sight of the fact that your only client here is the juvenile.

We take the view that persuasion — even in appropriate cases, a great deal of persuasion — is the legitimate and often necessary tool of the lawyer. The fact that one client may be more susceptible to persuasion than another doesn't mean that we should not persuade, and do it strongly if we truly believe in it. At the same time, we are mindful of the fact that for the susceptible client, persuasion can be tantamount to de facto decision-making. At some point, then, the brakes may have to be applied.

(b) Deciding "What's Best" for the Client:

Students tend to want to avoid this issue, choosing to answer that they would use strong powers of persuasion to get Joe to see it their way. The teacher may need to force the issue by making it clear that persuasion simply hasn't worked, and that Joe has stubbornly maintained his position. Teachers may wish to role play, with themselves in the role of the juvenile who has made up his mind that *this* is the way he wants it to be. The possibility of working out any kind of compromise should be eliminated. Finally, students will want to discuss whether the parents' home is a good place for Joe to remain. The teacher may want to have the students *assume* that the parents' home is fine, in order to eliminate the issue of a bad home environment.

Stripped of the other issues, the debate can then squarely focus on the question of whether, when push comes to shove, the lawyer will act in what he or she feels is the client's best interests, or whether the best solution is to provide a voice for the client's own wishes, misguided though they may be. **Sections 1** and **2** of the **Readings**, suggesting different forms of decisionmaking, may be helpful in framing this issue. So does the Tremblay article in the **Supplemental Readings**, an article many have found valuable over the years. We find it very useful to analogize between the *Mason* and *Deere* death penalty cases cited in the **Readings, Sections 4** and **5**, and the difficult if not impossible choices those lawyers faced, and Joe's circumstances.

This is such an difficult dilemma that it should be relatively easy for the teacher to play the devil's advocate, regardless of the perspective of the students who are speaking. We might ask these questions to students who say they would follow the boy's wishes: How can you justify taking this position before the court when you know it's not best for the boy? Doesn't that call into question whether you are really representing Joe to the best of your ability? Doesn't it make you little more than the caricature of lawyer as "mouthpiece"? How could you live with yourself were anything to happen to Joe at the Youth Authority prison?

To those who say they would ask the court for a disposition based on what *they* felt was best for Joe, the teacher can ask, "Then who speaks for Joe? Who expresses *his* desires, *his* fears, his perceptions and concerns if it's not his duly authorized representative?" The issue of "playing God" can and should be directly addressed with these students: "How are you so sure what is in Joe's best interests? Certainly, there are a few kids out there for whom a trip to the Youth Authority might be the best way to straighten out their lives."

Finally, if the students don't bring it up, we want to remind them of the distinction between tactical decisions and ultimate ones. Tactics have long been the province of the lawyer. The ultimate issue — going to the youth prison pleading guilty (see the **Notes** after *Deere* in **Section 5**), or even death, as in the case of David Mason — is generally the province of the client. We then ask whether this changes when the stakes are so high.

For those students who would choose to withdraw from representation if they ultimately fail to convince Joe to change his mind, the teacher can point out the difficulties with withdrawal that we have previously discussed in **Problems 4, 8, and 9**. Withdrawal from representing Joe is unlikely to accomplish more than passing the problem on to another lawyer, who may not be willing or able to consider the issue as carefully.

(c)   Client With An "Impairment," or "Disability":

Joe's relative youth and psychiatric difficulties would have an effect on all of us as we grapple with this predicament. These issues should be addressed in dealing with the question of the extent to which we are willing to make Joe's decision for him. The Hoffman article in **Section 8** of the **Readings** is helpful in evaluating this issue.

The teacher should be prepared to discuss how helpful — or unhelpful — the existing ethics rules are in dealing with these issues. **EC 7-12** and especially **MR 1.14** and its comments should be included in this discussion. Note that the **2002** version of **MR 1.14** marks a material change, including redefining the impairment as "diminished capacity." Only time can measure the effect of the rule's changes.

Students should evaluate whether **Rule 1.14**'s admonition to keep the client relationship as normal as possible, even in the case of a client disability, is workable in actual practice. Two cases explore this reality: the *Bolden* case (**Readings, Section 7**), in which the degree of impairment — the client believes members of his immediate family are inhabited by aliens — seems overwhelming, and the "Unabomber" case (see the article in **Section 6**), in which the extent of Ted Kaczynski's disability or "diminished capacity" is far less clear, and he had been found competent to stand trial. Finally, some would argue Mason and the defendant in *Deere*, like Kaczynski, are impaired simply by having to face the death penalty.

Finally, the students should discuss the *Colwell* and *Goldstein* cases (**Readings, Sections 6** and **9**). In *Colwell* the defendant wanted to die until he received the proper medication. In *Goldstein* the defendant's lawyers advised him to go off his medication so the jury could see just how "crazy" he could be. Lawyers and experts disagreed on whether this advice was ethical or whether a lawyer's duty includes to "preserve his client's health." The Goldstein case is a particularly difficult and compelling one. We ultimately believe that a lawyer's duty continues to be an advocate for the client. If it is in the client's interests to expose his mental illness, then with the client's consent, it is appropriate to do so.

(d)   Who Decides, You or Your Client?

A discussion of how to balance the decisionmaking between lawyer and client should include, in addition to the death-penalty cases, the three hypothetical situations set forth in **Section 3** of the **Readings**. How would students come out in evaluating these scenarios? These scenarios also back to the issue of "impairment" or "disability" discussed above.

Our view is to be most reluctant when it comes to taking decisionmaking out of the hands of the client, even when the client is acting under a partial disability. We tend to be sympathetic with the view that if we do not express what the client's personal desires are, then the client has no spokesperson of his or her own. We want to avoid "playing God" by inserting our vision of what is right for our client in place of the client's own views. Despite our greater experience and objectivity, we feel it is often presumptuous to claim to be certain we are right. It is, after all, our client's life.

We refer to the compelling speech made by Deere's public defender, quoted in *Deere* (**Section 5**), about his efforts to persuade but his ultimate determination to reflect his client's wishes. We take a similar view: we'll try very hard to persuade, but failing that, we'll do what our client wants.

We have used, as an example of the latter, an actual case one of us had. "Chuck," a criminal defendant, was convicted of robbery; he asks his appointed defense lawyer to concentrate argument at sentencing not on his own sentence but that of his wife, convicted of aiding and abetting because she

drove the getaway car. Chuck is concerned because his wife is represented by a lawyer Chuck perceives to be weak, and besides, he reasons that his own lawyer may be more effective arguing for his wife's probation than her own lawyer.

Students are initially disturbed by the defense lawyer carrying out these wishes, but often change their minds when the ramifications of the conduct are discussed. For instance, Chuck may understand that his sentence is not likely to be affected by a passionate argument, but that his wife's might be. In the actual case, we did as "Chuck" wished and his wife received probation. Similarly, with the battered woman, because she's an adult, and the children are hers, the ultimate decision of whether to seek custody of the children will have to be up to her. We urge all teachers to use their own experiences to illustrate the points that we raise in this difficult and challenging problem.

While we believe that this "mouthpiece" approach comes with the territory of being a lawyer, we end our class discussion by positing — and leaving for further thought — the situation of a seven-year-old child who is molested continually by both parents but who nevertheless insists that s/he wants to go home. The implication is that at some point, our view that we tend toward following the client's wishes and being a "mouthpiece" only goes so far. At some point, we too must draw the line.

PROBLEM 13

Practicing Law in a Multicultural World

THE POINT BEHIND THE PROBLEM:

This problem continues the issues raised in **Problem 12** about shared decisionmaking. This new problem was spun off from **Problem 12** for the Third Edition because we believe that the issues it raises are sufficiently distinct and important, and that warranted more specific discussion.

The principal point of this problem is simply this: If balancing decisionmaking is difficult under any circumstances, this balancing act is harder as the cultural divide between lawyer and client becomes greater. We have no definitive answers for bridging this divide, but several of the readings provide a good start. Our principal goals are to raise consciousness on the issue of cultural differences, and emphasize the vital role of communication and listening skills. Little effective lawyering takes place if the lawyer and client cannot find an effective, open, empathic way to communicate, despite disparate backgrounds — and the onus will almost always be on the lawyer to accomplish this.

While it may sound trite and, for that matter, outside the scope of an ethics course to preach tolerance, openness, and understanding, we are committed to encouraging students to emphasize these skills in situations such as those described in **Problem 13**. (We note that we have not named this client intentionally, as any name, and resulting ethnic identity, might tend to limit the discussion to one ethnicity or culture or another, which we wished to avoid.)

APPLICABLE RULES:

Model Rules:	MRs 1.2; 1.14; 1.16; 2.1.
Model Code:	DRs 5-107(B); 7-101; ECs 7-1; 7-7; 7-8; 7-11; 7-12.
CA Rules:	3-310(F); 3-500; 3-510.

SUGGESTED QUESTIONS TO ASK:

- How can JoAnne both empower her client and at the same time ensure that the client and her children save themselves from dangerous abuse?

- What is JoAnne's obligation in this situation to the client's children? How does that obligation change, if it does, depending on what JoAnne understands of the likelihood of the husband harming them?

- What if JoAnne's client speaks very little English and language communication is a principal issue? How is this best overcome?

- Do you believe that advising about the social and cultural implications of the client's actions is necessary, as Prof. Burton argues?

- Do you agree with Enos and Kanter that any traditionally "paternalistic" "best-interests" actions on the lawyer's part "can only be harmful," even if the client says "you decide"?

- How do you believe Enos and Kanter would resolve the dilemma of the battered woman if, once all the information was discussed, she determined to return to her husband? Would the effect on the children matter?

- How does the battered woman's situation differ from Joe's in **Problem 12**? How is it the same?

- Is there an argument that JoAnne's battered woman client should be considered "impaired" under **MR 1.14**? Should that affect the extent to which the lawyer helps empower the client to make her own decision?

- What can you do, given your cultural background, to make your client more comfortable in confiding her true needs to you?

- What can you do, given your cultural background, to make sure your client is able to express her complete story to you?

- What are the differences between **Parts I and II** of this problem? What means of communication do you see as different?

- How important is it that Kayla understands the other side's differences in culture? In modes of communication?

- How important is it that *Kayla's client* understands the other side's differences in culture and mode of communication?

- When dealing with an international business deal, must the lawyer advise the American client to accede to a different way of negotiating? Or might that be seen as a sign of weakness?

- What does Kayla's client have the right to rely on his way of doing things — e.g., "time is of the essence" — the way things have always worked stateside?

- How important is the perception of the United States among other cultures, such as Japan's, in determining how deals are best negotiated?

- How can Kayla use the communication skills discussed in the first part of the readings to advantage in the Japanese deal?

SUGGESTED ROLE PLAYS:

- Play the role of the lawyer interviewing the battered woman *without* sufficient sensitivity to her needs.

- Play the part of the battered woman while a student tries to do an empathy and enabling interview.

- Play the part of the battered woman who states that despite the lawyer's best advice she does not want to challenge custody, her husband, or the old ways. This is for the purpose of gauging how the student "lawyer" will deal with this difficult situation.

- Play the part of Kayla's very "American-style" client as the student acting as the lawyer attempts to explain why it makes sense to consider the Japanese company's negotiating style.

- Play the part of the Japanese company's lawyer explaining why the Westernized way of doing business will not work, as the student "lawyer" attempts to find a common ground.

SUGGESTED VIDEOS:

- Getting inside the client's head: *A Few Good Men* — rejecting the plea deal, DVD chap. 20, @ TBD.

- Understanding and communicating with a client with differences: *I Am Sam*, "My lawyer thinks I'm retarded," DVD chap. 11, 1:00:08 - 1:01:22.

THE DISCUSSION:

(a)   Communicating and Listening:

Before students can get to truly "client-centered" lawyering, it is vitally important to understand what it means to communicate — and perhaps more importantly to *listen* and *receive* communications — with someone who may be very different from the student herself or himself. Almost all of the **Readings**, especially in **Sections 1, 5,** and **6**, focus on this issue. Burton **(Section 1)** emphasizes communication in a more general way, gathering, analyzing and synthesizing, as she puts it on **page 352**. The Weng reading in **Section 5** points to the fallacy of using the traditional lawyer-client model, as it carries the baggage of preconception.

Weng's suggestions, many drawn from others, include allowing for other story-telling other than chronological, accepting the existence of distrust that is not paranoia, avoiding labeling our clients in standard but culturally stereotyped ways, and in all respects listening "actively" so the lawyer understands both "her own culture and the ways it affects her interactions with others." "Unless the lawyer understands her own culture and the ways it affects her interactions with others," writes Weng, "she risks perpetuating the status of others." The creation of a "cultural lens" is a valuable prism through which to view "the real client in her full context." We value this thoughtful perspective.

While to an extent, these articles are just rhetoric, the role-play examples set forth in the Dinerstein, et al. article in **Section 6** are extremely valuable in two respects. First, they bring life to the more theoretical pieces by showing how different cultural backgrounds lead to communications fraught with potential misunderstandings and mistrust. Second, the sensitive white male lawyer in the second role play demonstrates how communication difficulties may be overcome with empathy, lack of ego investment, and acknowledgement and acceptance of one's own mistakes.

(b) One More Preliminary Issue — "White Identity":

Professor Russ Pearce's thoughtful article in **Section 3** is an essential component to understanding both how to communicate and the concept of client-centered lawyering. Without the white, particularly the white male's, acknowledgement of his (or her) racial identity, it will be very difficult if not impossible for the lawyer to truly understand and accept the situation of a culturally different client. As Pearce notes at **page 356**, "we start by looking around the room and feeling like we belong," while many others, including the clients who are subject of this Problem, do not. Without Pearce's understanding of himself, the exemplary lawyer suggested in the Dinerstien piece, **Section 6**, would be unlikely to have the tools to respond as he did to the mixed race reporter in the article's second scenario.

The Watergate reading (**Section 4**) is included here in part because it has long been a part of this volume, and even 30-plus years later, it is important to remind ourselves of the genesis of the modern teaching of legal ethics — Watergate. More significantly, however, we use the article to show an example of a traditional white male attorney who was both principled and right about what was in his clients' best interests, but found himself without the means of communicating with his clients successfully enough to persuade them to change their course. The Cuban refugees, all operating under what they thought was the color of CIA authority, were — as attorney Henry Rothblatt suspected — being used by E. Howard Hunt and the other Watergate dirty tricksters. Rothblatt strongly stood up and refused to participate in what he perceived (correctly) was a set-up plea. But what he was unable to do was persuade his clients he was right. He had great sophistication about the political situation surrounding Watergate, but relatively little sophistication in the nuanced tools he needed to persuade his clients.

(c) How Should We Advise the Battered Woman?:

Once we have examined with our students both the significance of their cultural differences from the battered woman client and the means of communication they (or our lawyer, "JoAnne") can use to truly understand and empower that person, how then do we persuade, cajole, or convince the client to go through with actions against the husband? Or should we do this at

all? For if we do so, are we risking losing the client-centered model that many of the readings support?

Enos and Kanter (**Section 2**) most directly address this issue. They remind us to "address the client as a whole person," and to "see the abuse in the context of the client's life, rather than defining the client in terms of the abuse." Excellent advice indeed. But what happens when this newly-empowered client wants to return home to the abuse, out of fear not just of the husband but of the consequences back "home"?

Enos and Kanter make a clear statement in opposition to "co-opting" the client's power, one that is hard to argue with in theory, but with which we nevertheless cannot completely agree. When the client makes an informed determination, we believe, as we stated in **Problem 12**, that we must respect such a decision. But Enos and Kanter take this a step farther, saying that the lawyer must avoid deciding, even where the client wants the lawyer to make the call.

We question whether a lawyer making a decision *at the client's request* violates the notion of a client-centered approach. After all, the lawyer inevitably has expertise and objectivity that the client lacks. Empowering the client may include empowering her to put herself in the hands of an empathic and capable attorney. Perhaps "client-centered" lawyering more accurately means recognition that we, like Russ Pearce's "white guy," must manage our identity and avoid placing it in a superior position to that of the client? Is it reasonable to suppose that the client, like many others *without* cultural differences, makes a choice to trust her lawyer? We believe it is.

The teacher may want to take time to consider the interesting spin put on the concept of "independence of professional judgment" in **Section 1** of the **Readings**. The author point out, understandably, that "technical interpretation of the rules" is of little value here, which we saw as well in **Problem 12**. Burton also argues that the client has a duty to be aware of the social and cultural implications of her actions. That would presumably include her duties to protect her children. But we are unclear where this article comes out in terms of providing a client-centered framework. Does Burton intend that the client act in a socially valid interest rather than her own? The Weng article's reference to "rebellious lawyering" (**Section 5**) seems like a more fully-realized attempt to describe lawyering that places the client's background and experience as part of the consideration of what course of action should be taken.

Students should be able to engage in a lively discussion of these different perspectives, facilitated by the teacher playing the devil's advocate to counter whichever way the debate seems to move. Finally, if the hypotheticals set forth in **Section 3** of **Problem 12** were not previously discussed, this is an excellent opportunity.

(d)   Is the Client "Impaired" Within the Meaning of Rule1.14?:

Without repeating the discussion in **Problem 12**, we commend the teacher's attention to **Part (c)** of the Teacher's Manual for that problem. Here, as several of the readings suggest, it may be too facile for us, particularly those of us who are white and especially white and male, to see our battered woman client as "impaired." In light of what our students have hopefully learned in this problem, such a concern might be quite dangerous as well as unfair. Still, to ignore the issue completely would be to ignore the fact that at least in some circumstances, genuine impairment or disability within the meaning of **MR 1.14** might exist, as it might for a prisoner on death row.

(e)   Taking Multicultural Issues Into the Commercial Marketplace:

Part II of this problem is particularly important because it reminds us that multicultural issues — and the listening and communication skills we need to develop — need not occur only in traumatic situations. The relatively straightforward business deal addressed in **Part II** is made more complicated by the fact that two cultures are clashing. It would be hard to underestimate the importance of recognizing, dealing with, and resolving this culture clash. Students should recognize that Kayla will be charged with the responsibility to deal with cultural differences in a way that protects Kayla's client *and* the client's relationship with his new Japanese partner. That will undoubtedly call for respect for the new partner's cultural differences, as most of the readings suggest, as well as for the possibility of educating her own client.

Professor Terry's article (**Section 7**) gives us the facts on globalization, and they are both overwhelming and pervasive. It would be impossible to ignore the global nature of commerce in today's world even if we wanted to. The point for our students, as we see it, is to take the skills we have identified earlier in the **Readings**, and apply them here.

The Collins article (**Section 8**) is designed primarily to show what most of us suspect — that how the United States is regarded in the rest of the world can well have an effect on an American lawyer's negotiations with people from different places and different cultures. The questions asked at the end of **Section 8** are ones that can be taken seriously as a jumping-off point for this part of the discussion.

PROBLEM 14

How Far Should Richie Go to Get His Client Off?

THE POINT BEHIND THE PROBLEM:

This problem begins the part of this volume we have called "Balancing the Duty of Advocacy with the Duty to the Legal System." We see this balancing act as being the central ethical dilemma of the practice of law. We have found it useful to take some time with our students to take stock of what we have learned so far and where we are going. The first 13 problems in this volume, while they certainly raise the tension between representation of clients and obligations to our system of justice, are primarily about lawyers' obligations to their own clients. The tensions we emphasize are those among clients and between lawyer and client. Now, we directly confront the tension between obligations to clients and lawyers' duties to the justice system in which we operate.

The purpose of **Problem 14** is to put the conflict between the lawyer's role as an advocate and the citizen's duty to society in a practical context that happens frequently — representation of the apparently guilty defendant. Here we have added to it the fact that the defendant is unpleasant and thoroughly unlikable. Our goals here are several. First, in **Sections 1** and **2** of the **Readings**, we revisit the tension between advocacy and the truth, while in **Section 3** we present the case for "cause lawyering," the representation of the client as a tool for what the lawyer sees as social justice. Second, we provide a real-life context in which the lawyer as advocate must apparently act in a way that is clearly contrary to society's wishes, and may be contrary to the lawyer's own desires. Third, we discuss the extent to which the lawyer can decide, either because of the client's unpleasantness or because of his apparent guilt, that the lawyer can do something less for this client than he or she might do for another. We discuss both these ideas in **Section 4** of the **Readings.**

Fourth, we want to take a closer examination, through the writings of Subin, Mitchell and Freedman (**Readings**, **Sections 9** and **11**), of how far a lawyer is required to go on behalf of his or her client. Is anything less than the lawyer's full efforts ever justified, as Subin claims, given the harm that can be done to innocent people and to society as a whole? We believe that the answer to this is that the lawyer, *once having undertaken the representation*, must do everything possible within the bounds of the law to zealously represent the client in all respects. To do otherwise would not only put the lawyer in the position of judging his or her own client, it would deny the client the best the lawyer has to offer. To support this thesis, we offer Justice White's well-known words from *U.S. v. Wade* (**Section 10**).

All this makes the work of the criminal defense lawyer a hard job, and perhaps few should do it. Some students in the class will conclude from this class that this work is not for them, that they could never do it. We see that as something valuable learned. Part of the appropriate conclusions students can and should draw is that they should not be put in the position of doing work that they find morally indefensible. This is a far better solution than performing at anything less than one's full capabilities.

APPLICABLE RULES:

Model Rules:	MRs 1.1; 1.3, including Comment, paragraph 1; 3.1; 3.3.
Model Code:	DRs 7-101; 7-102; ECs 7-1; 7-2; 7-3; 7-19; 7-25; 7-26.
CA Rules:	3-110; 5-200.
CA B&P:	6068(c) and (d).

SUGGESTED QUESTIONS TO ASK:

- How helpful are the ethics rules in advising Richie how far he may or must go in representing Dirk?

- Should Richie's personal belief in Dirk's guilt have anything to do with how hard he tries to convince Dirk to plead guilty?

- Would it make sense if criminal defense counsel agreed to only go to trial with those people they truly believed not guilty?

- Which model of lawyering makes more sense to you, Rifkind's or Etienne's? Is there space in between for a middle view?

- Is it fair to a client if, as Etienne suggests, the lawyer is focused on a cause? Or can the "cause lawyer" actually help the client?

- Would Prof. Subin see a difference between the "knowledge" presumed in Question 2 and that in Question 3 once Dirk has made an admission? What about Mitchell and Freedman?

- How do you really "know" if Hopman is guilty in Question 2?

- If students believe they must pull out all stops on behalf of Hopman, what about the harm done to innocent witnesses such as those described by Subin and the New York Times article?

- Why does Freedman have difficulty with permitting vigorous cross-examination in all cases? Why does he ultimately conclude that such examination is necessary?

- Would it make a difference if Subin's rape victim was a prostitute who changed her mind about turning a trick? What if she had numerous drug charges and had also lost her child to family protection services?

- What do you think the average person on the street would think about the Michigan ethics opinion? What would Subin think?

- Should Richie go to trial with a client whom he is convinced is guilty?

SUGGESTED ROLE-PLAYS:

- Play the role of Richie advising his client about whether to plead guilty, once where the proof is strongly against him, and once where Richie is certain his client is guilty, even though the proof may be equivocal.

- Do a cross-examination of Rowena Soo, pulling out all stops, including accusing her of either lying on the witness stand or lying on her plea agreement form.

- Do Subin and Mitchell-style closing arguments, and then do one with "no holds barred" in support of Hopman's acquittal.

- Have students do a role-play in which they make a "reasonable doubt" argument, and then have them do an argument assuming they believe their client to be *not* guilty.

SUGGESTED VIDEOS:

- The purpose of criminal defense work: *Studio One,* conversation between father and son — DVD 42:45 — 45:36 or 20:30 — 23:21 without commercials.

- "Cause lawyering"?: *True Believer*, "everybody's guilty" — DVD Chap. 4, 16:50 - 18:42.

- The pain of the criminal defense lawyer: *And Justice for All* , the client I got off committed a murder — DVD chap. ___ (footage TBD).

- Cross-examination: *The Rainmaker*, damaging a damaging witness — DVD chapter 16, 1:46:05 - 48:23.

- Another cross-examination: *LA Law* — cross-examination of rape victim — DVD TBD.

- Using any tool at your disposal: *True Believer* — "Immigrants destroy the American dream," DVD chap. 15, 52:11 - 53:12.

- Popular fiction but unethical lawyering: *And Justice for All*, selling out the guilty client — last scene.

- Popular fiction but unethical lawyering: *The Devil's Advocate*, not defending the guilty client, DVD chap. 42, 2:15;14 — 2:16:26.

DISCUSSION:

(a) Revisiting the Purpose of Ethics Courses:

Time allowing, we encourage a "taking stock" discussion, beginning by recalling the **Introduction** and **Chapter One**, and our opportunity there to ruminate on the purpose of being a lawyer, or "what it's all about." We reevaluate the purpose behind ethics courses such as this one. Some teachers even see these readings as an opportunity to engage in further discussion of what law school is all about, and what law school should be teaching students.

(b) The Role of the Traditional Advocate:

Simon Rifkind's statement, excerpted in **Section 2** of the **Readings**, represents the view of the traditional advocate. While we have significant *theoretical* reservations about this view (which we find many students share), we find *as a practical matter* that as we negotiate our way through the next dozen or so problems, we often find ourselves taking the traditional advocate's point of view, especially when we are in the heat of battle in a case. Our students often experience the same thing.

As our discussion moves towards defining the term "ethical" and discussing its interrelationship with morality, it is sometimes too easy for students to shunt aside the traditional advocate's role. As teachers, we find it is important to validate this role for us all, even as we profess some disagreement with it. As a practical matter, the role of partisan advocate is why most clients hire us as lawyers; we should not abandon it too quickly lest we realize we need it in the far less theoretical circumstance of handling our client's case to the best of our abilities. Moreover, as the discussion moves to the question of ethics and morals, students should remember that to the extent ethics rules are society's — or the profession's — version of what is the "Right Thing" for a lawyer to do, the role of Advocate has received an important imprimatur.

The Etienne reading in **Section 3**, viewed superficially, seems to take a perspective diametrically opposed to the traditional view as exemplified by Rifkind. But on another systemic level, it is also true that the lawyer who believes in his or her cause is upholding a socially valid purpose. While Rifkind is suspicious of public interest lawyers, Etienne makes a good case that they make the best of defenders, in that their principles comport with their actions as criminal defense lawyers. And **Section 4** briefly states the general case for the role of criminal defense lawyer.

(c) Beginning With the Defense Lawyer's Role and Justifications:

We find that often it is helpful to begin a discussion of this problem with the justifications for representing criminal defendants set forth in the Babcock **Reading (Section 5)**, in addition to the perspective provided by Etienne in **Section 3** and the brief **Section 4** reading. We like to quote Babcock's reasons

and Judge Learned Hand's statement that "better 100 guilty men go free than one innocent man go to jail." We also discuss the criminal defense lawyer as defender of the oppressed and protector of the dignity of individual rights — something closely akin to the "cause lawyer." We point out that some criminal defense lawyers see their work as being "there but for the grace of God go I." The Lane article in **Section 5** is articulate justification of a public defender's work. We find this valuable in terms of setting the stage for what Richie is going to have to do on behalf of Hopman.

By way of further introduction, we also take a brief look at the rules which are used to assist our analysis. While the old Model Code talked of zealous advocacy within the bounds of the law (**DRs 7-101** and **7-102**), it is a quarter century out of date. The Model Rules moved significantly away from this emphasis on zeal. The Rules instead defined both competence (**MR 1.1**) and diligence (**MR 1.3**). While **MR 1.3** refers in the first paragraph of the Comment to acting "with commitment and dedication ... and with zeal in advocacy," that Comment also says that "a lawyer is not bound, however, to press for every advantage that might be realized for a client."

We usually briefly discuss whether there is a distinction between criminal and civil cases. We believe that there is. In fact, while **MRs 3.1 and 3.3** provide the brakes on a lawyer acting as advocate, the last point of **MR 3.1** is illuminating: "A lawyer for the defendant in a criminal proceeding ... may nevertheless so defend the proceeding as to require that every element of the case be established." The Michigan Opinion in **Section 5** of the **Readings** well illustrates this point.

But nothing in any of these rules make it clear how far Richie may, should or must go within the context of the facts presented in this problem. What, for example, does the quote from **MR 3.1** above mean? And how does one weigh commitment, dedication and zeal against an obligation which is "not bound to press for every advantage"? Thus, to an extent, Richie will have to deal with these difficult questions on his own.

(d) How Far Must Richie Go?

Question 1 is designed more to frame the problem than to result in lengthy discussion. Most students will agree that Richie must set aside or try to set aside his revulsion toward his client. However, some will feel that he should get Dirk to plead guilty if he feels that Dirk clearly is guilty. We ask whether Richie's belief in Dirk's guilt should make any difference in how he hard he pushes Dirk to plead guilty. This raises the basic issue of representing the known guilty client (an issue some teachers may have raised in the first class through the Mellinkoff reading in **Chapter 1**). But we feel that the strength of the lawyer's belief in the client's guilt is not an appropriate criterion for deciding how hard to push for a plea. Rather, the criterion should be how strong the case is, regardless of Richie's personal convictions.

The teacher can point out that students who believe that they should not successfully represent the clearly guilty client really reflect the views of society as a whole. But lawyers are not "society as a whole." It is important for students to recognize that they should either step aside from criminal defense cases, or be prepared to represent people they are convinced are guilty. After all, many, even most, of the criminal defendants represented by counsel are guilty of something. We ask if it would make sense if criminal defense counsel agreed only to go to trial with those people they truly believed to be not guilty. Again, we believe that the zealous criminal defense lawyer should look at evidentiary proof, not actual guilt.

(e)   Subin, Mitchell and Freedman:

Questions 2 and **3** can be analyzed by relating them to the debate between Prof. Subin and attorney Mitchell, and to Prof. Freedman's analysis. In **Question 2**, Richie sees a defense in which he does not believe, but which he feels may "work" to gain his client an acquittal. It will require a "both guns blazing" cross-examination. As students give their own views about this, it is useful to ask what Prof. Subin might do. Clearly, Subin would have questions about such a cross-examination, but here, he is not sure of Dirk's guilt. A review of Subin's analysis of what constitutes "knowing" a client is guilty is helpful.

The issue of "knowing" changes in **Question 3** because of Hopman's admission to his lawyer. Subin would likely see a difference between the "knowledge" presumed in **Question 2**, and conclusively understood in **Question 3**. But what about Mitchell and Freedman? Would this knowledge make a difference to them so long as Hopman does not testify?

The students' views should be compared to those of the commentators. If they believe that they "really know" that Hopman is guilty in **Question 2**, this hypothesis should be tested carefully by the teacher. If they believe that once they know Hopman is guilty, as in **Question 3**, they must withdraw from the case or not engage in vigorous cross-examination, they should be tested with Mitchell's and Freedman's hypotheses. If they conclude in a facile manner that they can defend Hopman no matter what as long as he does not testify, the teacher should test them by evaluating the harm to the innocent witness that Subin discusses. The New York Times article in **Section 8** of the **Readings**, which compellingly shows the horrors of vigorous cross-examination of innocent people, should also be mentioned.

Although Freedman's hypothesis will be discussed at length in **Problem 15**, this is an excellent time to preview it. It is valuable to some students to understand both his trepidation and his reason for going forward with vigorous cross-examination in any case. His concern has the same basis as Subin's — he would be excoriating a perfectly innocent victim. But his basis for going forward is a compelling one: that even when he knows his client is guilty, this

knowledge comes from confidences that he has sworn not to hold or use against the client. To fail to cross-examine vigorously, Freedman would argue, would in effect use the defendant's confidences against him. We personally find this argument most persuasive.

Students who agree with Subin's analysis might be given a changed set of facts. Instead of a rape victim, let us hypothesize a prostitute who changed her mind about turning a trick and was then raped. Would that change the students' views about vigorous cross-examination? What if the prostitute also had drug charges and had lost her child to family protection services? Would that make a difference? If it does, the teacher could then ask why, since the issue, according to Subin, is the ethics of a cross-examination that is intentionally designed not to seek the truth. As we modify it, the truth of the rape has not changed, though the extent of sympathy for the victim has.

(f)   Doing the Cross-Examination:

Lest we come too easily to the conclusion that we must vigorously cross-examine Soo, we like to do a role-play of the cross-examination, with ourselves as Richie and a student as Soo. We pull out all stops and take no prisoners. We show her her written plea agreement. We ask her whether she sees where she has written that she "personally committed great bodily injury on her own child." We ask her whether it is her signature on the bottom of the plea form. We ask whether she has written that everything in this form is true and correct. We then ask her, "Isn't it true, then, that you battered your own child?" When she says "no," we say "But didn't you admit that in this document?" If she hedges on her admission, we insist and go to the document again. Finally, if she says she did not really batter her child, we take this tack: "Are you saying then that you *lied* in your plea agreement?" If she admits it, we may stop, but if she denies it, we ask "Well, then, if you didn't lie there, then you must be lying now."

We do this to demonstrate the reality of a vigorous cross-examination. It often stops the class cold to see the cross-examination actually taking place. *Saying* that one will represent a client zealously and not accede to Subin's softer position can be a far cry from putting one's feelings aside, swallowing hard, and going ahead with "both guns blazing."

(g)   The Michigan Opinion and the "Right Thing to Do":

Before we get to closing argument, we think the Michigan opinion set forth in **Section 5** of the **Readings** is very valuable. This opinion uniformly troubles laypeople, but seems acceptable to most lawyers and law students. Since the known guilty client is being defended by *truthful evidence*, albeit evidence which is misunderstood to the defendant's benefit, students who are uncomfortable with suggesting false defenses or with vigorously cross-

examining truthful witnesses are far more comfortable with presenting this evidence.

The teacher might ask what students feel the average man or woman on the street would think about this opinion. They might ask also what Prof. Subin might think. Indeed, we see this opinion as an excellent example of how society's perception of what a lawyer's role should be differs materially from the legal profession's own perception. We are in complete agreement with the Michigan opinion, and further, we see a parallel between it and **Question 3** of our problem. In short, in vigorously cross-examining Soo, Richie, having undertaken the representation, must do his level best.

(h) Closing Argument:

We conclude with Richie's closing argument, a matter addressed at some length by both Subin and Mitchell. Subin argues that he should limit his closing argument to why the facts presented by the state do not sustain the burden of proof beyond a reasonable doubt. Mitchell goes further, even giving us a sample closing argument in the case of his client who stole an ornament for a Christmas tree. He relates the facts of the case to reasonable doubt, but does it in a "sanitized" fashion. Subin then replies to Mitchell, pointing out his sanitization, and giving a more direct closing argument before rejecting that type of approach as creating a false impression.

We believe that neither Subin's recitation of the state's failure to provide proof beyond a reasonable doubt, nor Mitchell's sanitized reasonable doubt argument works. But we — and we suspect Freedman — would go even further than the "false impression" argument which Subin suggests and then rejects. Again, we role-play here with our students either with the Christmas ornament case, or Dirk's case or both.

Again, for illustrative purposes, we make sure to pull out all the stops to intentionally shock the students about how a "both guns blazing" closing argument can actually sound. Thus, we might say, "Members of the jury, do you really believe that a mother would ever admit to battering her children like these children were assaulted if she did not actually do it? Do you know any mother who would lie in this horrible way? There is simply no proof that Dirk Hopman did this terrible thing, save for the testimony of Rowena Soo, a sworn liar and admitted perjurer."

The problem that we have with "sanitized" arguments, much less Subin's state-of-the-proof argument, is that they simply do not work. We invite students to try to construct arguments which raise reasonable doubt without arguing directly for a finding of not guilty. When we do, the obvious pulling of punches involved in this process is readily apparent. We compare the defense lawyers' job to that of an old-style carnival strongman. For a dollar, you can punch the strongman as hard as possible to see if you can knock him

down. If you swing anything less than as hard as you can, it defeats the very purpose of the exercise.

We try this test: When students who make the "reasonable doubt" argument are then asked to make an argument assuming that they believe their client to be not guilty, the difference is also readily apparent. The teacher can then point out that the difference between these two arguments is that only one of them truly involves the most zealous advocacy. In closing, we like to point out that we come to the same conclusion on **Problem 14** that we did on **Problem 12**. That is, ultimately the lawyer here must also serve as a "mouthpiece" for the client, reflecting the client's perspective regardless of personal belief and the client's repugnance.

Finally, we excerpt from our book, *The Moral Compass of the American Lawyer: Truth, Justice, Power and Greed*[*] the no-holds-barred closing argument on the Mitchell/Subin case that we wrote for Richie:

> Members of the jury, let's look carefully at the evidence the prosecution has presented against Martha. First, she walks out of the store holding the star in hr hand. Not in her pocket, not in her purse, not in a bag. *In her hand*. She didn't conceal the star, didn't try to hide it. In fact, that's why she was caught — because she walked right out of the store with the star in plain view, where everyone could see it. That's not how you steal something. That's what happens if you forget you have it. How many of you have ever absent-mindedly picked up something and started to leave without paying? Isn't that what this is about?
>
> Second, when the manager left her alone for five full minutes to deal with the fire, what did Martha do? If she had left, no one would have been the wiser. The manager didn't even have her name. But leaving is what a guilty person would do. Martha sat there and waited for the manager to come back. That's the behavior of someone who had nothing to hide, who knew she had not done anything wrong....

The argument would then go on to discuss the money in the defendant's pocket and her crying in similar terms.

Our fictional "Richie" would argue that he can't show reasonable doubt by *arguing* reasonable doubt. We believe that this view is correct.

PROBLEM 15

When the Client Insists On Lying

THE POINT BEHIND THE PROBLEM:

This problem, using the interesting and inflammatory framework of perjurious testimony, takes **Problem 14** one large step further. It presents what one might call the ultimate extreme of advocacy — putting on perjured testimony — in a balancing act with one's obligations to the legal system.

This problem is something of a departure from our norm in that it is based largely on scenarios developed by Prof. Monroe Freedman. Freedman's "perjury trilemma" has proven to be an abidingly valuable teaching model, both because students remember it and their discussion about it as one of the highlights of the class, and because it so graphically pits the advocacy for the client against the obligations to the legal system.

The goals of this problem are several. First, we want to reinforce the idea, expressed by former Yale Dean Calabresi (**Readings, Section 9**), that "any system breaks down in the extreme case." That is, there are no perfect solutions here; the solution of not putting on the perjured testimony, while it comports with the rules, has many of its own problems.

Second, students gain valuable insight into the difficulty of striking a balance when they understand why Freedman advocates putting on the perjured testimony — not merely because of the lawyer's role as advocate, but because of the promises made the client about confidentiality. Further insight is gained by understanding Freedman's point that this involves not a dilemma between advocacy and obligations to the legal system, but a *trilemma* that includes the lawyer's need to gain knowledge about the client's case in order to best serve that client.

The point in **Part II** is to demonstrate to the students the fine line between advising the client of the law, certainly one of the responsibilities of counsel, and actively assisting the client to come up with a false story. Freedman (and we) draw the line between the penknife scenario on one hand and *Anatomy of a Murder* on the other. Other commentators and students will draw it differently. But the exploration of the dynamics of giving advice to the client and answering the client's questions, while not assisting the client in the creation of falsehoods, is an important matter to be understood by students.

APPLICABLE RULES:

Model Rules: MRs 1.2(d), and Comment, paragraph 6; 1.6; 1.16; 3.3, especially 1983 Rules (a)(4) and (c) and 2002 Rules (a) and (b), and Comment, paragraphs 5-9 [compare to 1983 Rules]; 3.4.

Model Code: DRs 4-101, especially (C); 7-102(A)(1) (4) and (6) and
               (B)(1); 7-106; ECs 7-5; 7-6; 7-26.
CA B&P: 6068(d) and (e); 6128.
CA Rules: 5-200.

SUGGESTED QUESTIONS TO ASK:

- Is Freedman's justification for allowing the perjured testimony at all credible?

- Would refusing to allow the perjured testimony to go forward discourage clients from ever telling their attorneys the truth?

- Are the ethical rules satisfactory in dealing with this issue?

- Are you satisfied or dissatisfied with the alternative of allowing the client to testify in the narrative? Why?

- Why is withdrawal a helpful solution?

- To whom is a higher obligation owed, the client or the court?

- How do we know the client in Freedman's scenario is not guilty? Just because he tells us so?

- Does it change the justification for putting on the perjured testimony that the client is actually not clearly innocent? Why should it change?

- Why does Freedman reach the conclusion he does to allow the perjured testimony to go forward?

- Do you see a distinction between the actions of Pop Campbell's two lawyers?

- Is there any way to rectify perjured testimony without violating client confidences and/or damaging the client's case?

- Why does Freedman claim that putting on the perjured testimony is not *suborning* it, whereas performing the "Lecture" is subornation?

- Do you see a difference between perjury in the context of a criminal vs. a civil case?

SUGGESTED ROLE-PLAYS:

- Play the part of a client being told by the lawyer that if the client insists on testifying, the lawyer will tell the court it is perjury.

- Play the part of a client who, upon hearing that the lawyer insists the client tell the truth, explains to the lawyer why the testimony will not be *perjury* even when it is.

- Play the part of a client who is trying to get an answer to his questions about why how often he carries the penknife is important.

- Expand on the previous role-play, by playing the client, innocent of the crime, who is trying to guess the "right answer" to the question about how often he carries his knife. Let the students hear the client's thought processes.

SUGGESTED VIDEOS:

- The false explanation: *A Civil Action*, searching for the bogus alternative explanation in deposition, DVD chap 9, 31:07 - 32:01.

DISCUSSION:

(a) · Evaluating the Potential Perjury Itself:

Must a lawyer refuse to put on the perjured testimony? Is Freedman's justification for allowing the perjured testimony at all credible? We suggest beginning the discussion by directly confronting the perjury question. Freedman's "perjury trilemma" appears in **Section 3** of the **Readings**.

Students will often begin by saying that they will do everything that they can to talk the client out of committing perjury. The teacher may want to avoid too much discussion on this point. We probably can all agree we would use our best powers of persuasion to talk the client out of the perjury. This, we can point out, is what the public defender successfully did in the *Whiteside* case excerpted in **Section 6** of the **Readings**. The real problem is what happens where we are unable to dissuade the client.

Students will differ in their approaches. Many may feel that the whole justice system falls apart if they allow the perjured testimony to proceed. These students will likely opt for either advising the court, withdrawing, or allowing the client to testify in the narrative without further comment from the attorney. Each of these conclusions should be tested by the teacher. The teacher might argue that refusing to allow the perjured testimony to go forward may discourage criminal defendants from ever telling their attorneys the truth. Students also should be confronted with the fact that they represent an innocent man, as Freedman has advised us in his hypothetical.

At about this juncture, we think it is important to review the relevant rules, discussed by us at some length in **Section 2** of the **Readings**. In many respects, none of these rules is terribly satisfying. We are particularly critical of the solution of testifying in the narrative, for the reasons we describe in **Section 2**. Its hybrid solution seems the worst rather than the best of all possible worlds.

An entire class could be spent comparing the 1983 and 2002 versions of **Model Rule 3.3** and its related comments. We have set forth a very brief explanation at the end of **Section 2**, on **page 404**. Interested professors might want to go through a redlined version of Rule 3.3 to examine all its changes.

The teacher may point out that withdrawal is often not available to the attorney, and even if it were available, we tend to agree with Freedman that it may simply mean that subsequent counsel will not know the truth, thus permitting the perjury to go forward, hardly the goal the withdrawing attorney was seeking, except if the attorney just wants to pass the buck.

(b) Considering Putting On the Perjury:

Some students, perhaps more willing to take a risk (as well as having the safety of agreeing with a noted professor), will adopt Freedman's approach. These students too should be carefully tested on their conclusion. They should be forced to consider whether *anything*, even their clear obligations to their clients, should allow them to present matters before a court which they know to be false. The teacher should point out, as we do in **Section 5** of the **Readings**, that most commentators — most but hardly all — believe that of the two obligations, to the client and to the courts and justice system, the latter duty is higher.

Some students will point out that they know that their client is innocent, and that that makes a substantial difference. The teacher should press the students on this point as well. After all, we emphasized in **Problem 14** that whether the client was guilty should generally not make a difference in the zealousness of the representation. Moreover, how do we *know* the client in the Freedman scenario is not guilty? In reality, only because Freedman has told us, but how does *he* know?

In the "real world" even if Freedman thought his client was innocent, he would not know any more than we do. To that extent, the hypothetical is artificial. If we assume that we don't know for sure if our client is innocent, or know he is guilty, that changes the justification for allowing the perjured testimony for many students. But *should it*? We think that the innocence of the client is a red herring that Freedman has placed in our path; guilt or innocence largely begs the question on the actual issue of whether the obligation to the client to put on his testimony overrides those to the court.

(c) Prof. Freedman's Position:

Freedman's reasoning and justifications should be compared to the requirements of the stated rules. Students should be reminded of Freedman's two principal points. They are: (1) knowing of perjury and allowing the testimony to go forward is better than selective ignorance and not finding out as much as you can from your client; and (2) the bottom line is that when you

have promised your client to maintain confidences and secrets, you cannot abandon this fundamental assurance even in the face of perjured testimony, for to do so would destroy the very foundation of the attorney-client relationship. In a sense, the tension between those who agree with Freedman and those who agree with Burger (see *Johnson v. U.S.* at **page 409**) reflects the tension between two irreconcilable principles: putting the clients' needs first before those of the justice system vs. putting the needs of the justice system ahead of the clients.

Freedman would rather rely on the adversarial system to provide the opposing attorney with ample cross-examination and argument with which to impeach and destroy the perjurious client's testimony. We believe it contributes to Freedman's conclusion that he posits a criminal case, implicating constitutional requirements of due process and effective assistance of counsel.

We like to say in conclusion that Freedman is, in a sense, the ultimate radical conservative. That is, while he seems radical, he is really espousing the old-fashioned polarized system of advocacy at all costs, the same extreme of advocacy extolled by Rifkind and even Freedman's frequent opponent, former Chief Justice Burger. Freedman simply takes the advocacy component to its logical extreme of allowing the perjured testimony.

(d) Other Perjury Readings:

The Campbell and Drake case (**Readings, Section 1**) is valuable not merely as background, but also to compare the actions of Pop Campbell's two lawyers. One of these lawyers refuses to disclose Campbell's perjury after-the-fact, clearly protected by the rules. However, the other Campbell attorney apparently found out about the perjury before Campbell testified. (This distinguishes this situation from the selective ignorance Freedman so strongly criticizes.) Yet, the article makes little distinction between these two lawyers. Is that correct? If the rules themselves have not thoroughly been discussed with respect to the Freedman perjury scenario, they can be revisited here. (Again, see **Section 2** for the rules summary.)

Nix v. Whiteside also should be discussed, as should ABA Opinion, 87-353, which followed it. (See **Readings, Sections 6 and 7**.) We do have views about *Whiteside*; we agree with the minority, which believed that this should not be viewed as a case which sets ethical standards. We expressed these views in **Sections 6 and 7** of the **Readings**. Clearly, *Whiteside* on its face stands for the fact that when a public defender successfully *dissuades* a client from committing perjury, that lawyer has acted properly. Chief Justice Burger's dicta about a lawyer's other ethical obligations is entirely unnecessary to the opinion.

(e) Perjury in Civil Cases:

Before leaving the perjury issue entirely, it is important to compare criminal and civil cases and point out the differences between them. It is helpful to note that almost all of the writings on the subject of the perjury dilemma (see the **Supplemental Readings**) use the criminal model. The **Readings in Section 10**, and the *National Law Journal* article listed in the **Supplemental Readings**, provide a framework for the civil arena. It is useful to distinguish this arena, and also to point out, as McErlean does in his article, some of the different problems that occur in civil cases, where pre-trial deposition testimony is the rule, and the most frequent venue for perjury.

Because perjury is most likely to occur at deposition, and because deposition is usually held well before trial, there is ample opportunity for counsel to insist to the client that the perjury be rectified. Here, *Jones v. Clinton* (**Readings, Section 11**) is a valuable case in point. As the introductory note in **Section 10** of the **Readings** states, many jurisdictions require actual revelation of the perjury in addition to withdrawal if the client refuses to rectify. It is hard to imagine as much justification in any scenario for allowing a perjury to occur in a civil setting as in the criminal scenario posited by Freedman.

(f)   How Do You *Know* When Your Client Is Committing Perjury?

Knowledge, the essential prong of Freedman's trilemma, is the key to his perspective. It revisits the point Prof. Subin made in Problem 13. Freedman sees a clear duty to have lawyers educate themselves about the client's story. Without that, it is impossible, from his perspective, fully to advise the client.

Our own vision of knowledge is somewhat different. We find it easier to justify the position taken by the criminal defense lawyer "of our acquaintance" in **Section 8** of the **Readings**. Ironically, to us, ABA Opinion 87-353, and the courts and commentators who admonish us not to become the judge of our client's story, seem to agree with our perspective. Nevertheless, Freedman is greatly troubled by avoiding knowledge, calling it in his 1990 book (not included in the readings) the "Roy Cohn defense." Selective ignorance is an ethical issue, and not just a practical one. **MR 3.3** in its **1983** and **2002** versions can serve here as a useful example of whether a rule itself can help foster a lawyer's selective ignorance by talking about offering evidence "known to be false." Finding out what your client has to say remains the cornerstone of Freedman's trilemma.

However, many feel that 'knowing," or even defining what that word means, is nearly impossible. The standard of knowledge — even, according to the applicable attorney in *Whiteside*, is very narrow. We agree that 'knowing" can't involve conjecture, surmise, or even deduction. The *Long* and *Midgett*

cases cited in **Section 8** of the **Readings** help show the limits placed on a lawyer who does not really "know."

(g)   The Penknife and *Anatomy of a Murder*:

We begin a discussion of **Part II** with a review of "The Lecture" from *Anatomy of a Murder*, summarized in **Section 12** of the **Readings**. We often show the scene from the Otto Preminger movie quoted in that section.

Many students seem to feel that the *Anatomy* situation and the penknife scenario are ethically indistinguishable. We find that role-playing the "penknife" conversation is helpful in pointing out the differences. With the teacher playing the role of the client, the client can insist on straight answers to his questions.

This is particularly helpful where students want to lay out matters "objectively," and thus decline to explain to their client why carrying the penknife all the time is so important. (It is because carrying it on this occasion but not as a regular practice would tend to show the intent to use it.) In the dynamics of an actual conversation between lawyer and client, refusing to answer the client's questions becomes difficult if not impossible. We go so far as to play the part of a client who is not given the information by the lawyer, and who always carries a knife, but who tries to "guess" the "right answer," i.e., the one which will help his case the most.

(h)   Why the Scenarios Are Different:

We hope that playing out these roles demonstrates the difference between the two scenarios. We agree with Freedman that *Anatomy of a Murder* takes us over the line because the lawyer is actively assisting the client in coming up with a defense that he never would have imagined himself. On the other hand, we see the penknife scenario as answering our client's questions and doing our best to give legal advice.

We find our students deeply divided on these two scenarios. Many feel the *Anatomy of a Murder* lecture is ethical, while many more, perhaps the majority, feels that it suborns perjury. But again, many see little distinction between "The Lecture" and the penknife advice.

Since lawyers must be advisors as well as advocates, the point of **Part II** is to draw the line between advising and helping to create a false story. A comparison can be made between these scenarios and **Problem 4**, in which Roger Earl is confronted with a gun placed on his desk by the client. As in **Problem 4**, the teacher should emphasize **MR 1.2(d)** and **paragraph 9 (paragraph 6** under the **1983 rules)** of the **Comment** to the rule, which discuss the obligation to advise the client, even if the client may use that advice to further criminal objectives.

Again, as with Roger Earl, some students will be very uncomfortable with giving advice that may result in the client's fraudulent conduct. To those, the role-play of the penknife conversation can be particularly valuable, particularly if the teacher shows the client's frustration in not being able to get a straight answer to his questions.

Before closing, we like to point out that Freedman claims that putting on perjured testimony should be distinguished from suborning it. It is for this reason that Freedman will put on the perjured testimony of the client in Part I of the problem but refuse to suborn it in the manner of *Anatomy of a Murder*. The students may take issue with this position. The discussion of whether a legitimate distinction can be made between putting on perjury and helping create it can be interesting.

While we agree with Freedman that the *Anatomy of a Murder* situation is suborning perjury, and that the penknife scenario is not, being advice which a lawyer is required to give to a client, we think the teacher should reinforce the point that these issues are difficult ones, and that criminal defense lawyers (and sometimes others) must often perform a juggling act on a tightrope in order to make these distinctions.

(i)   Subordination in A Civil Context:

The now-famous Baron & Budd memo is discussed in the **Notes** in **Section 12**. If time permits, it's valuable to look at whether this is suborning of perjury or mere thorough horse-shedding. We discuss this memo further in **Problem 17**.

PROBLEM 16

Pushing the Envelope and Coming Clean to the Court

THE POINT BEHIND THE PROBLEM:

We divide the time on this problem roughly equally between **Part I**, and **Parts II** and **III** combined. If anything, we give the more complex **Part I** more time. The first principal point of **Part I** is to explore how a lawyer must engage in a balancing act between doing her level best for her clients, on the one hand, and going too far in creating claims for the client on the other. Just as in **Problems 1** and **2**, where lawyers have broad discretion in undertaking cases and choosing clients, lawyers have considerable discretion in determining what kinds of actions are appropriate to file on behalf of their clients. They also have obligations that extend beyond those to the client to investigate claims and refrain from filing frivolous or unsubstantiated ones. One of the major issues that students will have to resolve is how much investigation they must do in order to substantiate a claim.

Second, as we have come to see, there are different ways of measuring a lawyer's conduct. In the case of filing a frivolous claim, at least three different standards are used: the rules of ethics themselves; the tort standard of malicious prosecution; and the sanctions available under **Rule 11**. (See **Readings, Sections 1, 2, 4** and **5** for a discussion of all three.) Ethical standards are our primary concern. But from time to time in this course, other rules, similar to ethics standards in some respects but created for different purposes, may also be important to a complete understanding of the subject. Rule 11 is one such standard. Because Rule 11's standards are generally applied much more broadly than ethical, it is of particular importance to this problem.

Part II explores several facets of the tension between zealous advocacy for one's client and the obligation to the legal system. We include it largely to present a situation in which lawyers may commonly break the rules to fulfill the needs of their client — or their own desires — the last-second discovery of adverse law. It is important for students to recognize that, as a practical matter, the last-minute discovery of adverse cases usually occurs only in the deep, dark recesses of law libraries and Internet searches (or perhaps lawyers' minds). But when the more extreme of our scenarios take place, we believe most lawyers will violate black-letter rules in order to win their motion.

Additionally, the problem points to the clear irony that lawyers must give the court *case authority* which is on point, but need not reveal *facts* proving that, in actuality, their client's position is likely unjustified. The ethical rules clearly support this conclusion, even though students (and many practitioners) are uncomfortable that the fruit of their own labors, the case law adverse to their positions, must be revealed to the other side.

145

The final issue, about the propriety of closing argument, presents us with yet another question of semantics: how can a lawyer say there is no evidence to support the other side's conclusion beyond that other party's testimony when she knows of other evidence which contradicts her argument? Here, we examine the distinction between admissible evidence and actual reality.

APPLICABLE RULES

Model Rules: MRs 3.1; 3.3 (both 1983 and 2002 versions); 3.4, 8.4(d).
Model Code: DRs 1-102; 2-109; 2-110(B); 7-102; 7-106; ECs 7-1; 7-4; 7-5; 7-25.
CA Rules: 3-200; 5-200.
CA B&P: 6068(c) and (d).

SUGGESTED QUESTIONS TO ASK:

- Is Rule 11 the equivalent of an ethical rule? How is it different? The same?

- Does the liberalization of Rule 11 in 1993 change a lawyer's obligations under the rule? Or did it just change the punishment?

- Can Yetzi file suit even if Save Our Land does not really care about winning? Even if the suit is solely for the purpose of delay?

- Is filing a lawsuit for the primary purpose of obtaining a preliminary injunction sufficient grounds to proceed?

- Is Yetzi more justified in filing a lawsuit solely to delay because the purpose of the suit is to protect the environment? Should the nature of the lawsuit make a difference?

- Should Rule 11 serve to deny access to the courts for those who may not be able to substantiate their claims? Does the balance between protecting a plaintiff's rights and the rights of the prospective defendant shift where the plaintiff is infirm, does not speak the language, or is elderly?

- In evaluating whether to reveal adverse authority, should strategy or ethics govern your conduct?

- Is there a point at which you personally would not reveal adverse law, even if you discovered it? Where would you draw the line?

- To what extent can Annette avoid revealing adverse authority, on the theory, though unstated in her pleadings, that she is making a good-faith argument for extension of existing law?

- Does it make sense that a case with factual merit which nevertheless has a newly-discovered holding against it will fail, while a case which has little

factual merit may succeed, because the lawyer must reveal the law but not the facts?

- In making a closing argument, do the words Annette uses make a difference? Or is it just a matter of semantics, not substance?

- How would you argue the "facts" of Annette's case in a way that meets the letter of the rules while still being effective argument?

SUGGESTED ROLE-PLAYS:

- Play the part of Ernest Green, SOL president, with a student playing Yetzi, as Yetzi tells Green that she cannot file a lawsuit solely for the purpose of delay.

- Turn the previous role-play around, and play Yetzi explaining to Green why she cannot go forward.

- Play the part of a client after Friel tells you that she will have to go into court tomorrow to reveal authority adverse to your position, authority she just learned of at the last possible minute.

- Make Annette's closing argument for her, using better semantics than she uses in the text of the problem, in order to walk the fine line between misrepresenting the facts and jeopardizing her case. Or ask students to do the same.

SUGGESTED VIDEOS:

- Rule 11 sanctions: *A Civil Action*, DVD chap. **8**, 21:26 — 23:46.

DISCUSSION:

(a) A Brief Rule 11 Primer:

Rule 11 can have a broader application than the ethics rules. We like our Rule 11 discussion to begin with the question of whether abiding by the rule is tantamount to an ethical obligation. Such rules are best seen as being quasi-ethical in nature; while they do not directly involve potential lawyer discipline, they are rules developed by courts that govern the propriety of attorney conduct. But Rule 11 has a more important practical application than its ethical component: the financial sanctions against parties and their lawyers for filing or continuing unwarranted lawsuits.

Rule 11 has changed several times in the last generation, and some talk about future changes. Prof. Peter Joy begins our review with a thorough and readable recitation of the history and current status of Rule 11 (**Section 1** of the **Readings**), while the Davidson reading in **Section 2** shows how the rule might change if "tort reform" advocates have their way, but also points — as

does Joy's piece — to general judicial satisfaction with the rule in its current form. The **Section 2 Notes** show how Rule 11 remains a significant curb on lawyer' bad behavior.

Students may argue, as Davidson does, that since the December 1993 liberalization of Rule 11, lawyers' ethical obligations under this rule have diminished. We believe, however, that the substance of the rule is the same; it is the increased ability to avoid sanctions that has changed. We don't believe this changes any requirements of a lawyer's behavior, but only the *penalties* for such behavior. This can be an important distinction. Our perspective is that the 1983 — 1993 version, had an unintended result, high levels of Rule 11-generated litigation, as Joy describes, which clogged the courts and dissatisfied most judges. The current rule's safe harbor still serves to curb behavior, and its comparison with the former rule is why, in our view, judges' approval ratings of the current rule are so high.

While examining Rule 11, it is also useful to briefly mention the other ways that sanctions are meted out by courts (see **Readings, Sections 4** and **5**). We return to these other sanctions later in the class. Their import is significant: courts will keep and maintain a broad sanctioning responsibility and authority, and all attorneys should be wary.

(b) Save Our Land — Rule 11 In Context:

Save Our Land is a case filed without the goal of ultimately prevailing. SOL's president makes an overt statement to Yetzi that he doesn't care whether they win or not, but merely that the project gets tied up. The sympathetic environmental issue will strike some students as increasing Yetzi's justification to file, compared to non-political issues.

May Yetzi file suit even if SOL does not intend to win? Is that a legitimate standard? What about if she files suit for the purpose of delay or harassment? Delay and harassment seem to be the SOL president's stated purpose. **MR 3.2** is worth some discussion here. Its entire black-letter text, unchanged between 1983 and 2002, is "A lawyer shall make reasonable efforts to expedite litigation consistent with interests of the client." The students should evaluate what those "client interests" are.

The law is unclear how "technical" Yetzi can be in finding grounds on which to base a lawsuit on the lack of a hearing on the oak tree or a sufficient quorum. We feel better about the grounds that there was no hearing on cutting down the oak trees than the grounds that on one remote occasion, a city council quorum was lacking. But we are not sure why one technicality doesn't work as well as another.

We suspect, however, that ultimately, the question must focus on the substantive law issue; that is, "is there any reasonable hope that we will be able to prevail based on the theory of our case?" That issue — the tenability of

the claim — is at the heart of the matter. After all, there are innumerable instances where cases were won or lost based on "technicalities." Another point: If Yetzi is arguing in good faith for an extension or modification of existing law, the argument we discuss in the **Readings, Section 8**, her actions should be protected by **MR 3.1**.

Finally, it doesn't appear to us that Yetsi's *inaction* would violate Rule 11. If may run afoul of discovery (Rule 26) and other procedural rules, however, and is likely to incur the court's wrath.

(c)   Does the Nature of the Lawsuit or the Relief Sought Matter?

Is Yetzi more justified in filing a lawsuit solely to delay because the purpose of the suit is to protect the environment? Should the nature of the lawsuit make a difference? To test the hypothesis that an environment lawsuit *feels* different, we posit the example of a will contest, in which the family wishes to protest the will solely for the purpose of delaying the non-family beneficiary's receipt of the estate, or to make that beneficiary spend money in defending an unwarranted claim. Other troubling examples might be an adoption case where sufficient delay may mean that the best interests of the child will be to remain with the adoptive couple, or a tobacco or asbestos case where the defendant seeks delay in anticipation of the death of the plaintiff — and thus the likelihood of a lower award in most jurisdictions.

Under these facts, we feel less comfortable about filing the will contest than the SOL case, and so will most students. If we assume the will case has possible merit, what causes the discomfort? It may be that our personal belief in the will contest is much less, and may even be negative, compared to our personal belief in the legitimacy of saving old trees and open space. Besides, the impact to society of the environmental case is harder to ignore.

This is worth some discussion, because it shows how our personal beliefs again crop up in the decision-making process we use on behalf of our clients. Should this be the case? Perhaps not; this sounds a lot like "situational ethics." But it is difficult to sort out such beliefs and discard them completely.

Whatever the right conclusion is, either on the environmental case or the will contest, it is clear that the danger to Yetzi in filing a lawsuit comes not from the ethical rules but from Rule 11, and other similar state regulations, and the inherent powers of the courts to sanction attorneys within its discretion. As courts continue to exercise such discretion, and as rules of pleading and discovery continue to proliferate, the lesson our students should draw is that they must look beyond just the rules of ethics in determining how best to conduct themselves as lawyers.

What about filing a lawsuit for the primarily purpose of obtaining a preliminary injunction? Is that sufficient grounds to proceed? **MR 3.2** seems

to beg the question on this issue, because it juxtaposes its criticism of acting for the convenience of the *litigators* against the more appropriate goal of convenience of *clients*. Opposing parties are not the concern. Since a preliminary injunction is requested for the purpose of preserving the underlying lawsuit, one can reasonably argue that this is sufficient purpose to proceed, since there would have to be a legitimate underlying claim to get the injunction.

Students are likely to pick up the environmental theme and argue that since the delay would protect the environment, in the form of irreplaceable oak trees, this is a reasonable litigation goal, sufficient grounds to file the lawsuit even if solely to delay. These students may be right. When we drafted this problem, we had assumed that filing solely for purposes of delay would be impermissible. But our students have persuaded us that obtaining a preliminary injunction, for example, may indeed be a legitimate end of filing a lawsuit, particularly in an environmental case.

(d) Investigation and Reliance on the Client:

How much investigation is necessary before filing a claim? How much may a lawyer rely on the client's statements, even if unsubstantiated? Students will almost all agree that *some* amount of investigation is necessary. But what if that bears no fruit? If, after reading the *Hadges* case in **Section 3** of the **Readings**, the students conclude too quickly that a good-faith investigation that provides with no corroboration is sufficient, the teacher might play devil's advocate, pointing out the unreliability of uncorroborated allegations: "How can you file a lawsuit based on this without anything more?" Also, as the **Section 3 Notes** suggest, the liberal standard used in *Hadges* may not be used elsewhere. (Sadly, by the way, most of our students don't recognize the name William Kunstler. We give them a very brief bio. He appears again, as it happens, in **Problem 20** on contempt.)

On the other hand, if the students feel that more corroboration is always necessary, the teacher can ask how such corroboration is possible under some circumstances, since you get your client the way you find him or her. We posit an intersection accident in which there were no witnesses other than the two drivers. Should Rule 11 deny access to the courts in that situation?

(e) Tort Law and Rule 11 and Anti-SLAPP:

Section 4 of the **Readings** discusses the similarities between the standards of Rule 11 and the elements of the tort of malicious prosecution. The *Henigson* and *Sheldon Appel* cases are both valuable to understanding of the tort. Just as the ethical rules themselves are quite vague and narrow, tort theories are similarly narrow. (The teacher may want to refer to the Restatement 2d of Torts, sections 674 thru 681B, which hold that probable cause or honestly held belief after reasonable investigation of a tenable claim

is sufficient to successfully defend against malicious prosecution.) Nevertheless, the debate will continue; one of its most recent formulations is set forth in the Aneenson article (at the end of **Section 5**), and its interesting thesis about suits against attorneys.

In the past ten years, we have seen an important and emerging new remedy for litigation abuse: anti-SLAPP motions and other protections against so-called "SLAPP" suits, as described in **Readings, Section 5**. We see these protections — an increasing number of states now have anti-SLAPP legislation — as becoming more prevalent in the future, and worthy of discussion here.

(f) Overview of Parts II and III:

In general, we like to emphasize **Part II** of the problem, spending considerably less time on Question 1 of **Part III**, and closing with the more difficult second question of **Part III**, the way in which Friel may argue the case. In emphasizing Question 1, we like to suggest several shadings of the facts of the hypothetical, to test how far the students will go in acknowledging law directly against them. Our hypothesis is that, pushed to the limit, most students will acknowledge (as many practitioners do) that at some point they will *not* reveal adverse authority even though they know they must.

It is useful to begin by taking students through the black-letter rules point by point. The Pitulla article in **Section 7** of the **Readings** does this. Emphasis should be placed on **MR 3.3(a)(3)**. [Note the change in subsections of this rule noted in the text of the article.] However, note Pitula's citation of an ABA opinion that says the test should be whether the judge will feel misled. The last-minute discovery may not give rise to this state of mind by the court.

(g) What Will the Students Do with the Law Against Them?

Students will generally look for a way to explain why revealing the law against them really makes good sense. They will emphasize the strategic advantages of being candid with the court, or that the judge will respect their position and give them more credibility the next time. These responses beg the question. Strategy, while significant, is not what the problem is about. Students should be pushed to decide what they will do from an *ethical* point of view. They should assume that they will gain no strategic advantages. Moreover, how a court reacts to a lawyer the next time may be important to the lawyer, but it is not important to the *client* whose only case is this present case.

The ethical rule is clear — disclose the adverse authority. Students will look for ways to give this "right answer," even though they may not actually do it in practice. We do not believe that Annette violates a duty to the client by

revealing adverse case law because zealous advocacy is limited to lawful means. But the client, were he or she to find out about it, might well disagree.

Question 2 raises the question of "dicta." Students often distinguish between dicta and holding in a way that lawyers find more problematic. Nevertheless, they will be looking for excuses not to reveal the information. The first sentence in Question 3 is designed to state the extreme case in which Annette really has to do nothing in order to have a ruling in her favor confirmed. At this point, many students will likely acknowledge that they will do nothing, allowing them to win the motion. We confess, or at least one of us does, that there definitely comes a point where we are likely to do the same, ethical rule or not. Before we leave this issue, note the questions we ask in the **Notes** following the Pitulla article. Finally, note the civil sanctions that may occur from other rules of court, as the *Hendrix* case (**Readings, Section 7**) describes.

(h) Extension of Existing Law:

There is a relationship between this problem and **Part I**. One of the areas of similarity between Rule 11 standards and the ethical rule on disclosure of adverse authority is the question of whether counsel can argue for an extension of existing law. The extent to which a good faith argument for extension of existing law may be made is one which is the subject of some considerable debate, as indicated in **Section 8** of the **Readings** and our review of the fascinating *Golden Eagle* opinions, the ultimate outcome of which we do not necessarily agree. We believe that despite the *Golden Eagle* case, lawyers who make this argument, without acknowledging to the court they are asking for such extension of existing law, may be in dangerous territory.

(i) Dealing with the Facts of the Case:

Students will generally agree that they need not disclose adverse facts if they are not subject to discovery. We analyze the rules in this regard in **Section 9** of the **Readings**. We like to emphasize the irony of what the end result of the application of these rules can bring: A case with merit which nevertheless has a newly-discovered holding against it may fail, while a case which has little factual merit may succeed because the lawyer does not have to reveal facts in opposition to the claim. Indeed the lawyer *may not* be able to do so, given ethical requirements of keeping confidences and secrets. This remains counter-intuitive to us, though there is wide room for disagreement.

(j) The Closing Argument:

The point here is to show that while no factual disclosure adverse to the client is required of Annette, this does not necessarily mean she can argue that the adverse facts do not exist. Again, however, we believe that semantics play an important role, as they did for Roger Earl in **Problem 4**, and for the

Anatomy of a Murder and penknife scenarios in **Problem 15**, and as they will in several future problems.

We answer Question 2 of **Part III** this way: Annette may argue at trial that there is no evidence to refute her client's story, but not in the words chosen here. We suggest the teacher role-play Annette's argument and provide other words, or ask the students to do this. The students should evaluate whether those words would make a difference. For example, instead of "Unfortunately, no one witnessed the accident except the parties," what if Annette said "Unfortunately, there is no evidence about what happened at the scene of the accident except what the parties tell us." Again, this underscores the irony of having the factually-suspect case proceed with zealous counsel pressing her point regardless of the adverse facts known to her.

PROBLEM 17

Is Discovery The Survival Of The Fittest?

THE POINT BEHIND THE PROBLEM:

This problem, and the next one on negotiation, present issues of common, everyday practice in situations that could appropriately be called applied legal ethics. Dealing with these situations is a routine fact of life for many, if not most, lawyers.

The discovery approaches espoused by Clancy Garrett, while extreme, are a not unrealistic version of how some firms' litigation departments choose to conduct discovery. This problem has three purposes. First, it provides a forum for discussing how far a lawyer may go in protecting a client's interests. Second, and more importantly, it provides a framework for discussing two clearly distinct approaches to the practice of law: Garrett's strict advocate's view and a more temperate, humanistic approach that is still adversarial but more collegial. Students tend to have strong and widely divergent views on these issues. Finally, the problem is designed to help prepare law students for what most will experience as lawyers — both from their adversaries, and from the partners to whom they answer as law firm associates.

This problem tends to bring out strong feelings from many law students on what being a lawyer is all about. Some students admire Clancy Garrett and feel that he is the epitome of a lawyer who is doing the best possible job for the client. Others are appalled by what they see as his callous manipulation of the rules. Students may talk about the difference between what Garrett can "get away with" ethically vs. "doing the right thing" morally. These discussions should be encouraged, and enough time should be given to play out the issues the students raise.

We also contrast the discovery setting with the procedural tricks and devices discussed in **Problem 20**. We believe, and many of the students will appreciate, that procedural devices can be used on a relatively equal basis by both sides. Discovery, however, is more than just procedural trickery. It often involves substantive issues directly affecting the merits of the case. Moreover, for many types of litigation, such as products liability or employment discrimination, discovery in a particular case tends to be *unequal*, with one side attempting to gain information and the other side attempting to protect it. Finally, this problem serves as a reminder to our students that ethics is not just about discipline, and that other forms of sanctions — of which discovery sanctions are among the most prominent — can result from questionable ethical conduct.

APPLICABLE RULES:

Model Rules: MRs 1.2(b); 3.1; 3.2; 3.4(d); 4.4; 5.1; 5.2(b).
Model Code: DRs 7-101; 7-106(C)(1); ECs 7-1; 7-8; 7-9; 7-10; 7-25;
               7-27.
CA Rules: 3-200.
CA B&P: 6068(b), (c)

SUGGESTED QUESTIONS TO ASK:

- Is it merely talk to call litigation a "war" or is it the way the "game" is played?

- Isn't what Garrett is saying that if opposing counsel doesn't push the right button, they don't get the piece of cheese — that is, that any competent counsel should be put through the proper paces before getting discovery?

- On the other hand, isn't what Garrett is saying really tantamount to obstructing the proper functioning of the legal system by obfuscating the discovery process?

- How satisfactorily do the ethical rules deal with these kinds of discovery practices?

- What part of Clancy Garrett's behavior, if any, would be likely to result in sanctions?

- How is the tone of litigation set? Does a Garrett set the tone, to which the other side can merely react, or is the relative collegiality of a particular case a two-way street?

- Since all lawyers have had cases where they had good relations with opposing counsel, and others where they had bad relations with their opponents, what characterizes the "good" and "bad" experiences?

- How do you deal with discovery from the moral point of view? If discovery had to be moral, could you ever justify representing less than the perfect client?

- Doesn't your client have a right to protection against discovery disclosures if the disclosures are not properly requested?

- Do you believe that issues sanctions should be used more widely? Or are they too extreme a remedy?

- How does electronic discovery change the playing field when it comes to discovery wars? Or discovery abuse?

- Imagine yourself as an associate for Clancy Garrett; how would you deal with his demands about how you conduct discovery?

SUGGESTED ROLE-PLAYS:

- With the students, play the roles of counsel arguing "Clancy Garrett style" over filing a motion to compel.

- With the students, play out a more collegial style of arguing the motion.

- Play the role of a Clancy Garrett-style partner urging an associate to "stonewall" a document request, and have a student explain why he or she is not going to conduct discovery the Garrett way.

- Play the role of a young associate, using all available diplomatic and politically sensitive skills, explaining to the partner why he or she wants to use fewer "hardball" tactics than Clancy Garrett wants.

SUGGESTED VIDEOS:

- Telling the deposition witness not to answer: *A Civil Action*, DVD chap. 9, 25:37 — 29:29.

- Telling the deposition witness not to answer: *I Am Sam*, DVD chap. 11, 1:00:08 — 1:01:22.

- "You have to effectively destroy this witness" — the deposition as the senior partner sits in: *Class Action* DVD 49:22 — 50:43 50:44 — 54:42

- The arcane filing system — "Bottom line? It is within the letter of the law": *Class Action* DVD chap. To Be Identified (between depo scene above and burying scene below.)

- Burying the documents: *Class Action* DVD chap. 17, 1:10:15 — 1:11:50.

- "You guys are all the same": *The Verdict*, DVD chap. 12, 48:44 — 51:11.

- The impaired client: *I Am Sam*, DVD chap. 11, 1:00:08 — 1:01:22.

- Hiding the documents, disclosing the "bean counter" witness: *Class Action* — DVD chap. 26 1:40:48 — 1:42:56.

THE DISCUSSION:

(a)   Four Discussion Segments:

We suggest dividing discussion into four parts. First, we suggest allowing students to give their personal overall views of Clancy Garrett he's great, he's horrid, he's what every litigator should (or should not) be. This serves to show the wide divergence of student opinion, and gets it all out on the table at the earliest possible time.

Then, it is useful to go through the specifics of Garrett's conduct point by point, to analyze more concretely which of his tactics are appropriate, and which are not. After the specifics, it is useful to revisit the general global

discussion on tactics, to see how the students' analysis of Garrett's specific conduct affects their feelings about his overall attitude. Finally, it is useful to have students discuss what they expect to do as associates when they find themselves in a tough case to litigate, confronted with difficult adversaries and watched over by their own Clancy Garretts.

(b) Garrett's Specific Techniques:

After the students have spoken their minds — and spoken from their hearts — about their feelings toward Clancy Garrett, the teacher should force them to be more specific and analytical about Garrett's approach. Each of Garrett's techniques — each by the way, virtually identical to actual statements made to us by colleagues — should be evaluated on its merits. However, the language Garrett uses in describing his various approaches is subjective and vague. This makes the statements more realistic, and also provides a better forum for student discussion, since the "right answer" to many of his techniques becomes ambiguous and subject to interpretation.

Again, the student discussion is far more important than the concrete answer students decide on. They should be especially encouraged to argue about exactly what Garrett means when he says "litigation is a war of attrition," or "if you can argue with a straight face … then object." (Note, by the way, as to one of Garrett's techniques that in most jurisdictions, merely requesting emotional distress damages does not open the floodgates of medical record discovery.)

The specifics of Garrett's actions are also left sufficiently vague to show students that it is difficult to pigeon-hole this kind of practice into specific rules of professional conduct. While there should of course be reference to the rules during this part of the discussion, the teacher should assist students both by pointing out which rules may apply, and by noting that none of the rules is entirely satisfactory to deal with these issues.

The teacher should also discuss the relevance of discovery guides and other rules that may be more pertinent to changing a lawyer's conduct than rules of ethics. We have included several readings that discuss both monetary and issues sanctions — including the ultimate sanction of case dismissal. The *National Hockey League* case and the Rankin article about General Motors, and the *Abner* case in **Section 5** of the **Readings** all show how issues sanctions can result from discovery conduct. Other articles, such as those by Magistrate Judge Brazil and James Rooks on e-discovery, in **Sections 2** and **3**, discuss how the discovery process could be changed in a way that discourages abuses.

It is useful to discuss the techniques and requirements of proving discovery abuse and obtaining sanctions in the teacher's local jurisdiction; this will make the discussion more practical and less theoretical. Students should evaluate what parts of Garrett's behavior, if any, would be likely to result in sanctions.

While we generally discourage too many "war stories" during the course of a semester, some real life experiences of the teacher involving specific instances of Garrett-like conduct can be very useful here. Equally valuable are stories from the students themselves, who have worked as law clerks or "summer associates" and may have seen interesting discovery wars first hand. These stories bring home the point, in real terms, about what a fully adversarial relationship is all about.

(c) "What Kind of Lawyers Do We Want to Be?"

After Garrett's specific conduct is evaluated, we suggest revisiting the global issue of "what kind of lawyers we want to be." This debate can become something of a free-for-all, so the teacher should make sure that students focus on the basic differences in philosophy between those who take the traditional adversarial point of view and those who take a more collegial approach. Role-playing typical "discovery wars" of both kinds can be valuable in illustrating these differences. Play out the scenes both ways; the differences are magnified when actually seen in action.

Here, the ethical rules themselves are of little direct assistance, and the teacher may prefer to refer to the readings that address this issue. We intentionally filled this Problem with a series of readings focused on rather extreme behavior, largely because we find that behavior all too common. The now-famous "Dear Dr." letter described in **Section 1,** the off-the-charts behavior of the famed Joe Jamail in **Section 4**, and the "two extremes" of discovery abuse described in **Section 6**, and the modern-day E-discovery stonewalling described in **Section 8** all will help students gain ample understanding of how severe discovery conduct can become. For example, we find Bogle and Gates' refusal to provide a clearly discoverable memorandum by using a paper-thin semantic distinction, as set forth in **Section 1**, to be particularly disturbing. To us, the most significant part of the Bogle and Gates story are the positions of the firm's bevy of experts — so persuasive that the trial court refused to issue sanctions.

We suggest that during the course of the analysis, the teacher spend some time discussing the adversarial process itself. Among others, we suggest the following questions might be asked: How do law firms contribute to the culture of discovery? How is the tone of litigation set? Does a Garrett set the tone, to which the other side merely reacts, or is the relative collegiality of a particular case a two-way street? How do students feel the client will react to different attitudes about undertaking discovery? More generally, all lawyers have had matters where they had good relations with opposing counsel, and where they had bad relations with their opponents. What causes these relationships to be the way they are? How would we prefer them to be? Finally, do students believe some law firms use discovery practice as a "profit center?"

(d) Where the Authors Draw the Line:

There are no easy answers to the debates raised in this problem. We believe that the black letter rules of professional conduct are of little assistance in this area. However, some general truths for us include the following:

The "adversary theory" requires not giving up information unless asked appropriately. On the other hand, once appropriately asked, we would prefer a world in which the information is provided, with an adversarial relationship that is at least civil, if not cordial. This Problem should be contrasted with **Problem 10** where the rules are procedural, and provide a brighter line equally applied to both parties. In discovery, however, the playing field is not always level. Although it does tilt in both directions at times (see the *Abner* case in **Section 5** of the **Readings**), it is more common to see a single plaintiff represented by a single lawyer against a global company and a big law firm. Then, discovery, more than other parts of the adversary process, can involve significant *access* issues. We believe adversaries can protect their clients' interests to the fullest possible extent without engaging in practices which serve to inflame the other side *or* to deny access.

Against strong opposing counsel, Garrett's actions might ultimately be self-defeating, due to sanctions or reciprocal inflexibility on the other side. A Clancy Garrett is much less likely to get an extra extension of time or accommodation on deposition scheduling than a more collegial litigator. Since bad feelings tend to feed off each other (we'll focus on this in **Problem 20**), Clancy Garrett's litigation methods can become very expensive for both sides, in terms of time, money, and emotional capital, all ultimately paid by the client.

As to Garrett's specific techniques, we draw the line at those that are predominantly obstructionist rather than reasonable advocacy: "your job is to get in their way"; the "war of attrition" whose sole function is to wear the other side down or take advantage of a less aggressive or tenacious opponent; attempts to obtain unwarranted personal information, such as all medical records in all cases. It is in these areas that we see the discovery profit center clashing with access issues. While we find several other tactics somewhat offensive, we think that the actions themselves would be permitted in most jurisdictions, and are not, therefore, "wrong." Nevertheless, they do not foster the civility that we find to be the best course of conduct in discovery, and the course of conduct promoted by **MR 3.4**, specifically entitled "Fairness to Opposing Party and Counsel."

(e) "Ethics" and "Morality":

Time allowing, we encourage the teacher to return to the debate, first discussed in the first day of class, on the dichotomy of what a lawyer can "get away with" and still be "ethical" vs. what is the "right thing" to do morally. While this discussion is always very subjective, it is often — when guided by

the teacher — very productive. Law students and lawyers alike rarely take the time to reflect on these issues. As a result, we all tend to fall into patterns of behavior, learned from those with or for whom we practice, without having thought through what those behaviors say about how we have chosen to practice law. This problem provides a framework to encourage students to take a direct personal look at the kinds of lawyers they want to be.

On the issue of whether what's "ethical" is what a lawyer can get away with, we take — and encourage students to take — a larger view. We suggest, as we set forth in the book's introductory materials, that squaring one's own sense of what is legally ethical and what is morally right is an attainable goal. This does not mean that we find it wrong to argue on behalf of a client with whom we disagree, or to refuse to disclose damaging discovery where our client is clearly liable unless the information is properly demanded. Rather, we understand the rules of legal ethics as having an underlying moral base, and thereby see the representation of our client — in a real sense, acting as our client's shield and sword — as a morally justifiable position.

But we also believe lines must be drawn. The **Readings** in **Section 5** focus on two instances in which the line has clearly been crossed, and the GM and Baron and Budd memos, described in the **Readings, Section 5**, also step over the lines (and resulted in issues sanctions). Issue sanctions also occurred in the Morgan Stanley case described in **Section 8**.

(f)   The Students as Future Law Firm Associates:

Finally, the students — particularly those who are uncomfortable with Garrett's approach — should be asked to imagine themselves as associates in Garrett's firm. In discussing how they will act when confronted by the Garrett approach, many students may say that they would refuse to act in certain particular ways. The teacher will perform a valuable role by asking these students how they expect to survive in the firm's environment — or in their profession — if they refuse to comply with their superiors' directives. Role-playing can be most valuable here. The teacher can play the role of the partner who hears an associate refusing to object to the production of documents, or declining to ask certain aggressive deposition questions.

The teacher can also assist the students by explaining the balancing act that exists for associates in mid- and large-size American law firms. Associates must balance their youthful ideals with the practicalities of keeping their jobs. How this is accomplished is of enormous value to many students. If the students get stuck walking this tightrope, the teacher can continue the role-play, this time as the associate. The teacher should try to demonstrate how associates who present their concerns with diplomacy and political sensitivity may still get the point across without jeopardizing their positions. This discussion should contain a warning by the professor of the very real possibility of monetary and other sanctions for discovery abuse.

At some point in the semester, whether here or at another appropriate juncture, the teacher may want to invite practicing lawyer guests who have seen the pressures of law firm practice from both the associates' and partners' points of view. Their insights — and the students' opportunity to question them about their experiences — can be invaluable.

(g) E-Discovery — Here to Stay:

Before moving on, we commend to your attention the sections of this Problem, **Sections 3, 7,** and **8,** that deal with electronic discovery, each from a different perspective. All of these readings are new to this edition. **Section 8,** of course, points to the fact that whether through paper discovery or state-of-the-art high tech, cheating happens. And issue sanctions can and do result. The Rooks reading in **Section 3** went to press before E-Discovery rules were finalized. So did our third edition. It is our understanding that the rules discussed in Mr. Rooks' article were indeed approved by the new Roberts-led Supreme Court, effective December 1, 2006. Other rules, including a new Evidence Rule that would affect electronic discovery, are currently being discussed.

PROBLEM 18

The Fine Line Between Posturing And Lying In Negotiation

THE POINT BEHIND THE PROBLEM:

Negotiation, as the introduction to the problem says, inherently involves a certain amount of lying and a considerable amount of posturing and bluffing. There is a large gulf between attempting to apply theoretical ideals, such as those set forth by Prof. Wetlaufer (**Readings, Section** 1) and Judge Rubin (**Readings, Section 2**), and the practical realities of negotiating a deal or a settlement. We make this point in **Section 7** of the **Readings**. The new Temkin reading in **Section 6** attempts to bridge the theoretical and the practical. Again, the rules, particularly **MR 4.1**, leave us with more questions unanswered than answered. See our discussion in **Section 1** of the **Readings**.

Negotiation ethics, then, become largely a personal issue, as the negotiation roundtable in **Section 3** of the **Readings** — and the substantial differences expressed there by thoughtful and ethical lawyers — demonstrate. We have added a question to the problem itself that specifically calls for students to examine tow of the issues from that still-valuable roundtable article. The principal purpose of this problem, therefore, is to have students evaluate their own sense of how negotiations should be conducted, and how they will act themselves during the negotiation process. We see this as an opportunity for the students to ask themselves where they will draw the line, how far they are willing to go, and how much lying — or at least fibbing, posturing and puffing — they will allow themselves to do in pursuit of a "good deal." We also see this Problem as lending itself particularly well to role plays, which tend in our experience to be both instructive and a great deal of fun.

APPLICABLE RULES:

Model Rules: MR 4.1.
Model Code: DR 7-102(A); ECs 7-7; 7-10.
CA B&P: 6068(d).

SUGGESTED QUESTIONS TO ASK:

- How much lying, posturing or bluffing should be allowed in negotiation?

- How helpful are the rules, especially MR 4.1, in defining the limits of ethical negotiation?

- How would you balance the likelihood of being able eventually to produce the expert testimony or witness from Mexico with the fact that you do not have this information in hand?

- Do the semantics lawyers use in negotiation techniques make a difference in terms of how ethical that technique is? Or are the semantics secondary to the lawyer's intent?

- How would you interpret each of Ross David's techniques if you were Prof. Wetlaufer? Is Wetlaufer realistic or an ethics Pollyanna?

- How does failing to tell the truth about the extent of the lawyer's authority compare to misleading statements on other issues? Does it make sense that lying about the extent of authority seems to be an exception under the model rule?

- How can a lawyer represent a client without trying to have the client pay as little (or get as much) as the traffic will bear?

- Is there ever a time when a lawyer should not take advantage of a power imbalance in that lawyer's favor during the negotiation process? When or why?

- In judging the power imbalance in negotiation, does it make a difference who your client is? Should it?

- How do you think Freund would act in the situations posited by Fleischmann?

- Does it make sense to offer lawyers a "safe harbor" if they remain silent? On the other hand, does it make sense to require truthful speech once the attorney decides to speak, as Temkin suggests?

SUGGESTED ROLE-PLAYS:

- Play the role of Ross Davids demonstrating any of his techniques, particularly pointing out how different ways of phrasing things can increase or decrease the extent the statements mislead the other side.

- Role-play the semantic distinctions suggested by the Freund & Fleishmann articles.

- Role-play the going-out-of-business scenarios suggested by Temkin by taking his one-line exchanges and playing them out, exploring where they would go if continued.

- Role-play any techniques you or your colleagues have used in negotiation that would fuel discussion with the students.

- Role-play with a student a negotiation "end game," as set forth in the Lempest article where the issue comes down to how much each client will pay or receive.

- Pick a relatively simple case and role-play an entire negotiation — and the issue of "authority" — with a group of students.

SUGGESTED VIDEOS:

- Mutt and Jeff settlement tactics: *The Rainmaker*, DVD chap. 12.

- Prosecution puffery: *The Accused*, DVD chap. 4, to 29:46.

DISCUSSION:

(a) Dividing Up the Issues:

We suggest that the teacher begin with a general discussion of negotiation, and balancing negotiation with candor. **MR 4.1** and the sentiments of Prof. Wetlaufer (**Readings, Section** 1) and Judge Rubin (**Readings, Section 2**) can also be discussed. Some students will disregard their views as rose-colored, academic, and unrealistic. We have shortened the Rubin reading, but still believe his views are part of what our students should consider. These writers, like Prof. Postema, in discussing "moral costs" in **Chapter One**, take the moral high ground. And the *public* largely agrees with them.

After the introductory discussion, we suggest moving through the issues raised by the problem one at a time. We divide them generally into: dodging a question; puffing on the availability and use of experts; puffing on the availability of a corroborating witness; and statements made about the authority to settle a case or negotiate a deal. We move on to **Question II**, the student-chosen examples from the Lempert's negotiation roundtable article, making sure to touch on the issue of authority (see section (**c**) below), and give as much time as remains, often unfortunately brief, to **Question III**.

(b) Dodging a Question and "Puffing" About Witnesses:

Dodging the question by refusing to answer it is the easiest of these issues, and is really included more by way of introduction for the students, and the opportunity to discuss the rules that apply. It is hard to argue with Ross Davids' answering a question with a question, except as to how good a strategy that might be. But ethics, not strategy, is the focus here.

Puffing about the experts and the availability of the corroborating witness will give students far more trouble. After getting their views, we like to ask how the students feel members of the roundtable in **Section 3** would deal with these issues. When it comes to witness unavailability, the *Jones* case, though it relates primarily to prosecutors, is instructive (see **Readings, Section 8**). One would reason that if a prosecutor — whose obligation as an advocate is tempered by the role as a seeker of justice — may avoid revealing the death of a significant witness, then the civil litigator certainly need not disclose something similar.

Teachers should feel free to discuss their own experience and those of their colleagues about puffing in negotiation. Our own informal survey of mediators is set forth in **Section 7** of the **Readings**. We often tell our classes that when we have presented Ross Davids' methods to lawyers and mediators at

mediation continuing education seminars such as The American Arbitration Association, we find lawyers widely split on whether they would claim to have expert witnesses whom they have not yet fully lined up, or a corroborating witness who is in Mexico.

We describe to our class some of the variables raised by the lawyers evaluating these issues: the fact that they would be likely to produce the expert testimony in question, balanced against the reality that they have not yet obtained that testimony; the fact that the corroborating witness actually exists versus the witness' potential unavailability.

While students look to the teacher throughout the semester to provide the practical component of what "real lawyers" actually do in these situations, this is even more acutely the case with this problem. The ways in which lawyers negotiate are so idiosyncratic that students beg for personal perspectives on these issues. Teachers who do not have some experiences to relate off-hand might do well to survey some of their colleagues about these practices prior to the discussion of this problem in class.

Several times, we have mentioned the importance of semantics in grappling with difficult ethical issues. How much of a difference do semantic distinctions make in "puffing" situations? The teacher can role-play Ross Davids' "stretching the truth" in several different ways; some may be acceptable to many students, while others may not. The significance is this: the manner and mode of presentation will make a big difference in terms of how the propriety of the conduct is perceived. And, *the materiality* of the misrepresentation is also important to evaluating the conduct. We will see the materiality issue again in **Problem 19**.

(c)   The Authority to Make the Deal:

Of all of Ross Davids' behavior, obfuscating or failing to tell the truth about the authority to settle or negotiate a deal may arouse the most controversy and the liveliest discussion. Often, students will choose this example, Situation No. 1, to discuss from among the "roundtable" issues in **Section 3** — an excellent choice, for several reasons. First, the question of "authority" addresses the ultimate issue of the case, the value of the claim in question. Second, since it directly asks the question of whether the client has agreed to a particular sum, the answer may be a more direct lie or fabrication. While the Freund article (**Readings, Section 4**) suggests ways of avoiding this direct fabrication, we are not persuaded that such methods are effective. (Temkin, on the other hand, in the **Readings, Section 6**, favors silence and disfavors direct fabrication.) Third, MR 4.1 contains language which appears to specifically *exempt* such a fabrication from the general mandate of that rule.

Again, the experience of the teacher and others of the teacher's acquaintance can be valuable in helping law students evaluate this issue. In Situation No. 1 in the negotiators' roundtable, the group split down the

middle; although most agree that while a lawyer *could* lie, they personally would not. But we tell students that when we presented this issue at a mediation seminar, we asked mediators to raise their hands if they believed lawyers in mediation gave honest answers about the limits of their authority. Not a single mediator raised a hand. The mediators thus took for granted what MR 4.1 implies: that lawyers will not tell the truth about the limits of their clients' actual position on value, nor will they be expected to.

Role-playing a negotiation "end-game," where the issue is primarily how much the prospective clients will accept, will clearly demonstrate the problem that too much candor brings. Candor here can cost the client money. Students will ask (we do if they do not) how a lawyer can zealously represent a client without trying to have that client pay as little (or get as much) as the traffic will bear. It's an excellent question, and perhaps more than any other focuses on the principal dilemma of the negotiation process itself.

(d) Power Imbalances, the Roundtable, and Revisiting *Spaulding*:

The negotiation roundtable contains several valuable scenarios. We generally add, for the sake of discussion, a few others not specifically mentioned in the problem.

One of these is an issue raised by Judge Rubin's description of two lawyers of clearly unequal abilities negotiating in circumstances where the balance of power between them is far from equal. Rubin suggests that the more powerful, more astute lawyer should refuse to accept a resolution that is too unfair or unfavorable to the other side. In class discussion, however, students will find this difficult to accept. So, frankly, do we. The inequality that the judge cites is inherent in the advocacy system. Many students tell us that using their legal skill against another and prevailing is why they wanted to become lawyers. Where no rules are even arguably broken, it is difficult to get students or lawyers to agree that their clients should not be entitled to the benefit of their best efforts.

The teacher may wish to evaluate with the students whether it matters if the lawyer doing the negotiating is representing an individual or a corporation, a plaintiff or a defendant, a monied interest or a disadvantaged one. Who the client is may significantly affect things by changing the power balance between the sides.

For instance, many plaintiffs' lawyers feel that, as good as they may be, they always work at somewhat of a power disadvantage in negotiating a case with, say, an insurance company. This is because they are negotiating their individual client's only case, which means that they have to hedge their bets in order to avoid even a relatively slight chance of a negative result. But insurance companies or other entities who litigate on a mass basis can afford the luxury of "averaging out" their results, under a "win some, lose some" theory. Clearly, while this may work for the plaintiffs' *attorney*, it does not

work for his or her individual clients. Lawyers must take these kinds of issues into account in deciding how best to protect the client's interest.

Spaulding v. Zimmerman, the case we raised in **Problem** 4, and which is summarized again at **page 486-7**, is again an appropriate focus of discussion. Spaulding generated a great deal of comment in the legal community. Law professors wrote articles arguing that here <u>was</u> one case where surely a lawyer had a moral imperative to reveal the harm — and where lying by omission was just as serious as an affirmative lie. Yet one professor who had written extensively on the need to take personal responsibility voted for silence in the roundtable poll because "it's not my job to do their job."

(e)   Other Negotiating Techniques:

Time permitting, we bring up other negotiating techniques. We particularly like to discuss the "Mutt and Jeff" technique of using two lawyers to give different messages in the negotiation process. This technique, also referred to as "Good Cop, Bad Cop," in honor of its use in precinct houses and television programs alike to convince witnesses to talk to the police, raises interesting questions about misleading one's opponent. The technique involves one lawyer, or the client, taking the position that settlement is out of the question, or that the other side is not offering nearly enough money; the second lawyer takes a much softer position in talking to the other side, and suggests working together to bring the first person around to a more reasonable point of view.

Sometimes, of course, these positions reflect reality, and, for example, a lawyer may work with opposing counsel to bring both their clients around. But where this technique is set up in advance, "Mutt and Jeff" is almost inherently misleading in that it requires a certain amount of overt planning, a conscious willingness to confuse opposing counsel.

Other techniques and devices that we discuss given sufficient time are feigning anger or irrationality, terminating negotiations in anger and raising demands during the course of the negotiation process. Time allowing, it is both fun and useful to role-play a negotiation with the students. As it often does, a role-play will bring home the point in "real life" far more readily than a simple discussion.

(f)   The Obligation of the Prosecution:

Part III of the problem asks the students to evaluate whether the prosecution has an obligation of candor to opposing counsel or to the court. The *Jones* case in **Section 8** of the **Readings**, and our following comments, set forth both sides of this issue. Although *Jones* is the closest case we have found on point, we think its holding is difficult to justify. After all, if prosecutors are held to at least as high if not a higher standard than the average practitioner, and have some obligation to remain objective and see that justice is done (see **Problem 22**), given the due process rights of criminal defendants, one would

think that the District Attorney should disclose the truth about the eyewitness. We see misrepresentation by omission that is material to a plea bargain. We suggest that the teacher put the question which we ask in our closing note — how would the roundtable commentators, or Wetlaufer, view the prosecutor's actions in **Part III**, or in the *Jones* case?

(g) Personal Credibility and Individual Morality:

As we have seen in many problems in which the rules provide only part of the answer, the individual lawyer's perspective on what is right and wrong and the personal ethics of that attorney will be central to answering how each person approaches negotiation, particularly as it concerns the techniques described in this problem. Some students will rightly raise the issue of their ongoing credibility with their colleagues, a point made in several of the readings. But these credibility issues can often be successfully masked by polished negotiation techniques. To us, this problem's greatest utility is in providing students the opportunity to develop something of their own sense of the rights and wrongs of negotiation.

PROBLEM 19

"Honest Abe's" Trial Tactics

THE POINT BEHIND THE PROBLEM:

The goal of this problem is to provide an escalating series of tactics that are more and more difficult to justify, while also pointing out that many of these trial tricks of the trade, though some may consider them unscrupulous, are devices lawyers can and do "get away with." We want to show how the propriety of many of these tactics is not clearly covered by ethical rules. Those rules focus on making misrepresentations to the court. Clearly, lawyers who make false representations, present untruthful witnesses, or concoct false evidence can be sanctioned for their conduct. But many trial tactics don't fall so neatly into these categories.

What makes Honest Abe's trial tactics interesting to us is that his attempts to prejudice the jury are *indirect*. They do not misrepresent admissible material evidence, but rather do their handiwork in a more subtle way, raising questions about misrepresentation over collateral issues not part of the official evidence of the trial. Nevertheless, it would be foolish to believe that these collateral issues have no effect on the jury. Because of this, the students must extrapolate from the black-letter rules to interpret how those rules — and their *own sense* of fair play — should apply to these tactics.

APPLICABLE RULES:

Model Rules:	MRs 3.3, especially (a) (1) and (3) (2002 Rules), (a) (1) and (4) (1983 Rules); 3.4; 3.5, especially (a), (d) (2002 Rules), (a) and (c) (1983 Rules), and Comment, paragraph 4 (2002 Rules), paragraph 2 (1983 Rules); 4.1; 8.4(c).
Model Code:	DRs 7-101(A)(1); 7-102(A); 7-106(C), especially (1); ECs 7-1; 7-2.
CA Rules:	5-200.
CA B&P:	6068(b), (d) and (f).

SUGGESTED QUESTIONS TO ASK:

- What standard must Abe Dennison's tactics fail to meet in order to be considered "unethical"?

- Is it fair to object by making a speech that sounds more like argument than an objection? What about if the rules of the court require making objections by simply stating the evidentiary grounds?

- If dressing the clients for effect is questionable, what about having a criminal defendant wear a suit or other appropriate courtroom attire rather than the jail jumpsuit ordinarily worn? Or getting a shaggy and

bearded criminal defendant client a nice shave and haircut? Are those tactics any less misleading?

- Does placing the bus and subway passes in view of the jury amount to a direct misrepresentation?

- Is using Dennison's secretary's sister as the girlfriend of his gay client merely "leveling the playing field", or is it nevertheless an effort to mislead the jury?

- Don't both Abe's use of his secretary's sister and Wildman's tactic involve the same basic misrepresentation on the part of the lawyer?

- Is there anything different about Thoreen's use of a substitute as his "client" and the techniques ascribed to Abe Dennison?

- Is there any difference between what Thoreen did and what attorney Sotomayor did?

- In evaluating a lawyer's conduct, does it matter if the effort to prejudice the jury directly, or only indirectly, relates to the relevant evidence? *Should* this distinction make a difference?

- How can Dennison justify using a student's gender and racial background and even her being "attractive" in an effort to gain advantage for his client? Or, on the other hand, how can he avoid taking such action if it will benefit his client's case?

- Would the use of an attractive woman law student be less offensive if Dennison were defending a robbery case rather than a rape charge?

- With regard to all of Abe's tactics, what is the effect of the 2002 changes to Model Rule 3.3?

SUGGESTED ROLE-PLAYS:

- Act the part of Dennison with a student as opposing counsel, where opposing counsel attempts to get Dennison not to make a speech when he objects; try to make Abe's speech into a mini-closing argument, to highlight the effectiveness of this technique.

- Play the role of attorney Sotomayor deciding spontaneously to switch the location of his defendant and the substitute on entering the courtroom that day. For contrast, play the role of Thoreen, talking to his "client," and acting in all respects as if the person next to him is the client.

- Play the part of Dennison talking to a woman law student about hiring her to serve as the "attractive Chinese-American woman" who will appear friendly to the client during the trial.

- Play the role of a lawyer selecting a jury based on limited information, where the lawyer has to choose based on what the jurors (the members of the class) look like.

SUGGESTED VIDEOS:

- Client in a wheelchair?: *A Civil Action*, opening scene.

- "Razzle, Dazzle 'em" of trial: *Chicago*, DVD chapter 14, 1:19:19 — 1:24:33.

- Spying on the opposition: *The Verdict*, DVD chapter 16, 1:30:54 — 1:32:41.

- Voir dire of a crazed juror: *The Rainmaker, 20* 1:12:16 — 1:17:20.

- Jury consultants and racial profiling of juries: *The Devils Advocate*, DVD Chapter 6, 15:06-17:20.

- More jury consultants and racial profiling of juries: *Runaway Jury* DVD Chapter 6, 20:25 - 23:19.

DISCUSSION:

(a) Overview:

We believe it is best and easiest to go through Honest Abe's "tricks" one by one, in order. We also ask the students to evaluate the Clarence Darrow cigar trick and, especially, the particularly nasty "trick" of Max Wildman, both of which are described in **Section 1** of the **Readings**. We generally find we have more than enough to discuss without detailing the techniques described by Roger Dodd, also in **Section 1**, although we have included Dodd's tricks in our problem's **Question 2**. We use this reading more for Dodd's cavalier attitude about tricks than the specifics of his conduct. We generally conclude our discussions with Honest Abe's hiring of the law student, followed by the Wildman "trick," in which he hires an attractive young woman to interact in a friendly manner with the opposing party, because we find these two — and especially Wildman's — the most difficult to justify.

The basic question is whether these tricks are designed to mislead the jury. To that end, a careful review of **MR 3.3** and the significant 2002 changes to that rule is warranted. But there is a secondary purpose to almost all these misleading tactics — a subtle but important effect on the atmosphere in the courtroom.

Along the way, we specifically address the *Thoreen* and *Sotomayor* cases, where lawyers use false clients to fool the triers of fact. *Thoreen* is excerpted in **Section 2** of the **Readings**, while *Sotomayor* is referred to in the **Notes**. We

find replacing the defendant with another person particularly interesting in the context of this problem.

(b) Honest Abe's Tricks:

We deal with each of Honest Abe's tricks briefly in turn. We discuss his false bumbling persona first. We start here because, while students almost uniformly agree that this persona is acceptable behavior, they will admit, when directly confronted, that it is misleading at least to the extent it does not reflect who Abe Dennison really is. Nevertheless, few students if any will be troubled by Abe's acting in this manner. The import here is to point out that some posturing and exaggeration, while certainly misleading to an extent, is considered par for the course in any trial situation.

The teacher should ask about Abe's narrative method of objecting, which is really closer to speech-making than it is to stating an objection. Again, students will have few problems with this. The teacher might point out that mot rules of court require that objections be stated in the form appropriate to the rules of evidence. Students are unlikely to be swayed; if Abe can "get away with" his narrative and the court tolerates it, students will argue that then he is not violating the rules of ethics. This is a hard argument to dispute, since judges have the power to regulate the manner of objections in their courtroom. Nevertheless, most experienced trial lawyers would agree that making objections in this manner is a talent, even an art, and that not everyone can do it successfully and get away with it. Still it is difficult to fault Dennison for trying.

Having his clients dress down and buying them bus and subway passes that are placed so the jury can see them are techniques which students find more troubling. Again, however, their effect on the trier of fact is indirect. California professors might wish to point out **Rule 5-200(B)**, which forbids misleading by artifice." Students who complain that this amounts to a misrepresentation might be asked why criminal defendants are allowed to wear suits or other appropriate courtroom attire at trial instead of jail jumpsuits, or whether it would be appropriate to get one's shaggy and bearded criminal defendant a nice shave and haircut before trial.

While this is not completely analogous, since the efforts for criminal defendants are appropriately seen as a way of avoiding any prejudice by virtue of their status as pre-trial detainees, in some ways the comparison is apt. Worth discussing, but a less apt comparison, are the cases concerning clothing worn by the lawyers discussed in **Section 4** of the **Readings**. To us, these cases have more to do with balancing racial, religious and free speech issues with issues of a fair trial.

(c)   Materiality and Model Rule 3.3:

Most of Honest Abe's tactics don't rise to the level of "material" falsehoods, the standard required by the 1983 version of **MR 3.3**. This materiality standard is the same that we saw in **MR 4.1** in the previous problem on negotiation.

However, under the **2002 version** of **MR 3.3**, subsection **(a)(1)** of the rule no longer contains the word "material" in the phrase "make a false statement of [material] fact or law...." While the next, and new, phrase of the **2002 version** makes it clear that *rectification* of a falsehood is only necessary where materiality exists, the first phrase of the rule makes it clear that any false statement may be prohibited. Substantial changes to the Comments to this rule are consistent with its broader prohibitions. For example, new **paragraph 2** of the **Comment** states that a lawyer "must not allow the tribunal to be misled by false statements of law or fact or evidence the lawyer knows to be false."

But are Abe's tactics sufficiently clear falsehoods to be prohibited by even the 2002 version of the rules? The answer is not clear. The teacher might ask whether the bus passes, for example, amount to a direct misrepresentation to the court. These seem less justifiable than the clothing the clients wear. Nevertheless, they neither relate to admissible evidence, nor are they clear misrepresentations, in that no one is making a statement that the clients in fact ride the buses; rather the jury is allowed to draw that inference. These do not appear to be barred by the 1983 version of **MR 3.3**, but even under the 2002 version, it is unclear that the bus passes rise to the level of "false statements of law ... fact or evidence...." They have no evidentiary and marginal if any factual significance. And yet, they can be indirectly damaging.

This sums up the nature and effect of Honest Abe's tricks. The fact that they are so indirect protects Dennison from being sanctioned under the old version of **MR 3.3** and makes his conduct not much more than ambiguous even under the new version of the rule. These artifices allow him to manipulate the jury's impressions to form the opinions he wants. To that extent, a good argument can be made that the spirit and even perhaps the letter of the **2002 version of MR 3.3** is being violated. This is a close question worthy of discussion.

Teachers wanting to focus on **MR 3.3** should note that there are other material changes to the rule that broaden the prohibitions facing trial lawyers. New **subsection (b)** replaces old **subsection (c)** and substantially increases the duties lawyers have to take remedial measures to prevent inappropriate client conduct. Much of the **Comment** has been substantially revised as well.

A final note on this issue: Some students may argue that Honest Abe's tactics are a mistake not for ethical reasons, but for tactical ones. Again, as we have suggested in previous problems, the teacher should try to avoid too much discussion of strategy. Saying that these techniques don't work from a tactical

point of view is helpful for a trial practice course but doesn't get us to the root of the issue in an ethics course: the propriety of the conduct in question.

(d)   Dennison's Gay Client and Wildman's False Female Friend:

Many students will see Dennison's use of his secretary's sister to act as if he were the girlfriend of his client as merely "leveling the playing field" by avoiding any unfair prejudice to Abe's gay client. We ask whether leveling the field is all that is being done here. After all, it does not make the tactic any less misleading.

This is a good time to compare this tactic with that of Max Wildman, who hired an attractive young woman to sit behind the plaintiff in a wrongful death case and act in a friendly manner towards him during court recesses. The teacher might ask whether there is any real difference between the two. Both, one might argue, are used to mislead the jury, although on collateral, inadmissible points. If students see a difference between attempting to neutralize prejudice (Abe's tactic) and attempting to *create* prejudice (Wildman's tactic), the teacher can make the devil's advocacy argument that both involve the same basic misrepresentation on the part of the lawyer.

Students will nevertheless often see a difference between these two. We agree; Honest Abe is doing something *on behalf* of his own client, as opposed to something being done *to the opposing party*. (We also believe that Wildman's conduct raises questions about a lawyer communicating — through the young woman — with opposing party represented by counsel, something forbidden in all jurisdictions. See **MR 4.2** and **DR 7-104**.)

(e)   Thoreen and Sotomayor:

Before we look at Abe's last tactic, in the rape case, we like to examine *Thoreen* and compare it to the situation involving Illinois attorney Sotomayor. We ask the students two questions: Is there anything different about Thoreen and his actions in using a substitute to be his client and the techniques ascribed to Abe Dennison? Then we ask whether there is any difference between Thoreen's conduct and Sotomayor's.

The principal difference between Thoreen and Dennison is that Thoreen's conduct relates to a misrepresentation on an issue that is both *material* and *relevant* rather than one that is collateral to the proceedings and the facts of the case. This seems to be a significant factor in the court's decision to discipline Thoreen. It brings home the idea that prejudice to the trier of fact, when it is directly on an issue of relevance, will more likely bring sanctions than when it is indirect and subtle. But we are unpersuaded that Thoreen's actions are any less justifiable than the worst of Honest Abe's or Max Wildman's.

As the note following the Thoreen case indicates, we *do* see substantial differences between the actions of Sotomayor and Thoreen. Unlike Thoreen,

Sotomayor did nothing to overtly and actively mislead, nor did he represent over a continuing period of time that the substitute was his real client. Nevertheless, Sotomayor was also disciplined. The lesson here may be that much closer scrutiny will be placed on acts of a lawyer which involve *any* kind of misrepresentation *directly relevant* to the facts of the case.

We personally disagree with each other on how Sotomayor was treated. One of us believes that the potential to mislead, such as by changing the substitute's appearance to look like the defendant, is too great to allow. The other simply believes Sotomayor saw an opportunity and used it as best he could. This makes Sotomayor's tactic justifiable good lawyering, *less* questionable than many of the tactics described in the problem itself.

(f) Using Race and Gender to Advantage in the Client's Case:

We discuss Abe Dennison's hiring a young woman law student in the rape case and Arthur McCabe's jury selection techniques together. Both of them concern using people's race and gender for the ends of a case.

Abe's use of the attractive Chinese-American woman as his law clerk will offend many in the class. Some students, on the other hand, will find it totally justified so long as it is done to assist in the defense of his client. In either respect, the teacher can act as devil's advocate.

If students accept Abe's actions, the teacher can point out how overtly a student's gender and racial background, and even her being "attractive," are directly used, even to the point where she is instructed to touch the defendant. If students are unhappy (they may even be appalled) by Abe's idea, the teacher can argue that Dennison's job is to do his best for his client. The teacher can also point out that the student is undoubtedly a willing participant, since it would be impossible to successfully misrepresent his purpose to her. The teacher can ask whether the students would feel as strongly about the inappropriateness of using the student in this manner if it were an assault or robbery case rather than a rape.

Whether one would engage the services of a law student in this way is very much of a personal choice. Again, students will have to choose a balancing point between how far they are willing to go in their representation of a client and their own sense of propriety. This illustrates a central point of this problem, since it is unlikely that Honest Abe will get disciplined for *any* of his trial tactics. Personal choice, and a sense of fair play, is thus an important factor.

Students often ask whether we would use a technique like this in our own trial work. We emphasize that it is not for everyone, and there are good reasons to feel uncomfortable about doing this. We ourselves feel less than fully comfortable. However, if Dennison's job is to present his client in the best possible light, and the use of a *willing* law student who makes a choice to

participate in the trial in this manner will help, we do not see it as wrong. Indeed, it can be a very effective trial technique. We note, for example, how many law students have asked why there was not a woman lawyer on the O.J. Simpson defense team.

This query raises a similar point to that illustrated by Abe Dennison's actions. "Playing the race card" in the *O.J. Simpson* case (**Readings, Section 3**) should be discussed at this point to illustrate the importance of race in a trial. Particularly valuable is Judge Higginbotham's important article, especially the tension between color-blind rhetoric and race-conscious reality (**page 514**).

The jury issues raised by McCabe are often easier for students ("why not, if it's going to help him win?" is one typical comment) but more difficult for us. Students, of course, feel more directly involved in the situation of the law student than they do in picking a jury. Nevertheless, there is clear case law (including the U.S. Supreme Court's *Batson* case) prohibiting strictly racial decisions in jury selection.

The teacher should point out to the students that despite *Batson* the reality is that use of race-based decisions about jurors often occurs. This will likely be more subtle and not as overt or crude as those suggested by Melvin Belli in the **Note** after **Section 3** of the **Readings**. But some criminal defense lawyers will say, for example, that all other things being the same, they would prefer African-American jurors to Chinese-American ones, and some civil defense counsel might say that they prefer Chinese-American jurors to black or white jurors. Lonnie Brown's thoughtful article in **Section 6** acknowledges this reality and then argues forcefully for ethics prohibitions that parallel and support *Batson*.

(g) Expanded Discussion of Racial Issues:

Depending on the desires of the teacher, the gender and racial basis/bias issues raised in this problem can be expanded into a considerably detailed class discussion. We address the issue of bias and diversity in **Problem 28**. However, either the teacher or some of the students might also prefer to engage in a longer discussion now.

This discussion, if it takes place, can be a sensitive and difficult one. The question of whether racially-based decisions made by lawyers are tantamount to racist ones (or the same for gender-based decisions) raises difficult issues for us all. While the entire class will likely roundly criticize attorney Belli's attitudes, the larger issue of the use of race-based and gender-based tactics in trial remains. Ultimately, this issue comes down to some of the same questions that we asked in numerous contexts during this part of the course: how far should a lawyer go in representing the client? And how far should one's

representation of a client, rather than the best interests of society, govern the way lawyers handle their cases?

To illustrate the difficulty of being totally neutral about race, gender or personal appearance in picking a jury, we play the part of a lawyer picking a jury from the pool of the students in the class. Assuming that we have no specific information about any of them other than what they look like as they sit there before us, how do we make a decision about who to put on the jury and who to challenge? We discuss how we might choose one student over another based on the kinds of clothes they wear, the haircuts they have and so on.

We believe there are times when most lawyers, whether they will acknowledge it or not, will use ethnic, racial and gender characteristics to help them select a juror rather than the limited amount of information they were able to obtain during the voir dire process. Moreover, we feel that what a juror "looks like" may well affect the nature of the voir dire process itself. While we see this as a more questionable tactic than getting the knowing and intelligent cooperation of a law student, the reality is that sometimes the decision about selecting a juror is likely to be racially-based, at least in part. We end the class by discussing jury profiling and its pros and cons (**Readings, Section 5** and **6**).

PROBLEM 20

Civility, Contempt of Court, Free Speech, and Publicity

THE POINT BEHIND THE PROBLEM:

This is a rather long problem with many sub-parts. The teacher may want to pick and choose which are most appropriate for a particular course, or "pick off" several sub-parts in relatively rapid succession.

This problem explores the advantages and limitations of both lawyer civility and courtesy, and a lawyer's free speech. One of the principal points of this problem is to emphasize the desirability of lawyers acting with civility, courtesy and comity toward each other, while on the other hand to emphasize that, as the readings note, rules of civility, whether in ethical rules themselves or as suggested codes of conduct, generally won't protect against discourteous or uncivil conduct.

Certain techniques of the trade, particularly any advantages counsel has by using relationships with court personnel, are to be expected, and may well simply be good lawyering. Moreover, issues of civility and courtesy prove to be almost impossible to regulate; civility codes are largely hortatory.

The second principal point: When a lawyer's speech inside the courtroom is evaluated, contempt and other judicial sanctions may be just as significant in controlling the behavior of lawyers as the rules of ethics themselves. Outside the courtroom, the sanctions tend to be traditional discipline as governed by the ethical rules.

Finally, a third main point: Free speech by lawyers involves far more than the rules of ethics. The students must balance ethical requirements with the danger of contempt and other judicial sanctions inside the courtroom, and the constitutional freedoms of free speech is, for lawyers, a hybrid issue made up of one part ethics, a second part constitutional law, a third part, the contempt power, and a fourth part, dealing with out-of-court criticism of a judge, which returns us to the issue of civility and the difficulty in regulating civility.

APPLICABLE RULES:

Model Rules:	MRs 3.4 including 3.4(c); 3.5 (see changes referenced under Problem 19): 3.6; 4.1; 4.4; 8.2.
Model Code:	DRs 7-106; 7-106(C)(5) and (C)(7); 7-107; 7-110; 8-102; ECs 7-1; 7-3; 7-4; 7-9; 7-37; 7-38; 7-39.
CA Rules:	5-120.
CA B&P:	6068(b) and (f).

SUGGESTED QUESTIONS TO ASK:

- Why is the first Boyette scenario acceptable if the presiding judge is "reasonably available" the entire day other than the 15 minutes chosen by Boyette to seek the judge out?

- Is Boyette's getting the motion calendared on Monday involve lying or just using his long-time pleasant relationship with deputy the clerk?

- If the ethical rules do not explicitly prohibit judge-shopping, does that mean that this practice is appropriate?

- Would you act the way Courbasier acted if Boyette had not acted toward you the way he did?

- Does another lawyer's lack of civility justify your response in kind?

- How would you compare the two hypotheticals in the **Notes** at the end of **Section 4** of the **Readings**?

- In the second hypothetical, would you come to a different result if the clerk *turned back* the date stamp to accommodate the attorney?

- What may/can you do when you think the judge is acting like a jerk in open court?

- In evaluating Bethea's conduct, how much responsibility should fall on the judge for being peremptory in her attitude towards Bethea?

- Should contempt be a question of decorum and offensive personality, or an issue of whether the orderly processes of the court are obstructed?

- To what extent should a lawyer be entitled to "make a record" before having to be silent in court?

- Do semantics count? How important is how the lawyer says something as opposed to the substance of what is being said?

- Is being held in contempt tantamount to being found unethical? Are there times when a lawyer can be ethical while being found in contempt?
- Whose statements were more onerous, Gentile's or Mike Epstein's?

- How important is Epstein's use of imprudent language?

- What kind of a standard should Bethea be held to in speaking out to the press about the judge?

- In the final analysis, does it make sense to regulate civility, either in the case of Boyette and Courbasier or in the case of Epstein and Bethea?

SUGGESTED ROLE-PLAYS

- Play the part of Boyette to the clerk about calendaring the motion on Monday, to demonstrate how semantics, tone of voice, and "real life" interaction can affect the way in which this conversation is perceived.

- Role-play any examples of "home-towning" from your own or your colleagues' practices.

- With a student, role-play a conversation between Boyette and Courbasier that might lead to some "ground rules" that could have avoided the conduct that took place in this problem.

- Play the part of Bethea, who now gets to complete his interrupted sentences. Give these sentences the most innocent possible interpretations concerning the defendant corporation's actions rather than the judge's rulings.

- Play the role of Bethea taking a less inflammatory, softer approach to making his record, in order to show that such approaches are feasible.

- In contrast, play the role of the judge who simply does not have any interest in Bethea being able to make his record using a softer approach, to show that it is sometimes impossible to do things the "nice" way.

- Phrase Epstein's speech in a more semantically "careful" manner.

DISCUSSION:

(a) E. J. Boyette's Two Tricks:

We like to begin by comparing the two tricks of E. J. Boyette: first, going to the presiding judge in the 15 minutes when he is not available, and second, using his "schmoozing" with the clerk to get a matter set on a day when he will get a judge more likely to be favorable. These two scenarios seem to serve well as examples of the vagueness of the black-letter rules regarding such conduct. In evaluating Boyette's conduct, students refer most often, as well they should, to the ethical considerations in Canon 7 of the Model Code. But such ethical considerations do not mandate conduct, only suggest it.

In the many years we have been using this hypothetical, students almost uniformly feel that Boyette's conduct in the first scenario is sneaky but acceptable, while his conduct in the second is unacceptable. Students reason that since the rule of court refers to the presiding judge's "reasonable availability" and the P. J. is not available (by "P. J.", we mean the presiding administrative judge, *not* the judge assigned to hear the case to conclusion) at the time Boyette picks, this is okay. On the other hand, students are offended by Boyette's using his personal relationship with the clerk, and the ambiguous language he chooses, to have a motion set on a date when he can get a "softer"

judge. We find ourselves — and most lawyers and — at odds with this analysis.

We believe that Scenario #1 is inappropriate, while Scenario #2 is far more acceptable. Boyette's timed arrival for his order shortening time stretches to the breaking point the definition of the presiding judge's "reasonable availability." By picking the only 15 minutes when the P.J. is not available, we think Boyette has subverted and violated the local rule. Students will argue long and hard about this, however.

On the other hand, we see Scenario #2, and Boyette's carefully-chosen semantics ("It will make my life a whole lot easier") as within the bounds of at least the black-letter ethical rules. We come back to this second scenario when we later discuss "home-towning" and using the friendliness of court personnel to advantage.

(b) Judge-Shopping and Civility Rules:

Despite having long heard admonitions about judge-shopping, we do not find rules of professional conduct that address this issue. We ask students whether they have found such rules. Invariably, they say that they have not found any *specific* prohibition. Does that mean that judge-shopping is considered appropriate? If nothing else, it may violate rules of civility.

But both formal and informal rules of civility, such as the Texas Lawyer's Creed excerpted in **Section 2** of the **Readings**, only go so far in regulating attorney conduct. It is valuable to discuss why civility rules tend to be so limited. There are several reasons. One is that such rules are like modern-day ethical considerations, advising on appropriate conduct but not requiring it. Second, many of the rules have only unofficial or quasi-official status.

Third, civility rules by their very nature have self-defining limits. Most important among these is that as soon as the civility code becomes mandatory, it can be used aggressively as a sword, thus actually diminishing civility and increasing aggressive advocacy. It in effect becomes either an ethics rule or a formal rule of court. Thus, the Preamble of the Texas Lawyer's Creed ends by stating: "These standards are not a set of rules that lawyers can use and abuse to incite ancillary litigation or arguments over whether or not they have been observed...."

Fourth, as the *Wunsch* case **Section 3** of the **Readings** demonstrates, attempts to use civility language in a regulatory framework rarely meet with success. We choose to leave the overriding issue of whether civility should be sanctioned, raised by the Freedman article in **Section 4** of the **Readings**, until the end of the problem, though it certainly appropriate to discuss it earlier.

(c) "Home-Towning":

The two scenarios at the end of **Section 4** of the **Readings** are not the same. We are more comfortable with the first scenario, getting the reporter to type up some notes (a relatively common experience during trial), and considerably less comfortable with the second, convincing the clerk to allow the motion to be filed, since it involves an after-hours filing. Nevertheless, since the date stamp has not been changed to the new date yet and the clerk is still at work and willing to file the papers, we ultimately accept this behavior as well, while wondering what the judge would think. We ask students whether they would feel differently if the date stamp had already been changed. It would make a difference to us, because the affirmative nature of the special help being provided by the clerk seems close to favoritism, if not misrepresentation

Teachers are encouraged to provide their own "war stories" of how "home-towning" counsel have used their local courts and court personnel to their own advantage. This is a common occurrence, and is, in our opinion, best viewed as good lawyering, at least in instances where there is no misrepresentation. At this juncture, we often engage the students in a discussion of the element of ordinary human nature in the practice of law, which is demonstrated by some of Boyette's conduct. This is an important practical part of lawyering. While some of Boyette's conduct may be open to question, we don't advocate making the practice of law so antiseptic that tricks and devices that meet reasonable ethical standards must be avoided or even frowned upon.

(d) Part II — The Actions of Courbasier:

Students may feel that Courbasier's conduct is appropriate, particularly in light of what Boyette has done to her. They may take the attitude that maybe what she is doing is wrong, but they would do it anyway if they could get away with it, given what Boyette had done.

However, the actions of Courbasier in setting the hearing are more likely to directly violate modern local rules of practice. To us, this is more unacceptable than either of Boyette's efforts. These actions may go beyond civility issues to affecting the administration of justice, an ethical breach. We like to compare them as a prelude to the tactics of the hardball litigator conducting discovery whom we met in **Problem 17**.

The most important point here may be that Courbasier is reacting to the unpleasantries she has suffered at the hands of Boyette. Her escalation of the situation is partly the consequence of Boyette's lack of civility. Where there is no check on the conduct of an attorney acting discourteously, the likelihood that the other side will respond in kind substantially increases.

While Courbasier's conduct may be worse than Boyette's, it is certainly understandable. She may feel the need to act in self-defense. This does not excuse her conduct, however, but as a teacher may also raise the issue of

whether Courbasier, as a woman, may feel the need to "prove herself," or may feel that Boyette acted the way he did *because* she is a woman. We will examine this recurring theme closely in **Problem 28**.

But we also point out that when a lawyer engages in dirty tricks which she would never do if similar things had not been done to her, she may adopt a pattern of practice that has the danger of turning her into the kind of person she initially despised. If Courbasier refuses to respond in kind, she may enhance her reputation in the courts, and will at the very least maintain her own sense of integrity. We ask students whether it is worth trying to gain a minor tactical advantage or, in the long run, to try to build a reputation for fairness, honesty and integrity.

(e)   Boyette's Competence:

One final component of this part of the problem is the question of whether Boyette, having left his office entirely unattended, has performed competently on behalf of his client by failing to have someone cover his practice for him in his absence. It is collateral to the main issue, but the teacher may want to raise to remind students of the basic obligation of competence, which never goes away.

Sole practitioners in particular may run into this problem. There are numerous ways of dealing with it, including having an arrangement with other lawyers who will cover for Boyette as he will in turn for them. The problems of covering a sole practice also may argue for Boyette being more accommodating in his own practice to engender a similar attitude in Courbasier.

(f)   Miles Bethea and Contempt of Court:

The question of whether Bethea is in contempt of court is a close one, and ultimately turns on the way the judge interprets Bethea's actions. Students should be reminded that judges have wide discretion in such circumstances. Depending on the students' points of view, the teacher can play devil's advocate. If students say Bethea is clearly in contempt, the teacher can point out the frustration Bethea must feel hearing a series of adverse rulings while being unable to finish his statements before being interrupted by the court.

We find it interesting to role-play Bethea's interrupted sentences to see how he might have finished them had he the chance. The teacher can provide an innocent conclusion to what may at first sound like an offensive statement. For example, "*It's absurd to have dangerous* cars on the road without doing something to correct the condition. That is what Reliable Motors has done," would be a far cry from finishing the sentence in a way that is directly critical of the court. Similarly, "*It makes no sense at all to* have a car company which knows about a dangerous condition and does nothing about it" is a far cry

from "It makes no sense at all to rule on my motion without letting me speak." Since Bethea doesn't finish, we don't know what he is going to say.

These role-plays should demonstrate that perhaps Bethea was not being contemptuous of the court, given the text of what he was saying (or would have said). Rather, he may have been directing his comments at the defendant, which the judge never understood because she interrupted. The teacher should point out that judges, just like lawyers themselves, are not perfect and can also be guilty of losing tempers, acting abruptly, and the like. The teacher can question whether that has happened in this scenario.

On the other hand, if students defend Bethea's conduct, the teacher can emphasize the negatives of his behavior: his refusal to stop when requested by the judge; after his first comment, his lack of respectful language in addressing the court; and the wide judicial discretion given judges to regulate behavior in their courts.

(g) Other Factors to Consider in Evaluating Bethea's Conduct:

Sections 5 and **6** of the **Readings** raise a significant issue that students should address: whether contempt is a question of decorum and offensive personality (recall the *Wunsch* case in **Section 3**), or whether it is a matter of obstructing the orderly processes of the court. The *Breiner* case in **Section 6** (see **footnote 6**) provides a good illustration of the question of whether the lawyer crossed the line between decorum and obstruction.

A collateral issue is the extent to which a lawyer is entitled to "make a record" by having his or her argument recorded so that appellate reviewers will understand the point the lawyer was trying to make. Note that in the *Sacher* case (**Readings, Section 5**, see **footnote 6**), the U.S. Supreme Court advised that trial judges should give "due allowance for the heat of controversy." Since on appeal all presumptions will operate in favor of the rulings of the trial judge, making a record for appeal is vitally important. This would seem to argue in favor of allowing the lawyer reasonable leeway.

The *Friedland* and *Carrow* cases referred to in **Section 5** (and cited in the **Supplemental Readings**), underscore the importance of the manner of the lawyer's approach. The way in which lawyers make their statements or objections to the court can be highly significant in determining the propriety of their conduct. Thus, when attorney Carrow "respectfully submitted" that a trial had become a joke, he was eventually relieved of charges of contempt, whereas attorney Friedland, who called the trial a "farce" but did so in less respectful terms, saw his contempt upheld. We thus revisit a recurring theme: that semantics, how a lawyer says something, can have a significant bearing on the matter and the propriety of the lawyer's conduct.

Our view of Bethea's contempt is that the judge may have jumped the gun by assuming what Bethea was going to say while he was trying to complete

his record, an effort that generally should be accepted by the judge. On the other hand, had Bethea had an opportunity to finish what he was going to say, it may well have not come out as respectfully as our role-plays above suggest, and may have provided ample reason for the judge to hold him in contempt.

(h)   Is Being Held in Contempt Being Unethical?

We think it is important for students to recognize the difference between being held in contempt and being found unethical. A contempt citation is not tantamount to a violation of the rules of professional conduct, and would ordinarily would not lead to a disciplinary action. This does not mean, of course, that the two cannot overlap. But the sanction for inappropriate behavior in the courtroom, as that behavior is described in this problem, is contempt, not state bar discipline.

The teacher might point out that some lawyers feel that in extraordinary circumstances it is necessary for the attorney to "take a contempt" in order to make sure that the client's rights are preserved on the record of that court's proceedings. Some argue that this is not unethical at all but the very best in zealous advocacy on behalf of a client. For example, some criminal defense organizations prepare "contempt kits" for their member attorneys in case a judge sanctions them while they are trying to protect a client's record.

(i)   Epstein's Comments to the Press, and *Gentile*:

The issue raised in **Part III** also involves the lawyer's ability to speak freely. But the limitations on such speech are very different in kind. Students should recognize that these limitations flow from the rules, especially **MR 3.6** that prohibit speech that directly endangers the impartiality of the jury. The students should directly relate Epstein's comments to those of Gentile (see **Section 7** of the **Readings**). They might first compare the actual words of Gentile, and their context, to those of Epstein. Which most directly threaten the fairness of the jury?

Our belief is that Epstein's comments are more onerous, since they occur *during* the trial, rather than some months before. Moreover, they are relatively inflammatory in nature, stated as an opinion in a fashion that is unlikely to be similar to admissible evidence. By comparison, Gentile's charges against the police officer, eventually proven, were factually specific in nature. It would be difficult for anyone to prove either that McVie "took her life into her own hands" or is "looking for a deep pocket to pay her." Nevertheless, we favor a *narrow* interpretation of the publicity rule. If Epstein has done little more than give the press his closing argument to the jury, we don't see a reason to discipline him.

However the students come out on the issue of Epstein's accountability for his mid-trial press conference, the most important point for them to recognize is that sanctioning a lawyer for what is said *outside* the courtroom is as much a

matter of constitutional law as legal ethics. Some discussion of the complicated *Gentile* decision is important to assist students in understanding this difficult opinion, made more difficult because there is no true majority. We suggest tracking our analysis in **Sections 7** and **8** of the **Readings**.

Of particular significance to us is Justice Kennedy's use of the phrase "in the court of public opinion" to describe how prejudice might accrue to a client in addition to the courtroom itself. We see this distinction as a significant one, in that it would allow counsel to protect the client's reputation in the community as well as deal with any prejudice to the jury. We agree with this perspective.

(j)   Criticizing the Judge:

In **Question 2** of **Part III**, Bethea criticizes the judge's handling of the rules of evidence. Students should evaluate how this statement compares to those of D.A. Holtzman and attorney Westfall, the lawyer in the *Semaan* case (**Readings, Section 9**), and Stephen Yagman, described at length in Judge Kozinki's opinion in **Section 9** of the **Readings**. Some may feel that Bethea's comment is more onerous than Holtzman's; she merely adopted without further investigation the statement of her subordinate. On the other hand, it sounds less onerous than Westfall's comment, because it is not a direct attack on the judge's *integrity*. (Westfall accused the Judge of being "a little bit less than honest" to obtain a result he personally likes, a strong attack on the judge's honesty.)

At first blush, these comments seem far less onerous than those in *Semaan*, and the strong opinions expressed by attorney Yagman. *Semaan*, which described the judge as "a midget among giants," and *Yagman* lead us to the close conclusion that Bethea is merely expressing his own opinion in a way that does not directly demean the judge's truthfulness or integrity. Rather, the remarks criticize the judge's ability to apply the rules of evidence. These comments seem far closer to protected free speech than they do to sanctionable conduct.

On the other hand, it is a legitimate interpretation that statements like Bethea's *do* demean the court and reflect badly on the judicial system. Unlike Bethea's comments in the courtroom, there is no need to protect the record here; Bethea's remarks merely reflect frustration and discontent with the court, and do not advance the client's cause. Accordingly, the remarks can be seen as unnecessary, nasty, and possibly subject to discipline, since in the larger sense they may obstruct justice.

(k)   Can And Should Civility Be Regulated?:

Having evaluated the statements of several lawyers highly critical of the judge and our fictional lawyer Epstein's imprudent language in describing his

case against plaintive McVie, we return to Friedman's analysis in Section 4 of the Readings and discuss with the students whether civility is something appropriately regulated by rule or sanction, or better left to the sound discretion of individual lawyers — both those who don't act civilly and their peers who informally sanction their conduct by disapprobation at the cost these lawyers' reputations.

On balance, we tend to agree with Friedman's view that "dithering on about 'civility'" is not terribly productive, particularly when what is meant by "civility" differs from lawyer to lawyer. Students are often uncomfortable with this, because they would like to see more civil lawyering. A fruitful discussion could focus on the relative merits — and effects — of *dejure* and *defacto* (i.e., peer pressure) regulation.

PROBLEM 21

Advocates' and Mediators' Ethical Dilemmas in Mediation

THE POINT BEHIND THE PROBLEM:

This problem focuses on an increasingly important component of legal practice: mediation. The principal point of this problem is to familiarize students with how the ethics rules — and the ethical and moral mores of mediators — affect mediation practice. We also want to make the students aware, as we have in several other areas of law, that mediation is an underregulated area, where much is left to individual decisionmaking. We encourage students to view both from the point of view of the advocate and the mediator, since more and more practitioners are becoming trained in ADR. The first ethical issue, which dovetails with the increasingly bright spotlight shined on this subject, is whether lawyers should be required to suggest mediation to their clients.

A second principal focus is to explore the importance of two fundamental principles of mediation that are also ethical precepts: confidentiality and neutrality. These are discussed in **Sections 3** and **6** of the **Readings**, and addressed through **Questions 2** and **3** of **Part I**, on conflicts of interest and disclosure, and **Questions 1** and **3** of **Part II**, which deal with issues of neutrality, confidentiality in the mediation and confidentiality that extends outside the mediation room. A third issue is power imbalances — those addressed in **Part III** of the problem — which we see as a particularly important and somewhat subtle ethical issue, particularly for the mediator. We deal with this issue first, skipping **Part II, Question 2** of the **Problem**, where the issue is secret settlements (see next paragraph). We have placed the sections of the book relating to secrecy at the end of the **Readings**.

We have had occasion publicly to take a strong and rather widely-publicized position on secret settlements (**Part II, Question 2**). We acknowledge a bias about an issue we see as an important ethical and moral matter. Other instructors may or may not choose to teach this material, but we believe it to be current, relevant, and significant and an excellent opportunity to discuss another "trilemma" — client choice vs. social need vs. the balance between lawyer and client decisionmaking.

APPLICABLE RULES

Model Rules:	MRs 1.1, 1.2(a); 1.4; 2.1; 2.2 (1983 version); 2.4 (2002 version); 5.6.
Model Code:	DRs 6-101(A); 7-101(A)(1) and (3); ECs 5-14 — 5-16; 5-20
CA Rules:	none

SUGGESTED QUESTIONS TO ASK:

- Does mediation work well enough to require lawyers to suggest it to their clients?

- Should there be rules about maintaining confidences in mediation? What should they be?

- Was *Foxgate* rightly decided in the appeals court or the state Supreme Court?

- Can a mediator who is well known to one side ever be truly neutral?

- Might familiarity with the mediator actually work in favor of the "outside" party, since the mediator will have great credibility with the party or lawyer s/he knows well?

- How important is it that the mediator has no actual decisionmaking power?

- What would you do, if anything, to help Mr. Pottman if you were his mediator?

- What factors would you consider in deciding to help Pottman? How important are each?

- Are there other solutions than those suggested in the problem for Westport's dilemma? What are they?

- What is most important about the Stephens settlement — protecting your client's own financial interests or protecting the public against future harm?

- Who gets to make this decision, you or your client?

- Can you make an argument for a moral imperative to have your client refuse secrecy? What about the opposite argument?

SUGGESTED ROLE PLAYS:

- Have a student play the role of Justice talking to her client (you) about whether to accept Springer as a mediator to see the dynamics of how Justice's — and Stephens' — concerns play out.

- Play Springer attempting to show his neutrality by fully disclosing his relationship with Van Lund, to show that the mediator's candid disclosure might vitiate concerns about neutrality.

- Play either side in the conversation between Van Lund and Justice in which Van Lund makes his surprise offer.

- Play Pottman pleading with Westport for help, with a student in Westport's unenviable position.

- Play Stephens, who wants to settle, as Justice explains why Stephens should turn down the settlement for moral reasons.

- Play Justice where she advises Stephens to settle without describing the emotional and social consequences to Stephens, and focuses only on the economic advantage of settling.

DISCUSSION:

(a) What is Mediation?:

To the extent that this topic may be unfamiliar to at least some students, we suggest a brief review of the mediation process and the basic rules attendant to that process. The general information reviewed in the **Readings, Section 1** is relatively straightforward, as is **Section 2**'s discussion of the limited ethics rules that are currently in force. Note that the rule referred to in the Diemer article as MR 2.x has been changed and now exists as new **MR 2.4**. Former **MR 2.2** has been eliminated in the 2002 version of the Model Rules.

Before turning to the question of confidentiality, we prefer to skip to the issue of whether a lawyer should suggest mediation. Clearly, in most venues, neither ethics rules nor case law have reached the point where this is a requirement, as **Section 4** of the **Readings** indicates. As **Question 1** of **Part I** of the **Problem** implies, there are circumstances where an ethical, responsible lawyer may well feel that mediation is *not* appropriate. Nevertheless, as we suggest in the text before the Bickerman article in **Section 4**, each day brings an increasing possibility that one day, a lawyer will be found liable in malpractice for not suggesting to a client the possibility of mediation.

The Bickerman article itself presents ample evidence of why lawyers don't see it in their own firm's interests to offer mediation — as he puts it, "they viewed mediation as contrary to the business of litigation." This, of course, is a significant issue, harkening back to the self-interest of lawyers that we examined in **Problem 9**.

(b)   Confidentiality, Neutrality, and Conflicts of Interest:

The significance of confidentiality and neutrality in mediation cannot be overstated. **Questions 1** and **3** of **Part II** address different aspects of confidentiality — within the mediation as among the parties, and with respect to the outside world. Inside the mediation, the mediator's word should be a bond. This should ordinarily free a mediator to meet with whoever wants to meet with the integrity of the process preserved by following the wishes of the parties, and confidentiality being preserved by the trust vested in the mediator. A discussion of this collaborative process, particularly at this point in the

semester, when the students have discussed a variety of practice situations, can be most valuable.

The **Readings, Section 3** set forth some of the basics of confidentiality *outside* the mediation room, including California's strong statute, which some now see as a preview of things to come elsewhere, and the *Foxgate* case, which at first threatened to erode that statute. Neutrality of the mediator is just as vital. **Questions 2** and **3** of **Part I** focus on this issue.

As **Section 3** of the **Readings** notes, there is little if any by way of formal requirements that mandate what matters need to be disclosed to the parties in mediation. We suggest in the last paragraph of that section an approach that involves the widest possible disclosure for mediators, as well as for arbitrators and judges. The fact that mediators have no decision-making power is of obvious relevance, but the principle of full disclosure — one we have seen throughout the course book — is one which has the most advantage for the clients and their attorneys and which does no harm to the mediator, and may enhance the mediator's de facto power — i.e., to persuade or suggest.

Before moving on, we want to add a word about the importance of both the process of mediation, and of the concept of "symmetry," something more than "mere" neutrality. As we state in **Section 1**, mediators often talk about allowing the process to work. To many skilled mediators, the process has its own life force — one that can sometimes work if the mediator stays out of the way as "the process" progresses. One of the ways this happens is through this elusive concept of "symmetry." More than mere neutrality, it includes — as the text notes — fair dealing and equal treatment. We might also include the idea, inherent in both of the concepts discussed in this paragraph, that the parties themselves "own" the mediation and are thus in full ultimate control should they choose to be.

(c) Part III, Power, and True Neutrality:

Pottman, the party Westport encounters in the hallway is a sympathetic character indeed. It is not at all unusual to see, as here, marked power imbalances among the parties to a mediation, and/or the quality of their counsel. Students will naturally be inclined to help Pottman out. But may this be done, and if so, *how* can this be done? Mediators who find themselves in this situation recognize the no-win nature of their position. Many mediators would argue that they are powerless to do anything, or at most may stop the mediation but in no way "put a thumb on the scales" of neutrality. Others will take more liberties, perhaps to the point of suggesting Pottman find new counsel. Few experienced mediators are likely to go beyond this point, such as suggesting to Pottman their opinion on the "true" value of his case.

Yet this paramount goal of neutrality — indeed, many mediators call themselves "neutrals" — creates a moral dilemma that is worth at least some brief discussion, and perhaps some devil's advocacy and role playing: How

can a lawyer who is neutral sit back and watch this poor guy get hurt by the system and his own lawyer? Yet how, after all, can the neutral take sides? There is no clear-cut answer to these and other questions that these circumstances present. In time, and with more regulation of this emerging profession, such answers may become at least more focused.

(d)   The ABA Opinion, and Practicing Law:

We have included the recent ABA opinion on lawyers' truthfulness in mediation (**Readings, Section 5**), although its conclusion is hardly dramatic or even exciting. We find it worth including, however, because it both shows the similarity of mediation to any other negotiation, and also demonstrates the clear gulf between mediation and arbitration — a point that we make in **Section 2**. While we do not dwell on it in the text, we are critical of **MR 2.4**, which makes no distinction between mediators and arbitrators despite the obvious and very substantial differences.

In **Section 8**, we discuss whether neutrals are involved in the practice of law — a question the ABA ethics rules avoid directly answering, but a continuing matter of debate. While the answer is not as important as the question (a point we seem to return to in various contexts), some teachers may find a brief discussion of this issue interesting and enlightening to their students.

(e)   Secret Settlements:

Here, for the most part, the **Readings, Sections 9, 10** and **11**, speak for themselves. The issue itself is not a particularly complicated one. **Section 10** reviews the kinds of secrecy that commonly occur. **Section 11** contains a new reading by Alan Blakely that gives a few examples of the problems with secrecy — here, in both Catholic Church and products liability cases. We have used this reading to replace our own *Moral Compass* excerpt about the "fixed" Louisville Prozac trial, relegating that fascinating tale to the **Supplementary Readings, number 6**. While we love that story, we sought to avoid too much self-reference and to try to maintain some modicum of neutrality on the issue.

Reasonable minds differ about the resolution of this issue, of course, though increasingly — with the Firestone/Explorer cases and the church molestation scandals, public opinion — and, we find, the large majority of our students — has turned more in the direction of preventing secrecy. Most recently, in 2007, the Zyprexa settlements — like Prozac, also involving Eli Lilly — caused a substantial stir, with the issue still pending as we print this Teacher's Manual. (Richard Zitrin wrote a February 8, 2007 op-ed piece for the Los Angeles *Times* on this new secret settlement, for those who may be interested.)

We reiterate that here, far more than anywhere else in the course book, we have a point of view. We see the issue much as we ultimately came out on **Problem 25**, the in-house whistleblower. We have endeavored to present an

objective analysis in **Section 11**, including there an excerpt from the most articulate proponent of the need for privacy in the resolution of disputes, Harvard professor Arthur Miller.

However one ultimately comes out on this issue, the subject affords an excellent opportunity to compare once again ethics rules (there are none preventing secrecy as of this writing) and moral imperatives, along with a dose of the issues we examined elsewhere: in **Chapter 1**, in which Prof. Postema weighs moral costs, **Problem 19**, where Judge Roger Miner argues against getting every last dime through every possible advantage, and in **Problem 12**, which raises the always tough issue of whether the lawyer or the client should decide, and how objectively the lawyer should be in laying out the alternatives. Should the plaintiff's lawyer, for example, be telling the client about all the money s/he is being offered in settlement, perhaps even that it's a premium amount (because of the secrecy it buys)? Or should the lawyer take a more holistic view and explain to the plaintiff the non-monetary effects that "secretizing" the information might have on future victims?

PROBLEM 22

Must A Prosecutor Play By Different Rules?

THE POINT BEHIND THE PROBLEM:

The most important point of this problem is to emphasize that district attorneys and other prosecutors have both a unique responsibility in their dual role as advocates and seekers of justice and truth, and an incredible amount of power with which to perform these roles. They, unlike most advocates, retain an independent obligation to maintain objectivity, seeking a conviction only in those cases where they believe it warranted. This is a direct contrast to criminal defense lawyers, their usual opponents, who are charged with the responsibility of trying to win their clients' cases even where those clients may be guilty. (See **Problem 14**.)

Indeed, the role of prosecutor is different from that of any other advocate; only prosecutors must believe in the cases they litigate. We have seen that even civil litigators need not necessarily believe in the merits of their clients' claims in order to represent them. This problem displays that unique prosecutor role in two different venues — the decision about whom to charge and under what circumstances to prosecute, and the question of seeking conviction against a particular defendant at trial.

This unique role means that prosecutors are asked to abide by different rules — in some cases higher standards of behavior — than other attorneys. But at the same time, substantial questions have arisen in the relatively recent past about prosecutorial accountability. Two important and related questions that students should address are whether prosecutors' unique roles as advocates and objective seekers of justice (1) entitle them to answer to the ethical mandates of their superiors, rather than the ethics rules of their state; and (2) entitle them to reach their own conclusions about the merits of a prosecution, rather than accede to the mandates of those superiors. The first question has a recent and rather colorful history (see **Section 6**), while the second is the subject of an important 2006 United States Supreme Court opinion (see **Section 7**). Finally, given the breadth of issues concerning prosecutors and the current events as the third edition went to press, we have included a somewhat broader group of Supplemental Readings.

APPLICABLE RULES:

Model Rules: MRs 3.8; 4.2, and Comments paragraphs 1-5 to the 2002 Rule (substantially amended from 1983 Rules).
Model Code: DRs 1-104(A); 7-103; ECs 7-11; 7-13; 7-14; 7-18.
CA Rules: 5-110.

SUGGESTED QUESTIONS TO ASK:

- Can you argue that selective enforcement is not only acceptable but necessary?

- Do you find the ABA standards of prosecutorial conduct helpful in articulating the unique standing of prosecutors?

- Is acceding to the wishes of the Mission District citizens giving them preferential treatment, or a matter of the "squeaky wheel getting the grease"?

- In the case of Leonard Sheldon, how do you balance the problem of selective enforcement with the need to get "bad guys" off the street?

- What if the loitering statute was being applied to people of Muslim and Arab descent? Is there a post-9/11/01 justification that allows the application of the statute more generally, rather than just to one individual?

- In the statute in the Sheldon matter were more equivocal and political — a anti-sodomy statute, for example — would your answer be the same?

- Can district attorneys prosecute all felonies as vigorously as others, for example robberies vs. small quantity sales of marijuana? Should they?

- What factors should a prosecutor consider in determining whether to prosecute?

- May prosecutors exercise blanket discretion and refuse to prosecute certain crimes at all, or is it better to exercise discretion on a case-by-case basis?

- What duties do prosecutors owe to their own view of "the interests of justice" and to what extent must that view and the discretion they exercise given that view be modified in the event of a superior's disagreement?

- Is it appropriate for a United States Attorney General to set standards of behavior for his or her deputies? Or is it necessary that these deputies abide by the ethical requirements of their particular states?

- Did deputy DA Pautler's simply go too far, or does he have a point that his failure to act might have cost lives?

- How convinced does a prosecutor have to be before trying to prove guilt at trial?

SUGGESTED ROLE-PLAYS:

- Take the part of a Mission District Safe Neighborhood leader who goes to the district attorney's office to request assistance in dealing with

problems in the neighborhood. Or take the role of a DA who refuses to help. The dynamics of such role-plays can clarify to the students why DA responsiveness may well be appropriate.

■ Role-play a supervising DA working with a group of deputy DAs to discuss "enforcement priorities," i.e., how prosecutorial discretion will be exercised.

■ Play the role of a prosecutor who is uncertain of Sish's guilt, yet believes he may be able to get a conviction.

SUGGESTED VIDEOS:

There are myriad movies and television shows that explore the behavior of prosecutors and, by inference or direct discussion, their ethics. We invite the teacher to choose from among these wide choices. We suggest being mindful of those examples — perhaps exemplified by the Law & Order TV shows — where prosecution and conviction, and a certain measure of sanctimony, seem to play a larger role than the more difficult ethics issues we attempt to confront in class.

DISCUSSION:

(a) Part I — Must the D.A. Prosecute Loitering?

Many students, despite the clear discretion vested in prosecutors (see ABA Standard 3-3.9 in **Section 1** of the **Readings**), will argue that Heather Headlines cannot refuse to enforce a law completely. The teacher may point out reasons why such selective enforcement is not only acceptable but can be necessary, due to allocation of resources. Before moving on, we review the ABA standards in order to emphasize the unique position of prosecutors.

This problem is also an excellent opportunity to seek direct input from local prosecutors, either before class or by asking them to join the class to describe how prosecutorial discretion works in practice. Most prosecutors will agree that without being able to make choices on minor crimes, it is impossible, given budget constraints, to successfully prosecute major felonies to the fullest extent of the law.

Such choices are the kinds of decisions which take place around the country on a daily basis. Some students may object that Headlines is acting out her own agenda because she made a campaign promise to stop prosecuting such crimes. While this is true, we see nothing wrong with it. Indeed, here we have a politician *keeping* her promise.

(b) Part II — Comparing No Enforcement at All with Selective Enforcement in the Mission District:

Some students will argue that whether or not the DA can refuse to apply the law at all, the selective enforcement in one area of the city alone is unfair. Students should evaluate whether it is the mobilized efforts of the Mission District citizens that make for this selective treatment, or whether it is their suspicion that other areas of the city have made similar requests that have been ignored. Many will see this as a squeaky wheel getting some grease. We agree. But selective enforcement where all those who complain have an equal voice.

A second issue here relates to the problem of the homeless itself, and whether loitering statutes are an appropriate way of dealing with this difficult question. Again, district attorneys are vested with considerable discretion. **Questions 2** and **3** ask whether it would matter if the constitutionality of the loitering statute had just been upheld, or if the statute had actually not been used for fifty years. It would be difficult to argue that dusting off a statute after that period of disuse is an appropriate exercise of the prosecutor's discretion.

About this juncture in the proceedings, we ask the students to turn to the ethical rules that govern prosecutors' conduct. It is important for students to recognize that **MR 3.8**, while it relates directly to the role of the attorney as prosecutor, says little about discretion in enforcing the law. However, ABA Standards 3-3.4 and 3-3.9, excerpted in **Section 1**, relate directly to this issue. Standard 3-3.9(b) is particularly significant in that it gives a "laundry list" of seven factors that the prosecutor "may properly consider" in exercising discretion.

(c) Selective Prosecution of Drug Lord Leonard Sheldon:

Question 4 of **Part II** asks whether it would be appropriate for the district attorney to prosecute only reputed drug lord Sheldon with a statute that has not been used for fifty years. We see this question as distinct from the earlier questions that relate to more general enforcement of a law across the city or in specific neighborhoods. The **Readings** in **Section 3**, including the summaries of the positions of professors Freedman and Uviller, together with our description of San Francisco's attempted homeless law enforcement and, especially, the "celebrity justice" cases involving the Marion Barry "sting", Martha Stewart, and former governor Ryan, are useful in evaluating this issue.

Our view is that here, what is happening is more than paying attention to a neighborhood coalition group. It is singling out somebody for prosecution with a statute that has not been used for half a century. We think this strains credulity and, given the supposedly objective, even-handed way that prosecutors should conduct themselves, is not an appropriate use of prosecutorial discretion. DAs of our acquaintance generally agree. But many students do not, arguing that if law enforcement has an opportunity to get a "bad guy" off the streets, they should do it. Standard 3-3.9 leaves enough

room to prevent a definitive black-letter answer to this question. Still, we believe Sheldon may have a strong motion to dismiss on constitutional grounds.

A valuable — one might say vital — piece of this question is some discussion of the effect of our post-9/11/01 world on the idea of selective enforcement. Students will have a wide variety of responses to the issue of whether people of Muslim or Arab descent may be detained under still-viable but little-used statutes. Teachers should be mindful of encouraging student responses that shed the politically correct views in favor of those honestly held. See our discussion of the Mayfield and *Alameh* cases in at **pages 589-590**.

(d) Part III — Whit Moore's Identification of Benjamin "Butch" Sisk:

The purpose of **Part III** is to show the broad prosecutorial discretion DAs have in filing particular charges against a particular prospective defendant. The first question, which of Mike's musings should be considered, is one we intend to have answered by considering *all* factors. Students may determine to file charges or not; our point is that regardless of that ultimate decision, the district attorney should objectively evaluate both the factors pointing to guilt and those raising significant doubts.

The teacher can serve as devil's advocate by asking why certain factors were considered rather than others or not considered at all. The factors we have isolated are the following: (1) the "coincidence" (unless the ID is wrong) of Sisk's showing up at a bar clear across town just a few days after the robbery; (2) Moore's questionable eyesight and the fact that he had had two drinks in a bar; (3) Moore's relative unfamiliarity with African-American men; (4) Moore's generally accurate physical description, except his inaccuracy about height; (5) Sisk's lack of prior record and the fact that he has a decent job; (6) Butch's brother's arrest (Question 3); (7) damaging but inadmissible evidence (Question 4); and (8) Moore's certainty that Sisk is the person who robbed him.

Prosecutors we have asked tend to consider most of these factors, though some are uncomfortable with those relating to Sisk's background, his lack of a record, or his good employment record. Nevertheless, we believe these factors are significant and should be considered. This is particularly true for an African-American male who, statistics show, is more likely to be stopped by police even if he did nothing wrong, than a male of a different race or a woman. Prosecutors will agree uniformly not to use any information about Sisk's brother, since it has no relevance to Sisk himself. However, many in fact, most will consider the illegally seized evidence in deciding whether to charge, because it is clear evidence of guilt in the minds of the prosecutors themselves, even though it will not be introduced at trial.

It is important to recognize that once the decision is made to charge Sisk, the DA's role as advocate will undoubtedly predominate. Once filed, cases often have a life of their own. This is perhaps understandable, since it is hard to seek conviction while continually looking over one's shoulder at abstract notions of "truth." Nevertheless, if Sling harbors significant doubts about Sisk's guilt, we believe his best course is to dismiss the case. One could reasonably argue that the district attorney would better serve the criminal justice system and the defendant if the discretion on whether to charge the case was exercised at the beginning of the case rather than at the time of trial. Note the reference to a district attorney's "reasonable doubt" in the *charging* part of the case, set forth in **Standard 3-3.9(b)(i)** (see **page 521**). We would expect that even where DA Sling has some doubts about the identification, if the case goes to trial he will argue the strength of the identification as forcefully as he would if he were absolutely certain. That is to say, at trial, the advocate's role will clearly predominate.

(e)   Other Points About Prosecutorial Discretion:

There are several other points about prosecutorial discretion worth discussing if time allows. The teacher may want to role-play a supervisor meeting with a group of deputy DAs (students) to discuss "enforcement priorities," i.e., how prosecutorial discretion will be exercised. (Be mindful here of the new US Supreme Court case of *Garcetti v. Ceballos* in **Section 7**, which deals more systemically with independent discretion and accountability — see below, **section (h)**).

Among the issues district attorneys must decide on a daily basis are these: Can they prosecute all felonies as vigorously as others, for example, robberies vs. small quantity sales of drugs? Some prosecutors feel that a general announcement that certain statutes will not be enforced is an invitation for the populous to commit those crimes. They point to examples of prostitution being allowed to take place in "red-light" districts or instances in which municipalities have allowed the personal use of marijuana. They say that a blanket prohibition against prosecution has the effect of defeating all efforts at deterrence. While this is more a matter of strategy than ethics, they would argue that exercising discretion on a case-by-case basis, or at least not making an announcement that certain laws will not be prosecuted, is far more preferable.

Some prosecutors question the factor, set forth in Standard 3-3.9(b), concerning a victim's willingness to testify. They note that, for example, victims of severe domestic violence cases are often reluctant to testify. DAs will want to forge ahead anyway because of the harm being done. Finally, prosecutors emphasize the difference between entrapment and selective prosecution, pointing out that entrapment is never acceptable.

(f) The Thornburgh and Reno Memoranda:

Although the Thornburgh and Reno memoranda are not directly a part of **Problem 22**, their inclusion in the **Readings** (in **Section 6**), along with the discussion of prosecutorial accountability in **Sections 2** and **6**, and the continuing debate over multijurisdictional practice (see **Chapter 13**) make discussion of this ethical issue important. We focus on whether it is appropriate for a U.S. Attorney General to set standards of behavior for his or her deputies.

Such standards, by their very nature, serve to supersede the standards of the state bar to which the lawyers belong. We are most uncomfortable with both the Thornburgh and the Reno memoranda, and take the position that we ascribe in the text to the majority of ethics commentators: Prosecutors must be subject to the same laws affecting all other attorneys. The ABA has come to agree. In 1995, the ABA amended **MR 4.2** to change the word "party" to "person," thus broadening the rule's application. Moreover, a new ABA ethics opinion held that prosecutors were required to follow this rule just as any other lawyer. While this opinion came from a split committee with a strong dissent, the 2002 version of **MR 4.2** reiterated its application to prosecutors, while carving out an exception for actions authorized by law or court order.

(g)   Starr, Pautler, and Abuse of Power:

Students will want to examine the investigation of President Clinton by special prosecutor Kenneth Starr. We see an issue of prosecutorial discretion and selective prosecution that has been widely discussed. More significant in our view as the way in which Starr and his office abused their power that was widespread and enormous. We see the story of the innocent bystander Kramerbooks, forced to spend hundreds of thousands of dollars defending an important right to privacy principle as the most unambiguous example of that abuse.

Ethical standards must apply across-the-board to the Starrs and Pautlers (see **Readings, Section 5**). A discussion of Pautler is particularly valuable, because unlike Starr, he was not a high-profile national figure, and his argument — compelling superficially — will strike some students as more than ample justification while striking others as similar to what they see as post-PATRIOT Act prosecutorial arrogance. Some teachers may want to relate this to the so-called "torture memorandum," which we discuss at greater length in both **Problem 24** and **Problem 26**, and for which we have included **Supplemental Reading No. 9**. Others may want to reference the actions of senior attorneys in the Gonzales Justice Department regarding the dismissal of US attorneys on seemingly political grounds, an issue that came along after our book went to press.

(h) Accountability:

It seems reasonable that abuse of power is inevitable without accountability. Pautler, for example, acted with his superior's consent, and thus can argue he is not accountable. We like the quote by Scott Turow at the end of **Section 5** of the **Readings** about prosecutors who help the evidence along. If superiors sanction bad behavior, accountability — and, in our view, ethical behavior — inevitably suffer. On another front, the point of the *Kojayan* excerpt in the **Readings, Section 8** is obvious: A "sanitized" opinion about a prosecutor who failed to tell the truth will not be likely to result in accountability.

We believe that the issue of *personal* accountability is of particular importance in an ethics class, particularly if there are future prosecutors in attendance. The standards for prosecutors in **Section 1** of the **Readings** — and, of course, virtually all rules of professional conduct — apply to lawyers individually. The recent US Supreme Court case of *Garcetti v. Ceballos* has a material effect on personal accountability, and not, in our view, a positive one. While Ceballos' actions may be somewhat over the top, his effort to "do the right thing" cost him significantly. While this is not the lesson we want to teach, it would be imprudent at the very least to ignore this important case.

PROBLEM 23

What's A City Attorney To Do?

THE POINT BEHIND THE PROBLEM:

We really take the title of this problem seriously: "What *is* a city attorney to do?" As much difficulty as students — and law professors — have in identifying the appropriate role for a corporate or partnership attorney (see **Problem 8**), the difficulties are magnified when the lawyer is a government attorney. Much of the purpose of this problem is to demonstrate the complexity of the situation that the average city attorney or county counsel faces daily. At the outset we recognize that there has been relatively little "hard case law" available on this subject, and that the rules of professional conduct are inadequate to deal with many of the problems inherent in a government attorney job. As we note in the introduction to the problem, the dilemmas commonly confronting such attorneys have largely been ignored by legal ethics experts, at least until very recently.

These dilemmas are multi-dimensional. But they center, ultimately, on this problem's first major point — defining the client. The government attorney must first determine whether the client is the entire government or the agency of the government with whom that attorney works. He or she must determine whether there are particular individuals within the agency to whom the lawyer answers — the "real person" representatives of their client — and who is entitled to a confidential relationship with the lawyer.

A second major point is whom the city attorney can successfully *advise* (see **Parts I** and **II**). This is a different question than on whose behalf the city attorney can *litigate* (see Part **III**). Circumstances may allow giving advice, even differing advice, to two agencies of the city. But it may not be possible to represent both these agencies should the matter get to litigation. In both instances, a conflict of interest analysis must be done, but as the Readings point out, this analysis is different than if it were taking place in the private sector. We also examine whether it is possible to represent both the city and its employee, a question that follows a more traditional conflicts analysis. A third point is to evaluate limits on the governmental attorney-client privilege and confidentiality, and to consider when, if ever, whistleblowing outside the agency is appropriate.

Finally, it is important to explore the extent to which government attorneys can work with their respective governments, and the agencies within those governments, to self-define lines of responsibility and accountability, and thus develop guidelines for their future conduct.

APPLICABLE RULES:

Model Rules: Scope, 1983 rules, paragraph 4; MRs 1.6, Comment, paragraph 8 (1983 version; the last sentence of Comment paragraph 5 in 2002 version); 1.13, including Comment, paragraph 6 (1983 version), or paragraph 9 (2002 version), including comparison of substantial changes in this comment

Model Code: ECs 5-18; 7-14.

CA Rules: 3-600.

SUGGESTED QUESTIONS TO ASK:

- Who is Joe Hannah's client?

- Who does Joe "answer to"? The assessor? The assessment appeals board? Or both?

- If he only gives advice on evidentiary matters, to what extent does Joe represent the appeals board?

- If the appeals board can make its own decisions on appeals that are not subject to review, is the board just an agency of the city? Or is it at least quasi-independent?

- Is it possible Joe can *advise* both the assessor and the appeals board even if the city attorney could not represent both in litigation?

- Does it matter whether Joe believes the comparable values are or are not admissible?

- Would it help if Joe could bring in another city attorney to *advise* the appeals board while he advised the assessor? How would this other city attorney know of the faulty assessment?

- Does deputy assessor Shostrand have a reasonable expectation of confidentiality? Or may Joe disclose Shostrand's comments to the assessor?

- What if Shostrand were the chief assessor? May Joe go *outside* the agency to reveal Shostrand's misconduct? To whom should he go?

- Who is the client in *In re Lindsey*?

- If Joe goes outside the Assessor's Office to disclose wrong-doing, is that whistleblowing or merely taking it up the governmental ladder to the entity of the city itself (e.g., to the City Council)?

- What happens when the mayor (or city council) and the assessor disagree about how to deal with extortion in the assessor's office?

- What factors can a city attorney use to self-define the government lawyer's role and the lines of authority that the government lawyer should follow?

SUGGESTED ROLE PLAYS:

- Play the part of the assessor when she hears that against her wishes, Joe is going to tell the appeals board about the incorrect assessment.

- Play the part of a member of the appeals board at the hearing on the Sturges assessment who is dissatisfied with Joe's disinclination to give direct advice and asks him probing questions about the admissibility of evidence about the assessment.

- Play the part of Hannah, believing the comparable values admissible, advising the appeals board of this (and assume the assessor is present).

- Play the part of deputy assessor Shostrand, who has the expectation that what he tells Joe is confidential; or play the part of Joe advising Shostrand to be forthcoming with what he knows.

- Play the part of the assessor if Joe refuses to tell her what Shostrand told him.

DISCUSSION:

(a) Approaching this Complicated Problem:

In dealing with the problems of Joe Hannah, we generally concentrate our efforts on **Part I** of the problem, working through the questions — at least 1, 2, and 3 — in turn. Joe must first decide whom he answers to. Is it the assessor? The assessment appeals board? Both? Must he also answer to, for example, the city council? The basic problem is stated in the **Readings, Sections 1** and **2**, describing the dilemma of the Los Angeles city attorney who finds himself giving conflicting advice to two different agencies of the city about what to do with Police Chief Gates. While doing this was criticized by at least one ethics expert, former city attorney Pines argues persuasively that the city attorney represented the city as an entity itself, and a traditional conflict analysis, at least as between different agencies of the city, does not apply.

In determining which entity or entities he represents, Hannah will find little help from the ethical rules. **MR 1.13** has already proved very difficult to apply when a lawyer tries to define the lines of authority representing a private entity (see **Problem 8**). It is even more difficult here, a fact which **Paragraph 9** of the **Comment** to that rule (**2002 version**) recognizes. Indeed, some teachers may want to point out the difference between **Comment Paragraph 6 (1983 version)** and the newer comment. The 1983 Comment at least suggests a

possible answer to the who-is-the-client dilemma. The 2002 Comment flatly calls this issue "beyond the scope of these rules."

If this seems scary to our students, we can say little but agree. It is important that teachers reassure students, as we did in **Problem 8**, that their difficulty in finding clear answers to the problems confronting Joe Hannah is understandable, even expected, in light of the complicated and virtually irresolvable situation presented. We advise our students that they are not responsible, after all, for the fact that the ABA rules offer little guidance, and are even moving in the direction of less guidance. While this may be scary indeed, it underscores the importance of addressing this problem in our classes, and reminds our students that sometimes we can only ask questions and grapple with answers as best as we can under the circumstances.

(b) "Clienthood," Confidences, and Taking Orders:

Commentator Lowry (referred to at the end of the **Readings, Section 2**) suggests that rather than evaluate the "theoretical" question of who is the client, the lawyer should determine from whom to take direction. We believe Hannah should also consider which city officials are entitled to expect a confidential relationship with him. The Pendlebury article (**Readings, Section 10**), which we have placed at the end because it deals with the federal government giant, suggests a similar test: With whom does the government lawyer work closely in an ongoing relationship? The *Lindsey* case in the **Readings, Section 3** assumes that Lindsey is the attorney for the Office of the President, not some wider governmental entity. If these tests are used, the students may conclude that Hannah is really attorney for the assessor, or at least the Office of Assessor, and should therefore do the assessor's bidding at the hearing. It can reasonably be argued that he advises the appeals board only as to evidentiary matters, and accordingly should do the assessor's bidding in not revealing the mistake about Sturges' assessment.

This analysis works reasonably well until the evidentiary issue presents itself. If no one presents the information it appears that Hannah has represented the assessor (or her "Office") without conflict. But if Sturges' lawyer presents the expected comparable values and — let us suppose — Hannah believes the information is admissible, can he tell the appeals board this, or must he now withdraw? On these facts, the situation is quite similar to the Gates controversy in Los Angeles, except that Hannah is exactly the same individual dealing with both "sides." We don't see particular utility in informing a higher authority other than buck-passing, unless it is to get a separate city attorney — as was the case in L.A. — to "buffer" the conflict. (We should remind students that while this might work in a government lawyer context, it generally won't in private firms — see **Problem 10**, and see further discussion in **section (e)** below. But there are problems everywhere; a new deputy city attorney may have little or no familiarity with the issue of admissibility of the "comps."

It is useful to note that many city and other local public attorneys' offices, except perhaps the very largest, represent various city or county agencies *horizontally*, wearing various representational "hats" depending on the circumstances. Federal agency attorneys, on the other hand, tend to work vertically, for one particular agency. The question of whom such lawyers represent may benefit by this vertical vs. horizontal analysis. Entities such as Ossias', California Office of the Insurance Commissioner, are somewhere in between, though they seem to have more in common with federal agencies in that such attorneys are *hired* by the agency rather than by some centralized attorney office, and structured vertically, as opposed to the office of a state attorney general.

Role-plays in which the teacher first plays the part of the assessor, and then a member of the appeals board who is dissatisfied at the hearing and is asking Hannah probing questions, or an angry assessor unhappy with Hannah's advice, may show both the assessor's reasonable expectations that Hannah works for *her*, and the appeals board's reasonable expectations that Hannah will advise *them*. These role-plays will demonstrate that Hannah has no perfect solution to his problem. It argues rather strongly, in our view, for a separate lawyer to advise the board, even if from the same city attorney's office.

(c)   Limits of Confidentiality:

Both the *Lindsey* case (**Readings, Section 3**) and the Ossias matter (**Readings, Section 4**) are worthy of discussion here. *Lindsey* expressly limited the privilege afforded government lawyer working for President Clinton in his official capacity. Ossias was allowed to breach confidentiality when the head of her agency was the malfeasant.

It is important in discussing these matters that the student recognize that the limits on confidentiality for government attorneys are different than those for private counsel. *Lindsey* emphasizes that public policy may require disclosure by a governmental attorney, and while the California State Bar's position on Ossias is not conclusive, it stands as a strong defense of her conduct on public policy (see the Bar letter's second determination, at **page 617**).

While we believe that these cases may have implications broader than just in the governmental context, it would be premature to reach such a conclusion. It is worth taking note of the cases cited in the **NOTES** following the Ossias reading. Nevertheless, it would be interesting to revisit particularly the Ossias case when discussing **Problem 25** concerning whistleblowing by an in-house attorney.

(d)   Two Issues We Try to Avoid:

Some students may see a duty to property owner Sturges, since the city attorney is, after all, a servant of the people. They may see a duty to "blow the whistle" to the property owner himself. While this is an understandable point

of view, we believe it unduly complicates an already complicated issue. Things are tough enough for attorney Hannah without throwing in this element as well. We would discourage looking too closely at this idea as a viable solution. If the ultimate client is the city, it is the city as an entity, not as a collection of its citizens.

Other students, particularly those who may have studied municipal governments, may raise the issue of the city charter, and what it says about the relative responsibilities of different city agencies. This is a good point, certainly one worth noting. City charters often do define, at least in part, how a city and its attorney work. But they generally will not serve to resolve Hannah's problem. While they are certainly worth mentioning, we try to avoid spending too much time discussing charters and other similar documents. They don't answer the ethical questions.

(e) The Appeals Board's Independence and the Use of Screening:

It can be argued that the appeals board, which makes its own decisions on assessments which the city government cannot overturn, is the same kind of quasi-independent municipal agency as the San Diego County Civil Service Commission (see the case excerpt in **Section 5** of the **Readings**). This independence argues in favor of requiring a separate attorney if the matter goes to litigation. But as we discuss in the readings, it does not necessarily mean that the city attorney's office (the office, not the same lawyer) cannot *advise* both the assessor and the appeals board. It is useful to point out to students that there may be a difference between these quasi-independent agencies of local government and departments which have no independent decisionmaking authority.

It is also useful to discuss the possibility of screening, a subject which we discuss in **Sections 5** and **7** of the **Readings**. Courts appear to be more liberal on the issue of screening for government attorneys than they are with private law firms. Some students may argue that if Hannah could bring in another city attorney to advise the appeals board, at least some independence of advice would be possible; Joe would not be put between a rock and a hard place, having to do the assessor's bidding on the one hand and advise the board on the other. Although all members of the city attorney's office are part of one law firm the same as a private law firm, this argument has some merit, as we've stated above.

We emphasize the practical realities of providing independent private counsel in every instance of conflict in public entity representation. This is probably the most likely reason why courts are willing to consider screening solutions for government attorneys when they refuse to do so for private attorneys. The teacher might ask whether L.A. city attorney Hahn would have been better off had he at least found two different deputy city attorneys to advise the police commission and the city council respectively. At least those

individuals would have understood to whom they answered and whom they advised.

(f)   Part II — Joe's Duty to the Assessor's Office and to Individual Assessor Shostrand:

We like to save for this part of the problem the issue of how city attorneys, and their deputies, can self-define their roles and responsibilities by working together with municipal officials and agencies. We feel that the discussion fits well here because of the issue of whether Joe owes Shostrand the duty of confidentiality. The problem seems to imply that Shostrand thinks he has spoken to Joe in confidence. The students may presume that this is the case, and go on to the issues of what Joe should do next and whether he can represent both the city and Shostrand. But does Shostrand have a reasonable expectation of confidentiality? Are his comments confidential, or may Joe disclose them to the assessor, for whom he directly works?

Our view is that Shostrand's comments are not confidential as to him personally, and would be appropriately disclosed to assessor Ferrara. But what has Joe done to tell Shostrand what the "ground rules" are for his speaking candidly? The confidentiality issue can expand to a larger discussion about how city attorneys can, by defining lines of authority and lines of confidentiality, develop a method for minimizing (never eliminating) conflicts in their roles as counsel for municipalities, their subdivisions and their individual employees.

(g)   Actual Representation of the Assessor and Her Individual Deputies:

The questions in Part III show why we believe that joint representation of the assessor and the city and the individual deputy assessors presents a direct conflict of interest. The *Barkley* case in **Section 6** of the **Readings** does a good job of articulating the conflict between the city as an entity and its individual employees. Here, the conflict analysis is much more traditional than when dealing with the municipality and its constituent parts or agencies.

We believe that this more traditional conflict analysis is why the *Barkley* court refuses to allow screening to permit one part of the city attorney's office to represent individual police officers while another represents the city itself. The teacher may want to point to the *Dunton* case and the other cases referred to in **Section 6** to help explain why the division between a municipal entity and its individual employees is different than juggling among the municipality's various entities. In these circumstances, we might also point out that the city acts much as an insurer would; the responsibility to pay independent counsel is similar to the obligation that may be required of an insurer (see **Problem 11**).

(h) The Pressure from the Mayor and the Need to Define Ground Rules:

The pressure Hannah feels from the mayor, or from the city council — we see little effective difference — brings us back to the city-as-entity issue that began our analysis. The mayor's office is a subdivision of the city government. Hannah, however, generally answers to the assessor. We believe that Hannah can take into account the mayor's views. But what happens if the assessor and the mayor disagree?

This is an opportunity to reemphasize the need to define the role of the city attorney's office in general, and the role of particular city attorneys specifically. If Joe is deemed to be the attorney for the assessor, then the mayor can seek the help from those city attorneys assigned to assist his or her office, or the chief city attorney. Interestingly, when we asked a student recently who Hannah represented, the student replied, "Well, he *doesn't* represent the Mayor." We found this analysis a useful one. The same may pertain to evaluating whether Shostrand is Hannah's client. That is, it may be beneficial to analyze whom a lawyer clearly does *not* represent rather than having to figure out with whom counsel does have an attorney-client relationship.

We conclude by asking the students what "ground rules" they can think of to assist deputy city attorneys. Among the most helpful readings is the Pendlebury article in **Section 10**. We agree with the comments made there by Charles Ruff that a uniform ethical rule applicable to all lawyers and all government representations is unrealistic. Clearly, for example, if the lawyers for the CIA or NRC quoted in this article had to consider the entire federal government its client, the consequences would be disastrous. We think it is more sensible to look for self-defined solutions that govern the particular governmental institution involved.

Among the factors we suggest the teacher consider if the students do not mention them are: what are the lines of authority to be followed by a deputy city attorney; whom does the particular deputy or city attorney unit represent; who may expect to impart confidences to these lawyers within the course and scope of their employment; from whom will specific city attorneys take direction (i.e., from what agencies and from what persons within them); and to whom may confidences from one individual be passed on within the "client unit"?

These efforts at self-definition, obviously, will only go so far. While we don't see them as providing anywhere near a complete solution, we believe they are more than a little helpful.

The pressure Hannah feels from the mayor brings us back to the city-as-entity issue that began our analysis. The mayor's office is a subdivision of the city government. Hannah, however, generally answers to the assessor. We believe that Hannah can take into account the mayor's views. But what happens if the assessor and the mayor disagree?

This is an opportunity to reemphasize the need to define the role of the city attorney's office in general, and the role of particular city attorneys specifically. If Joe is deemed to be the attorney for the assessor, then the mayor can seek the help from those city attorneys assigned to assist his or her office, or the chief city attorney.

We conclude by asking the students what "ground rules" they can think of to assist deputy city attorneys. Among the most helpful readings is the Pendlebury article in **Section 8**. We agree with the comments made there by Charles Ruff that a uniform ethical rule applicable to all lawyers and all government representations is unrealistic. Clearly, for example, if the lawyers for the CIA or NRC quoted in this article had to consider the entire federal government its client, the consequences would be disastrous. We think it is more sensible to look for self-defined solutions that govern the particular governmental institution involved.

Among the factors we suggest the teacher consider if the students do not mention them are: what are the lines of authority to be followed by a deputy city attorney; whom does the particular deputy or city attorney unit represent; who may expect to impart confidences to these lawyers within the course and scope of their employment; from whom will specific city attorneys take direction (i.e., from what agencies and from what persons within them); and to whom may confidences from one individual be passed on within the "client unit"?

These efforts at self-definition, obviously, will only go so far. While we don't see them as providing anywhere near a complete solution, we believe they are more than a little helpful.

(i) Bosses, Employees, and Part-Timers:

These three issues, discussed at the end of **Section 7 (top, page 624)** and in **Sections 8 and 9**, are significant issues with ethical components. We find that the extent and subtlety of this problem often does not leave time for much discussion of these issues (except *Garcetti*, which we examine in **Problem 22**), but they are included in the text because they each make significant points about this difficult area.

PROBLEM 24

What's Most Important — What You Say, How You Say It ...
Or Whether You Should Say It At All?

THE POINT BEHIND THE PROBLEM:

As the Chapter 9 title indicates, we now focus on the lawyer's role as advisor. The first purpose of this problem is to evaluate how far the lawyer may or should go in giving advice, and where the line should be drawn between giving advice on the law and assisting in the client's fraudulent conduct. The client clearly is entitled to complete legal advice, but is not entitled to advice that explains how to break the law.

A second point relates to the distinction between the two scenarios in this problem. We see a clear distinction, but many, perhaps most, students have great difficulty in seeing this difference. Drawing the distinction between advising about the law — which every client will expect of a lawyer — and assisting in the creation of fraudulent conduct is a difficult but necessary task. This, in the words of the **Comment** to **MR 1.2 (Paragraph 6, 1983** version and **Paragraph 9, 2002** version) that we have cited before (see **Problems 4 and 15**), is a "critical distinction."

A third purpose of this problem is its use as a vehicle to distinguish between passive advice and actively assisting the client in what the lawyer knows or should know is fraudulent conduct. A fourth and related purpose is to examine the distinction between the lawyer acting as adviser and as advocate — and to evaluate where the line between these two very different roles should be drawn. To these ends, we summarize two celebrated scandals from the 1980s and 1990s, the O.P.M. Lincoln Savings & Loan cases, before we address the new millennium's major corporate scandal — Enron. The law firms' actions in each of these cases can be compared to Pomeranian's assistance to Tovarich.

APPLICABLE RULES:

Model Rules:	MRs 1.2(d), including Comment, paragraph 6 (1983 Rules) paragraph 9 (2002 Rules); 1.4; 2.1.
Model Code:	DR 4-101(c), DR 7-102(A)(6) and (7); ECs 7-3; 7-5; 7-6; 7-8.
CA Rules:	3-210; 3-500.
CA B&P:	6068(d), (e), and (g).

SUGGESTED QUESTIONS TO ASK:

- Do you see a difference between Scenario #2 and a reply from Lonnie that said "Here's the law, here are the possible consequences of violating the law, and here are your options and the risks involved"?

- Have you assumed that Pomeranian's motives in advising Tovarich in Scenario #2 are the same as in Scenario #1? Is the lawyer's intent an issue at all in Scenario #1 and #2? Why?

- Have you concluded that if he marries Elena, Tovarich is definitely committing a fraud on the INS? How can you be certain?

- Might not Tovarich's marriage to Elena be a desirable thing for him, something he really wants to do for himself? Not all marriages are based only on love. Would this legitimize the marriage?

- Is the advice Newman discusses in his article similar to that given in the Bybee memo? Does it matter that Bybee was a government lawyer, or that the memo discussed matters of national security?

- What do you think of the actions of Singer, Hutner and Kaye, Scholer? Were these firms merely giving advice, or did they cross the line and assist their clients in the commission of ongoing frauds?

- How does the behavior of the lawyers at Vincent & Elkins on behalf of Enron compare to that of Singer, Hutner or Kaye, Scholer?

- In assisting Solomon and Elena, what does Lonnie "know" of their intentions? Does she have to quiz her own client about these intentions?

- How much investigation must Pomeranian do about her own client and her client's motives? Or is it sufficient for her to simply rely on the assurances of Tovarich?

- At what point does Pomeranian become "litigation counsel"? Can a lawyer be "litigation counsel" in anticipation of litigation? If so, when?

- How much of a difference should it make to a lawyer's ability to advise the client that the lawyer is "litigation counsel," or acting as an advocate?

SUGGESTED ROLE-PLAYS:

- Play the part of Solomon Tovarich seeking Pomeranian's advice, showing why Solomon will be unlikely to be satisfied with anything less than a complete answer to his inquiry.

- Role-play the "innocent" Tovarich: when the student, as Pomeranian, advises Tovarich that what he is thinking about would violate the law, "Tovarich" responds by saying that he really does want to marry Elena, and that it sounds like a good idea to him for a number of reasons besides her immigration status.

- Role-play Pomeranian laying out the law, the possible consequences to Solomon of violating the law, and Solomon's options "objectively and dryly" to see if this would satisfy the students if they were Tovarich.

- Role-play a group of lawyers at Kaye, Scholer or Vincent & Elkins, assigning roles to reflect various perspectives, and have a debate about whether the firm is acting appropriately.

DISCUSSION:

(a) Advising Solomon Tovarich:

We spend most of our time talking about **Question 1** of this problem. Particularly, we concentrate on the difference between Scenarios #1 and #2.

Students readily see that the first scenario is more blunt, and more direct in advising Solomon how to "break the law" than the second scenario. But many students see this as a technical distinction without any substantive difference. However, we — and most practicing lawyers we have surveyed — see a *clear* distinction between Scenario #1, which points the client directly toward how to defraud immigration authorities, and Scenario #2, which we believe advises the client about the law.

Students accept the idea that advising about the law is appropriate, but often argue that Scenario #2 does more than this. They see the appropriate advice as limited to "Here's the law, here are the possible consequences of violating the law, and here are your options." We see little difference between this approach and Scenario #2, except that this dry approach may be less than what Solomon wants. But students see a substantial difference.

There are several ways in which we highlight the distinctions between the two scenarios and answer the questions and arguments raised by students. First, the Newman article in the **Readings, Section 1** points out the need to fully advising the client. Second, we role-play the part of Tovarich to explore why he is unlikely to be satisfied with anything less than a complete answer to his inquiry. This recalls the pen-knife role-play in **Problem 15**, which we cite in **Question 2**. Finally, we evaluate the motives of both attorney Pomeranian and client Tovarich. Frequently, students *assume* what their motives are in a negative way that is not necessarily correct. We review each of these points in turn.

(b) The Newman Article (and the Bybee Memorandum):

In Prof. Newman's article (included long before the Enron/Andersen matters gave new meaning to the term "audit') he makes it clear that he would advise a client fully on the fact that the taxpayer audit rate is low while also telling that client that what he wants to do may be illegal. Newman argues that to not advise a client of the consequences of his actions — even if it means telling him he is unlikely to get caught — is part of a lawyer's duty to that

client. He has a good point, but as the **NOTES** after the article explain, his argument strikes us a mite too facile, and fails to address the abuses of this type of advice raised in the Baker article in **Section 8**. The bottom line is that the lawyer must avoid cheating for the client or assisting the client's fraud, while making sure that the client has been fully advised. It is important that students recognize that at this preliminary stage, there is no question of participation in a client's crime.

While we will revisit the famed "torture memo" in a different context in **Problem 26**, we think it valuable to examine the differences between the advice suggested by Prof. Newman and that given by Jay Bybee. The questions in the **NOTES** in the **Readings, Section 2** after the Liptak article frame the discussion. While we question whether Newman's advice parameters are a bit too broad, the Bybee memo appears to us to be much more clearly over the line, particularly given the argument that the OLC should provide "disinterested" advice.

(c)   Role-Playing the Part of the Client:

It is easier for students to see why a client would be dissatisfied with less than a Scenario #2 response if the teacher plays the role of Solomon. Students who feel that the advice given in Scenario #2 goes too far may be invited to play the part of Pomeranian. The teacher should be sure to require that "Pomeranian" answer all the questions put to the lawyer, and that Tovarich will not be satisfied by anything less. Most students will readily see, as we did, that clients will not be satisfied by lawyers whose advice they have sought if those lawyers repeatedly dodge the very issue that the clients have asked about.

We are fond of citing the words of one of the public members of our California State Bar ethics committee. She has told us often that if Lawyer A won't do what she asks, "I'll take my business down the street" to a lawyer who will. The reality of client expectations is that when the client asks the lawyer for advice on an issue, the lawyer's duty is to give it, not dodge it.

(d)   Judging Pomeranian's and Tovarich's Motives:

Some students assume that the motives of attorney Pomeranian are the same in Scenario #2 as they are in Scenario #1. This may be because we begin with the first scenario, where the lawyer seems to be consciously advising Tovarich how to commit a fraud. It is important for the teacher to point out that in the second scenario, while students might assume these "bad motives," that is nothing more than an assumption.

Of perhaps greater significance is the assumption many students make of *Solomon's* impure motives to circumvent USCIS regulations to get Elena into the country. The concepts of paternalism raised in **Problems 12 and 13** are

relevant here. So are the ABA opinions that discuss the duty to investigate (**Readings, Section 4**), which we mention below in **section (f)**.

If the students believe Solomon has fraudulent intent, the teacher may wish to play devil's advocate by pointing out all the reasons other than love for which people get married. May/December marriages, while they may not be fashionable or "politically correct," certainly occur. Why do students conclude so firmly that Solomon's comments about Elena only mean that he wants to marry her for the purpose of helping her escape her native land? After all, might not this marriage be a very desirable thing from Tovarich's point of view?

Role-play can also be useful here. For example, the teacher can suggest that a student playing Pomeranian advise the teacher, as Tovarich, that what he is contemplating would violate the law. The teacher can respond by saying that he really wants to marry Elena; that it sounds like a good idea to him for a number of reasons.

In short, we think it may be necessary for the teacher to emphasize that neither Pomeranian nor the students should jump to conclusions about Tovarich's intent and must look carefully at what he says in the context of the situation. Again, we reach a recurring theme of this course — the admonishment not to judge one's own client too quickly. If students are to assume that Tovarich's motives are benign, we would take a different tack, and emphasize that Solomon's motives are, at the least, suspicious. We have somewhat differing views about this ourselves: on one side, far more suspicious of Solomon; on the other, thinking that Lonnie must not presume that Solomon wanted to break the law.

(e) The Parallel Between *Anatomy of a Murder* and the Pen Knife Scenarios:

We do see a parallel between Scenario #1 and *Anatomy of a Murder*, and Scenario #2 and the pen-knife scenario discussed in **Problem 15**. This allows us to revisit another recurring theme of this book: that sometimes, seemingly small semantic distinctions may make all the difference.

There are, however, several distinctions between this problem and **Problem 15** that the teacher may want to point out. Here, no crime has yet been committed. Moreover, Pomeranian is acting solely as an advisor, and is neither "litigation counsel" nor an advocate. This, as we discuss in the **Readings, Sections 6** and **7**, may give Pomeranian somewhat less leeway than if she were litigating a case on behalf of Tovarich. As applied to this scenario, we see these as small distinctions. The lawyers in **Problem 15** were acting as *advisors as well as trial counsel* when they met with their clients.

(f)   May Lonnie Help Tovarich Help Elena?

This distinction between the lawyer as advisor and advocate brings us to **Question 3** of the problem. It is here that the OPM, Lincoln Savings, and Enron cases are valuable analogies. The OPM case, summarized in **Section 3**, remains a suspenseful, colorful tale invaluable for its description of how one law firm could collectively stick its head in the sand and continue to represent a client committing fraud after fraud. Many would argue that Vincent & Elkins (**Readings, Section 5**, on Enron) and Kaye, Scholer (**Readings, Sections 6** and **7**) did the same thing.

In addition to determining whether Lonnie can assist Solomon in his efforts on behalf of Elena, students should address: (1) what Pomeranian "knows" about Tovarich's intentions; (2) how one measures what an attorney "knows" (see our discussion of this issue in **Problems 14** and **15**); and (3) what duty Pomeranian has to inquire into or investigate Tovarich's intentions. The two ABA opinions cited in the **Readings, Section 4** both address these questions. Particularly, both concern what duties a lawyer has to inquire into the client's version of events before assisting that client in asserting a claim or position.

The teacher might ask what duty Pomeranian has to inquire whether, for example, Tovarich has ever engaged in similar conduct in the past with other women he helped to enter the country. The students should discuss the extent to which such inquiry has to be made, and the extent to which the client himself must be cross-examined. For example, is it sufficient for Pomeranian to say what Kaye, Scholer said about Lincoln Savings, that it relied on what the client told the law firm? There is a fine balance between taking the client's word and sticking one's head in the sand without doing *some* investigation.

(g)   When Does the Law Firm Become Advocate or Litigation Counsel?:

At what point does Pomeranian become "litigation counsel"? Does it happen when Pomeranian is still assisting Tovarich before the USCIS has taken action against him? Can she argue as Kaye, Scholer did (with Prof. Hazard's support, **Section 6** of the **Readings**) that she can be "litigation counsel" *in anticipation* of litigation? Or, as Vincent & Elkins did in writing documents that supported fraudulent transactions in Enron, that she was an advocate for her client? The ABA opinions, as the last paragraph in **Section 4** notes, seem to say no. But another ABA opinion, 93-375 (see **Section 7** of the **Readings**), seems to exonerate Kaye, Scholer. And much of the case against V&E has now evaporated. (The California opinion cited in **Section 4** is notable for its contrasting view.)

We see a natural progression from Prof. Newman's advice to the Bybee memo through the advice and actions of the law firms in the three scandals we examine. The Gordon article (**Section 5**) discusses how Vincent & Elkins' lawyers assessed and advised about risk management for Enron, not unlike

Newman's assessments on the likelihood of his client being audited. There also seems to us a substantial amount of risk management in the Bybee memo.

We also see similarities among the Bybee memo, Singer, Hutner's actions, and especially Kaye, Scholer's and Vincent & Elkins' behavior. Prof. Hazard's case for "litigation counsel," like V&E's claim of client advocacy, means lawyers who, it may be argued, as Gordon's article puts it at **page 647**, are "loyal to the law seen as the outer boundaries of the arguably-legal." Some feel this would be an excellent description of what the torture memo tried to accomplish. And Prof. Simon (**Readings, Section 7**) describes Kaye, Scholer's behavior in similar terms, noting their blurring of the line "between factual assertion and argument." (See **Supplemental Readings 9** for Simon's take on the Enron scandal's lawyers.)

(h) Question 4: *Now* There's Litigation Counsel:

Clearly, by the time the situation reaches the point set forth in **Question 4** of the problem, Pomeranian is litigation counsel. Students should evaluate how much of a difference this makes. Students should also be asked to evaluate the ways in which litigation counsel may act to protect a client about a past wrong. Finally, they should also be asked if they are persuaded that litigation counsel should be given more leeway in defending a client than in giving advice.

When actual litigation is reached, we agree with Hazard that the lawyer's role has changed and become liberalized, since litigation counsel's role is to defend the client about what has occurred in the past, and not to affirmatively assist in any wrongdoing. But there can be a fine line between advising the client about *potential* wrongdoing and protecting the client from *past* wrongdoing. We note finally that Lonnie the litigator must be careful that Lonnie the advisor is not a witness in the USCIS case.

PROBLEM 25

Advising The Corporate Client That's Made A Mistake

THE POINT BEHIND THE PROBLEM:

There are two principal issues raised by this problem. The first is the extent to which corporate counsel has a duty to prevent the corporation from acting fraudulently or dangerously, even to the point of "blowing the whistle" on the client in an extreme circumstance. We move rather quickly through a non-dangerous defect in **Part I** to a defect that could cause death or grave bodily injury in **Part II**. In addition to the difference in the gravity of the harm, this problem also points to several other factors that may affect how an attorney faced with these circumstances should act. Among them are: the predictability of future harm; the gravity of the harm; whether the lawyer's client acted fraudulently; whether the lawyer's work product was used in connection with that fraudulent conduct; and whether the harm is in the past, in the future, or ongoing. The issue of future versus past harm is particularly important; students must recognize that *past conduct* (whether it is the creation of a defective car CD player or the use of a defective brake fluid distribution system) can cause *future harm*.

In order to have a solid understanding of the issues raised by this problem, it is necessary to engage in a thorough review of the rules and regulations that apply. No regulatory scheme relating to any problem in this Third Edition has changed more — or is in greater flux. Not only has the past several years brought Sarbanes-Oxley and new SEC regulations but *two* important ABA Model Rule changes,— to **MRs 1.6** and **1.13**. And these rules changed *twice*, in 2002 and 2003 (**Readings, Sections 3** and **4**). Moreover, because states don't adopt the Model Rules in an instant, there is still an unusually wide disparity of ethics regulations covering the subject of this problem. We recommend use of a rules book such as our *Legal Ethics: Rules, Statutes, and Comparisons* that has a "redlined" copy of the ABA Model Rules changes.

Our second principal issue remains the moral questions raised by a life-threatening danger and a regulatory scheme that in many, perhaps most, jurisdictions still does not allow for overt "whistleblowing." While going outside of the corporation is now permissible in narrow circumstances in some states, students are still confronted with a situation in which the rules of ethics take us only so far, and a sense of personal morality may play a part in deciding what to do. This is the argument urged by Prof. Luban in **Section 1** of the **Readings**.

APPLICABLE RULES:

Model Rules: MRs 1.2(d), and Comment, paragraph 6 (1983 Rules), par. 9 (2002 Rules); 1.4(b); 1.6, especially 1.6(b), with substantial variation between 1983 and 2002-03 Rules, and compare 1983 Comment, paragraphs 9, 10, 12 and 13 and 2002-03 Comment, paragraphs 6, 7, 8, 9, and 12; 1.13 especially 1.13(b), with substantial variation between 1983 and 2002-03 Rules, and compare 1983 Comment, paragraphs 3, 4, and 5 with Comment, paragraphs 3 through 8; 2.1.

Model Code: DRs 4-101(C); 7-102(A)(7); ECs 4-2; 4-5.

CA Rules: 3-600.

CA B&P: 6068(e).

SUGGESTED QUESTIONS TO ASK:

- Isn't the CD player a defect that could easily and inexpensively be fixed?

- Does it amount to a fraud on the public when a car company knows of a defect such as the faulty stereo system and fails to correct it or disclose it?

- Isn't it true that the gravity of the harm of losing the stereo is not terribly great? Does this matter in terms of how Ernie advises Giant?

- Should Valencia defend on the merits of each individual brake fluid defect claim? Does this conflict with the advice he gives regarding recalling the cars because of the brake fluid defect?

- What do the rules of your jurisdiction allow Ernie to do about blowing the whistle on the brake problem?

- What is the effect of Sarbanes-Oxley and the SEC's regulations on Ernie's ability to blow the whistle?

- At what if any point should Ernie be required to take Prof. Luban's perspective regarding moral imperatives?

- What will be the consequence to Ernie of refusing to be silent in the face of a dangerous brake fluid condition that the company will not reveal?

- Isn't it true that some price is always placed on human life, whether by the government or by corporate entities? Does one death mean that the defective brake system has to be recalled or revealed no matter what?

- If you were Ernie Valencia, how would you approach Giant Auto in an effort to encourage the company to recall the cars?

- How much can Valencia emphasize "doing the right thing" in advising Giant to recall cars and how much should he rely on other factors, such as economics and good public relations?

- Could you, should you, and/or would you reveal the defect to the public if Giant refused to disclose? Under what circumstances?

- If you would consider "blowing the whistle," *how* would you do it?

SUGGESTED ROLE-PLAYS:

- Role-play the part of an upper-level Giant Auto executive who is being told by Valencia that it is necessary to recall and replace the tape decks. (Note that the economic consequences of replacing 2.4 million tape decks at $82 each is very high.)

- Role-play the part of a lawyer about to engage in whistleblowing, or a lawyer advising a colleague about the consequences of doing this.

- Play the role of Valencia appearing before a board of directors for the purpose of persuading the board to recall the vehicles.

SUGGESTED VIDEOS:

- Whistleblowing and its consequences: *The Insider* (entire movie)

- The dangerous car and the advice of dishonorable counsel: *Class Action*, entire movie, especially DVD scene 16, 104:32 — 107:39.

DISCUSSION:

(a) Part I — The CD Player

We use **Part I** primarily to contrast it with **Part II**. We find that it is not terribly helpful to dwell too long on **Part I**, since the most substantial issues are raised in **Part II**. In this part of the problem, the students are confronted with a clear defect, but one that causes only limited property damage. In answering the questions, students will most likely come up with a range of appropriate responses for attorney Valencia from advising that all the stereo systems be recalled to doing nothing other than what is necessary to respond to affirmative customer complaints. Students are also likely to see the harm done as a *past* rather than *future* one.

If students take the view that they need do nothing other than defend the company against claims and settle them as may be strategically or economically advantageous, the teacher can take the position of devil's advocate by asking a series of questions: Is it not a defect that could easily and inexpensively be fixed; doesn't it amount to a fraud on the public when the car company knows of the defect and fails to disclose it to the customers who bought the car; isn't the harm a future or at least an ongoing harm? Despite

these points, many students may feel that the nature of the harm, coupled with the clear attorney-client confidential relationship, means attorney Valencia should take no action.

If students too easily agree that their responsibility is to have the company correct each and every defective CD player, the teacher can closely examine the students from the opposite perspective as to why they feel such action is necessary under the ethics rules. The substantial differences among states are useful to note and revisit in **Part II**. Contrast, say, the narrow rules in California or Michigan — where auto companies are headquartered — with New Jersey, with its broad disclosure rules. In support of their position, students may cite to the article on corporate criminal guidelines (**Readings, Section 5**). But does this justify disclosing the defect?

We find it useful to play the role of an upper-level Giant Auto executive who is being told by Valencia that such action is necessary. Note that the economic consequence of replacing 2.4 million tape decks at $82 a piece is very high. We argue as devil's advocate that the *gravity* of the wrong here, as opposed to in **Part II**, is not great. That doesn't make the defect any greater or less negligent, however. The question may be whether acknowledging clear errors to the public turns on the gravity of the harm or a general obligation to disclose one's mistakes. One more issue: It does not appear that any of Valencia's work product is involved here, so that **MR 1.6(b)(2) and (3)**, amended in **2003**, does not seem to impact **Question 4**, but it is significant to recognize this important rule change. (See much more on rules changes in **section (d)** below.)

(b)   The Brake Fluid Distribution Defect:

First, students will often try to point out that fixing the brake distribution system is in Giant Auto's best interests strategically. This in fact may be a good argument and one that Valencia might be well-advised to use. Selling a client on "doing the right thing" solely because it is the right thing to do is more difficult than convincing the client that it is in the client's own best economic interests. But we suggest that the teacher not allow the students to dwell too long on this strategic solution, since it too easily avoids the principal *ethical* question, which is what Valencia may, should and/or must do if the Giant executives refuse to act to recall the vehicles.

Many students will also feel that Valencia can litigate each claim as it occurs, on the basis of proximate cause, contributory negligence or any other legitimate legal defenses available to him. We agree with this position. Here, Valencia is acting as litigation counsel (as we saw in **Problem 24**), and is entitled to put the plaintiffs to the test in proving their case.

The central issue in **Part II**, however, is not what to do with each individual claim, but how to deal with the dangerous defect on a global basis. The defect may or may not have caused the accident in a particular individual claim; other

possible causes, such as driver error or use of alcohol, may provide the car company with a defense. But while these individual cases are being litigated on their own merits, what should Valencia do to press for a recall?

(c) What Should Valencia Advise About a Recall and What Should He Do if the Company Refuses? The Regulatory Requirements:

Because the ethics and SEC regulatory schemes have changed so dramatically in the last several years and are still in flux, we suggest that there be some substantial discussion of the applicable ethical requirements. We prefer to discuss this part of **Question 5** before we get to the moral issues suggested by Prof. Luban. Some students may initially feel that the harm caused by the defect is a "past harm," since the defective system is already in place. But by now, most are likely to have come to understand that while the defect was in the past, the *harm* is in the future, since it is ongoing.

Students should discuss the different approaches suggested by Sarbanes-Oxley and the SEC, and go on to examine the various versions of **MR 1.13** and **MR 1.6** when it comes to revealing a past act that will cause future harm. It will be important for the teacher to have on hand the applicable rule(s) in the state(s) where most students will practice.

Section 307 of the Sarbanes-Oxley Act and the SEC regulations that "SOX" mandated **(Readings, Section 3)** have substantially increased the responsibilities of in-house counsel. By *mandating* behavior, they move well beyond the requirements of both **MR 1.13** and **MR 1.6**, which allow the lawyer to exercise discretion. As the **NOTES** at the end of **Section 3** state, the SEC regulations go beyond SOX requirements; the responsible legal officer *must* conduct an inquiry, provide notification of the results, and take reasonable steps to ensure that the corporation engage in remedial measures.

Significantly, however, neither SOX nor the SEC regulations allow, much less require, the lawyer to report *outside* the entity. While an SEC proposal to change this remains alive **(top page 667)**, it has been in the proposal stage for several years. Moreover, while the SEC regulations cut a reasonably wide swath, they by no means cover all general counsel in all corporate situations, much less those counsel — as in **Problem 8** — to partnerships and other entity types. While we do not want to underestimate the significance of these regulations — there is some evidence that other regulatory schemes might "model" the SEC's — neither do we want to overestimate them. They are neither universal nor as pervasive as the ABA Rules.

Regarding those ABA rules, **MR 1.13**, in its **2003** formulation, *does* allow corporate counsel to report outside the corporation under certain narrow circumstances. This is a significant departure not only from the 1983 Rules but from the 2002 rules amendment, as the Manson article **(Readings, Section 4)** describes. An examination of a redlined copy of Rule 1.13 demonstrates how materially changed this rule is.

Nevertheless, as set forth in **MR 1.13(c)**, the window of whistleblowing outside the entity structure remains rather small. It requires that (1) the matter has gone as far as the organization's highest authority; (2) the highest authority's act or refusal to act is "clearly a violation of law"; and (3) the lawyer is "reasonably certain" that disclosure is necessary to prevent "substantial injury to the *organization*" (our emphasis). Disclosure must be limited to the minimum necessary to protect the organization. This is hardly license for Ernie Valencia to blow the whistle to protect *the public* from the dangers of Venezia brake failures.

Students should also explore whether the more permissive language in the **2002-3** versions of **MR 1.6** alters what Valencia may do under the rules. **MR 1.6(b)(2)** and **(3)** were changed in **2003** and raise an issue with respect to **Part I** of the problem as well as being added fodder for **Part II** disclosure. As we have discussed in several other places in this Teacher's Manual, **MR 1.6(b)(1)** has been materially broadened; this subsection has several changes (see a redlined version), particularly its recognition that slowly developing harm is just as serious and deadly as "imminent" harm — a change that directly affects **Part II**.

Two other issues should be discussed before leaving our rules discussion: first, whether either of these two key rules trump the other; and second, recognition that the **2003** amendments to these two rules are not nearly universally adopted. It is clear on the face of the **2003** amendment to **MR 1.13(c)** that disclosure is permitted regardless of whether it would be allowed under **MR 1.6**. It is less clear on the face of the rules whether this works the other way — i.e., that disclosure permitted in **MR 1.6** overrides any **MR 1.13** prohibition. However, the logical structure of the rules causes us to conclude that this is the case.

While focusing on these major rules amendments, we must remain mindful both that many states have not adopted (or not yet adopted) the newest versions of the **MR 1.6** and **MR 1.13** changes, and that both rules are *permissive*, not mandatory, in the vast majority of jurisdictions. As we've noted before, most states either already had a rule like the *2002* amendment to **MR 1.6(b)(1)** or have conformed their rules. California is a notable exception.

(d) What Should Valencia Advise About a Recall and What Should He Do if the Company Refuses? The Moral Imperative:

While the rules have come much closer to Prof. Luban's position (**Readings, Section 1**) than when this book was first written, this problem remains one that is designed to go beyond the boundaries of the ethical rules. Luban argues strongly that counsel must sometimes do more. The teacher should encourage students to discuss Luban's perspective. They should be required to state at what point, if any, they will refuse to be quiet in the face of the company's refusal to recall dangerous vehicles, regardless of how the rules

are interpreted. They should think about whether and when they will make some kind of disclosure to the public, noting Roger Tuttle's experience — and the self-described "courage" he initially lacked (**Readings, Section 2**).

Students should therefore *carefully* evaluate whether and to what extent the number of accidents and the cost of repairs will make a difference in what they do. Students who would refuse to allow even one possibly fatal accident to occur per year should be closely questioned about whether they would really make a disclosure at that level of danger.

The teacher should be prepared to take either side. For example, if students take the view that disclosure is necessary to prevent deaths, would they really not be affected at all by a very small number of potential fatalities and the $2.7 billion price tag that would put Giant Auto out of business and tens of thousands out of work?

Revealing a client confidence, even to save lives, is a most serious issue, even if the ethics rules justify it. Students should not get away with undertaking this action lightly. The deadly defect may be far less clear than as the facts are presented in this problem. Students should also look at the economic realities for the workers at Giant, as well as the dangers to the purchasers of Venezia vehicles. The teacher can take the position of devil's advocate and legitimately make the argument that if the car company is driven out of business, many thousands will lose their jobs, the economy of the region will go to pot, and the adverse consequences to society could be *greater* than the loss of a very small number of lives. (Note the discussion of this cost-of-human-life issue, analogous to military evaluations, in the Lavelle article, **Supplemental Readings No. 1**.)

(e)   Moral Decisions and Practical Arguments:

Teachers might ask the students how they would approach Giant Auto in an effort to encourage the company to recall the cars. On some level the issue of what the lawyers should do becomes, as Luban suggests, a moral one for many students. But it is useful also to look at the practical question of how a lawyer's moral position can be translated into a persuasive but realistic argument.

The teacher might role-play the part of Valencia appearing before the board of directors for the purpose of persuading the board to recall the vehicles. The argument that Giant should "do the right thing" is a more difficult sales pitch than that the right thing will lead to a sensible economic solution which is also good public relations. To this end the corporate sentencing guidelines (**Readings, Section 5**) and the government's frequent insistence on cooperation (**Readings, Section 8**) can be persuasive. (As to that last section we note the double edge of the issue — see the **NOTES** section at the end.)

Nevertheless, there is no reason for the lawyer to ignore the moral component when speaking to the board. The board should not automatically be viewed as being oblivious to the significance of moral suasion and moral decisionmaking. (For this purpose, we have included Arthur Miller's *All My Sons* in the **Supplemental Readings** as an example of one businessman who failed to make a moral decision at great personal cost.)

(f) The Practical Dangers of Blowing the Whistle:

Many students will soon be associates in large firms where they may be asked to do things on behalf of clients that make them very uncomfortable. They will then have to balance that discomfort with the need to keep a job, fulfill career goals, feed a family, and so on. The fundamental question is not only how they will balance the ethical rules of confidentiality against any moral feeling that they must disclose the dangers of this car, but also how they will balance their personal needs and goals against what they may consider a moral imperative.

Clearly, there is a danger in blowing the whistle, and in particular, little cover for those working in-house, where the client is also the employer. In **Section 6** of the **Readings**, we describe the horrors that befell attorney Roger Balla when he was fired after telling the president of his company that he would do whatever was necessary to stop distribution of faulty kidney dialyzers. In what appears to us to be a counter-intuitive decision (we have included a brief excerpt from the dissent that eloquently states this case), the court found the fired lawyer had no cause of action. Results elsewhere **(Readings, Section** 7) have been mixed at best. The students should understand that even where a cause of action exists, the limitation on the use of confidential client-lawyer communications can operate as a Catch 22 vitiating the protection afforded by a lawsuit.

Outside lawyers don't have this problem, though they may not have clear sailing either, as we will discuss in **Problem 26**. Clearly, though, those in-house have a tougher row to hoe and a tougher decision in balancing morals and the practical realities of survival. Finally, note that the corporate attorney-client privilege is not as strong as it once was, as **Section 9** of the **Readings** discusses. We believe the corporate transgressions described in this section are both a significant factor on the issue of privilege and interesting reading for students. (Note the **typographical error** in the first paragraph of this section — "the Salomon Brothers case" should refer to the Arthur Andersen case.)

PROBLEM 26

The Senior Associate's Serious Dilemma

THE POINT BEHIND THE PROBLEM:

This problem moves beyond the questions raised in **Problems 24** and **25** about how to advise a client, and along with the next two problems focuses on the political and intra-firm "cultural" difficulties of being an associate, particularly in a firm of some size. Here, the associate is placed in the situation of being told to write an opinion letter in which he does not believe, and finds himself confronted by two separate issues.

We focus first on examining the lawyer's conduct from the point of view of the pressures he will naturally feel as a law firm associate who wants to keep his job and his standing on the partnership track. Among other things we want students to examine are the practical realities of this associate's circumstance and some practical ways to possibly get around his ethical conundrum.

We then move to the second, more substantive part of the problem: the propriety of writing an opinion letter in which you do not believe. Since this letter specifically calls for Steven's opinion, students must address the issue of whether an "opinion letter" can ever reflect an opinion that the lawyer does not genuinely hold. We see this as the logical extension of Problems **24** and **25** and this substantive issue, and the logical prelude to **Problems 27** and **28** on the more subjective issue of the lawyer's interrelationship with the firm's culture.

APPLICABLE RULES:

Model Rules:	MRs 1.2; 1.6(b)(2) and (b)(3) (as amended 2003); 2.3; 5.1; 5.2; 8.3; 8.4.
Model Code:	ECs 7-3; 7-5; 7-6; 7-8; 7-17.
CA Rules:	3-210.
CA B&P:	6068(c) and (d).

SUGGESTED QUESTIONS TO ASK:

- How would you define an opinion letter?

- Is what Steven is being asked to do as serious in nature as the "seriously unethical" conduct that Prof. Hazard describes?

- Can you think of a practical solution if you find yourself in a dilemma like Steven's?

- What is the significance of Steven not being sure that his opinion is correct? Does this mean that he can write the opinion letter?

- If Steven is not sure about his opinion, shouldn't the client's wishes govern?

- Is there a significant difference between an opinion letter and other forms of advice?

- Is the opinion letter Steven Green is asked to write analogous to the Bybee torture memo? How is it similar, and how is it different?

- Is there a significant difference between an opinion letter and a brief?

- In giving an opinion, does it matter whether Steven is an advisor as opposed to defending a claim in litigation?

- Does Steven have any other viable alternatives to writing the opinion letter that the client and Sheila request?

- Recall the readings about the statements and opinions provided by Vincent & Elkins and Kaye, Scholer in Problem 25 — is there any analogy between those law firms' actions and what Steven is being asked to do here?

- Are the new subsections ((b)(1) and (2)) of ABA **MR 1.6** relevant to the issue of Steven's writing this letter? What happens *after* the letter is written?

SUGGESTED ROLE-PLAYS:

- Play the role of a law firm partner who is asking a reluctant Steven Green to write an opinion letter, and react when Steven protests.

- Play the role of law firm associate Green, who is convinced that writing an opinion letter is inappropriate, and must persuade the partner in a way which is sufficiently delicate so as not to cost him his job.

- Play the role of a client who reads an opinion letter which does not quite measure up to what the client had in mind (either because it hedges by laying out the pros and cons, or stops short of saying Thorzac is safe, or has Sheila's signature rather than Steven's).

SUGGESTED VIDEOS:

- Only following orders — an international law defense?: *Judgment at Nuremburg* Scene 32, 2:43:15 - 46:19.

- "I quit!": *Legally Blonde Two, Red, White and Blond*, DVD Chap. 7, 11:38 — 13:02.

- "I do more good than harm": *Changing Lanes*, 1:22:52 — 1:24:15.

DISCUSSION:

(a) Preliminary Considerations:

We suggest focusing first on the pressures that the law firm associate feels, and then, once that issue is thoroughly aired, turning to the substance of writing the letter itself, and the nature of opinion letter advice. This method follows the path of the readings. Before digging into these issues, we find it useful at the outset to explain in general terms what an opinion letter is. To the extent possible, it is helpful to use examples from one's own practice or those of one's colleagues. We examine the special nature of opinion letter advice later (see **section (e)** below.)

In any event, we think it important to describe the opinion letter process: that is, a formal recitation of a lawyer's legal views on a legal subject and on which we would expect a client to rely. Those teachers who have written opinion letters on legal ethics issues should certainly refer to such letters. They are excellent examples of this kind of legal work.

(b) Walking the Tightrope Between Writing a False Opinion and Keeping One's Job:

The first two **Readings** in **Sections 1** and **2** provide ample evidence of the problems law firm associates can find themselves in when they "rock the boat." Life was hard for Peter Kelly after he blew the whistle, and the lawyer he accused was a criminal and a fugitive. Prof. Hazard's direct recognition of the problem — "how many children do you have and how big is your mortgage?" — puts the situation in clear perspective. But is what Steven Green being asked to do the kind of "seriously unethical" conduct of which Hazard writes? We think not. We have intentionally made this opinion letter a bit more ambiguous.

Some students will see this ambiguity as helping to solve their dilemma, since they may be able to "get away with" writing it. Others may feel as we do, that it makes their task *more* difficult since it is not crystal clear that such an opinion letter is inappropriate, even though Steven feels it is.

We see this as an opportunity to talk with our students about what they will confront when they enter the "real world" of legal practice. Earlier discussions along these lines, in **Problems 2** and **14**, for example, turned on the question of choosing the kinds of people we want to represent. Here, however, writing this opinion letter is not a matter of representing the "good guys" or the "bad guys" but rather a question of the *substance* of what Steven is being asked to do. In short, this could happen to anyone.

So, too, could being put in a position like Peter Kelly and others similarly situated, where they believe they have an ethical duty to blow the whistle on another attorney in the firm. See the **Readings, Sections 1** and **3**. Events have not treated the lawyers whose stories are referred to in **Section 3** kindly, and

either, for the most part, have the courts. The situation is not quite as bad as having your employer as your client (see **Problem 25**), but the lawyers who have reported wrongdoing in their firms have had at best mixed success in their own careers.

(c) A Discussion of Possible Solutions to Steven's Dilemma:

We find it may be useful to bring into class a partner and associate who have worked together in a larger firm to discuss their interrelationship as it relates to Steven's problem. In the alternative, the teacher may wish to role-play the part of a law firm partner, and later turn it around and role-play the part of the associate.

It may also fall to the teacher to offer possible practical solutions to students who may find themselves in a dilemma similar to Steven's. Among the solutions we suggest, or have heard other practitioners we have invited to our class suggest, are the following:

- Don't wait for this opinion letter or something similar to happen. Learn about the people you work with, who you can trust to go to when confronted with a dilemma like this, and which partners you may wish to try to avoid. Experienced associates frequently talk about staying away from certain partners who are more likely to ask them to do things which they would find unacceptable. Walking the associate's tightrope through a firm is not easy, but may be much easier than dealing with a situation like that which confronts Steven.

- Try to avoid being bullied; try to be firm in your resolve while still maintaining appropriate respect and decorum toward the partner. Review the suggestions made by Hazard; of particular value is going to someone within the firm who can help you and whom you trust, such as a partner other than the one who is asking you to do the "bad deed."

- In this situation, Sheila is a real estate partner, and is unlikely to be the partner who is Steven's principal "boss." If possible, Steven should seek out that partner's thoughts about how to deal with the situation, and even enlist that partner's aid in dealing with Sheila.

Finally, we tell students to be aware of some things they should *not* do: attack the partner, either directly or indirectly; "end run" the partner, or go over her head, which would be strongly resented; say "absolutely not" without providing a context or reason. This last can become a problem if students feel it means they are acknowledging that they will not absolutely refuse to write the opinion letter, but will look for some alternative solution around it. Still, we believe it's possible to *determine* not to write the letter Sheila wants without *saying* "no" directly.

(d) How to Deal With Writing (or Not Writing) the Opinion Letter:

The above discussion leads directly to the main issue: What should Steven do about writing this letter? In addition to the pressure from both client and partner, students should consider several other issues relating to the legitimacy of the advice itself. First among them is that Steven is not absolutely sure that this letter is incorrect. As such, it is different from the serious ethical breach described by Hazard. Steven may feel that it is "wrong" and may not reflect his "true opinion," but even in his conversation with his partner, Sheila, Steven talks about what he "thinks," rather than what he is sure of. We have made this language intentionally equivocal; even more equivocal is the situation in **Question 2**, where Steven's lack of certainty is acknowledged.

Many students will feel that under such circumstances, Steven can legitimately write the opinion letter anyway since it is not clearly wrong. He can argue, as does Sheila, that no one can be certain what the state will eventually determine. Students may also argue that so long as a claim is supportable, the client's choice about what to do should govern. These points are well-taken, although we, who have frequently written opinion letters for other lawyers, take a different point of view.

Our different point of view is the long view. If Steven writes this opinion letter, he will be stuck writing opinions he doesn't believe in for the rest of his career. The question, to us, is not whether he should refuse to write a letter that is not *his* opinion — he should — but how he can hold his ground and avoid doing what he knows he shouldn't do without it damaging his career.

(e) The Difference Between an Opinion Letter and Other Forms of Advice:

We see a material difference between an opinion letter and other forms of advice. An opinion letter is one on which a client will rely, based on the lawyer's considered opinion of the propriety of certain conduct. We believe that this is one time when Steven's beliefs and opinions about the right course of conduct *are* the key since the purpose of the letter is to give *one's own opinion*, rather than an opinion which is "defensible."

Other authorities may disagree with this point of view, arguing that an opinion letter is designed to serve the needs of the client within the bounds of the law. If the teacher has had occasion to serve as an expert witness, or otherwise write opinion letters, the students will benefit by hearing that personal perspective. The question really becomes how much one may — or is willing to — "stretch" his or her beliefs in writing such a letter.

It is here that the Bybee "torture memo" and Prof. Clark's article **(Readings, Section 4)** are valuable. The torture memo is, of course, a matter of considerable public interest and debate. As such, it helps shape a discussion about a lawyer's true opinion and a lawyer's defensible position. Note that

despite its usefulness here, the Bybee memo is *not* an opinion letter like Steven's. As Prof. Clark notes in the beginning of her piece, one would not expect the torture memo to reflect Jay Bybee's or John Woo's personal opinions. But the issue of "how far can you stretch?" still applies. In Prof. Clark's and many others' views including our own, the Bybee memo stretches beyond a defensible, objective, within-the-facts-and-the-law document to one that — as Clark puts it — reflects "what the authors wanted the law to be."

(f) Revisiting the Advocate/Advisor Distinction:

The advocate/advisor distinction that seemed to make a significant difference in the Kaye, Scholer case, particularly to Prof. Hazard (see **Problems 24** and **25**) is significant here as well. **Question 4** of the Problem asks whether if Steven Green is an advocate, might his opinion more appropriately be "stretched" to reflect a colorable position of a client.

We believe that there is, indeed, a difference, as we did in **Problem 25**. As an advocate, one has the responsibility of defending one's client within the bounds of the law. We can't see how this is the case with the opinion letter, where Steven is dealing with questions regarding disclosure *before* real property may be sold, rather than litigation *after the fact* of such a sale. We find this distinction an important one. But we note that others (again, see the Kaye, Scholer matter) might draw the line that distinguishes advisor and advocate in a different place than we do.

To crystallize this issue, the teacher might ask if the students' views of whether Steven could write an opinion letter would differ if he were writing the letter — or a brief — *after-the-fact* to assist the firm in an arbitration over the client's sale of the property to a third-party purchaser who was not given disclosure about Thorzac.

(g) Does Steven Have Any Other Viable Alternatives?

Students may be uncomfortable writing the opinion that Sheila wants, but are understandably reluctant to simply say no. Among the alternatives we have heard students propose are: (1) drafting a qualified opinion letter that hedges its opinion, or talks objectively about the pros and cons as to whether Thorzac is a hazardous subject; (2) an opinion letter that is firmer but which stops short of saying that the client does not have to disclose Thorzac as a hazardous subject (for example, one which emphasizes that Thorzac has not yet been found to be a hazardous substance, while avoiding Steven's own position); and (3) writing the opinion letter but insisting that Sheila sign it.

None of these solutions will be entirely satisfactory to the client. The teacher may wish to role-play the part of the client reading one of these three letters, and getting on the phone and talking to Steven and Sheila about his discontent. As a practical matter, all of these alternatives leave something to

be desired from the client's perspective, and are not likely to satisfy Sheila either.

Nevertheless, we argue that if Steven takes a *strong but reasoned* position with Sheila, that is as far as any reasonable attorney should go in acceding to her requests. Others will argue that Steven can play semantics with the language. For instance, Sheila has focused on a "hazardous substance, *as that term is now defined.*" It is possible that Sheila will accede to a letter of this type (even though the client will likely still be unhappy). After all, clients don't always get what they want in litigation, nor will they always get what they want in terms of advice.

There is a solution that Steven might try with more success, based on Reynolds' potential liability. If he can persuade Sheila that the firm may be liable to Reynolds and even (see **Readings, Section 5**) possibly to third parties should any harm occur on the property, Sheila may agree that protecting the firm is more important than serving Reynolds' needs. Here is the mock conversation as we wrote it in *The Moral Compass of the American Lawyer*:

"Sheila," Steven began, "I'll give you the letter George wants if it's still what *you* want, but I think it could hurt the firm." When Sheila asked what he meant, Steven began: "You know that I think it's a sure thing the state will eventually say Thorzac's hazardous."

"I thought you understood your personal beliefs are not the issue here," snapped Sheila.

"I understand that," continued Steven, "but if the state does rule on Thorzac anytime soon, and I'm right — which I'm sure I am — then the buyer is going to go after Reynolds Realty, maybe even sue. And Reynolds is going to wave our letter around and say they relied on *us*. If Reynolds gets sued, we're going to be next."

"So you think George is getting our letter just to cover his behind?" asked Sheila.

"Yes," replied Steven, "but you know him best. What do you think?"

"OK, rewrite it," said Sheila, now beginning to thaw. "And don't worry about George. I'll deal with him; I'll just tell him this is as good as it's going to get."

(h)   Relative Responsibilities of Supervisory and Subordinate Lawyers:

As Prof. Hazard notes, ultimately the associate may resort to the fact that "an arguable question of professional duty" may be resolved by a supervisor, and the subordinate lawyer may rely on it under **MR 5.2**. How effective that is here may be open to debate in light of the fact that Steven is being asked to sign this opinion letter himself. But this rule makes it relatively clear that if Sheila signs the opinion letter and takes responsibility for it, Steven may be

"off the hook" at least for disciplinary purposes. (This is *not* currently the case in California.)

On the other hand, the cases in the **Supplemental Readings** concerning securities offerings indicate that lawyers writing opinion letters which turn out to be false may accrue liability to the *third parties* who rely on them, at least when they are in the form of securities offerings described in those cases. This could potentially put Steven right back "on the hook" as the author of the letter, whether or not he or Sheila signs it.

(i) Disavowing Work Product Under the Newest Parts of MR 1.6:

As we discussed in some detail in the **Teacher's Manual** for **Problem 25** (especially **section (c)**), the **2003** changes to **MR 1.6(b)(2)** and **(3)** — described in **Section 4** of the **Problem 25 Readings** — may have a significant effect on Steven Green's situation. These subsections permit a lawyer to blow the whistle notwithstanding the ordinary requirements of confidentiality to prevent or help rectify a crime or fraud that results in "substantial injury to the financial interests or property" of another. It is limited to those situations where the lawyer's work product is being misused to further the crime or fraud. After years of in-fighting that included a fight before the original 1983 Model Rules were passed, a 1992 ABA ethics opinion known as the "noisy withdrawal" opinion, a defeat of these provisions in the ABA House of Delegates in 2002, and a very close win the next year, it seems that this rule is here to stay. Again, the number of states that will adopt it is not yet clear. The year after the "noisy withdrawal" opinion, the same ABA considered the Kaye, Scholer situation also described in **Problem 25** and essentially concluded that that law firm had not acted inappropriately.

The application of these subsections to this problem is not entirely clear. Thus far, Reynolds, the client, has done nothing fraudulent. If he gets Steven's imprimatur, he will be able to say that his notice to the seller was done following his lawyer's advice, and the advice will comport with Reynolds' actions and substantially attenuate any fraud claim. But if Steven gave an opinion, say a more equivocal one, that Reynolds was poised to use in a way that avoids any disclosure, these subsections of **MR 1.6** would seem to apply.

(j) Law Firm Discipline and Law Firm Culture:

We like to end our discussion of this problem with a discussion of the effect of the opinion letter on third parties (**Readings, Section 5**) and the Schneyer article on disciplining law firms (**Section 6** of the **Readings**). (Note the editing typo in the first sentence in **Section 6**; we no longer focus on the "noisy withdrawal" opinion.) We also direct our attention to the development of a "law firm culture" that could make it possible for a Steven Green to address the propriety of an opinion letter such as this one without risking losing his job. In so doing, we also revisit the Bowen McCoy article in **Chapter One**

and, as our note following Schneyer's article mentions, draw a parallel between McCoy's lesson of the sadhu and Schneyer's perspectives on the ethics infrastructures of law firms.

We believe that a discussion of law firm cultures and law firm ethics is an important one, and it is one that recurs throughout the last third of our course. It is important to us that students understand the significance of such cultures, both in terms of how they may affect the students once they too become associates, and also in terms of the importance of selecting a firm that has a culture or sense of ethics that comports with that student's beliefs. **Section 7 of the Readings** concludes this problem. While light in tone and designed to amuse, the Greedy Associates article has a serious point: that many young lawyers go outward to their colleagues at other firms to seek healthier cultures than the ones they find within their own four walls. In **Problem 27**, which follows, the second excerpt of Schlitz's "Happy, Healthy" article makes a similar point.

PROBLEM 27

Billing Practices at Prager & Dahms

THE POINT BEHIND THE PROBLEM:

Billing is the name of the game for lawyers, a day-to-day necessity that never goes away. The principal point here is to expose students to a variety of billing techniques, including some of the more outrageous ones described in the readings, each to be considered in turn. The purpose of this is to enable students to evaluate whether the fees are excessive or reasonable under various ethical rules and opinions.

It is also important for students to recognize that a determination of whether specific billing techniques are appropriate will rest largely on whether the client has consented to the particular practice. Client consent will solve many ills; the absence of client consent will cause far more skepticism about the validity of a fee arrangement, particularly on the part of lay juries who must judge a fee dispute.

We address two other issues here. The first of these is the use and abuse of "billable hours," a concept that started as a reform to require lawyer's bills to reflect the time they spent, but which many now feel needs reform itself. Second, we continue our examination of the plight of big-firm associates, who face large billable hour quotas, and pressure to keep up with their peers in billing what sometimes seem like an ever-escalating number of hours.

APPLICABLE RULES:

Model Rules:	MRs 1.4(b); 1.5; 1.15, especially Comment, paragraph (2), 1983 rules, para. (3), 2002 rules; 7.1(a).
Model Code:	DR 2-106; ECs 2-17; 2-19; 2-20.
CA Rules:	3-500; 4-100; 4-200; 4-210.
CA B&P:	6068(m); 6147; 6148.

SUGGESTED QUESTIONS TO ASK:

- What constitutes an excessive fee?

- May at least some time spent in the shower be billed if Billy comes up with useful material?

- May Carrie bill for time spent walking the dog while putting her thoughts in order about the next day's opening statement?

- May Billy bill for long runs in the park during which he organizes his motions and discovery practice?

- What if Carrie gets a great idea in a dream and wakes up with a new strategy on her big case? Can she bill time?

241

- May Carrie bill for assisting another lawyer to copy and organize a trial binder?

- Would it be more appropriate on the plane to halve each client's billing rate if billing for travel and work done on the flight?

- If billing is based on the idea that time is money, how can one hour spent by a lawyer translate into more than one hour billed?

- Isn't it true that each separate piece of Billy's two phone messages billing method is a reasonable way to bill? Isn't the bill therefore reasonable?

- Aren't there times when the value of a service performed by somebody who is familiar with the specific issues is worth considerably more than the amount of time spent?

- How can the value of special services be fairly compensated if not by "value billing"?

- Have Prager's clients truly given their informed consent to his two-hour minimum court appearance? To his billing three clients at the same time?

- In your work experience, have you seen any examples of lawyers who "churn" files by spending too much time on them? Have you seen other billing horror stories?

- How does the current bonus system compare with Prager's proposal? Do either of these serve to increase or decrease the pressure on associates?

SUGGESTED ROLE-PLAYS:

- Play the part of the client quizzing a lawyer about how counsel can spent one hour in the air and bill two separate clients for the entire hour.

- Play Billy or Carrie explaining how h/she managed to bill for time in the shower or jogging?

- Play Billy Shears attempting to justify to the client the half-hour bill for two phone messages.

- Role-play a lawyer explaining to the client why the client will receive good "value" for billing greater than the lawyer's hourly rate, because of the lawyer's particular expertise on the complex antitrust matter in question.

SUGGESTED VIDEOS:

- "If you even think about a client, I want you to bill it!": *The Firm*, DVD Scene 5, 17:25 — 18:15.

DISCUSSION:

(a) Introduction and Excessive Fees:

We generally approach the billing techniques in the problem by going through each in turn. Before we begin, we briefly discuss with the students what constitutes — or does not constitute — an excessive fee. We are assisted by the Margolick article and the **NOTES** that follow, in **Section 2** of the **Readings**, which present the more horrendous examples of fee charging methods, and the Goldhaber article in the **Reading, Section 3**, which focuses on some high-end billing atrocities that Prof. Lerman has studied in depth. You might also refer back to the Zitrin article in **Problem 9** and note the comment that there is an inherent conflict of interest in almost any a fee arrangement.

(b) Billing for Thinking While Showering:

One would think students would find Billy Shears' billing for his showering time an outrageous example of a billing abuse. In fact, in our experience, they break down rather evenly on this issue. If Billy comes up with useful material that he then takes time to memorialize, we see no problem billing for the time he spends writing it down. Otherwise, so long as the purpose of the shower is exactly that — to *shower* and not to think — billing this feels absolutely improper.

Before passing on to other issues, we play devil's advocacy on this subject. For example, what if a lawyer takes the dog for a long walk on the eve before trial to put together her thoughts about opening statement and voir dire? May she bill for the hour spent? What if a lawyer routinely takes long runs in the park during which he organizes his motions and discovery work in his mind on his big case? May this time — or at least some of this time — be billed? Try taking Billy's idea to the extreme: What about great ideas in dreams (clearly, we think, a completely outrageous and unjustifiable idea)? What should the test be? We think a reasonable test is whether the time is being spent specifically — or at the very least predominately, to allow billing *some* amount of time — for the benefit of the client's case. Another element, of course, is to what extent a client consents to the practice. But there is no bright-line test justifying billable time.

Students should understand that "strategizing client's case" and "evaluating tactics for trial" are red flags to a client that is monitoring or auditing the law firm's bills. Auditing has become an increasingly common practice in the last decade, as Margolick describes. Students should be reminded to prepare their

bills as if they will one day be reviewed by an auditor. Moreover, that auditor may be on a contingency fee. The auditor may look at the attorney's draft timesheets as a whole to discern whether there is evidence of double billing. As the Goldfaber and Coster pieces in **Section 3** show, overbilling is quite common. But an associate may be surprised to discover that the firm will likely deny all responsibility for encouraging overbilling if the associate is "caught."

(c)   Question 2 — Billing up in the Air:

Billing one client for a cross-country flight while working on another client's case while up in the air — and billing the second client too — is actually a common practice in much of the country. Students may well feel that this is justified despite the ABA opinion excerpted in **Section 4** of the **Readings**, which specifically forbids this practice without client consent.

The teacher may wish to role-play the part of the client quizzing a lawyer who is trying to justify spending one hour in the air and billing two separate clients for that same hour. There are arguments the student can make that justify this practice. We make one such argument in the **NOTES** following the ABA opinion. While we do not agree with this argument, it is at least colorable. But why not cut the lawyer's hourly billing rate in half as to both clients? Wouldn't that be the easiest and most equitable thing to do? Or charge a flat per diem travel fee for travel to Client 1 rather than an hourly rate with the understanding that counsel could bill another client for work done during that time.

(d)   Question 2, Billable Hours, and the Pressures on Young Lawyers:

It is helpful for the students to pause to consider how the concept of billable hours is used, and how it is changing. As **Section 1** of the **Readings** points out, the use of billable hours began as a reform movement to prevent lawyers from charging whatever they deemed reasonable. Charging only for the amount of time spent was considered a vast improvement.

But billable-hour pressure at law firms has become enormous. That is undoubtedly part of why the concept of billable hours has been stretched to include showering and dog-walking time and billing two different clients each for the same hour. If the whole concept of "billable hours" was created to reduce things to a time-is-money analysis, how can one hour spent translate into more than one hour billed? This frankly troubles us. We discuss these concerns with the students directly to see if it affects their points of view.

At some point — now is as good a time as any — we want students to discuss with us the larger issue: the extraordinary pressure that lawyers, especially newer lawyers, feel to bill as much as possible. To many, billing their requisite hours is a matter of survival. For many, survival is not just a

financial issue but involves remaining a viable part of the firm and possible partnership candidate. Others feel trapped in the vortex of the firm's culture.

To help our analysis we revisit Schiltz's important article, excerpted in **Readings, Section 5**. This time, in contrast to the first segment in **Problem 2**, Schiltz's outlook is bleak, but not without reason. We don't want to pull our punches with our students, and Schiltz certainly doesn't. This excerpt of Schiltz's article is one of the longest readings in this book. However, we find ourselves trying to temper his "stick" with some "carrots" for balance.

We find that our discussion with our students about the expansion of the concept of "billable hours" is always interesting. The effect on billing of escalating salaries should be obvious, but the **Readings, Section 6**, discusses this explicitly. We also find it beneficial to discuss other billing methods, such as those enumerated in **Section 7** of the **Readings**. These methods can be compared to the "expanded" billable-hours concept in terms of their fairness to the client.

Before leaving **Question 2**, we raise one more issue — what the client expects of the lawyer. We broach this issue here, but leave it for fuller discussion until **Question 4**. This issue represents the key to understanding the fairness of billing practices. It is for this reason that we suggest a role-play in which the teacher take the part of one of the two clients paying Billy Shears' full billing rate.

(e) Question 3 — The Half Hour 2-Minute Phone Calls:

Although Shears' billing techniques in **Question 3** sound horrible when put in the context of two one-minute phone calls resulting in a half hour of billing, some students will justify this practice. They will point out that each part of the practice seems justifiable by itself; we are largely in agreement with this. That is, a quarter-hour minimum is appropriate at least in some instances, and setting some reasonable minimum time is a virtual necessity. Moreover, there are times when leaving a voice mail message, what with gathering the file and pulling it out and making a notation in the file, warrants billing the minimum amount. But, it would be double billing.

Our problem with **Question 3** is the *cumulative* effect of all these things together: 15-minute minimum, billing for the voice mail message and then billing another full 15 minutes for a second voice mail message later in the day and doing this over and over again for their clients.

(f) Question 4 — The Special Project and "Value Billing":

The practice of "value billing" is billing for the reasonable value of the work accomplished, even though that "value" may be much greater than the actual time spent on a specific case. This concept is being used more and more frequently by law firms for exactly the reasons expressed by Billy Shears.

Again, students will likely see the justification for such a practice; they can certainly appreciate the value of long hours of research and the value of the special knowledge that has been gained.

There is indeed some basis for this point of view. But students should again be confronted by the issue of client expectations. These expectations are usually one hour paid to counsel for one hour spent by counsel. Again, the teacher can play the part of a client who is not expecting value billing who learns that the "extra time spent" was actually not spent on the client's own case.

We find this the most appropriate time to address the issue of notice to the client and the client's informed consent. When the teacher broaches this issue with the students, they generally readily accept that it would be best to obtain the client's informed consent, just as lawyers have done for many of the conflicts of interest described in other problems. (Indeed, in **Problem 9**, we addressed consent as it directly related to the lawyer's economic interests.) With such informed consent, some value billing might well be appropriate.

Once more, the teacher — or one of the students — can play the part of a lawyer explaining why "value billing" for specialized knowledge will be used and why that specialized knowledge will cost the client X dollars, a figure much larger than the hourly rate for the amount of time that will actually be expended. There is an understandable reason for such a billing practice; when it is explained to the client, the client might well agree. Indeed, as Shears suggests, the client may still be getting a bargain, at least compared to any other firm which would have to start the project from scratch.

(g)   Part II — Prager's Fixed Fee Court Appearances:

Students may have trouble with this billing procedure unless they fix on the issue of informed consent. Prager makes it clear what he charges. Less clear to us is whether his clients understand that he may double or triple bill for work done for several clients. The primary question, to us, is whether the clients have truly given their informed consent. If they have, the next issue is whether his fees — we calculated $2,100 for all three clients for an hour and 15 minutes of work — are unconscionable or unreasonable. In light of the *Brobeck* case, however, Prager may well be entitled to these fees *so long as he has his clients' clear informed consent* to his 2-hour minimum *and* to his double billing.

Without consent, in many states Prager's likely fee will be quantum merit: the reasonable value of the lawyer's services. This will generally mean, at most, payment at the firm's hourly rate for actual time spent on the matter.

(h) Prager's Bonus System:

This bonus system may sound perfectly acceptable to many students. They reason that it will make associates work hard to generate fees for the firm. We have difficulty with it, however. It seems to raise the temperature of the billable-hours pressure-cooker even higher. It also encourages associates to work hardest on those cases where they are billed out at the highest possible rates.

Rates for law firm associates and partners can vary widely depending on the type of case. Insurance defense cases, for example, often have compensation scales which are significantly below the rates for other kinds of cases. Prager's bonus scheme will encourage lawyers to work on certain clients' cases, while giving relatively short shrift to others. This raises in our minds the question of whether the law firm's fiduciary duties are being performed on behalf of all its clients. And it creates a culture of overbilling at Prager & Dahms because it rewards overbilling.

In conclusion, we ask the students for other "war stories" from the offices in which they work. We find that many of them have seen interesting and, to them, strange and inappropriate billing practices. This discussion can often do as much as the problem itself to bring home the point about billing practices in a cogent fashion.

PROBLEM 28

Is There A Glass Ceiling As Lawyers Climb The Law Firm Ladder?

THE POINT BEHIND THE PROBLEM:

The point here is to address the issues of racial and gender bias and diversity as candidly as possible within the confines of the classroom by a vehicle familiar to many lawyers and some law students — deciding whether a particular lawyer makes partner. Our goals are relatively modest: to get out on the table in as honest a way as possible issues that deal with the factors of race and gender assumptions, stereotyping and latent issues which can affect, even unintentionally, the way we view others.

We acknowledge from the outset that this can be a very difficult subject to teach. We find that when we acknowledge this difficulty, and our own discomfort with some aspects of these issues at the outset, students relax and can more easily recognize *their* own discomfort, which in fact is one of the points behind the problem itself.

Some have asked whether this problem belongs in an ethics class. We believe that not only does it belong, but this course may be the *only* place these issues are likely to be raised. They are of fundamental moral importance; indeed, race has often been termed America's defining issue. The difficulty most of us have in talking about these issues is proof to us of the importance of engaging in this discussion. Otherwise, the discussion might not take place at all.

By asking students to list factors they have considered in deciding whether to make Sharon Chau partner, we attempt to open up the discussion up to *anything* related to her performance, participation in firm events, "personality" and background that may possibly come to mind. The goal is to remain as non-judgmental about these factors as possible, and then to return to them to evaluate what they may say about Sharon as a woman, a single mother and an Asian-American. (We have made Sharon Asian partly because we saw that as being "easier" for many than if she were African-American. But we intend here to address *all* issues, all races, sexual preferences, and disabilities as well as gender.)

APPLICABLE RULES:

Model Rules: Preamble, paragraphs 5 and 6, 1983 rules, paras. 6 and 7, 2002 rules.
Model Code: (None).
CA Rules: 2-400.

SUGGESTED QUESTIONS TO ASK:

- What factors — whether they *should* be considered or simply come to mind — occur to you when considering Sharon Chau for partner?

- Doesn't it concern you that Sharon has substantially lower billable hours than most other associates?

- Does it bother you that Sharon leaves the office so early and does so little socializing? Are there good reasons for her doing that? Insufficient reasons?

- Do you think men would be asked the same kinds of questions about family life and responsibilities that Sharon is asked by her two partners?

- Can you think of ways in which we can all agree that men and women are treated differently as lawyers?

- What is meant by the following factors, which may have been mentioned in considering Sharon for partner: "She is not a team player"; "She doesn't hang out with us"; "We question her loyalty to the firm"; and "She just doesn't seem to fit in"?

- Do the factors above make sense without regard to racial and gender issues? Might they nevertheless demonstrate a relationship to race or gender?

- If Sharon is not given partnership, should she have been warned about any shortcomings in her performance in previous annual reviews?

- Should the law firm consider a part-time partnership position for single parents like Sharon?

- What are some good reasons — not just a matter of political correctness — to increase diversity in a law firm?

- Do you think Jacob Herring's comments about stereotyping go too far or hit the mark?

- Why should Sharon have to deal with the insensitive remark from her senior partner at all? Would a white male, for example, have to deal with it?

- Is Taylor's invitation to dinner an innocent effort to help Sharon make partner? Or is he asking her out on a date?

SUGGESTED ROLE-PLAYS:

- Role-play the partnership meeting, with the entire class becoming the partners who are deciding Sharon's fate.

- Play the role of a judge in two different scenarios, being requested by a male and then a female lawyer to leave a settlement conference a little

early to pick up a child at day care, in order to demonstrate the different ways men and women attorneys are likely to be treated.

- Play the head of the litigation department talking to another partner about concern that Sharon neither socializes with the rest of the unit nor adequately entertains the clients of the firm, to point out both business and other issues this raises.

- Play the part of either the offending partner or another partner in **Question 4**, to help demonstrate the clear awkwardness (at best) of the situation.

- Play partner James Taylor one of three ways, or all three: interested in helping Sharon, interested in dating her, or ambiguous.

SUGGESTED VIDEOS:

- Discrimination confronted and understood: *Philadelphia*, entire movie, and see DVD scene 11, 25:11 ffl.

- Making a pass: *Legally Blond*, DVD scene 26, 1:13:06 — 1:16:30.

DISCUSSION:

(a) Background Thoughts About Teaching This Material:

We consider this problem one of the most ambitious we address, both because the issues it raises can be difficult to talk about, and because we — like most teachers of legal ethics — began teaching this without much particular training in teaching bias and diversity issues. While training in teaching such issues is increasing by leaps and bounds (for example, we know of the emphasis on such training among clinical professors), it is not yet that widespread. Now, much more experienced, having taught this material on numerous occasions and having also used this material on several occasions as a continuing education program for lawyers, we will try to give you the benefits of what we've learned to date.

One thing that is quite clear to us is the extent to which many people are sensitive on the issue of gender bias, and even more sensitive on the issue of racial or ethnic bias. We feel, therefore, that it is very important to make it clear from the outset both that these are very difficult issues (this is one occasion to use the adverb "very"), and that most of us, if not all of us, have some significant discomfort in discussing them.

There is no perfect way to address this matter, however. We have found, for example, that particularly with lawyers, many deny *any* feeling of discomfort whatsoever, and are sensitive about that. (We think this proves our point.) We have also found that it is easy with this subject matter for us to misstate and mischaracterize unintentionally, or to be viewed as having misstated and

mischaracterized something of importance, despite having exercised an abundance of care. Things said about issues of bias do not, and perhaps cannot, always be articulated in a way that is acceptable to everybody.

Because of the heightened sensitivity of this issue, and the time it takes to get to some of the more fundamental elements of gender and race bias and the purposes of diversity, we often leave extra time for this problem. Sometimes, we have used an entire three-hour seminar session for a discussion of these issues. And while we recognize some of the difficulties and discomforts of discussing this problem, some of our greatest rewards have come from discussing Sharon Chau's partnership with our students.

(b)   One Approach to This Problem:

We generally approach the problem by role-playing the partnership meeting, with the entire class becoming the partners who are deciding Sharon's fate. We focus on the first two questions in the problem, spending the vast majority of our time on these. We get to the other questions only to the extent there is time, except that we use **Question 4** for the specific purpose of showing the significance of Sharon's ethnic background, should the students resist acknowledging its importance. (We discuss this below.)

We have designed the problem to make Sharon's partnership a close question. She has some discernible strengths and discernible weaknesses, many of which have little to do with her gender and ethnic background, some of which have everything to do with these issues, and some of which relate to her background in a subtle or latent way.

(c)   Putting the Factors on the Blackboard:

We suggest an approach in which we, teacher and students alike, meet as a partnership committee to consider Sharon, and articulate as many factors as we can about her which seem to have *any kind of relevance* at all to our decision. We try to avoid prioritizing these factors or judging them. We try to emphasize not what factors *should* be considered, but what factors will come up about her in our own minds or might cause in the minds of our "partners," *whether or not* we ultimately consider them as pros or cons in our decision to make her partner. Thus, we look to cast the widest possible net.

Students occasionally object to inclusion of some factors on the board, because they insist that they have not considered them. Nevertheless, if the teacher maintains the position that everything about Sharon which comes up, whether regarding her partnership or not, will be put on the blackboard, students will generally acquiesce. By being over-inclusive about these issues, and by allowing the debate to focus on both "significant" and "insignificant" factors, issues about Sharon's gender and race are allowed to "float" to the surface during the course of the discussion.

We find that this gradual focusing on gender issues, and even more gradually on racial and ethnic issues which may lie deeper under the surface, allows students to adjust to the discussion. We believe this helps increase the students' candor, and perhaps even student awareness about some of the more subtle issues involved, while minimizing the students' feelings that they are threatened by the discussion.

Nevertheless, drawing the students out on some of the factors to consider about Sharon Chau can be difficult. The teacher should take the same devil's advocate role used in other problems. For instance, if Sharon's fewer billable hours have not directly been addressed as an economic issue, this discussion should be encouraged. If the nature of Sharon's early departure from the office, and the feeling that she may not be a "team player," has not directly been addressed, then this should be brought out. The teacher might role-play the part of the head of the litigation department talking about his or her own concern that Sharon neither schmoozes the clients nor goes out drinking with the litigation unit. (In some firms, as we will see in **Problem 29**, not only going out together but going out *drinking* together is important.)

(d)   Some Gender-Related Issues:

Often, gender issues will come out relatively early in the discussion, usually well before racial issues. In our experience, these issues have often been volunteered by a woman student or a group of women students who may express something like "Well, it is obvious — what's going on here is all about gender."

The teacher should help facilitate a discussion about these gender-related issues. Among them are, most significantly, those concerning Sharon's single motherhood. This may help explain why she leaves the office when she does, and does so little socializing. It is also appropriate to raise the propriety of the questions Sharon is asked by two of the partners regarding her family life and responsibilities. Men should be asked, honestly, whether they would expect to get the same kinds of questions.

We believe it is beneficial for the students to engage in a discussion about how men and women lawyers are treated differently, not only in seeking a partnership but on an ongoing basis. **Sections 1, 2,** and **3** of the **Readings** largely focus on women lawyers, and provide ample evidence of the different treatment women and those with family responsibilities are accorded. (Note also the experience of minority women lawyers described in the **Readings, Section 7.**) When we focus on men with "mommy track"-like duties — Stuart Hanlon's compelling piece and the brief story that precedes it — it can show the different, more *advantageous* treatment men get.

We are particularly fond of the paragraph just before the Hanlon piece, which compares the single father who needs to leave court early with the

single mother in the same situation. As we suggest in the note, we have tried this test empirically and found a clearly sexually-skewed response. Men simply get much more leeway in such circumstances than women do. Not all law students will have sufficient in-court experience to appreciate the truth of this story. But we have found that when we use this story with lawyers, some male lawyers acknowledge — many for the first time — the significantly different treatment accorded men and women. For this reason, we find this a valuable illustration.

Teachers should draw closely on their own experience. For example, our own personal experience has been that when one of us refers a case to another one of us, *he* is often asked how old or experienced *she* is, with concern being expressed that she might be "too young." But when the other of us refers a case back, *she* is never asked about *his* age or credentials. This speaks volumes about the tougher road women have to travel to generate business.

(e)   Some Subtle Issues That Can Have Double Meanings:

Our experience is that many of the issues related to Sharon being a woman, including those related to her being a single parent, frequently come out early in the discussion. Students tend to be much more reticent about the racial and ethnic issues. For example, on several occasions when we have done this problem, a large number of factors about Sharon Chau have been put on the blackboard, and the fact she is Asian-American has not been mentioned by anybody.

We have intentionally come up with a set of facts, many of which translate into "factors" for inclusion on our blackboard, which have both a straightforward and possibly a more subtle meaning. Among these factors, as they are often phrased by the students, are the following: "She is not a team player"; "She doesn't hang out with us"; "We question how loyal she is to the firm"; and, perhaps the most significant, "She just doesn't seem to fit in."

All of these factors make sense without regard to racial and gender issues. If Sharon were a white male, for example, all these factors could and probably would be mentioned. A white male who spends his free time singing in a barbershop quartet may also be seen as not fitting in, compared to a white male who plays golf with his partners. Nevertheless, we believe that there also may be latent gender-related and ethnic-related components to these statements. Once these factors get mentioned, and other more direct gender-related issues have been thoroughly discussed, we sometimes find it useful to concentrate on what students mean by these terms.

It has often proved the case that at this point in the discussion, minority members of the class have volunteered their perception that they have felt that others considered them "not a team player" or someone who "did not fit it." If this perspective is not volunteered, the teacher may gently suggest this

interpretation, which may encourage those students in the class who appreciate this point to help move the discussion along.

We add this caveat: The fact that a lawyer "doesn't fit in" does not signal either racial or gender bias. Socializing with one's colleagues is important. Everyone has an understandable desire to practice law with people they feel comfortable with and like. What we want to do is recognize at least the *possibility* of another ingredient in these comments about Sharon.

(f)   Some Specifics Raised by Students:

Performance Reviews. We have found that students often raise issues which the teacher should try to address. Some students point out that Sharon should have some kind of warning about any shortcomings in her performance, particularly her low billable hours, if it is going to be brought up in considering her partnership. They want to see her annual performance reviews. This is a point well taken, although good performance reviews as an associate and elevation to partner may involve legitimately different criteria.

Kids, Part-time Partnerships, and Timing. Another point raised by students is the availability of less than full-time partnership tracks. This is an issue, mentioned in passing throughout the readings, which is receiving increasing attention. Part-time partnership tracks allow custodial parents to maintain their dream of law firm partnership and their dream of raising a family at the same time. A small number of more progressive firms have begun permitting such partnerships. But they are still quite unusual. They are also unproven; some believe that "mommy-track" partners work 40-hour weeks instead of 60 or 70, but only get paid for 20. Nevertheless, the validity of the idea, and the underlying relationship to gender issues, is significant. Some younger writers on women's issues have suggested that women return to the method most often used by the "pre-liberation" generation of woman professionals: Have kids first and then return to the law after the kids reach an appropriate age. Of course, this is hardly equality, but it is a strategy worth some discussion.

Law Firm Culture. On occasion, a student will want to defer the list of factors until the partnership group can decide what kind of partners we are looking for, or what kind of firm we are — in short, what our firm culture is like. This is a very perceptive approach. In fact, the firm's goals and culture have an enormously important role on our perceptions of whom we want as a partner, and our perceptions of Sharon Chau. But to allow the exercise to play itself out, we usually ask this student to defer consideration of these issues until the end, when we address them directly.

It's Not Just About Gender. We have mentioned that on several occasions a woman student or students have, near the beginning of the discussion, pointed out that "this is very much about gender." As we have also mentioned, the racial issues often do not get addressed for a long period of time. Once we have discussed the matter for some time, we have found it useful to return to

ask these women, who usually have exhibited a high degree of social awareness, whether there are issues other than gender that come into play. They often readily agree that it is *not* just about gender, but about race too, providing us a smoother entry into that area.

(g) Justifying Racial and Ethnic Diversity:

Once the discussion begins to focus on Sharon's ethnic and racial background, the issue of whether it is a worthy goal in itself to foster racial diversity among the partners will undoubtedly come up. This can be a difficult issue. First, students may at this point feel the need to be "politically correct" by acceding to diversity for its own sake. Other students may argue that Sharon's being Asian will afford them an opportunity for business, such as "Pacific Rim" business, that they did not have before. But there is no clear evidence that she is likely to bring in such business.

In short, students may search for a way to see her racial background as a strength, and in doing so may resort to a formulaic approach, without working through the reasons why diversity will ultimately be a strength. We see diversity as a strength for several reasons. While it's true that it may enhance business opportunities and help a law firm meet the "buzz word" test of diversity, it also assists the law firm to show that its population more closely approximately the society in which the law firm operates.

Perhaps more important, it allows for significant broadening of a law firm's perspective. We all bring our cultural experiences and background to the table with us, along with our formal education and professional experience. We believe that the more diverse backgrounds and perspectives present in the partnership room, the larger the wealth of our collective knowledge. This helps us, as a law firm, to guard against insularity and maintain a broader perspective about the affairs of humankind. Finally, diversity says something about the law firm's culture, and its statement to the legal community and to the firm's partners and employees about the kind of environment that the firm wishes to foster.

Another racial issue which students may want to address — or that the teacher may want to look at — is the issue of "tokenism" and the need to move beyond tokenism to a truly diverse professional setting. One look around many law school classes will demonstrate how small the number of minority students in our law schools often is. This is even more true at law firm partnership meetings. The Pfaff, Baynes, and Wilkins articles (**Sections 4** and **6**) speak strongly to this issue. The Wilkins excerpt is long, but full of significant empirical information. These pieces echo the readings in the **Introduction** about the elitism of the late nineteenth and twentieth century bars, and the warnings of the Higgonbotham, et al. article in **Problem 19**.

We particularly commend the teacher's attention to the Herring article (**Readings, Section 10**) that closes the problem. This experienced teacher of

bias and diversity issues pulls few punches in talking about the racial and gender stereotyping which is systemic in our world. Herring intends to deal with it by confronting it. For a similarly plain-spoken approach, we recall Prof. Pearce's "white guy" perspective in **Problem 13**. We agree with Herring's proposition, and with his optimistic conclusion that law firms could become among the best-equipped organizations to deal with these kinds of issues.

(h) Question 4: The Offensive Remark:

Despite our discussions, some students will remain unconvinced that Sharon Chau's race plays any part at all in her role as a lawyer. For those students, we have included **Question 4**, the purpose of which is to bring home the issue of race as it relates to Sharon.

This question, in which one of the named partners makes an offensive remark about a Chinese company, asks what actions Sharon should take after hearing the remark. Students will readily engage in a discussion about her alternatives — going to her own partner, confronting the partner who made the remark or even doing nothing. The point is not so much what Sharon is best off doing, but rather the fact that she has to do anything at all.

A white male overhearing the same conversation could make the choice whether to confront it or to let it go. If the white male confronted the issue, he would not be doing it on "his own behalf" but because he found the remark racially or ethnically insensitive. For Sharon, however, the stakes are different. The remark relates to her personally, at least in the sense that she too is Chinese-American. It is our hope that, for those students who do not perceive the significance of her ethnic background, this question will bring the point home. The teacher can, if desired, engage in a role-play in which the teacher plays either the offending partner or another partner. This will help demonstrate the clear awkwardness (at best) of the situation.

(i) Sexual Harassment:

We have made the facts regarding the dinner invitation intentionally ambiguous. Neither we nor Sharon, nor our students, can tell exactly what is meant by the dinner invitation. Is it an innocent effort to help Sharon out? Is Taylor using her pending partnership as a vehicle to ask her out on a dinner date? Taylor's different approaches, which may depend entirely on tone of voice, demeanor and attitude, can be role-played by the teacher if time permits.

Our purpose here is to point out both the ambiguity and the danger of the situation. If students too readily assume that this is harassment, the teacher can take the counterpoint view. On the other hand, if students too cavalierly shrug it off, the teacher can emphasize the dangers. Either way, the teacher will be helpful by giving some advice to students about how to deal with situations like this.

Long experience has taught us that in this situation, it is best to take a middle course, between accepting the invitation oblivious to its potential danger and telling the partner to "get lost." The reality of law practice is that these situations are more likely than not to occur at some point. The lawyer who wants to remain employed in the good graces of her firm will try to find a way of dealing with such situations in a manner that protects both the lawyer's professional standing and personal wishes. That may mean changing the dinner invitation to lunch, or going to dinner with Taylor directly from work and keeping the focus on business.

(j)   Bias as an Ethical Issue, and Law Firm "Culture":

We like to end our discussion, time permitting, with a brief look both at the question of whether bias is an ethical issue and at the importance of law firm culture. The **Readings, Section 8**, briefly address the first issue. More and more states have rules prohibiting bias among their lawyers. But the larger reason for such rules may be, as D.C. lawyer Isbell states, their "hortatory purpose."

In this respect, the rules relate directly to a law firm's image of itself. As we said above, students sometimes raise the issue of a law firm's "culture" during the course of our discussions. This "culture" may be enabled, in part, by the fact that our Supreme Court is not yet a level playing field. (See the **Readings, Section 9**.) We like to return to these issues at the end of the discussion, because where there is a strong law firm goal or culture, it makes dealing with the "issue" of Sharon Chau far simpler. If all the partners in the firm know what they are looking for in a new partner, and what kind of direction and attitude about diversity they want their firm to take, the decision on making Sharon Chau partner may become much easier.

PROBLEM 29

A Lawyer In Trouble And His Friends On The Spot

THE POINT BEHIND THE PROBLEM:

The point of this problem is to address as candidly as possible within the classroom setting the reality of substance abuse and other impairments, including depression and gambling, and their effects — on our colleagues, ourselves, our practice and our clients. We have materially expanded the scope of discussion in several ways, most significantly by including a new reading in **Section 1** that focuses on disturbing statistics about depression in the profession, and the Krieger article in **Section 6** and its holistic approach to health and satisfaction among law students.

The issues in **Problem 29** have expanded significantly in importance and breadth since we first addressed them in our first edition in 1995. First among the major issues is the extent to which we owe it to our colleagues and to our law firm's clients to insist that our colleagues with these problems seek assistance. Second is the effect of substance abuse and related impairments on a lawyer's competence, and the potential breach of fiduciary duty to clients represented by that attorney.

The third issue relates to the significance of destructive behavior as a force in itself in the lives of our friends and colleagues, and perhaps ourselves. A related fourth issue is the difficulty we all have in recognizing the signs of impairment in those close to us and especially in ourselves. Finally, a fifth key issue, eloquently presented in Prof. Krieger's article in **Section 6**, is that losing our personal and professional health and integrity has a substantial effect on our wellbeing. These last three issues must be coupled with a dose of reality — that the practice of law, combined with the relative powerlessness of law firm associates, *is* stressful, and can even foster a certain amount of alcohol and drug use, much of which may be termed "abuse," but some of which may not be.

In raising these matters with law students, it is important for the teacher to avoid a "holier than thou" attitude, and to appreciate the practical realities of the stressful life of both law students and lawyers. This is the final point we wish to raise: We should all recognize the peer pressure to engage in certain potentially destructive behaviors, and the fact that it can be very difficult for partner and associate alike to take the steps advised in the readings to insist that a colleague get help. At the same time, we recognize the overriding importance of attempting to solve these problems.

APPLICABLE RULES:

Model Rules: MRs 1.1; 1.3; 5.1; 5.2; 8.3.
Model Code: DRs 1-103(A); 7-101; 9-101; EC 9-2.
CA Rules: 3-110.

SUGGESTED QUESTIONS TO ASK:

- Is "Rabbit" Worthington's behavior in **Part I** sufficiently clear to warrant his colleagues taking action?

- Is "Rabbit" an alcoholic? Is alcohol affecting his performance?

- When should the law firm intervene in Rabbit's situation? When he loses clients? Or stops bringing in business?

- Should the firm not intervene in Rabbit's case until he is no longer competently representing clients?

- Should the point where the law firm intervenes on Rabbit's behalf depend more on his personal situation than on his representation of clients?

- How many students would talk to Worthington? How many think Chenier will discuss the problem with Worthington?

- If Chenier talks to Worthington, should it be as a managing partner, or a friend?

- To what extent does potential incompetence raise the ante for intervening in the case of a possible substance abuser?

- When must the clients be informed about a lawyer who seems impaired in performance?

- In taking steps to intervene or inform clients, does it matter whether the lawyer's impairment stems from alcohol, or gambling, or depression?

- How strongly must Jane Diaz consider her status in the firm before deciding what to do about Rabbit's problems?

- What alternatives does Diaz have to simply "blowing the whistle" on Rabbit?

SUGGESTED ROLE-PLAYS:

- Role-play a group of partners discussing the issue of an "intervention" for Rabbit, with the teacher as one partner, and the students leading the discussion as other partners.

- Role-play Jane Diaz examining the alternatives she has and some practical avenues she might take. For example, Jane might talk to a partner in the firm whom she trusts.

- If students are willing, ask a small group of them to role-play a discussion or intervention with a fictitious law-school friend suffering from serious depression or substance abuse problems.

DISCUSSION:

(a) Part I, What Should Chenier Do?

Students should begin by evaluating how clear a problem "Rabbit's" behavior is in **Scenario I**. To us, even at this earlier stage, the extent of Rabbit's alcohol use seems quite clear. What is somewhat less clear is the extent to which his problem affects his representation of clients. Still, it appears to us there is enough to conclude that Rabbit's condition means he has a significant alcohol problem and is no longer an asset to the firm or its clients.

The **Readings** in **Section 3** state the clear case for intervention at the earliest possible time. The Temple Law Review article argues strongly for the idea that when it comes to substance abuse, "if you are not part of the solution, you are part of the problem." The **Readings** in **Sections 1** and **2** sound out warnings, perhaps most loudly about *early recognition* of depression or substance abuse. The strong last paragraph of the Mounteer article explains why the typical "lawyer-type" has particular difficulty in recognizing the need for help. And the freefall of David Demergian shows how rapidly a lawyer can descend into a pit of substance — and lifestyle — abuse.

Nevertheless, the teacher should be wary of students who too easily reach a conclusion that Rabbit definitely needs outside assistance. The practical realities of the law firm setting, the daily pressures from colleagues and the realities of natural human interaction make Chenier's decision to intervene at this stage a difficult one at least on a personal basis. What we try to encourage is a full and fair evaluation of the options that face Chuck Chenier.

(b) Why Should a Lawyer Intervene?

The teacher might wish to inquire of students what the principal issue is in terms of the law firm's intervention. Should intervention occur when Rabbit begins to lose clients? When he stops bringing in business? Should the firm wait until he is actually not competently representing his clients? Or should it depend more on his personal situation?

We note before moving on that the two ABA opinions discussed in the **Readings, Section 4** offer fewer solutions than they avoid, as our synopsis makes rather clear. Opinion 429, which requires law firms to create a plan to prevent impairment from adversely affecting clients, leaves unsolved the

problem of self-recognition. In a larger firm context, the behavior of someone like Rabbit will certainly raise flags, whether codified or not. But *recognizing* that a problem exists will be far more difficult among small law firms and solos.

Assuming a firm of some size, we like to role-play a group of partners discussing this issue, with the teacher as one partner, and the students leading the discussion as other partners. In this way we can engage in a roundtable about what we should do, and why it is that we are (or are not) doing it. We also are mindful of the ultimately personal nature of this issue, which is brought home by **Part III**.

The **Readings** in **Section 5** make a strong case for intervention in appropriate situations. But students also need to be made aware that the lawyer's family may not fully support the intervention. That is because even if impaired, the lawyer is earning money, and will have no income while spending what could be as long as three to six months in rehab. We found this surprising, but a lawyer of our acquaintance told us that after one intervention, the family was more angry at the loss of income and status than concerned about the welfare of the lawyer.

(c) Part II: What Is Diaz's Responsibility?

Again, in **Part II**, the students should review how clear Rabbit's behavior is, and how clear the apparent substance abuse. Again, the same reasons for intervention should be reviewed. Here, however, it appears that Rabbit's competence is directly affected. To what extent does this raise the ante for intervening? Indeed, Diaz — and her firm — could incur liability for doing nothing while watching Worthington's possible malpractice.

The competing consideration is Diaz's status as an inexperienced associate. As a second-year associate, she has almost no power within the firm. It would be normal for Diaz to consider her status in deciding how to deal with Rabbit's situation. Her problem is a real one. If she goes directly to Rabbit and he denies there is a problem, it may be more difficult to go to Chenier. If she goes to Chenier, however, she is going over Rabbit's head. Worthington may take that out on her in her annual evaluation. She's in a no-win situation. Only Chenier can get Jane off the hook, because he's in a better position as managing partner to do so.

The teacher can assist by role-playing Diaz and/or examining the alternatives she has and suggesting some practical avenues she might take. For example, as we suggested in **Problem 26**, Jane can talk to a partner in the firm whom she trusts and present the problem to that partner.

It is important, however, to recognize that in most states, under **MR 8.3** or a similar rule (California is an exception here), a lawyer has an obligation to report to the bar regulatory authority the incompetent conduct of a colleague.

This, of course, is what got attorney Kelly in trouble, as we saw in the readings to **Problem 26**. This rule may be honored more in its breach than in its implementation, but it remains a lawyer's obligation. Further, there remains a duty to supervise subordinates. This may not apply to Worthington, but could to a subordinate with a substance abuse problem.

(d) Part II — Chenier's Duty Revisited:

Students may argue that for Diaz, since she is a subordinate lawyer, her obligation to report Rabbit is mitigated by her supervising lawyer taking her off the hook. (See the contrast between **MRs 5.1 and 5.2**.) No such defense will be available to Chenier, on whose shoulders clearly fall a responsibility not only to report incompetence, but also a fiduciary duty to clients of the firm not to allow them to be represented incompetently.

On another level, however, Diaz's dilemma point up the problems with the effect of Chenier's failure to act back in **Part I**. Had Chenier decided to act — to do *something* — Diaz wouldn't have found herself in a no-win situation in **Part II** — another good argument for early intervention.

(e) Drugs, Alcohol, and Your Friend (or You):

Part of the purpose of this problem is to bring home the reality of substance abuse to each law student, not only about their colleagues, but about their friends and potentially themselves. This is something we intend to do gently, and in a way that tries to avoid being too "preachy." For this reason, for example, the Allan article in **Section 5** of the **Readings**, and our text in **Section 6** talk about instances of alcohol use that are appropriate, and instances of drug use that may not interfere with a lawyer's performance.

We suggest that the teacher remain mindful of the realities of practicing with colleagues who go out for a beer after work, and that all of us must deal with the stress of modern law practice. At the same time, we believe the teacher has here the opportunity of returning to the recurring theme of a law firm's culture. Some firms foster substance use and even drug abuse through peer pressure that makes the teen-age variant look mild by comparison.

When we refer to stress (see some examples in **Section 6**), we neither want to minimize it nor overstate it. Rather, we want to acknowledge it, and point out the downside risks of giving in to it in inappropriate ways. According to studies we have read, this is of particular concern to women. One study showed that 20% of women lawyers in California had six or more drinks a day. This may well stem from the additional pressure felt by women who want to succeed as equals in the legal marketplace, as we saw in **Problem 28**.

(f) Satisfaction, Integrity, and Law Students' Mental Health

Before closing our discussion on this Problem, we have two more stops to make. First, students should be afforded an opportunity of telling their "war stories" about the use and abuse of alcohol and drugs in legal circles. Many law schools may be guilty of fostering at least an environment of alcohol use, if not one that actually fosters abuse. This is a serious concern, worthy of serious consideration.

Finally, we encourage a thorough and frank discussion of Prof. Krieger's important perspective (**Readings**, **Section 6**). While Krieger's thesis is that personal integrity leaves to health and wellness, we believe he has managed to transcend mere "happy talk" about the subject. His article affords students real lessons in the importance of personal integrity, and the reality of why following "intrinsic" values and motivations will bring far greater satisfaction and wellbeing than extrinsic values like money and the trappings of superficial success.

Krieger's has given his arguments a logical resonance; when they are bolstered by his citations to empirical studies and the now-readmitted David Dermagian's comment about power and money vs. happiness (**page 786**), a strong case has been made. Finally, we find Krieger's definition of professionalism (**page 785**) to be one of our favorites.

PROBLEM 30

Counselors In Action Go For The Gold

THE POINT BEHIND THE PROBLEM:

There are three principal points here. First, the Supreme Court's efforts to define commercial free speech have largely taken over from the ethical rules in this field. What a lawyer can "get away with" in advertising has become a matter largely defined by the Court, not by ethical rules, some of which are obsolete, and some of which, although new, may be constitutionally overbroad.

The second point is that the test of whether advertising, and even some forms of solicitation, is impermissible will almost always come down to the question of whether it is "misleading." One of the major points that students will have to examine is how the term "misleading" should be defined. Finally, with respect to the solicitation issues which have so significantly broadened the scope of advertising, students should try to define the limits set by the Supreme Court. These limits are relatively narrow, as our review of several Supreme Court cases in the **Readings, Section 6** indicates.

Third, few subjects have not been affected by the Internet. Not surprisingly, the Internet has had a dramatic effect on advertising and solicitation. We expand our previous edition's introduction to this issue by including a significant new problem — unsolicited clients obtained from lawyers' websites, sometimes with severe consequences. See **Readings, Section 5**.

APPLICABLE RULES:

Model Rules:	MRs 1.5(e); 1.18; 7.1; 7.2; 7.3; 7.4.
Model Code:	DRs 2-101 through 2-105; ECs 2-8 through 2-15.
CA Rules:	1-400, and Standards Authorized by 1-400.
CA B&P:	6152.

SUGGESTED QUESTIONS TO ASK:

- What does "the most qualified lawyers in town" mean? What does having "many" lawyers from prestigious law schools mean?

- How can one quantify how qualified the "most qualified lawyers in town" are?

- Is "you can count on C.I.A. to win" really tantamount to a guarantee?

- If Weir really received a trial lawyer award, does it matter that it is an award of small significance in the legal community?

- Is it misleading to say that a client "pays nothing" for a case that is lost, if the client is responsible to reimburse costs?

- Is an ad misleading if the matters asserted, while true, are significantly or even grossly exaggerated?

- Does the issue of whether an ad is misleading turn on whether the copy itself is misleading in the abstract, or whether the public which reads the ad is in fact misled?

- If everyone knows that the two actors portraying lawyers in a TV ad are in fact actors, is the ad misleading because they are not identified?

- What factors should be used in evaluating the propriety of the phone call described in Question 3?

- How can a law firm avoid the conflict of interest that could be created by an unsolicited email from a prospective client containing confidential information and asking for representation adverse to a current client?

- To what extent should advertising regulations be designed to protect the dignity and decorum of the profession?

- How effective will advertising *guidelines* be in encouraging more dignified ads if they do not have the force of ethical requirements?

- How much does the emphasis on dignity and professionalism in advertising serve to mask the same pro-establishment attitude that was the basis of our profession's historic opposition to advertising?

SUGGESTED ROLE-PLAYS:

- Play the role of C.I.A.'s bar defense counsel showing that the ad copy used by the law firm in **Question 1** has not been proved to be "misleading."

- Play the role of a lawyer talking on the phone to a prospective client in a way that proves (or disproves) the overreaching and coercive nature of the phone call. Try playing the role so that an immediate "yes or no" about the lawyer's services is required.

- Play out a debate in a law firm over whether an unsolicited email inquiry that contains sensitive information about the sender turns out to create a conflict with one of the firm's existing clients.

DISCUSSION:

(a) A Discussion of the Interrelationship Between the Rules of Ethics and the Supreme Court's Views on Free Speech:

We discuss **Questions 1** and **2** in turn, saving our analysis of Supreme Court cases until our discussion of **Question 3**. We suggest that along the way, the teacher and students take some time to discuss the gulf between the

Supreme Court cases and the ethical rules, and the distinction in this problem, perhaps more than all others, between *ethics* and *case law*. Here, case law clearly controls.

It is also worth noting that many state bars have advertising and solicitation regulations which may be much broader than the Supreme Court would allow, but which are in place anyway. These regulations (the standards supporting California Rule 1-400 are an excellent example) can have a substantial chilling effect on attorneys who do not want to be test cases every time they advertise. Accordingly, some overbreadth on the part of state bar regulators is perhaps to be expected.

This last point raises the issue of why the rules of ethics seek to regulate what amounts to lawyer "dignity." This echoes a theme which we raised in the **Introduction**: that traditionally, rules of lawyers' ethics had a certain exclusionary purpose, i.e., to keep out the legal "riff-raff" that established lawyers felt lowered the standards of the profession. The teacher might ask whether ethical rules about advertising and solicitation may serve this same purpose at least in part.

(b)   Going Through the Specifics of Garcia, Weir and Lesh's Conduct:

The principal issue will be whether the law firm's advertisements are misleading. We have found that students will tend to see misleading aspects where at least the Supreme Court would not. Moreover, as far as state bars are concerned, many of the "misleading" aspects seen by the students will probably not result in enforcement.

It will be important for the teacher to test the students as to why they claim that certain advertising approaches are misleading, and test whether these are sufficient to warrant a disciplinary violation. For example, the name Counselors in Action may be seen by many students as misleading. But few states would try to regulate this name in light of modern rules about commercial free speech. The issue of whether this name is misleading provides a good introduction to these issues.

Interestingly, it appears to us that if anything, recent years have brought about a more stringent, less open view of advertising. While the constitutional issues have not changed, the perception seems to be — from our subjective vantage point — that more regulation is permissible in the interests of ... well, we are not sure of precisely what interests. Whether this reflects a temporary change or a clear course correction remains to be seen. See our discussion in the **Readings, Section 7**, and particularly the **NOTES** section, for some thoughts you might focus on if this is an issue that you want to discuss with your students.

(c) The Ad Copy in Question I:

We suggest dealing with each ad copy in turn. In *Advertisement (a)*, students will question why C.I.A. says "the most qualified lawyers," how they justify saying that "many of our lawyers attended prestigious schools," and, finally, how they can give a seeming guarantee by saying "you can count on C.I.A. to win." There is ample justification to consider these matters misleading. But they are largely misleading in their ambiguity. What does "the most qualified lawyers in town" mean? What does "many" lawyers from prestigious schools mean? And will anyone seriously believe that counting on these lawyers to win is tantamount to a guarantee?

Thus, while students often see clear ethical violations, we see the issue as a close one. The teacher can bring this home by role-playing the part of C.I.A.'s bar defense counsel, pointing out the equivocal nature of these statements. "This," bar counsel might say, "is what advertising copy is all about. For example, the phrase 'the most qualified lawyers' is not quantifiable." Nevertheless, we are bothered by "many" prestigious school attendees, and most of all by the guarantee. On balance, we find the copy of this first ad misleading.

Some of the same problems exist in *Advertisement (b)*. Again, the question is largely one of semantics ⤷ another of our recurring course themes. Again, many students see a clear ethical violation. But to us the misleading elements are thin.

If Garcia has in fact won his last 12 trials, this is factually accurate, even if most of them were minor or uncontested matters. If Weir received the Trial Lawyer Network's award, it may matter little that this is an award of small significance to most of the legal community. The *Peel* case (see the brief summary of the case in **Section 6** of the **Readings**) seems clearly to allow this. We have the most problems with the statement about Lesh. His last six jury successes may have been out of twenty cases tried, not a very good percentage at all. But absent proof that this is indeed misleading, it will be difficult for a bar enforcement agency to discipline Lesh even for this last comment.

Again, it should be part of the teacher's role to point out that this enforcement problem does not make these statements pristine, dignified or appropriate in the eyes of most lawyers. Rather, since the question of their propriety must account for commercial free speech and thus rests entirely on a finding that they are in fact "misleading," it merely points out that it leaves bar enforcement authorities with relatively little flexibility.

The statement in *Advertisement (c)* was designed by us to be relatively close to *Bates* (see **Section 2** of the **Readings**). Nevertheless, some students will take exception to this statement as well, asking what is meant by a "simple divorce" or a "simple will." They suspect, perhaps, a bait-and-switch operation. But nothing in the statement itself indicates that those fears are

justified. Of greater significance is the one place we departed from the careful language of the *Bates* ad: The assertion that clients pay nothing for personal injury cases if they don't recover, since they may still be liable for costs. Some states have tried to show that where the client is expected to reimburse costs, saying that the client "pays nothing" is misleading.

(d) How to Define "Misleading":

At some point, and this juncture might be as good as any, we ask the students again to define the term "misleading" as it relates to lawyer advertising. Some of the questions we ask are the following: Is the ad misleading if the matters asserted are true, regardless of how stretched or exaggerated the significance of those matters may appear? Does the issue of whether an ad is misleading depend on the copy itself viewed in the abstract by a state bar regulator, or is it the effect it has on the person who reads the ad? For example, what if nine out of ten prospective clients surveyed did not view the statement about "counting on Counselors in Action to win" as being a meaningful guarantee; would this defeat any claim that the copy was misleading?

(e) Hiring Actors to Portray Lawyers (Question II):

Here as well, the standard remains whether the advertisement is "misleading." Since the actors are not actually lawyers working for C.I.A., a good argument can be made that such an ad would be misleading. If students too easily come to this point of view, the teacher can argue out to the contrary: if everyone knows that these two television actors are really the stars of the latest hot TV show, the fact that they are playing roles may be obvious to the vast majority of viewers. Again, if the public does not perceive the actors as lawyers, then perhaps this ad is not misleading.

Nevertheless, many states have successfully argued that in order for actors to portray lawyers in advertisements, it must be clear that they are actors and not actual lawyers. (This may be the reason for the famous ad in which the actor says: "I'm not a doctor, but I play one on TV.")

The fact that states have successfully required that actors portraying lawyers be identified as such provides a good vehicle for pointing out the distinctions between what may be considered misleading in professional advertisements, such as for lawyers, and the greater leeway afforded advertisements for other services. Students can come up with their own examples of local late-night TV advertising for hair salons, camera stores or auto repair shops where actors could freely portray the principals. And everyone will recall Madge the manicurist and the Maytag repairman. No one would even think of requiring that they be identified as actors.

(f)   Question III and the Supreme Court's Decisions:

Question III, which raises the issues of personalized direct mail and personalized phone calls, provides the best opportunity to review the string of Supreme Court cases set forth in **Section 6** of the **Readings**. We believe that it is useful for students to follow the line of cases after *Bates* to develop a sense of how the Supreme Court expanded the doctrine of commercial free speech in the years after 1977.

The *Shapero* case is very close to the direct mail scenario suggested in Question 3. Students should cite to this case in dealing with this question. But the more interesting issue to us is the phone call. It goes further than any Supreme Court case, and is clearly beyond direct mail, since it involves a personal contact directly with the prospective client. On the other hand, the phone call is considerably less intrusive than the actions of attorney Ohralik, which represent the extreme in intrusion when the Supreme Court first ruled the conduct was not protected.

In evaluating the phone call, students should ideally look at the factors cited by the court in *Shapero*, including the "condition" of the prospective client and the extent to which the vulnerability caused by that condition was exploited by the communication. Also of value is the *Zauderer* case, which emphasizes that an advertisement may be acceptable at least in part because no immediate yes or no answer about hiring the lawyer is demanded, as it was in *Ohralik*.

It is not terribly clear whether a phone call would require such an immediate yes or no; obviously it is a lot easier to simply hang up the phone than it was for the prospective clients in *Ohralik* to get rid of that intrusive and overreaching attorney. It is difficult to say how the Supreme Court might come out on this issue. But as the **Readings** (last paragraph of **Section 6**, and **Section 7**) suggest, there is some reason to believe that the Court may be inclined to narrow rather than further broaden the range of commercial free speech for lawyers.

Went For It, discussed at some length in the narrative at the end of **Readings, Section 6**, upheld Florida's regulation requiring a 30-day cooling off period after an accident. This case is not only important for a discussion of the direct mail scenario in **Question 3**, but also emphasizes the likely shift of the Court on advertising issues. We believe *Went For It* may well be the beginning of a regulatory trend that will manifest itself in future cases.

(g)   Question IV:

The Internet is being used more and more as a way to lure clients. And the advertising rules differ in many states. Thus, what may be proper in one state may violate the advertising rules of another, where the potential client resides. The ABA has opined that internet advertising by itself is not improper, but it is false or misleading, it will not pass muster. You may want to recall **Problem 1**

to remind the students of how easy it is to create an attorney-client relationship, and **Problem 6**, regarding the damages of a law firm picking up a "client" on its website.

Of greater or at least more complex significance is the unsolicited email received through the law firm's website, as described in Prof. Hricik's article in the **Readings, Section 5**. Note that Hricik correctly, in our view, points to the problems of both a "we don't take clients" disclaimer and an "it's not confidential" disclaimer. While Hricik's solution is the hybrid disclaimer inspired by **MR 1.18**, we are not certain how well even this thoughtful idea will work. **MR 1.18** was newly adopted in 2002, and does not yet have firm and clear judicial interpretation.

We like a more practical solution that some law firms have begun to adopt: the availability on the website of emailing not the lawyers directly, but only the law firm generally. These emails can then be administratively reviewed for conflicts before any substantive review by an attorney. Disclaimers on the website can explain the email limitations, and suggest limiting content. Of course, this solution is also not without problems. There is no guarantee that even these emails will protect against every conflict or potential disqualification. Of greater concern to practitioners is a practical consequence: Shielding the lawyers' email addresses on the website will interfere with communications from opposing counsel, or even other lawyers looking to refer a case. And ours is a potential solution likely to make every law firm marketing person unhappy.

(h) Question V:

Question V raises two issues: the propriety of a referral fee, and "baiting and switching" of clients from the C.I.A. referral service by siphoning them off to the private practice of the three lawyers. We briefly address the issue of the propriety of private referral services in **Section 4** of the **Readings**. Note that, just as with advertising and solicitation, what is permissible may turn more on issues of constitutional free speech than the ethical rules limiting participating in such services.

Ethical rules have long prohibited the receipt of a referral fee from lawyer to lawyer. (See **MR 1.5 (e)**.) However, it is unclear whether the proposed operation would be a referral service or would result in a lawyer-to-lawyer referral fee. The paramount point is this: there are many tricks and devices which lawyers can and probably will think of to attract business. Many of these have not yet been tested. Garcia, Weir and Lesh have come up with two, set forth in **Question V**. Only time will tell how courts deal with these issues. What is important here is to recognize that the efforts of lawyers to attract business and money will continue to present us with an ever-changing landscape.

(i)   The Gulf Between What Is Ethical and What Is Dignified:

We find it useful to close our discussion of lawyer advertising and solicitation by looking again at the gulf between what one can "get away with" and what is considered by most lawyers to be a dignified approach to the profession.

Several readings are useful references in this regard. Justice White's opinion in *Zauderer* (see **Readings, Section 6**) made it clear that while he might like to consider "dignity and decorum" in determining whether Zauderer's newspaper ad was improper, he simply did not have a constitutional reason to do so. Put another way, Prof. Gillers tells us in the article about "ambulance driving" (**Readings, Section 3**) that whether something is "tacky" and whether it is ethical have become two separate and distinct issues.

Justice Blackmun, writing in *Bates* in 1977, clearly never anticipated how undignified and tacky lawyer advertising might become. But how much does the emphasis on dignity and professionalism serve to mask the same pro-establishment attitude that was the basis of our profession's longstanding opposition to advertising as being "unethical"? And how much do certain restrictions on advertising such as *Went For It* have the potential to endanger the rights of those injured, in need of a lawyer, but not knowing one feeling pressured to speak directly to the insurance company? We see this danger, discussed in the **Readings, Section 8**, as quite real.

PROBLEM 31

The Economics Of Legal Services For Indigent Clients

THE POINT BEHIND THE PROBLEM:

We emphasize that the fact this problem comes last does *not* make it the least. In fact, because of the importance we place on lawyers doing pro bono work, we specifically "save" our last class for this subject.

The purposes behind the problem are twofold. First, we want students to understand the difficult, perhaps impossible choices legal aid attorneys must make on a daily basis in deciding which cases they can take, and which they simply don't have the time to handle. We encourage the students to understand that these attorneys must have broad discretion to allocate their resources as they see fit.

The second and even more important purpose of this problem is that it gives us the opportunity to advocate our belief in the need for all lawyers — and law students — to do pro bono work. This is important for three reasons. First, we see this as the ethically (and morally) right thing to do, and believe that each of us should consider ourselves *required* to do it, whether or not it is deemed mandatory by our bar. Without being too dogmatic or "holier than thou," we try to articulate our reasons for this view during the course of our last class. Second, we have come to believe, as the eloquent Fleischer article in **Section 5** of the **Readings** points out, that it can be the most rewarding work young lawyers do. Sometimes, as on Lubet's Eleventh Floor (**Readings, Section 9**), it can elevate an entire courtroom. Third, of course, without this work being done, important legal interests of scores of millions of people go unmet.

At the same time, it is important to recognize the difficulty some lawyers will have in performing this work, because of the lack of sympathy of their firms, or lack of support from their colleagues. This raises the "law firm culture" issue that has been a recurring theme throughout the course. For this reason, and perhaps because of a more sympathetic "culture," we also want to address with our students the possibility of mandatory pro bono at the law school level.

APPLICABLE RULES:

Model Rules:	MRs 3.1; 6.1; 6.2.
Model Code:	ECs 2-1; 2-2; 2-3; 2-16; 2-24;2-25; 2-26; 2-27; 8-1.
CA B&P:	6068(c), (h); 6210 et seq.

SUGGESTED QUESTIONS TO ASK:

- What factors will you consider in deciding what cases to handle? What is the relative importance of these factors?

- What troubles you about the methods used by the Gold County Legal Aid staff in deciding what kinds of cases to handle?

- Do you believe that legal aid will ever be able to serve the needs of all those who require help?

- If more people need legal aid than Legal Aid can provide, how else will these people get legal help?

- Can you come up with reasons why, as Schell says, lawyers, "unlike groups such as plumbers or manufacturers of can openers," should engage in pro bono work?

- Should doing pro bono work be mandatory?

- Should a law firm be allowed to discharge its pro bono duty by having its younger associates do all the pro bono work?

- What is the significance (if any) in having *all* lawyers, old and young, leaders and followers, including the great or famous, like Albert Jenner, doing pro bono work?

- Should lawyers in the public sector be excluded from having to do pro bono work?

- Should lawyers be able to "buy out" of doing pro bono work by paying a fee?

- How would you define what the term pro bono means? Must it be legal work? Must it deal with the poor as opposed to improvements in the administration of the legal system? Can civic good works suffice?

- Do you believe that law students should be required to do pro bono work? Could they do it through their clinical programs?

- Is pro bono an ethics issue?

SUGGESTED ROLE-PLAYS:

- Turn the classroom into a legal aid board of directors meeting, and discuss how you will make choices about what kinds of cases to handle.

- Play the part of a law firm associate talking with a partner about doing pro bono work for which he or she gets "credit" within the firm.

DISCUSSION:

(a) Legal Aid Means Making Tough Choices:

In addressing the first part of **Problem 31**, we often role-play by turning the classroom into a legal aid board of directors meeting. We ask the students to take the lead in making the choices about what kinds of cases to take and in determining both which factors should be considered and their relative importance.

Students will have different perspectives on some of these variables. Some may be troubled by going only with "winning cases," because that in effect makes the lawyer the judge of the client's cause. After all, they point out, although most of the custody cases are unsuccessful, 18% are successful. Without legal aid representation, almost all of these cases will be lost. Some students will be troubled in general by the time/cost analysis suggested in **Question 2**. Others will be troubled by concentrating on landlord/tenant and housing issues, while others will be concerned about whether a survey is an appropriate way to decide what kinds of cases to take.

In this discussion, the teacher can serve two significant functions. First, we can validate the students' concerns about making such difficult choices, and the legitimate reasons why one or another way to choose should be used. Second, however, the teacher can point out that all of these methods, while valid, do not change the fact that choices have to be made. The bottom line is that these are insoluble choices, and perhaps like Sophie's Choice, someone worthy is going to lose out.

(b) The Tie-in Between Tough Legal Aid Choices and Doing Pro Bono Work:

As the **Readings** in **Section 2** and **3** point out, making these tough choices comes with the territory of being a legal aid attorney. It doesn't make these choices any easier but it points to the tie-in between the legal aid and the pro bono aspects of this problem. Students will readily recognize — and if they don't, the teacher can encourage the perspective — that the burden of providing these legal services cannot possibly fall solely on the Gold County Legal Aid Program. These lawyers simply could not do the whole job, even if they worked 24 hours a day.

Our perspective is that if there are individuals with worthy cases in need of legal assistance, the burden of providing most of that help will have to come from other lawyers providing free legal services, or it will simply not come at all. Since in analyzing the legal aid caseload, we have agreed that there are more worthy cases to handle than lawyers to handle them, the need should be clear.

Lest this be all doom and gloom, we begin our readings with the inspiring story of career legal aid attorney Robert Doggett (**Readings, Section 1**). We first "met" Doggett when he was profiled in a 1991 *Texas Lawyer* article. We have kept up with him over the years and updated his story in the more recent piece excerpted here — an article in which he is one of five profiled lawyer "heroes." And there are the rays of hope in **Section 3**, especially the 2004 *Brown* case reaffirming IOLTA funding.

(c)   The Argument in Favor of Pro Bono Work:

The **Readings, Sections 4** and **5**, address opposite perspectives on the need for pro bono. The Fleischer article (**Section 4**) describes how one Wall Street associate found himself gratified to have "a client who needed me." We have found few if any more compelling arguments for pro bono. The satisfaction this young lawyer has gotten from his pro bono work is palpable. The article in **Section 5** (see **section (e)**, below) points to a far harsher reality.

We have moved Prof. Lubet's "Eleventh Floor Principle" piece to the end of this Problem (**Readings, Section 9**) because we wanted to use it to sum up what happens when *all lawyers* participate in pro bono work, even the "great" Albert Jenner. This article directly speaks to the point that when pro bono, whether mandatory or not (see **sections (e)** and **(f),** below), includes everyone from all segments of the bar, the professionalism and credibility of lawyers are enhanced. We agree with Lubet's perspective on this score, and also agree with him that the system, and its resident judges, clerks and lawyers, can become inured to a particular set of behaviors which do not truly serve the ends of justice, particularly justice for the poor.

We have used for many years the statement of Orville Schell before Congress   30 years ago (**Readings, Section 6**) because we think it compellingly states the case for pro bono. Specifically, we take Schell's statement that lawyers are "unlike groups such as plumbers [or] manufacturers of can openers." We then try to isolate reasons or factors why this statement is true.

We encourage students to come up with reasons why lawyers are different, in the sense that they have responsibilities others do not to assist those who need but cannot afford their services. Based on our students' responses over the years, we have come up with a list of about ten factors which we like to point to as justifying this special status. Every teacher's list of factors will undoubtedly be different; indeed, teachers may disagree about the extent to which pro bono work should be required. However, we give our factors here as a sample based on our experience.

We do note at the outset, however, that giving lawyers a "higher obligation" than plumbers or the makers of can openers may also encourage attitudes of "elitism," "parentalism" or even noblesse oblige. This is a danger which in its

more negative aspects causes some lawyers to feel that other workers in the system, such as paralegals, are less worthy than they. By recognizing this danger we hope successfully to deal with it for the most part. We can then move on to some legitimate reasons why lawyers may have a higher obligation than people in other occupations to assist those who have a need of their services.

(d) Factors That Distinguish Lawyers from Plumbers:

We have polished and reworded the most useful factors our students have provided us over the years, and have come up with the following ten factors:

1. Professionalism and the fact we are licensed.
2. The special confidential relationship we are permitted to have with our clients, unique to our profession, ministers and physicians.
3. The fact that we render personal services to individual people, not to things (such as plumbers).
4. The obligation we have to ignore our own self-interest (which we call fiduciary duty).
5. The duty stated in our rules to improve the system of laws, and therefore, implicitly, society as a whole.
6. The fact we have a monopoly on our profession (and do-it-yourself lawyering can be difficult, although we readily acknowledge that, for us, do-it-yourself plumbing is probably more difficult).
7. The extent to which our unique skills mean people require our services to translate the legal system into intelligible terms.
8. The fact that most of us, most of the time, serve monied interests. While President, Jimmy Carter said that "90% of lawyers serve 10% of the people." To a significant extent, he was correct, since those of little or modest means can hardly afford the expense of legal services. His statement may be even more true today.
9. The fact that we operate under a mandate to help, is set forth in our ethics rules. While these rules are not mandatory, their clear import is to provide legal services to those who cannot afford it. Only in this way do lawyers truly become service providers to all people.
10. The last factor we cite, which brings our own class and course to a close, is the very existence of ethical rules themselves. We know of no plumbers' code of ethics, nor one for the manufacturers of can openers (though we note the increasing use of business ethics among enlightened business people). To give credence to these ethical rules — and the concept of professionalism which underlies them — is to take responsibility for our profession by providing services to all those who need them.

(e)   Should Pro Bono Be Mandatory Rather Than Permissive?

Most students in our course readily agree that doing pro bono work is the right thing to do, and they say they are going to do it. But most, in our experience, feel that it should not be mandatory. Many feel that the phrase "mandatory pro bono" is an oxymoron. Semantically, they may be right. However, making pro bono mandatory could assist the lawyer in **Part II** of the problem by taking the pressure off the young associate and putting it on the firm. So we encourage the students to engage in the debate over whether pro bono work should be mandatory.

In this discussion, we first examine need. In the post-stock-market-boom-days — and those days come in every generation — big law firms cut back severely on pro bono, as described in the New York Times article in **Section 5** of the **Readings**.   Second, we examine the failure of a Colorado proposal (**Readings, Section 7**), the milder approaches of the Florida court and the newer Illinois proposal (**Readings, Section 8**), and the similarly milder CLE-credit approaches under the new Colorado rule (**NOTES** at end of **Section 7**). As the author of the *Chicago Lawyer* piece notes, "Notice what is not recommended?"

Many legal services lawyers of our acquaintance oppose mandatory pro bono because they do not want attorneys who are being forced to give their time. They prefer to rely on those whose pro bono commitment is heartfelt. They reason that lawyers who are forced to help the poor have little inclination or incentive to do a good job on behalf of these clients.

We have enormous respect for our legal services colleagues. But we disagree with their position. Perhaps we are too idealistic, but we believe that if lawyers were all required to do pro bono, and could not "buy out" of it, doing the work would soon be part of the culture of being a lawyer, *any* lawyer in any work situation in any place. We liken it to mandatory continuing legal education. Lawyers may grump about MCLE for a while, but after a period of time they will just do it, and many will start to enjoy it. On balance, we agree with Mr. Schell's call.

(f) Defining What Pro Bono Means:

An important component of doing pro bono work is defining what that term means. A key question is whether service to the legal profession as a whole qualifies. We think that the Florida plan came up with a rather good definition of what constitutes pro bono work.

This definition, in the **NOTES** at the end of **Section 8**, involves work for the poor or the "working poor," which could possibly include non-legal work so long as the work is "predominantly designed to address the needs of poor persons." Others would define the work more narrowly, requiring it to be legal work. Still others would want a far more general definition, including civic

good works, service on boards of directors of artistic associations and the like. We believe this last definition is too broad.

There are other issues for the teacher to consider a discussion of the pros and cons. One is whether, as is allowed in Florida, the law firms can collectively discharge their pro bono duty by having some of their lawyers (most probably younger associates) do all their pro bono work. On one level, this would give less experienced lawyers, those most like our law students, the opportunity to do pro bono work. On the other hand, it defeats the idea of Lubet's Eleventh Floor Principle.

A second issue is whether lawyers can opt out of pro bono by paying a fee, which the Florida system also allows. The advantage to this is that lawyers who do not want to engage in pro bono have a relatively inexpensive alternative by simply paying money which will be used to further legal services. But there are disadvantages: this too defeats the Eleventh Floor Principle; and it doesn't give these lawyers the opportunity to learn how rewarding pro bono work can be.

(g) Pro Bono for the Large-Firm Associate and Law Firm Culture:

Once we have discussed our "ten factors" and the other issues concerning mandatory pro bono, we return to **Part II** of the problem. It is important for us to recognize, given all the reasons we articulate in favor of doing pro bono work, that a law firm culture may simply make doing pro bono work for a young associate very difficult, given the billable hours pressure.

While requiring mandatory pro bono is one way of changing the law firm culture by "force," there are other ways in which associates can, at least little by little, change the culture. Finding a sympathetic partner who will support the associate's efforts may be the best place to start. While it is difficult to impose too many of our own beliefs on law students who may find themselves in such an unfriendly environment, we encourage them to try. We recognize that this is more difficult during a period of economic downturn, but ironically more necessary.

(h) Mandatory Pro Bono for Law Schools?

We think the last question of part **II** of our **Problem** is particularly important — whether law schools should require mandatory pro bono work. (See **Readings, Section 10**.) Again, many of the students take issue with the proposed mandatory nature of the requirement. We point out, however, that the increasing use of clinical programs, the more favorable attitude of law students towards doing pro bono (when compared to lawyers), and their greater time availability make law schools a good place for pro bono work to start. Moreover, as opposed to law firms, the chances of developing a law *school* culture which is favorable to pro bono work are far greater than

changing a law *firm*. In this way, the habits of today's law students can become the habits of tomorrow's lawyers. Indeed, today many *high schools* have pro bono community service requisites.

(i)   Is This an Ethics Issue?

We believe that this is clearly an ethics issue, and point to the ten factors we isolated earlier as evidence. We understand many students, and indeed many teachers of legal ethics, will not agree with our perspective on this issue. Also, we remain aware of the dangers of sounding too "preachy." Nevertheless, a discussion of the pros and cons of doing this work, together with an evaluation of whether the issue is an ethical one, is valuable for all concerned.

CHAPTER 13

Admissions, Discipline, And Some Other Rules of Lawyering

THE POINT BEHIND THE CHAPTER:

Chapter 13 is included in the text to make sure that full coverage of legal ethics issues is provided by this volume. We do not use the problem approach here. Rather we try to provide an overview of some basic issues not addressed elsewhere: (1) admission to practice; (2) discipline; (3) the unauthorized practice of law; (4) multidisciplinary practice; and (5) the role of non-lawyers.

We each handle this material differently, as, of course, any teachers should, adopting one's own methodologies and preferences. We often find that we generally do not have time for a lengthy discussion of these issues in our course. We adopt a lecture format and summarize the material contained in the chapter with a minimum of interactive discussion. Some teachers choose to begin the semester with this material. Many may want to spend more time on these issues, particularly admissions and discipline, two subjects that are likely to be most interesting to law students. We note particularly the issues of defining "good moral character" (**Part A, Section 4**), and multijurisdictional practice (**Part A, Section 7**). In keeping with one of our book's principal themes, we examine the issue of race and admissions in both **Sections 1 and 3** of **Part A**.

Of special interest, particularly for those teachers who want to engage in robust discussion and debate — or in role-play — is the six-page Matthew Hale "file" contained in **Section 5**. Hale is the self-avowed racist whose well-publicized effort at admission to the Illinois bar was rejected in 1999. In the years since, Hale later exposed himself as a felon unworthy of bar admission in almost everyone's view, but at the time, both sides of the Hale debate had strong proponents from the legal ethics world. Hale's story forms an excellent basis for discussing how bars may and should apply the standard of "good moral character."

Bar enforcement and discipline issues (**Part B**) tend to interest students greatly. While we may not spend much time on these questions, other teachers have had great success using the disciplinary arena as a focus for explaining ethical behavior, often with the help of a guest lecturer from the state bar's disciplinary counsel.

Unauthorized practice and multidisciplinary practice are two issues that have gained much attention in the last decade, although as we sent this third edition to press they had faded a bit from the spotlight, perhaps because the pace of observable change has slowed considerably in the last few years. We remind that we spent a few pages addressing MDPs in the context of "unbundled" legal services and confidentiality in **Section 4** of **Problem 5**, and

looked at an issue beyond unauthorized practice — international practice — in **Sections** 7 and **8** of **Problem 13**.

DATE DUE